Interventions: New Studies in Medieval Culture
Ethan Knapp, Series Editor

Revivalist Fantasy

Alliterative Verse and Nationalist Literary History

RANDY P. SCHIFF

THE OHIO STATE UNIVERSITY PRESS
Columbus

Copyright © 2011 by The Ohio State University.
All rights reserved.

Library of Congress Cataloging-in-Publication Data

Schiff, Randy P., 1972–
 Revivalist fantasy : alliterative verse and nationalist literary history / Randy P. Schiff.
  p. cm.—(Interventions : new studies in medieval culture)
 Includes bibliographical references and index.
 ISBN 978-0-8142-1152-6 (cloth : alk. paper)—ISBN 978-0-8142-9251-8 (cd-rom)
 1. English poetry—Middle English, 1100–1500—History and criticism. 2. Alliteration. I. Title. II. Series: Interventions : new studies in medieval culture.
 PR317.A55S36 2011
 821'.1093581—dc22
                    2010047838

This book is available in the following editions:
Cloth (ISBN 978-0-8142-1152-6)
CD-ROM (ISBN 978-0-8142-9251-8)
Paper (ISBN: 978-0-8142-5683-1)
Cover design by Larry Nozik
Type set in Times New Roman

Contents

Acknowledgments   vii

INTRODUCTION
REVIVALIST FANTASY: ALLITERATIVE NATIONALISM, FROM
MODERN TO MEDIEVAL   1

1   BEYOND THE BACKWATER: ALLITERATIVE
REVIVALISM AND NATIONALIST FANTASY   17

2   CROSS-CHANNEL BECOMINGS-ANIMAL:
PRIMAL COURTLINESS IN *GUILLAUME DE PALERNE*
AND *WILLIAM OF PALERNE*   45

3   DESTABILIZING ARTHURIAN EMPIRE: GENDER AND ANXIETY
IN ALLITERATIVE TEXTS OF THE MILITARIZED MIDLANDS   72

4   BORDERLAND SUBVERSIONS: ANTI-IMPERIAL ENERGIES IN
THE *AWNTYRS OFF ARTHURE* AND *GOLAGROS AND GAWANE*   100

5   BAGS OF BOOKS AND BOOKS AS BAGS: POLITICAL PROTEST,
COMMUNICATIONS TECHNOLOGIES, AND THE *PIERS
PLOWMAN* TRADITION   128

EPILOGUE
EPOCHAL HISTORIOGRAPHY AND RE-ENGAGEMENT WITH
ALLITERATIVE POEMS   157

Notes   163
Bibliography   229
Index   255

ACKNOWLEDGMENTS

FIRST AND FOREMOST, I would like to thank Aranye Fradenburg, whose insights and enthusiasm have been at the heart of this work. My adviser when this project began, Aranye has remained a key source of counsel, encouragement, and inspiration.

I owe a special debt to Jerold Frakes, who has counseled me on matters great and small in my development of this book. I am grateful for his continued mentorship.

To Carol Braun Pasternack I owe great thanks for her searching commentary on my work, in both its early and later stages. I wish I could thank Richard Helgerson once more for all his care and cheer in responding to my dissertation. The memory of his warmth and wisdom will always enrich my work.

I must acknowledge my unique debt to Patricia Clare Ingham and to the other, anonymous reader who responded to my manuscript. Their extraordinary insights have enriched my argument, and their careful analysis has saved me from much error. Any infelicities in the present work are my responsibility.

I am very grateful to Malcolm Litchfield, Maggie Diehl, Martin Boyne, and everyone else involved at The Ohio State University Press for helping bring my manuscript to print. In this respect I also owe a singular debt to Ethan Knapp for enabling this wonderful venue for my work.

To Jim Holstun I am very grateful for feedback on so much of my work, which is all the stronger for his having engaged with it. I must also thank Graham Hammill, for his rich readings of two chapters and his sage advice on my general project.

Reflecting on the road leading to this book, I owe a singular debt to Carolyn Dinshaw, who inspired me to pursue medieval studies and who gave me my first, fateful taste of alliterative verse.

An earlier version of portions of chapter 2 appeared in *Exemplaria* 21 (2009); I am grateful to Maney Publishing for allowing me to reprint this expanded and updated version and to the editors, Patricia Clare Ingham, James J. Paxson, Tison Pugh, and Elizabeth Scala. An earlier version of portions of chapter 4 appeared in *Speculum* 84 (2009); I thank *Speculum* and its editor, Paul E. Szarmach, for permission to reprint the work.

For providing access to manuscripts that I consulted in my research, I owe thanks to all at the British Library; the Bodleian Library, Oxford University; and the Cambridge University Library. For financial assistance in my archival research, I must thank the English Department and the College of Letters and Science at UC Santa Barbara and the English Department and College of Arts and Sciences at SUNY Buffalo. For help with the cover design, I am grateful to the Pierpont Morgan Library and to the Julian Park Publication Fund.

For feedback on my general project, I am grateful, among many others, to Rachel Ablow, Barbara Bono, Jeffrey Jerome Cohen, Siobhain Calkin, Jody Enders, Laurie Finke, Geraldine Heng, Kathy Lavezzo, David Marshall, Carla Mazzio, Cristanne Miller, Michael O'Connell, David Schmid, Martin Shichtman, Scott Stevens, Andy Stott, Joseph Taylor, Katherine Terrell, and Candace Waid.

For comments on chapter 1, I owe thanks to Ruth Mack; Thomas Hahn, who invited me to present before the Early Studies Group at the University of Rochester; Russell Peck; Alan Lupack; and Susan Eilenberg, who invited me to address the SUNY Buffalo English Department. For chapter 2, I am grateful to my anonymous readers at *Exemplaria;* Patricia Clare Ingham; Elizabeth Scala; and Molly Lynde-Recchia, for inviting me to present at the 2008 Kalamazoo congress. Regarding chapter 3 material, I am indebted to Mili Clark; Mark Amodio, who invited me to present at the 2007 Medieval Academy meeting at the University of Toronto; Kurt Heinzelman; and Sue Niebrzydowski, who invited me to present at the 2008 NCS congress at Swansea University.

Regarding chapter 4 material, I am grateful to Paul Szarmach; my anonymous readers at *Speculum;* Jacqueline Brown; Sandro Sticca; Steven Deng; the students in my 2006 Pre-Postcolonialism Seminar at SUNY Buffalo; Scott Kleinman, who invited me to present at Kalamazoo in 2003; and Ned Lee Fielden, who invited me to present at the 2005 MAP meeting. For chapter 5, I am grateful to Frank Grady; Robert J. Meyer-Lee, who invited me to present at the 2001 MLA meeting; Aranye Fradenburg, who invited me to present at the 2006 NCS congress; and Daniel Hack, who invited me to present before the SUNY Buffalo English Department.

I am very grateful for the support of my family and friends, especially my parents, Barbara and Neal Schiff.

More than anyone, I thank my wife, Maki Becker, and my sons Duncan and Desmond, for all their loving support. This book is dedicated most especially to you three.

INTRODUCTION

Revivalist Fantasy

ALLITERATIVE NATIONALISM, FROM MODERN
TO MEDIEVAL

IN AN 1868 ESSAY on alliterative verse, Walter W. Skeat argued that, to move forward in framing the "rules and laws of English prosody," literary critics must cast their eyes inward, reconsidering their discipline's foundational assumptions.[1] Critiquing the "absurd and mischievously false terminology" produced by applying concepts from "temporal" classical verse to the "accentual" English corpus,[2] Skeat urged scholars to generate "genuine English terms" for the study of "English" poetic works.[3] While Skeat is concerned primarily with meter rather than politics, it is telling that he turns to a nationalist rhetoric of uniqueness and authenticity when considering alliterative prosody. Although Skeat's terminological suggestions did not reshape prosodic studies—we still speak of the *iamb* and *trochee,* for example, rather than Skeat's "genuine English terms," *Return* and *Tonic*[4]—his insistence on retooling a classically oriented criticism of alliterative meter led to considerable standardization. Indeed, Skeat's key claims concerning alliterative verse—that of a four-stress line, with two caesura-divided half-verses, each marked by two major stresses, with the stresses tending to be marked, in various patterns, by alliteration—still form the basic framework within which most literary historians work.[5]

Skeat's call for literary critical self-critique has been echoed in recent medievalist work.[6] Critics practicing the New Medievalism have turned increasingly to self-reflexive studies of literary criticism's institutional context. The New Medievalist writing of "the history of medieval studies from within the perspective of the discipline itself"[7] has been aptly described as an "Oedipal" project that directs critical violence against the enduring work of foundational scholar-fathers.[8] Narrating the "family romance" of medieval studies, New Medievalists have foregrounded the epochal nineteenth-century transition from amateur to professional literary criticism[9] and thus have called attention to the often hidden ideological legacy generated by the institutionalization of literary studies.¹⁰ As I shall argue, nationalism proves the most powerful paradigm of this nineteenth-century critical inheritance.

Tracking the development and continuing impact of the literary historical concept of an Alliterative Revival, *Revivalist Fantasy* participates in such disciplinary history. I will define Alliterative Revivalism as the dissemination of the theory that the Old English alliterative line re-emerged in a mid-fourteenth-century Middle English literary "efflorescence" practiced by a single, nativist "school" that competed with French-influenced, syllabic poets associated with the English South.¹¹ I will maintain that the Alliterative Revival is a medievalist rather than medieval phenomenon that originates from, and continues to sustain, Western nationalist interests linking British, American, and Continental scholars. Tracing the Alliterative Revival only so far back as the nineteenth century, I will argue that Euro-American nationalists project modern racialism into the Middle Ages, using the fantasy of an atavistic alliterative movement to narrate the rise of a Chaucerian proto-modernity.

In foregrounding critical fantasy, I do not claim an objective vantage point from which the folly of past scholars can be isolated and removed, exposing a stable medieval corpus beneath. *Revivalist Fantasy* has its own desires, which dictate the directions in which I steer criticism after identifying Alliterative Revivalism's continuing literary historical life. Operating according to the historiographical assumption of the modernity of the Middle Ages—the artificial pastness of which James Simpson traces back to the sixteenth-century epochal "period map" drawn by state and ecclesiastical interests that consolidated themselves by narrating a "negative" medieval past¹²—I will present Revivalist prejudice as a critical horizon within which we continue to receive late-medieval alliterative texts.¹³ Revivalist discourse tells a fundamentally nationalist story: linking alliterative verse with a factitious Germanic antiquity, Revivalist critics tie literary and national modernization to the spectacular collapse of a unified alliterative movement. Identifying the Revival as a racialized fantasy, I will demonstrate the ways in which the totalizing vision of a neo-Saxon alliterative movement inhibits us from appreciating the engagement of alliterative poems with matters of current concern. My own critical desires and cultural moment drive both my critique of Revivalism and my recovery of perspectives obscured by a nationalist literary historical lens. I will arbitrarily select poems that speak to my own post-nationalist, anti-imperialist critical priorities. Such arbitrariness is obligatory: since my primary argument is that the Revival is a monolithic narrative that blinds us to alliterative poems' local contexts, my own story is deliberately multiplex and discontinuous. Redirecting alliterative texts away from the Revivalist fantasy of a moribund neo-Saxon tradition, I seek to re-open lines of communication between particular alliterative poems and issues of current critical fascination, such as transnational identity (chapter 2), gendered economic power (chapter 3), borderlands culture (chapter 4), and subversive communication networks (chapter 5).

My aim is to identify and thereby disengage layers of disciplinary prejudice that have rendered alliterative texts fundamentally retrograde, by analyzing a racialized rhetoric that sustains a nationalist *grand récit*. The Alliterative Revival has had a long literary historical life. Offering material evidence of Kathleen Biddick's observation that "medieval studies is still intimately bound to the fathers" responsible for literary criticism's nineteenth-century professionalization,[14] Revivalist discourse continues to inflect our reception of late-medieval alliterative texts. This ongoing impact is nowhere clearer than in vexed efforts to escape Revivalist historiography. In his critique of "Old Historicist" investigations of alliterative verse, Ralph Hanna argues persuasively that "identifying the poetry with its verse-form renders it particularly Other in a literary context increasingly dominated by syllabic (and especially Chaucerian) verse" and marginalizes alliterative texts according to assumptions of "defiant regionalism" and "negative reactions to centralizing tendencies."[15] Yet even as Hanna attacks the limitations of this "Othering" gesture, he participates in an "Old Historicist" insistence on a monolithic and self-conscious alliterative movement: for Hanna, "alliterative poems" are "always concerned" with the sociopolitical implications of lordship; "alliterative narrative" is "inherently exemplaristic" and "soberly turned towards values which will endure"; and history is for "them"—evidently for *all* "alliterative" poets—a "longing for a new beginning."[16] By the end of the essay, Hanna holds that "alliterative poetry" is indeed "Chaucer's Other," in terms of "consciousness," if "not of geography."[17]

Insisting that the nostalgic pose associated with the alliterative poet is a literary historical rather than literary phenomenon, I will argue that the fantasy of a nativist Alliterative Revival contributes to a nationalist effort to retroactively arrest the play of late-medieval ethnic, linguistic, and regional identities. By manufacturing a monolithic metrical school obsessed with a native past, Revivalist critics consign poets producing alliterative works to a static antiquity against which a Chaucerian modernity is projected. Alliterative verse becomes linked repeatedly with pastness and with death. Much as Hanna reveals a totalizing vision in revising Alliterative Revivalism, so does Christine Chism disclose the continuing influence of Revivalist literary historiography. Chism's powerful analyses of the social and cultural contexts of alliterative texts are framed by a Revivalist paradigm:

the "single current" Chism pursues in *Alliterative Revivals* is "the revival of the dead and the past performed."[18] Generations of Revivalist criticism literally cast a pall over the readings, with alliterative poets portrayed as primarily backward-looking, their postmortem eyes turned resolutely toward the Saxon past. As I shall argue throughout this book, the structural metaphor of revival that Chism inherits derives from a nationalist narrative of double death: a doomed fourteenth-century aesthetic movement appropriates the prosody of a doomed Saxon England. By reviving the allegedly native strong-stress line, with the re-animated prosody expiring after its spectacular, but short-lived, literary moment, alliterative poets suffer a second death in Revivalism's writing of the rise of a Chaucerian English modernity.

If Alliterative Revivalism inflects even such searching studies as Hanna's and Chism's, it is because its fantasy is deeply embedded in the discipline, with its nationalist, racialized narrative reproducing itself in numerous literary histories. Each of the elements constituting Revivalist discourse merits terminological discussion. In turning to fantasy as a conceptual tool, I investigate the ideological vision that projects a coherent historiographical picture onto a Middle Ages made to stage English modernity's rise. Medievalist scholars have deployed what L. O. Aranye Fradenburg calls the "power of fantasy to make history" for various purposes, ranging from the ethical installation of state welfare systems to programmatic nationalist activity.[19] I will locate the rise of Revivalism within the nationalist philological culture in which Middle English studies evolved. If Stephen G. Nichols is correct in arguing that nineteenth-century "romantic historiography" fashions an "essentially 'modern' Middle Ages wherein might be discerned the origins and identity of current practices and institutions,"[20] then it is crucial to note that Revivalist criticism writes this modernity into the close of medieval English literary history, with Chaucer winning the field after the final, failed stand of a nativist, provincial poetics.

Alliterative Revivalism turns to ethno-history to manufacture this medieval modernity, picturing a Chaucer who triumphs over purist neo-Saxons by fusing native bluntness with a Francophile sophistication. Such racial logic is a key innovation in post-Romantic literary criticism. As Reginald Horsman demonstrates in his study of the nineteenth-century shift from "environmental" understandings of racial difference to the pseudo-scientific taxonomies of discrete races, blood-based narrative played an integral role in both the British and American brands of imperialism that sustained Revivalist theory.[21] Spawned in this racialized nineteenth century, Revivalism fantasizes the continuation of eleventh-century Saxon–Norman struggles on fourteenth-century metrical battlefields, with neo-Saxon alliterative poets revolting against French-influenced (though English-speaking) syllabic competitors.[22] While Revivalism depends upon racialist logic, it remains largely aloof from explicit racism. Far from serving to sustain the Anglo-Saxonist ideology key to Anglo-American imperial aggression,[23] the Revivalist narrative ultimately depends upon a barbarization of Saxon identity, whose backwardness is used to highlight the English ascent to a racially hybrid modernity.

Revivalist criticism involves a literary historical writing of English exceptionalism and the deployment of "cultural capital" to "constitute retroactively" a "pre-national" culture on which to ground the modern nation.[24] A fantastically ancient Saxon culture and a nativist artistic rebellion against a syllabic foreignness become the narrative ingredients of a nationalist myth of triumphant aesthetic assimilation. Alliterative Revivalist imagination involves a retrospective installation of what Dipesh Chakrabarty calls the "not yet": much as nineteenth-century historicists display a Western-biased evolutionary model of history that deems non-Western cultures not yet civilized enough for self-rule, so do critics theorizing a doomed reflowering of alliterative verse imagine fourteenth-century Saxons as noble barbarians in need of the civilizing supplement of a French-influenced, but nevertheless English, Chaucer.[25] To build the story of a modern England, Revivalists narrate the meteoric rise and collapse of a medieval one.

Just as Revivalists write a nineteenth-century notion of race into late-medieval alliterative culture, so do they project a modern notion of the nation into the Middle Ages. Throughout this book, I will understand the nation as a fundamentally modern phenomenon, generated by a nationalist ideology that saturated the nineteenth-century development of literary criticism. I will contend that, despite recent efforts to stretch the nation's history back into the medieval period, we should see the Western Middle Ages as pre-national, with the imperial state a preferable model for late-medieval British literary history. How we are to understand the nation in such a chronology remains controversial. Some discussion of what Walker Connor calls the "terminological chaos" in the theorization of the nation, in which arguments range from a people to a state, and from vaguely contoured, subjective communities to precisely delineated polities,[26] will help contextualize my understanding of Revivalism's nation as a fundamentally modern construct.

The "notoriously slippery meaning" of the word "nation," as Kathy Lavezzo notes, precludes us from meaningfully tying this "fantasy"-saturated concept to a determinative etymological analysis.[27] However, it is instructive to examine two related ethno-historical arguments for a medieval nation, which depend on racial and linguistic associations. If we were to rely merely on historical uses, then the word "nation," as a term connoting a community bound together by notions of common blood—rooted in the Latin *natio,* for "birth, origin," and extended to mean "breed, stock, kind, species, race, tribe, set"[28]—would be of great antiquity. The *Vulgate* Bible offers a particularly influential use of *natio* in its enumeration of the various descendants of Noah's three sons, Shem, Ham, and Japheth (Gen. 10:1–32), in a catalogue appropriated both by medieval genealogists and by nineteenth-century race theorists.[29] If we regard the nation as signifying merely the perception of common birth and culture, then nations must be seen as polities of great antiquity, with roots stretching well beyond historical memory. Influenced by Romantic notions of cultural particularity, some critics emphasize language as the primary force binding individuals into a nation. As in the case of race-based views of national identity, the criterion of linguistic solidarity leads to claims for numerous nations, with each possessing the same primordial antiquity as the language with which it is conflated.[30]

Neither racial nor linguistic bonds produce the nation as I understand the term. I do not mean to discount the importance of ethnic identity in late-medieval Britain, though I do seek to work against a recent trend of extending the nation's genealogy lineally back into the Middle Ages. I will suggest that, rather than providing space for medieval nations, late-medieval Britain featured a range of non-congruent entities—regnal (and imperial) states; transnational communities based on religious and class affiliations; and what Anthony D. Smith calls *ethnies,* ethnic groups sharing common culture, origin myths, and sensibilities about territory.[31] While modern nations are qualified by ethnic roots, according to Smith, they are nevertheless distinct from these ethnic identities, requiring the homogenizing mechanisms of the bureaucratically centralized, post-Enlightenment, post-industrial state.[32] In suggesting that we speak of ethnic communities and states as separate entities, while seeing religious and class identities as constantly complicating individual political loyalties, I join certain theorists of the medieval nation in critiquing teleological understandings of national development.[33] My focus on empire, for example, aligns my work with Patricia Clare Ingham's study of late-medieval British political fantasy. While I share Ingham's vision of a dynamic Britain in which competing visions of community included various combinations of regional and ethnic identities,[34] I differ in choosing to break from the vocabulary of a medieval nation in my investigation of radically other forms of political community that bear uncanny resemblance to the transnational present.

In calling attention to the nationalist motives at the heart of the Alliterative Revival, I rely particularly on two theorists of nationalism. For Benedict Anderson, the rise of a nation like England was part of a second phase of the nationalist age, as nineteenth-century European states produced sovereign and limited "imagined communities" imitative of originally Creole models, with the latter polities formed out of former administrative units of empire.[35] The nation required significant cultural development, as a fixed vernacular gradually became standardized by, and then became the primary vehicle for, print-capitalist culture.[36] Despite this material prehistory, the age of the nation represents a new sociopolitical epoch. Whereas the homogenization of a national print language and the related reduction of other dialects to "regional" status are, Anderson holds, "largely unselfconscious processes," nationalists regularly make it their business to manufacture a teleology out of such developments.[37] As I shall argue, Revivalist critics use the narrative of an alliterative school's rise and fall to imagine a metrical civil war that yields a single literary tradition for a late-medieval nation. Revivalists obscure their nationalist motives, stressing radical difference through a racialized dialectics, even as they distract attention from the shared nature of the field in which these ethnic others compete—that of vernacular Middle English. Revivalism's fantastically aged, nativist neo-Saxons compete with a Francophile but English-speaking Chaucer in a struggle that marks the foundational literary history of England as English. Channeling language's unique capacity to provide a powerful, but virtual, sense of "contemporaneous community," Revivalism conflates the English nation with an English language that "looms up imperceptibly out of a horizonless past."[38]

Revivalist critics insist on such continuity, in order to obscure the post-industrial rupture that, according to Ernest Gellner, produced the nation.[39] Emphasizing the modern nation's faux-antiquity, Gellner argues that nationalism is "*not* the awakening of an old, latent, dormant force, though that is how it does indeed present itself," but is rather the product of new forms of "social organization" demanded by industrial capitalism.[40] According to Gellner, modern industrial societies, seeking constant market growth, require socioeconomic mobility and cultural homogeneity, each of which is precluded by the primacy of class-based and religious affiliations in the medieval and early modern worlds. While breaking away from the fundamentally class-striated, pre-national past through the cultivation of a general education system, the industrialist-capitalist nation still exploits emotive ethnic attachments.[41] Literary history proves a key channel through which nineteenth-century nationalists exploit ethnicity's homogenizing power. Producing the evolutionary narrative of a hybrid English identity generated by competing, racially encoded prosodies, Revivalist critics linked an alliterative movement's collapse with the imagined rise of an English modernity destined to become the cultural center of a larger and later British imperial state.

In emphasizing Alliterative Revivalism's nationalist modernity, I do not mean to suggest an absolute medieval–modern divide. As Jeffrey Jerome Cohen argues, we need not "choose between continuist and alteritist approaches" as "metanarratives," insofar as each vision offers useful perspectives in interrelating the medieval and the modern.[42] While I maintain the alteritist view that the medieval nation is a modern projection, I insist on placing late-medieval Britain within an ongoing imperialist history that stretches back at least as far as the era of Edward I.[43] Urging critics to consider the imperial, rather than national, state as the analytical unit for late-medieval English and Scottish political history, I aim to link this pre-modern political world with post-national "Empire," as seen in Michael Hardt and Antonio Negri's vision of a global movement beyond static nation-states and into a world of unbounded, corporate, and biopolitical power.[44] In order to indicate the dynamic sense of community formation in the Middle Ages, I avoid use of the term *international,* which implies a modern, static disposition of uniformly defined nation-states, and instead deploy the term *transnational.* Drawn from postcolonial critics' efforts to work against nation-based critical methodologies, the concept of the transnational enables our identification of networks of meaning that defy boundaries traditionally tied to nations.[45] Undoing nationalist Revivalist frames allows us to juxtapose the medieval and post-modern periods' similarly transnational empires.

Besides forging connections between contemporary and medieval polities, an alteritist view of nationalism works against the marginalization of the Middle Ages in traditional periodization. Medievalist critics have often been wary of alteritist views of the nation, sensing that modernity constructs its identity precisely against a medieval past. In arguing that English nationhood stretches back to King Alfred's reign, for example, Kathleen Davis contends that Anderson systematically ties modernity to the "decline" of medieval culture, with the "shift" to the nation requiring decisive movement away from medieval dynasticism, transnational religious community, and a "providential" sense of time.[46] While Davis is right to critique Anderson's generalization that the medieval sense of time is non-calendrical—Geoffrey of Monmouth's systematic synchronization of British historical events with Roman and Judeo-Christian histories clearly counters this view[47]—it is worth noting that Anderson's argument for late-eighteenth-century Creole nations undermines traditional literary histories that locate modernity in the sixteenth century.⁴⁸ When we follow Gellner's even later dating of the nation's rise, falling well into the industrial nineteenth century, it becomes clear that the modernist theory of the nation allows us to reconfigure traditional literary histories, grouping the medieval, early modern, and Enlightenment periods in a pre-national epoch.

In insisting on Revivalism's nineteenth-century, nationalist origins, I systematically explore modern literary historical materials as filters through which late-medieval alliterative texts are encountered. Analyzing educational institutions' powerful role in producing the homogeneity key to the modern nation, Pierre Bourdieu isolates literary history as a key means by which the school system constitutes a "dominant culture" as the "*legitimate national* culture."⁴⁹ Revivalist discourse participates in precisely this process of "inculcating" the cultural ingredients of the "national image,"⁵⁰ by narrating modern English literature's rise after the ruin of a reactionary, nativist movement. Much as, for Derek Pearsall, the Chaucer associated with the foundations of Englishness is a product of nineteenth-century nationalism bearing little resemblance to the class-conscious and Continentally minded medieval poet,⁵¹ so is the stereotype of the alliterative poet as a neo-Saxon struggling against foreign newness generated by post-industrial, Western nationalism. Gellner's and Bourdieu's focus on the education system's homogenizing effects informs my choice of medievalist materials for analysis. I engage not only with literary historical monuments, such as those of Hippolyte Taine and George Saintsbury, but also with little-known works used in secondary schools or aimed at a general readership that also participated in inculcating the Revivalist narrative. While it would be impossible to give exhaustive coverage of such literary histories, my engagement with a range of Revivalist arguments exposes the mode of reproduction of this nationalist fantasy of opposition and nativism that obscures the various motives driving late-medieval alliterative poems.

As I shall argue, not only the Revivalist vision of an agonistic relation between alliterative and syllabic prosodies but also an emphasis on a self-consciously "alliterative" culture are medievalist rather than medieval phenomena. Only by resisting the Revivalist fantasy of a nativist alliterative school can we re-engage with the poems' current concerns. Just as we do not read Chaucer as obsessed with a specifically syllabic identity, so should we avoid reading poets working in alliterative meter as primarily focused on prosody.⁵² Indeed, almost no medieval evidence exists of the metrical struggle posited by Revivalism. Chaucer produces only a single unambiguous reference to alliterative poetry,⁵³ when the Parson insists, "But trusteth wel, I am a Southren man / I kan nat geeste 'rum, ram, ruf,' by lettre" [But believe you me, I am a Southern man. I don't know how to tell stories "fe fi fo," by letter].⁵⁴ The Parson defines "Southern" literature negatively, distinguishing it from the alliterative line by encoding the three alliterating stresses in the most common alliterative verse-pattern, *aa ax,* as "rum, ram, ruf."⁵⁵ Chaucer elsewhere makes clear that he sees Britain as a realm with a wide variety of dialects and, indeed, prosodies: knowing that there is "so gret diversite / In English, and in writyng of oure tonge" [such great diversity in the English language and in its orthography], he prays that no one "myswrite" [mis-write] or otherwise "mysmetre" [mis-versify] his text.⁵⁶ In referring to alliterative verse, Chaucer's Parson seems to anticipate Revivalist rhetoric through his reduction of the prosody to a single set of barbaric sounds: *rum ram ruf.*

However, Chaucer's Parson is virtually alone in such isolation of an alliterative tradition. While Chaucer's single snipe at alliterative meter should indeed be seen as part of an effort to magnify his own poetry's prestige,⁵⁷ both the innocuous nature of the attack and its conventionality speak strongly against linking it with a national metrical struggle. The literature-disdaining Parson is hardly an ideal spokesperson for un-ironic literary criticism: indeed, the Parson moves immediately to state that "rym holde I but litel bettre" [I consider rhyme only slightly better] (X.44). Moreover, while the buttressing of identity through a process of "self-alienation" from past "barbarism" has been linked with the early modern "writing of England,"⁵⁸ another late-medieval use of the trope elicits evidence against its application to alliterative culture. In the *Goldyn Targe,* William Dunbar thanks "reverend Chaucere," along with the Southerners Lydgate and Gower, for bringing the flowers of rhetoric to a Scotland that was before "bare and desolate," thus improving "our rude langage" and "imperfyte" [imperfect] speech (253–70).⁵⁹ If Chaucer's Parson was tasked with communicating that alliterative verse was barbaric, then Dunbar clearly missed the message, for his "longest and most ambitious work" is the fully alliterative (yet Chaucer-influenced) *Tretis of the Twa Mariit Wemen and the Wedo.*⁶⁰

If little evidence exists for Chaucer's conscious competition with alliterative poets, there is even less in extant alliterative poems. Explicit statements by alliterative poets either about their own or about a competing prosody are virtually nonexistent.⁶¹ The exceptional, indeed singular, status of Chaucer's Parson's comment on alliterative verse casts doubt on the Revivalist fantasy of opposed meters locked in mortal combat. The Revivalist assumption of alliterative poets' regional and linguistic alienation also seems overstated, considering recent work that suggests that a strong sense of dialect emerges only after generations of standardization produced by print culture and its grammars, dictionaries, and stable literary idioms.⁶² With such doubt concerning the primacy of medieval dialectal self-identification, and with so little alliterative evidence of metrical self-consciousness, the Parson's potshot at alliterative poets seems too slim a piece of evidence to support such militaristic Revivalist visions as Saintsbury's view of an armed alliterative "rebellion" against the syllabic "foreigner."⁶³

While the Alliterative Revival is a medievalist fantasy, it derives from a medievalism very different from that of nineteenth-century utopianists seeking escape from post-industrial alienation. Examining a late-eighteenth- and nineteenth-century "medieval revival," Alice Chandler argues that both "naturalist" and "feudalist" medievalists, hostile to utilitarianism, set about "reanimating the spirit of the medieval past," in order to locate a "home" absent from a mechanistic, materialistic modernity.⁶⁴ No such Romantic utopians, Alliterative Revivalists were not fleeing from, but were essentially invested in, the consolidation of the post-industrial nation. Rather than looking to alliterative culture for a more authentic past to inform a morally deficient present, Revivalists imagined a retrograde past as the antithesis of a proto-homogeneous modernity. Manufacturing a national Saxon–Norman struggle that persisted into the fourteenth century, Revivalism highlighted the doomed nature of a unidimensional nativism, with the fantasy of a proto-national race war culminating in the triumph of Chaucer's hybrid poetics.

Alliterative Revivalists, building upon the racialized literary historical foundations laid by critics such as Taine and Thomas Warton, did not share with nostalgic medievalists such as the Pre-Raphaelites the vision of an ideal medieval order, with neatly organized social classes harmonized by a larger, supervisory Catholic Church.⁶⁵ Rather, they saw a pre-modern inheritance that provided material useful for the nationalist mythology of cultural continuity. As we shall see (chapter 1), Revivalist racialism emptied the fourteenth-century prosodic proving ground of all competing ethnic identifications save the Saxons and Norman French. As F. V. N. Painter chillingly argues, invading "Teutons . . . supplanted the native Celts as completely as their descendants exterminated the American Indians," thereby ensuring that in "the character of these Teutonic tribes are to be found the fundamental traits of the English people and of English literature."⁶⁶ American Revivalist critics such as Painter, every bit as invested as British scholars in a primordial Saxon Englishness,⁶⁷ participated in the construction of an ethno-historical narrative in which a neo-Saxon subculture survived the Norman Conquest, only to disappear into Chaucer's assimilative English modernity. The evolutionary essence of Revivalism's nationalist, agonistic literary history could be encapsulated as the conviction that that which does not kill Chaucer makes modern English stronger.[68] Working against the grain of the more virulent forms of Anglo-Saxonism that sustained racist discourses in both Britain and America, Revivalism valued hybridity over purity, using its narrative of a crushed nativism to portray England as both strengthened and unified by ethnic diversity.[69] While we may cringe at hearing the racialist logic of Reuben Post Halleck's description of Saxon "dough" mixing with Norman "yeast" to make a single English "race" that produced the world's pre-eminent poetry,[70] hybridity is here valorized in such a way as to distance Revivalism from the Teutonist emphasis on Saxon superiority that Clare Simmons has shown to lead directly to twentieth-century racism.[71] As we shall see, Alliterative Revivalists insist on the futility of efforts to cultivate a nostalgic, race-based nativism.

Along with ethnic identification, regional difference plays a significant role in my analysis. Recognizing Revivalism's unremittingly diachronic pursuit of the racialized origins of a single alliterative movement, I will re-engage with alliterative texts as individual poems by conducting synchronic analyses. I have not sought to map out a detailed history of late-medieval alliterative verse; indeed, it is my basic contention that the Revivalist production of a single explanatory model blinds us to the current concerns of poems composed in the meter. In the final three chapters, I propose regional models for exploring select alliterative texts. In referring to *alliterative zones* I build on N. F. Blake's revision of a monolithic Alliterative Revival through the conception of "revivals" in the Southwest Midlands, Northwest Midlands, and Scotland, with none "in total isolation" and yet each featuring a unique audience.[72] While I argue that we need to discard the concept of "revival" produced by generations of critics artificially binding alliterative poems to a fantasized Saxon past, I follow Blake's lead in imagining relatively distinct sociopolitical contexts. I do not suggest that these alliterative zones are finite in either number or location,[73] nor do I attempt to provide exhaustive coverage of alliterative works within a region. Heuristic rather than deterministic, these alliterative zones map out the range of local, regional, and transnational contexts inflecting poems that happen to be composed in alliterative verse. I do not seek to offer the final word on the regions that I assess. My engagement with Yorkshire, for example, a region that could command its own study considering York's thirteen-line alliterative tradition and the prodigious output of the West Riding scribe Robert Thornton,[74] does not presume a totalizing reading, but serves primarily to enrich our contextualization of *Sir Gawain and the Green Knight* (chapter 3).

Attention to regional difference and instability, along with my focus on empire and transnational class loyalties, undermines Revivalism's assumption of late-medieval national identity. Theorists of a medieval nation have produced powerful visions of English unity, such as Adrian Hastings's argument for a late-medieval vernacular literature forging national identity from insular territorialism and from a religious English exceptionalism that dates back to Bede's eighth century,[75] and Michael Clanchy's argument that a cultural Englishness surviving the Norman Conquest became the basis for thirteenth-century processes of governmental centralization that treated England as a national territory.[76] My analyses of alliterative poems released from Revivalist filters call such national unities into question. I critique such cultural homogeneity as Hastings asserts, by examining a transnational aristocratic culture that defies attempts to equate English community with the territorial population (chapter 2); and I argue that such elitist interests render the state Clanchy describes as imperial rather than national (chapter 4). As I will systematically maintain, Revivalist critics exploit the powerful narrative appeal of teleological historiography, positing a stable, primordial ethno-linguistic presence as the foundation for a stable English territorial state. While centralizing tendencies can indeed be located, we need to be wary of projecting static notions of English (or Scottish) nationhood back into the medieval period, since regional, class, and religious loyalties overrode the capacity of centralization to produce either territorial or demographic homogeneity.[77] Joining with critics who emphasize such socioeconomic and regional fissures,[78] I work against the retrospective, post-Romantic gaze of a Revivalism that projects national unity into discrete social and cultural historical data. *Revivalist Fantasy* seeks to redirect our critical attention to the contemporary engagements of alliterative works unconcerned with Revivalism's ethnonationalist nostalgia.

In chapter 1, I introduce Alliterative Revivalism, tracking its development from the early phase of amateur medievalism to its explicit racialization and regionalization by critics participating in the disciplinary formation of literary studies. I collapse the distinction between critics who see the significant fourteenth-century output of alliterative poems as the resuscitation of a long-dead Anglo-Saxon line and those who interpret that re-animation as an illusion produced by manuscript attestation of an essentially oral meter:[79] each perspective is predicated upon a modern rather than medieval desire for continuity with the Saxon past. Tracing the development of racialist literary history, I argue that Revivalist critics imagine a unified, neo-Saxon alliterative movement that struggled in vain against a syllabic, Francophile South that Chaucer shepherds into modernity. After demonstrating the survival of such a militaristic, monolithic vision of alliterative meter, I turn to *Wynnere and Wastoure* to explore the limitations produced by Alliterative Revivalism. Revivalist insistence on Saxon sternness and nationalist nostalgia blinds us to the *Wynnere*-poet's sophisticated, playful engagement with transnational issues of class, consumption, and pleasure.

In chapter 2, I explore Revivalist anxiety concerning French culture, arguing that medievalists project Francophobia into a late-medieval period in which transnational solidarities precluded nationalist loyalties. Examining *William of Palerne*, a fourteenth-century alliterative translation of the twelfth-century Old French *Guillaume de Palerne*, I explore a ritualized animal allegory that bridges the French and English aristocratic worlds. Working against Revivalism's ethno-linguistic nationalism, I track the poet William's use of translation to sustain elitist interests. In becoming animal, whether as werewolves or as dressed in animal skins, these romances' aristocratic youths ritually mark their social power. William intensifies his source's elitism due to his anxieties concerning the prestige of Middle English, pressured by his patron's transnational aristocratic class rather than by any anti-French nativism. William also intensifies female participation in the ritual transformation of each noble youth into the *homo sacer,* as women wielding clerkly power supervise the animalized allegory of aristocratic exceptionalism. Excluding an Eastern prince from the closed circle of aristocratic becoming, William indicates that pan-European cultural ties override anything like nationalist identity, suggesting empire as the model for late-medieval English political identity.

In chapter 3, I turn to *Sir Gawain and the Green Knight* and its transnational context. The *Gawain*-poet's milieu transcends the militarized Northwest Midlands, to include a Northeast Midlands bound by bibliographical and economic links, as well as Welsh, Manx, Scottish, and Northern English territories connected by mercenary warfare. Noting Revivalist critics' tendency to privilege male conflict due to an obsession with a Saxon spirit motivating alliterative work, I investigate critical resistance to the vital roles accorded to Morgan and the Lady. Anxiety about such powerful female figures derives from the considerable legal and economic power open to all English women being magnified by the massive wealth and sparse population of militarist culture. Such economically empowered female agents also stir unease in regionally proximate poems by John Clerk and the *Morte*-poet. Considering literary critical efforts to reduce the Lady's and Morgan's roles through aesthetic fault-finding or doppelgänger fantasies, I conclude that such reactions reveal both medievalist and medieval unease with the socioeconomic instability generated by the English war machine, and that such female empowerment undermines Revivalism's masculinist, neo-Saxon ethos. Finally, I maintain that Morgan encodes her political pre-eminence through an allegory of ages, disguising herself as an elderly widow in order to signal her superiority both to her middle-aged emissary, Bertilak, and to her young competitor for transregional power, the young Arthur.

In chapter 4, I explore two alliterative Arthurian romances, analyzing Anglo-Scottish marcher culture as a transnational context obscured by Revivalism's nation-based literary historiography. Examining two poems in the thirteen-line stanza, the *Awntyrs off Arthure* and the *Knightly Tale of Golagros and Gawane,* I investigate borderland sensibilities produced by the collision of the Scottish and English empires, in which shared narratives of imperial aggression and practices such as side-switching belie attempts to link either poem to a single national provenance. I call attention to the *Awntyrs*-poet's anti-imperialist imagination of Arthurian aggression and assess the ethnic ambiguities of Galeron, Gawain, and Galloway. The poetics of land-grants with which the poem closes highlights the Arthurian war-state's transnational status. Turning to the ostensibly Scottish *Golagros and Gawane,* I argue that, far from figuring a Scottish love of freedom through a lord's effort to remain independent, the poet highlights the arbitrariness of imperial Arthurian aggression in a fluid, marcher world. Golagros's final lordlessness signals the purely romanticized status of his independence in a borderland driven by brutal, transnational expansionism.

In chapter 5, I turn to poems of the *Piers Plowman* tradition that undercut Revivalist claims concerning the geographical and cultural provinciality of late-medieval alliterative verse. Situated in a Southwest Midlands–London nexus that connected an allegedly outlying region with the scribal and administrative circles of the Greater Westminster area,[80] the Langlandian tradition forces us to abandon the center–periphery rhetoric at the heart of Revivalist discourse. While Revivalist critics often link alliterative poets with cultural and technological backwardness, the poets of the *Piers Plowman* tradition prove to be on the cutting edge of communications technologies. I assess a canny conception of book production among Langlandian poets, examining the *Crede*-poet's recursive media analysis and the strategic use of anonymity for political communication in *Richard the Redeless.* Tracking the narrator's movement in *Mum and the Sothsegger* from idealism to pragmatism, I explore a systematic deployment of media and authors in a recursive allegory of political discourse. Langlandian poets' sophisticated understanding of social networks and textual media is obscured by Revivalist efforts to read alliterative poets as neo-primitives looking ever backwards into a moribund, oral, and Saxon past.

In the epilogue, I discuss the literary historiographical implications of undermining Alliterative Revivalism. Arguing that my modernist view of the nation involves an epochal rather than teleological model of historical change, I maintain that the disengagement of nationalist desires structuring the reception of alliterative texts exposes medieval motivations that often mesh with current critical priorities. By identifying Revivalism's monolithic discourse (chapter 1), clarifying the transnational context for alliterative poems (chapter 2), and then exploring the diverse local contexts obscured by a reductive Revivalist vision (chapters 3–5), I expose the considerable, yet often unconsidered, weight of nationalist fantasies. It is only by disclosing Revivalism's racialized and nationalist rhetoric that we can recover what Gabrielle Spiegel calls the "social logic" of literary works as "lived events" that "are essentially local in origin."[81] By identifying and thereby disengaging layers of reductive criticism that have accreted to critical assessments and editions of alliterative texts, I seek to forge dynamic links among late-medieval and current concerns.[82] *Revivalist Fantasy* re-engages with what has been left out of the nationalist fantasy of a doomed, nativist metrical rebellion, re-imagining communities and commitments occluded by the deeply rooted discourse of Alliterative Revivalism.

1

Beyond the Backwater

ALLITERATIVE REVIVALISM AND NATIONALIST FANTASY

WHEN THORLAC Turville-Petre theorized a single "school" of late-medieval alliterative poets in his 1977 *The Alliterative Revival*,[1] he was not offering a fundamentally new literary historical view. Turville-Petre's monolithic model has a long scholarly lineage, with the proposal having been reiterated enough times by 1906 for a revisionist William Henry Schofield to refer to "the so-called alliterative revival."[2] Writing the history of English prosody in 1910, George Saintsbury devotes several sections to the "Alliterative Revival," imagining a single poetic army with Langland its chief "rebel," who set a "revived alliterative prosody" against a syllabic verse-form imported from the Continent.[3] And even as he recognized some regional differences among participants in this "Revival," J. P. Oakden envisioned a single "alliterative school" confined largely to "the west."[4]

By the mid-twentieth century, the concept of an Alliterative Revival had been so frequently deployed as to appear unavoidable. Feeling compelled to entitle her survey "The Alliterative Revival," Dorothy Everett nevertheless critiques the implication of a "suddenness" that is only "apparent,"[5] while Derek Pearsall notes that, though "revival" should be replaced by either "renewal" or "reflourishing," he will "nevertheless" continue using the term.[6] Literary historical repetition had produced its own momentum. Indeed, even critics of the theory of a "revival" of Old English metrical practice tend to assume a single alliterative "school." While Hanna critiques the "Alliterative Revival" as "Old Historicist," he still assumes a single "alliterative movement" and generalizes that "alliterative narrative is inherently exemplaristic."[7] Such reduction of the variety of contexts and desires informing late-medieval alliterative works demonstrates the continuing influence of Alliterative Revivalism, a discourse rooted in and sustained by the nationalist foundations of Middle English studies.

Two influential eighteenth-century literary histories provide a critical prehistory for Revivalism. In Thomas Percy's 1765 *Reliques of Ancient English Poetry,* an amateur antiquarian work that leads directly to Middle English literary criticism's nineteenth-century professionalization,[8] alliterative verse is linked genetically with Anglo-Saxon prosody. For Percy, Langland did not in *Piers Plowman* practice a "new mode of versification," but rather "retained that of the old Saxon and Gothic poets; which was probably never wholly laid aside, but occasionally used at different intervals."[9] Percy here offers the earliest consistent ethnic literary history that will influence the later Alliterative Revivalism. Not only does Percy foreground the question of continuity with Anglo-Saxon metrical practice, but he also treats alliterative prosody in recognizably modern terms. Much as Hanna emphasizes that alliteration is of secondary metrical importance, merely helping mark the essential factors of four stresses in heteromorphic, caesura-separated lines, so does Percy state that the "harmony" of *Piers Plowman*'s meter comes "not so much from its alliteration, as from the artful disposal of its cadence, and the contrivance of its pause."[10] Percy's ethno-historical vision of alliterative practice provides a framework that is amenable both to those critics who maintain that alliterative verse had a continuous existence in oral channels, and to those who assume the early medieval death and late-medieval resuscitation of a meter defined by its "Gothic" origins.

The question of continuity of alliterative practice proves crucial to both the narrative and the reception of Thomas Warton's seminal *History of English Poetry.*[11] Warton's anxiety over how to historicize Anglo-Saxon England suffuses his preface. While investigating "the savage condition of our ancestors" in order "to mark the steps by which we have been raised from rudeness to elegance," Warton concludes that Saxon culture is anterior to English literature.[12] For Warton, the Norman Conquest is the threshold to "the progress of our national poetry," marking an English epoch "when our national character began to dawn."[13] Yet however much Warton contends that the "mighty revolution" of Norman conquest "obliterated almost all relation to the former inhabitants of this island," he reveals an uncanny sense of an identity that pre-dates this "national" dawn, as when he claims that before the arrival of the Normans "we were an unformed and unsettled race."[14] Such anxiety about ethnic continuity will be central to Revivalist theory. Though Warton structurally invokes rupture with the Saxon past, he cannot resist integrating its after-life into English literary history.[15] Making a claim that Skeat removes and attacks in an 1871 edition,[16] Warton argues that Langland consciously adopts the "style" and "alliterative versification" of the "Anglo-Saxon poets," having "rejected rhyme" and instead adopted the "affectation of obsolete English."[17] Without using the word "revival," Warton anticipates Alliterative Revivalism by portraying a deliberate late-medieval appropriation of a traditional meter as a reaction against the predominant prosody.

With the transition from eighteenth-century antiquarianism to the increasingly professionalized academic medievalisms of the nineteenth century, the groundwork for an explicit Alliterative Revivalism began to be laid. The crucial factor in generating Revivalism was the epochal shift to nationalist discourse. Theorists of the re-animation of alliterative prosody imagined an English exceptionalism that marked Anglo-Saxon roots as the native origins of an England-dominated British imperial state.[18] Nationalist critics racialized history, manufacturing continuity with an idealized Germanic past by narrating the meteoric rise and collapse of a native alliterative poetics. This ethno-historicizing fantasy of the doomed Revival project shapes the modern reception of late-medieval alliterative poems. A medieval modernity is built on the ashes of alliterative culture, as a dying neo-Saxon poetic school gives way to Chaucer's triumphal blending of Norman wit with Germanic vigor.

Despite its emotional appeal to ethnic and territorial attachments that seem to stretch beyond historical memory, the nation is for some theorists an exclusively modern phenomenon. According to Anderson, the earliest nations are Creole communities carved out of late-eighteenth-century imperial provincial states, with European nations coming later in a nineteenth-century wave of imitative construction.[19] The rise of the nation is dated even later by Gellner, who links nationalism and its product, the nation, with nineteenth-century industrial capitalism's need for social and economic homogeneity to sustain growth.[20] The Alliterative Revival offers literary historical aid in such national consolidation. By imagining a fierce opposition between ethnically marked prosodies, while downplaying the shared linguistic terrain upon which this struggle was played out, Revivalist critics participated in the production of what Anderson calls the "ellipsis" of simultaneous remembering and forgetting required for nation-building.[21] Much as English educators introduce William the Conqueror as a "Founding Father" and yet sidestep the conclusion that this French-speaking warrior might best be described as the "Conqueror of the English,"[22] so do Alliterative Revivalist critics portray modern English literary history through a dialectics of memory and difference, generating a homogeneous English literature from ethnically distinguished, but linguistically continuous, poetic competitors.

If nationalism always precedes the nation, as Gellner asserts, then Revivalist discourse has participated vigorously in manufacturing the shared past required for nation-building. Linguistic and ethnic identity prove the key ingredients of Revivalism's contribution to the "invention of tradition" that enables the modern nation to imagine its roots reaching into "remotest antiquity."[23] Alliterative Revivalists, by presenting late-medieval literary history as a conflict of two Middle English dialects, exploited the power of the vernacular to encode as English pre-modernity's "immense antiquity behind the epochal sleep."[24] Revivalists selectively mined the historical inheritance, constructing a homogeneous nation efficiently mobilized for capitalist growth and international competition.[25] Various platforms helped sustain Revivalism. Disseminating itself in nineteenth- and early-twentieth-century literary histories, anthologies, and editions, Alliterative Revivalism inculcated a notion of Englishness as a uniquely hybrid blend of putatively pure Saxon and Norman camps whose cultural competition generated modernity.

Racializing Prosody
Revivalist Fantasy and English Exceptionalism

With the nineteenth-century development of European nationalism, the vexed nature of mapping ethnic identity onto the complex terrain of British history intensified. Despite the complex ethnic history of pre-modern England's waves of Celtic, Roman, Scandinavian, Anglo-Saxon, Norman, and Flemish immigrants, there emerged what Deanne Williams calls the modern "national pastime" of "smoothing out" this ethno-historical complexity through a "simple binary of Saxon and Norman."[26] From as early as the seventeenth-century launching of the Norman Yoke myth, according to which a freedom-loving Anglo-Saxon culture was displaced by an absolutist, feudal society installed by French-speaking invaders, generations of literary histories foregrounding this native–foreign binary laid the foundations for Alliterative Revivalism.[27] As Krishan Kumar argues, the "historical fantasy" of the Norman Yoke requires that we posit "two nations," Norman and English, while also assuming an absolute class division between a Norman elite and an English nation of commoners.[28] Much work is required to sustain such a myth of ongoing Saxon–Norman struggle. The Norman Yoke fantasy works both against our general understanding of the assimilative habits of the "chameleon-like" Norman "diaspora,"[29] and against William I's clear record of cultivating continuity by self-consciously appropriating an English crown and its related institutions.[30] As literary studies professionalized in the nineteenth century, scholars engaged in nationalist philological work elaborated the myth of a nationally divided

Britain.³¹ As we shall see, Revivalist critics eschew the most virulent forms of racist Anglo-Saxonism, since their nationalist narrative of alliterative output requires a presentation of neo-Saxon culture as retrograde and ultimately unsuccessful.³² More interested in propagating a myth of English exceptionalism through cultural hybridization, Revivalists emphasize the fall of an allegedly ancient line of native metrists in order to frame Chaucer as the first English poet to transcend the Saxon–Norman *agon*.

Given that one of the requirements of nations, according to Anderson, is that its members recognize their own nation as one among a number of separate, sovereign, and limited territories co-existing in the homogeneous, empty time of modernity,³³ it is hardly surprising that key elements of what would become a national myth consolidating English national identity come from both non-English and English scholars. Indeed, what is to my knowledge the earliest explicit use of Alliterative Revivalist terminology comes from the American George Perkins Marsh's 1862 *The Origin and History of the English Language*.³⁴ As Horsman demonstrates, Marsh, who insisted that Americans and Englishmen were linked by descent from the "Gothic" (Germanic) race that had successfully displaced Rome, was a key propagator of racialized mythological history in the United States.³⁵ The explicit language of revival is also seen in the Dutch-born, German-language philologist Bernhard ten Brink's 1877 *Geschichte der englischen Litteratur* [*History of English Literature*].³⁶ Finally, the French scholar Hippolyte Taine's racialized rhetoric of native genius and foreign encroachment launches what I will call Revivalism's militarization of meter. Far from a parochial, partisan discourse, Alliterative Revivalism proves a multi-national project sustaining nineteenth-century nationalism and racialism. While nationalist critics may come from various, even competing backgrounds, they share the methodological insistence on the nation's primacy in the post-industrial West.

In his 1863 *Histoire de la Littérature Anglaise* [*History of English Literature*], which Henry Louis Gates, Jr., has described as providing the "great foundation upon which subsequent nineteenth-century notions of 'national literatures' would be constructed,"³⁷ Taine pursued a positivist program of historicizing literary works through the categories of *"race," "milieu,"* and *"moment."*³⁸ With no single determinative factor, Taine's literary historiography interrelates epoch, surroundings, and race in assessing the "elementary moral state" informing a civilization's works.³⁹ Taine shared with a number of Victorian English scholars, particularly archaeologists, an arbitrary view of national growth, in which invasions are seen as the primary factor in pre-national change, up until a singular invasion ends this dynamism and stabilizes national and ethnic identity; in the case of English literary history, the Norman Conquest comes to ground English ethnic identity.[40] As with the ideology of what Patrick J. Geary calls "primary acquisition" transcending waves of invasions to mark certain territory as thereafter the possession of an objectifiable ethnicity,[41] Taine's narrative fantasizes a historical moment transforming both race and place. As David Wallace shows, geography is pressed into service in Taine's ethno-historiography: Taine's Anglo-Saxons live barbaric lives as virtual hunters and gatherers in a gloomy Saxon Britain, only becoming "leavened into English" when Normans deliver the "sunny, civilizing powers of Gallicism."[42] Such a nationalist view of the French as the civilizing supplement for barbaric Saxons will prove central to Alliterative Revivalism.

Despite his claim for the essential role of "*moment*," Taine produces a literary historiography that collapses temporal differences in the assertion of deep racial continuities. We are told that "Milton's Satan exists already in Caedmon's, as the picture exists in the sketch; because both have their model in the race [*modèle dans la race*]," with Caedmon finding "his originals [*matériaux*] in the northern warriors, as Milton did in the Puritans."[43] Taine's interrelation of the earliest identifiable Anglo-Saxon poet with a canonical voice of Protestant England projects modern English identity into insular antiquity. This fantasy of an always already Protestant England anticipates the prominent role of religious independence and English exceptionalism in a number of histories of nationalism.[44] Taine's fourteenth century resembles Gellner's industrial nineteenth century, in which the nation is generated through a general education that levels local differences:[45] post-Conquest England experiences ongoing racial conflict, with literature a central battlefield, as Norman "conquerors" cultivate a literature "purely French, purged from all Saxon alloy" [*bien française, bien purgée de tout alliage saxon*], going so far as to send their children to France to "preserve them from barbarisms" [*barbarismes*].[46] That very barbarism helps Saxon identity endure: since Saxon "dullness" [*lourdeur*] renders this conquered race incapable of learning a "foreign language," the stage is set for their ethnic survival.[47] Imagining the Saxon tongue, "English," as a kind of "contagion" [*contagion*] that spreads among the Normans over generations, Taine cites the dangerous contact with commoners required for the maintenance of aristocratic life: the Normans "breathe" the Saxon language, encountering it via "foresters in the chase, the farmers in the field, the sailors on the ships."[48] Modern English becomes a product of contamination, generated by the mingling of aristocrats with a "coarse" [*grossiers*] yet vocal Saxon under-class.[49]

Taine's literary ethno-history of political rupture and return anticipates Alliterative Revivalist narrative, though he does not fully nationalize the fourteenth century. Arguing that Saxons "remembered their native rank [*rang natal*] and their original independence" during the period of "long bitterness with which they continually recalled their ancient liberty [*liberté antique*]," Taine confers racial memory on a subaltern Saxon class who survive the Conquest and live on into Langland's fourteenth century.[50] For Taine, facial hair becomes a site for national memorial: Saxons cultivated "long beards from father to son in memory of the national custom [*coutumes nationales*] and of the old country [*patrie*]."[51] Literature also enters into this ethno-historical pastiche. Anticipating much Hollywood anachronism, Taine imagines fourteenth-century Anglo-Saxons sharing tales of Robin Hood oppressing clergymen and freeing commoners.[52] Ethnicity and political victimization combine in Taine's vivid resistance narrative: "suddenly, amid the pleasant banter or the monotonous babble of the Norman versifiers, we hear the indignant voice of a Saxon, a man of the people and a victim of oppression, thundering against them."[53] This exemplary Saxon is the author of "Piers Ploughman," a poem revealing "traces of French taste" while betraying few such "vain foreign phantoms," with its "national, and true to life" [*national et vivant*] poetic "body."[54] In Langland the "old [*antique*] language" and "the old meter" reappear, with rhyme giving way to "barbarous [*barbares*] alliterations."[55] Linking Luther and Langland through "Teutonic [*germanique*] conscience" and "English good sense" [*le bon sens anglais*], Taine portrays the alliterative poet in terms that will inform Revivalism—as a native, liberty-loving rebel who appropriates an old, barbaric meter in protest against his Francophile age. However, Taine hesitates to project the modern nation fully into the medieval period, preferring to locate Langland and Chaucer in an epoch pre-dating the two "national outbreaks" [*explosions nationales*] of Renaissance and Reformation.[56] Pointing toward the modern, but failing to attain it, Taine's fourteenth-century Saxons foreshadow generations of racialized, Revivalist literary history.

With ten Brink's seminal description of "the revival of alliterative poetry" [*das Wiederaufblühen der alliterirenden Poesie*],[57] Revivalist narrative becomes clearly formulated. At first sight, ten Brink seems to eschew ethnic or dynastic politics in a purely aesthetic history. Speculating that in late-thirteenth- and fourteenth-century monasteries of the Welsh Marches there were poets producing rhymed works with pronounced ornamental alliteration in the style of *Juliana,* ten Brink concludes that "a secular poet of that region [*Gegend*]" must have through sonic exposure become "conscious of the advantages of the alliterative long line [*Langzeile*]" over "romance-poetry" [*Romanpoesie*].[58] For ten Brink, the poet reviving alliterative verse had only to look around him, for "formulas of alliteration [*Alliterationsformeln*] were plentiful in the poetry of his home [*Heimath*], in the folk-song [*Volksgesang*] as well as in the erotic lyrics of the clerks."[59] Linking a new literary movement to a single poet's innovation, ten Brink imagines saints' lives as the venue in which alliterative prosody was formed by removing rhyme and increasing the "strictness" [*Strenge*] of alliteration.[60]

Revived due to this single poet's aesthetic pragmatism, the literary innovation of alliterative meter evolved rapidly into a movement. For ten Brink, the appeal of this simultaneously "old" and "newer form" lay in its "national character" [*nationalen Charakter*] still being "felt" [*empfand*].[61] Citing ethnic conflict as the background for the prosody's popularization, ten Brink racializes alliterative meter as neo-Saxon. In ten Brink's Revivalist vision, the prosodic adaptation occurred "at a time when the native life [*heimliche Wesen*], as a whole, was beginning powerfully to react against the foreign [*gegen das fremdländische mit Macht zu reagiren begann*]."[62] When ten Brink claims that "something old-fashioned [*Altväterisches*] and serious, a touch of austerity [*Sittenstrenge*] or of piety [*Frömmigkeit*] pervade the poems,"[63] he inaugurates a Revivalist insistence on neo-Saxon seriousness and conservatism, while manufacturing a unitary field of study through the question-begging assumption of "the poems" about which he proceeds to generalize.

Combining ten Brink's sense of an aesthetic program of revival with Taine's dramatic narrative of ethnic conflict, George Saintsbury's *A History of English Prosody, from the Twelfth Century to the Present Day* (1906–10) emerges as the next Revivalist landmark. Through a focus on technology, Saintsbury produces a seminal portrait of a culturally backward neo-Saxon underclass with their backs to the provincial, late-medieval walls. For Saintsbury, alliterative poets compete valiantly but futilely in a poetico-military struggle every bit as binary and uncompromising as the Saxon-Norman hostilities imagined by Taine. This "late fourteenth-century battle between the older and newer schools of English prosody" was fought for no lesser stake than that of becoming the sole standard meter of modern English literature.[64] Saintsbury's militaristic literary history is suffused with the inevitable triumph of the sense of rhyme. Considering the thirteen-line stanza form of the *Awntyrs off Arthure,* in which alliterative long lines are structurally combined with rhyme,[65] Saintsbury could have conceived of compromise—a metrical marriage of Saxon Robin and Norman Marian, if you will. However, he asserts that the "really useful lesson" of such poems is to show that the "charms of rhyme were felt to be too great to resign" even "in the very moments of the alliterative reaction."[66] For Saintsbury, such hybrid prosody serves merely to indicate the relentless spread of regular foot-patterns into the prosody of cultural and technological latecomers. When working exclusively in the native long line, alliterative poets are imagined as a rebel army of "bowmen" fighting against poets armed with "gunpowder"; when they arm themselves with rhyme's "arquebuses and firelocks," the alliterative school is presented, not as intensifying its campaign, but as submissively signaling through such metrical hybridization that the "rhythm of the foreigner has triumphed."[67]

In depicting a technologically backward alliterative movement, Saintsbury studiously avoids a simple racial calculus: Langland is no pure Saxon, but already a hybrid. Echoing Marsh and Skeat, Saintsbury insists that, while Langland was ever ready to deploy "dialect and now obsolete English," he was "no less copious in French words" than Chaucer.[68] This portrait accords with then-current understandings of the post-Norman English as of mixed racial descent. In his 1900 *History of English Literature,* Reuben Post Halleck reveals the dialectic of hybridity used by Revivalists to explain English literature's particular power. According to Halleck, the Normans benefited from the "intermixture of Teutonic and French blood" that gave them "the best qualities of both races"—the Norman's "nimble-witted" imagination and "northern energy," and the Saxon's "dogged perseverance" and "good common sense."[69] The further blending of Norman and Saxon was like "joining the swift spirit of the eagle to the strong body of the ox," with Norman "yeast" interacting with Saxon "dough" to enable "English literature" to become "first in the world."[70] Saintsbury's Revivalist history insists on this fantasy of post-Norman hybridity as a frame for both the "Titan" of the "alliterative revival" (Langland) and his "literary contemporary," Chaucer.[71] Assuming that the combination of Germanic and French traits explains the exceptional status of the English, Saintsbury presents an evolutionary vision of the colliding "older and newer schools of English prosody," with Chaucer's gravitation toward Frenchness giving him the decisive edge in this inter-ethnic struggle.[72]

Associating alliterative verse with a more primitive technology than the cutting-edge weapons systems used by rhyming, syllabic poets, Saintsbury neatly obscures his assumption of a shared and stable field upon which the allegedly "native" alliterative and "foreign" syllabic forces struggle—namely, vernacular English. In Saintsbury's agonistic model, Chaucer's modern poetics synthesizes antithetical Saxon and "foreign" prosodies. With a resolutely teleological vision, Saintsbury portrays the Alliterative Revival as a "backwater or loop" within the "single stream" of English poetry.[73] This "reactionary rebellion," besides being "very curious," proves a crucial evolutionary moment, revealing Chaucer as both competitor with, and heir to, the alliterative tradition's ethnic spirit.[74] Saintsbury's "genius"

Chaucer "mustered and co-ordinated the literary resources of the whole country, North as well as South," producing a body of work that would eventually become nationally definitive.[75] By the sixteenth century, Chaucer would be recognized as the "Lycurgus of the laws of English poetry" who provided the "foundations of all future building," by "co-ordinating" the "ragged, uncouth, unkempt dialects of his predecessors into a real standard English of poetry."[76] In literary terms, then, Saintsbury's modern English nation arises in the late fourteenth century.[77]

Saintsbury's insistence that Chaucer's "blending of Teutonic and Latin matter and machinery" was a "retrospective exploit"[78] reveals the nationalist tactic of teleologically rewriting past cultural events.[79] No Romantic medievalist-escapist, Saintsbury looked to the past to project his historical moment, writing the rise of English modernity by fashioning past poets who were themselves obsessed with the past. By describing an alliterative backwater, Saintsbury makes clear that he has no desire to re-animate such prosody and so separates himself from medievalist scholars and artists who sought to escape the uniformity and alienation of industrial life by reviving medieval forms.[80] Quite to the contrary, Saintsbury's evolutionary model of alliterative verse participates in the nationalist agenda that Gellner sees as central to post-industrial nationalism, which requires the erasure of ethnic discontinuities in order to create and sustain a homogeneous, anonymous, and literate population.[81] By invoking an ethnically marked alliterative difference only to foreclose its possibilities as already disarmed and displaced, Saintsbury participates in the Revivalist myth of a hybrid English nation destined to exploit its powerful Saxon-Norman blend.

Alliterative Arms Races, from England to Scotland to America

Carrying on the racialized fantasies of the late nineteenth and early twentieth centuries, a second phase of Alliterative Revivalism applies the militaristic logic of Saxon–Norman prosodic conflict to more immediately nationalist concerns. As we have seen, Revivalist discourse was launched by critics from multiple national backgrounds. If nationalism always precedes a nation,[82] then so must a general theory of the nation sustain any nationalist discourse: Revivalist critics insist first and foremost on *the* rather than their nation as the basic literary historiographical unit. As we shall see, Scottish and American critics join English scholars in fashioning a Revivalist discourse that justifies an English-dominated British state. While patriotic Scottish critics sometimes compete with English colleagues in ethnonational literary historiography, some Scots contribute explicitly to Anglo-Saxonism.[83] Meanwhile, American medievalists utilize regionalist models to produce virulently nativist Revival narratives, reinforcing English critics' myth-making about systemic, late-medieval Saxon–Norman conflict.[84]

Nationalist interests emerge clearly in a critical competition to claim virtually all alliterative poetry as either Scottish or English. Considering patriotic critical inquiries into the historical context for the poet Huchown, Pearsall asserts that "the whole early interest in medieval alliterative verse was carried forward on a wave of fervent Scotticism."[85] Our only evidence concerning the enigmatic Huchown comes from Andrew of Wyntoun's *Original Chronicle* (c. 1420). Andrew attributes from three to five works to the single hand of "Huchown of the Awle Ryale," who "mad" [composed] in "metyr" [meter] a number of "dyte" [songs], including "a gret gest of Arthure" [a great heroic poem about Arthur], "þe Awntyr of Gawane" [the Adventure of Gawain], and "þe Pistil . . . of Suet Susane" [the Epistle of Sweet Susanna]; Andrew elsewhere links Huchown with a "Gest Hystoryalle" [Historical Heroic Poem] and the "Gest of Brutis aulde story" [Brutus's ancient story].[86] The ambiguous nature of nearly every aspect of Andrew's claims inspired manifold attempts to link poems to Huchown and thereby seize for the critic's nation the signal honor of this fantastically prodigious poet's provenance. Besides uncertainty over how to interpret the name "Huchown" and where to locate the "Awle Ryale," most of the titles Andrew lists are vague enough to be applied to numerous Arthurian works. Even if the *Pistill of Susan,* a late-fourteenth-century alliterative poem attested in five manuscripts and usually assigned to the North, can be safely attributed to Huchown, the dialectal evidence still allows space for debate concerning provenance, since Northern and Scots dialects are often difficult to distinguish.[87]

The battle royal over Huchown of the Awle Ryale began innocently enough, with competing claims concerning dialect. In his 1839 Bannatyne Club anthology, *Syr Gawayne,* Frederic Madden identified a number of texts as "*genuine* Scotish poetry"—*Sir Gawain and the Green Knight, Pearl, Cleanness, Patience,* and the Alliterative *Morte Arthure,* each of which he ascribed to Huchown, as well as the *Awntyrs off Arthure* and *Golagros and Gawane,* which Madden claimed to have been composed by another Scot, Clerk of Tranent.[88] In the first publication of the Early English Text Society, Richard Morris's edition of the poems of Cotton Nero MS A.x, Morris argues on the basis of dialect that the works Madden and others had attributed to a Scottish Huchown were actually composed in the West Midlands.[89] Though Morris displays no overt patriotism in identifying the English origins of this significant poetic corpus, the venue for his arguments sends strong nationalist signals. The Early English Text Society, founded in 1864 by Morris and Frederick James Furnivall in reaction to the social exclusivity of the Roxburghe Club, sought to make available to the masses "their forefathers' speech and thoughts" in the form of low-priced editions.[90] Furnivall's 1871 address to the EETS Committee reflects the Society's nationalist background: Furnivall foregrounds "the love of Fatherland" in describing the EETS agenda; cites Professor John Robert Seeley's 1868 address to the Society, which identified the "study of native literature" as "the true ground and foundation of patriotism"; and asserts that EETS "workers" owe a "duty to England."[91] A glance at the EETS's first publications suggests that alliterative verse seemed particularly well suited for this patriotic project of disseminating such "native" antiquities. Within its first six years, the EETS followed up its inaugural anthology, *Early English Alliterative Poems,* with editions of *Sir Gawain and the Green Knight,* the Alliterative *Morte Arthure, Pierce the Ploughman's Crede, Joseph of Arimathie,* and the 1867 inaugural edition of the Society's Extra Series, *William of Palerne,* as well as the first several installments of Skeat's seminal series of *Piers Plowman* editions. Morris's dialectal argument against Madden's Scottish claim acquires a nationalist edge in the context of an Early English Text Society that signaled through its very name the desire to publicize the Englishness of as many literary "forefathers" as possible.[92]

Describing the often-vituperative literary critical debate concerning the "mysterious" Huchown's national origins, Henry Noble MacCracken aptly chooses the language of nationalist militarism.[93] Foregrounding George Neilson's Glaswegian background, MacCracken argues that Neilson's claims for some "40,000 lines of the very meat of Middle English literature" as the work of his "beloved" fellow "Scotchman" Huchown pressured "English scholars to assert their rights."[94] MacCracken's Neilson makes a "sortie into the enemy's country" in order to protect the "fortress" of his Scottish Huchown from the "shot" of Henry Bradley's and Israel Gollancz's "English forces."[95] Exploiting the shadowy nature of Huchown's identity to shore up nationalist claims for an alliterative pre-modernity, the participants in this debate share the Revivalist predilection to steer all evidence toward a fantasy of singularity. For Neilson, Scotland plays a major role in English literary history, with virtually all extant late-medieval alliterative verse traced to the "single superbly appointed pen" of Hew of Eglintoun.[96] When Neilson argues that "we have waited long, with unrewarded patience for any suggestion of the constitution and *personnel* of such a joint-stock company of genius" that produced this body of work, he clearly did not recognize that Alliterative Revivalists were already patiently manufacturing just such a literary "school."[97]

The Scot F. J. Amours's study of Huchown reveals the often arbitrary, tactical nature of Revivalist nationalism.[98] Citing Moritz Trautmann's work on the Alliterative *Morte Arthure,* Amours argues that its poet's Englishness is precluded by his portrayal of France as the "flour" [flower] and "heuede" [head] of "rewmes" [realms]: such sentiments are for Amours self-evidently beyond the pale for an Englishman.[99] Even as Amours links such "epithets" to the Scottish Huchown's "love" for France, the "old ally of his country," he proves ready to abandon nationalist rhetoric when considering the *Morte*-poet's numerous references to "Arthur's army" as consisting of "oure" [our] men.[100] Claiming that "those British warriors were never considered as Scottish," Amours shifts theoretical ground, denying that medieval nationhood informs Arthurian romance, the "world" of which he claims to be "above, or at least outside, the world of strife and bloodshed of contemporary history."[101] Amours's foray into alteritism, however, is brief—a reservation soon forgotten on his way to territorializing Huchown's works as unambiguously "written in Scotland."[102]

If Huchown-obsessed critics drastically reduced the diversity of late-medieval alliterative verse, a later wave of Revivalist scholars leveled alliterative difference despite positing multiple authors, by envisioning a single, politically charged movement. The year 1932 proved to be a seminal one for Alliterative Revivalism, with the English critic R. W. Chambers channeling decades of racialized literary history, while the American scholar J. R. Hulbert moved Revivalism into resolutely regionalist terrain.[103] While Chambers makes explicit use of Saxon–Norman struggle, Hulbert marks a shift away from explicitly racial formulations. Much as, according to Gates, race does not disappear from Anglo-American literary criticism dominated by New Criticism's insistence on a timeless and trans-cultural canon, but rather becomes "implicit" in post-Eliot methodologies,[104] so does the racialized rhetoric of post-Saintsbury Revivalism move underground in theories that mark alliterative difference in regional rather than ethnic terms.

Encoding his argument for a continuity of Anglo-Saxon and late-medieval English culture with ethnic rhetoric, Chambers continues the late-nineteenth-century conflation of language and race.[105] Denying that Anglo-Saxon culture was in a state of decadence before the Norman Conquest, Chambers asks why the "resultant nation" was not "Norman-French," and why, after a "long struggle" between Saxons and Normans, what "comes at last to the top is not merely the English language, but essentially an English, not a French civilization; an English mind, not a

French."[106] For Chambers, alliterative verse is inherently linked with an "English" ethnicity continuous with the "Anglo-Saxon": when alliterative verse "reappears" in the fourteenth century it is one of a number of "national triumphs" in a "struggle" over whether England would be English or French.[107] Insisting that the "correct technique of the alliterative poet must have been handed on from poet to poet" since Anglo-Saxon times, Chambers argues that the Alliterative Revival, which produced "two of our three greatest Middle English poets," demonstrates ethnic continuity at the heart of the English nation.[108] When Chambers argues that late-medieval alliterative verse provides a "link between Old England and Modern England," with monuments such as *Piers Plowman* revealing "the English spirit as it still exists," he adds to a chorus of Revivalist voices retrofitting modern English nationalism with the fantasy of an ancient Englishness surviving Norman attempts at ethnic cleansing.[109]

While Chambers envisions alliterative continuity primarily in ethnic terms, he also broaches the subject that moves to the center of alliterative studies, speculating that "there must have been some parts of the country" where "the alliterative school . . . maintained an energetic life."[110] The Iowa-born critic J. R. Hulbert sought to localize this alliterative heartland. In an influential model of an oppositional Alliterative Revival, Hulbert hypothesizes a regionalist patronage aimed at supporting provincial, magnate power-bases against the rising influence of Southern, Francophile courts. Hulbert's sociopolitical narrative eschews the explicitly racialistic focus on Saxon continuity and instead looks back to the reign of John I and the English "baronial opposition," whose continuing desire for "local independence" drove the Revival.[111] Arguing that fourteenth-century barons were, like their forebears, "historically conscious," cultivating a "tradition of opposition to government by the royal household," Hulbert claims that the "historic, national associations" of late-medieval alliterative texts allowed barons to maintain a "patriotic" and "distinct" literary culture separate from that of the Southern "court."[112] Joining with Oakden in presenting alliterative poetry as distinctly provincial,[113] Hulbert injects political oppositionality into the deliberate revival of a meter associated with a national English heritage.

Hulbert's argument for a baronial patronage of an alliterative school that set martial, provincial Englishness against effete, Southern Frenchness has been decisively critiqued. Noting that late-medieval magnates possessed multiple and discontinuous holdings, and that their households led itinerant lives that precluded rigid regional identification, Elizabeth Salter undermines Hulbert's confident localization of baronial life.[114] The monolithic impulse of Revivalism nevertheless shapes Salter's response. Claiming that patrons of alliterative verse had "national" rather than regional motives, she insists that Revival poetry derived from fourteenth-century baronial libraries well-stocked with French and Latin manuscripts of Continental texts.[115] Hulbert's focus on magnate households is also dismantled by Turville-Petre, who demonstrates that the vast majority of surviving alliterative poems were "copied into unpretentious, workmanlike and unadorned manuscripts," suggesting gentry rather than aristocratic patronage.[116] Once again, the monolithic nature of Revivalist discourse limits this revisionary work. By linking "alliterative poetry" to a single socioeconomic provenance, Turville-Petre reduces the range of possible audiences for poems that he uniformly traces to a single "school."[117]

Along with its reductive view of reception, Hulbert's oppositionalist hypothesis reveals an anachronistic projection of English nationalism. According to Gellner, nationalism is a "theory of political legitimacy" that "requires that ethnic boundaries should not cut across political ones," and that "ethnic boundaries within a given state" should not "separate the power-holders from the rest."[118] By portraying late-medieval magnates as patronizing a "native" meter that asserts their "continuity of blood and neighborhood" against a Chaucer whose work and world would have appeared "French,"[119] Hulbert fantasizes modern nationalists acting on xenophobic impulses, fearful of any rupture to the "cultural continuum" between "rulers and ruled."[120] Ignoring the clear cultural overlap between putatively provincial magnates and their Southern counterparts, both in terms of social class and of participation in French-language literary culture,[121] Hulbert retroactively creates a rigid and oppositional cultural divide. As we shall see (in chapters 2 and 5), alliterative texts often resist Revivalist efforts to obscure the socioeconomic hierarchy that links the alleged opponents in a metrical civil war.

Turning to Charles Moorman's American Southern Anglo-Saxonist narrative and its discursive links with nineteenth-century justifications of slavery,[122] we can see the dialectics of remembering and forgetting of "reassuringly fratricidal wars" that Anderson sees as central to "nationalist genealogies."[123] Discussing Ernest Renan's 1886 claim that members of a French nation must have forgotten such horrors as the St. Bartholomew's Day massacres or the destruction wrought by the transnational Albigensian Crusaders who descended upon the multilingual occupants of Catharist Provence, Anderson argues that nationalist mythology manufactures French unity out of complex, heterogeneous, pre-modern traumas.[124] Renan provides the insight that forgetting is productive in the modern manufacture of national identity: moments of suffering and division are fashioned into unexamined strands that consolidate a French populace no longer fissured by region or ethnicity.[125] A similarly selective, institutional processing of national mythology is effected, Anderson argues, via "English history textbooks" that transform the French-speaking William the Conqueror into a "Founding Father," and by American textbooks that compel students to "remember / forget the hostilities of 1861–65 as a great 'civil' war between brothers rather than" its actual status as a war between "two sovereign nation-states."[126] Traumatic divisions serve memorialistically to bind a later populace into national community.

With his Revivalist narrative of the Saxon alliterative long line surviving the Norman Conquest and biding its time in oral channels before seeking vengeance, Moorman presents an uncanny conflation of such institutional acts of forgetting and remembering. For Moorman, the Norman Conquest is analogous to the United States Civil War: each conflict "scratched away the innocence of its defeated victims and robbed them of their homes, drove them back to the land and to the heritage" and to "whatever fragments might be shored against their ruin, a Delta or a Wirral forest, a primitive Baptist meeting, or Gawain's 'corsedest kirk.'"[127] In Moorman's narrative, the "lingering effects" of the "agony" of conquest were "very real" in the provincial "West."[128] Addressing the unlikelihood that "English" grievances would remain fresh centuries after the Norman invasion, Moorman invokes temporal alteritism, contending that "time passed more slowly in the Middle Ages than now."[129] Even as Moorman temporally separates the medieval and modern epochs, he reintegrates them through reassuring myths of civil war that simultaneously divide and consolidate the English and American nations.

Building a Backwater
Alliterative Revivalist Singularity and Marginalization

Working with an ethno-historical fantasy of native Saxons struggling with foreign Normans, Revivalist critics engaged not in antiquarian escapism, but in a nationalist enterprise. Revivalist genealogy used a racial fantasy to bridge the medieval–modern gap, imagining stern, warlike neo-Saxons who continued to resist Normans into the liminal period of late-medieval England, which witnessed the second death of the alliterative past and the simultaneous birth of syllabic modernity.[130] To portray a unified Saxon reaction against a foreign other, Revivalist scholars required more than just the collapsing of centuries of historical difference; they also required the myth of a single alliterative tradition working with a single alliterative meter. As we shall see, Revivalism's monolithic presentation of alliterative prosody posits an essentially outmoded poet, who plays the role of literary straw man displaced by a forward-looking, soon-to-be modern Chaucer.

With his representation of "the alliterative poet" in his "homely and wholesome English guise," Geoffrey Shepherd exemplifies the Revivalist reduction of regional and temporal variety that enabled a nationalist underwriting of Chaucer's modernity.[131] For Shepherd, the "alliterative poet" has read "old, good books," and stands alongside those "backward-gazing" poets "drawing upon the oldest traditions of European poetry."[132] The traditionalism that Shepherd attributes to the "alliterative poet" separates him from his Southern, syllabic contemporaries and transforms him into a temporal anomaly—a holdout from an ancient and dying Germanic tradition. The critical lineage of this aged and untimely alliterative poet can be seen in W. P. Ker's 1904 *The Dark Ages,* which imagines an epoch beginning around 1100 when French and Provençal literature became ascendant and proceeded to exterminate all "Dark-Age" forms, including "Teutonic" literary traditions in Germany—with the signal exception of "the survivals and revivals of Teutonic alliterative verse."[133] For Ker, the late-medieval English poets who deployed alliterative verse were reproducing a moribund tradition of a "Dark Ages" that was "really and not merely conventionally separate from what came after."[134] Portraying alliterative poets as stillborn literary remnants, Ker limits their interest to the presentation of philological data concerning ancient literary practice. Shepherd's alliterative poet, dressed in English ethnic garb, gazes backward into Ker's curiously past and present Teutonic epoch—an era lost, save for the atavistic alliterative enunciation of Englishness that coincided with Chaucer's busy construction of a brave, new syllabic modernity.

To tie alliterative meter to a single ethnic category, Revivalist criticism must develop a monolithic model of alliterative meter and a unified aesthetic. As we have seen (in the Introduction), scholars have long employed a generally stable definition of the alliterative long line.[135] It is clear from the work of Thomas Cable that the early notion of the *same* alliterative line reappearing in the fourteenth century is a fiction[136]—with the only reviving agent being numerous critics' longing for a cultural continuity that bridges the Anglo-Saxon and late-medieval periods. The principal subjects of scholarly dispute concerning late-medieval alliterative meter are the extent to which the number of syllables intervening between stresses may vary; whether stress and alliteration must always coincide; and the number of permissible stress-patterns. Hypotheses regarding stress-patterns reveal the impact of monolithic understandings of the meter, for a key Revivalist legacy is its insistence on seeing the *aa ax* stress-pattern,[137] the most common disposition in Old English prosody, as the sole pattern for an authentically "alliterative" line.

For Skeat, the *aa ax* pattern, while certainly the most frequently attested line, is by no means definitive. A number of alternate stress-patterns are allowable, "provided that the *swing* of the line was well kept up by the regular recurrence of loud syllables."[138] Even lines lacking alliteration are for Skeat "quite admissible *as a variation*," with the four-beat rhythmic "swing" the decisive factor.[139] Skeat's view of a flexible meter that by its very nature admits various patterns of stresses accords well with much manuscript evidence and supports conservative editorial principles that caution against rejecting scribal readings that do not fit the *aa ax* mold. In de-prioritizing alliteration among his criteria for "alliterativity," Hanna allows for just this sort of fundamental flexibility: as long as the line has four stresses and a caesura, and is composed in heteromorphic form[140]—that is, as long as it's got Skeat's "swing"—it counts as "alliterative."[141]

With his argument that, rescued from scribal interference, each alliterative line must conform to the *aa ax* pattern, Hoyt Duggan reveals an editorial approach inflected by Revivalism's insistence on singularity. While it is beyond this book's scope to provide exhaustive treatment of Duggan's metrical arguments, I will examine Alliterative Revivalism's continuing impact by considering the database Duggan deploys to generate laws governing even the minutest fluctuations in unstressed syllables. Coincident with his interest in resisting the conservative editorial trend of avoiding the emendation of scribal readings, Duggan uses a database that favors the delivery of expected, if not desired results—for it includes lines of verse from *editions*,[142] such as Israel Gollancz's 1920 *Winner and Waster*. As Stephanie Trigg demonstrates, Gollancz in this edition conflated his "interpretative and editorial tasks in the manner of an interfering and meddlesome scribe, with enormous effects on subsequent readings of the poem."[143] The use of such a heavy-handed edition suggests that an aspect of *petitio principi* is woven into the database, which consists, not of raw manuscript data, but of readings produced according to long-standing Revivalist assumptions about alliterative prosody: with earlier editors having regularly emended on the basis of an *aa ax* standard, it is hardly surprising that their processed readings support an argument for prosodic regularity.[144] Revealing the Revivalist urge for a single framework to filter all variety, Duggan chooses to pursue his quest, against the preponderance of manuscript evidence,[145] for a rigid *aa ax* standard as the "single unified poetic" that has been hidden from us by medieval scribes who were less familiar with alliterative patterns than we are.[146]

Alongside arguments for a single prosodic pattern, theories of a unitary aesthetic also reveal the influence of Revivalism's reduction of late-medieval alliterative variety. Assuming a single "alliterative 'aesthetics,'" Susanna G. Fein explores the predilection of this "school of poets" for imagining the "weird and ghastly."[147] Images of the "horror of physical decay" in alliterative works are said to deliver "the poems' comprehensive message—that mankind is caught in time, moving inexorably from naive, carefree youth to sadder, wiser old age, to death."[148] While a powerful guide to such grisly productions as the *Awntyrs off Arthure* and the *Siege of Jerusalem,* Fein's vision of a uniformly grim alliterative aesthetics casts a pall over any poem composed in the meter. Even for critics insistent on the regional, temporal, and prosodic diversity of alliterative verse, the influence of Revivalism's monolithic vision seems apparent. While David Lawton argues compellingly for the need to abandon reductive historical arguments concerning alliterative poetry's origins, insofar as paleographical, dialectal, and literary historical evidence suggest multiple centers of production,[149] he elsewhere insists on filtering such diversity through a single aesthetic—"penance" as an omnipresent theme.[150] Grounding his literary historical claim in late-medieval reception, Lawton argues that *Piers Plowman*'s seminal status provided a vernacular precedent for a penitential alliterative poetics, shaping the "tastes of a common audience" for the alliterative "movement."[151] For Lawton, alliterative prosody became so suffused with Langland's Christian project that the very "choice" of the meter conveys a "spiritual value."[152]

As I shall argue throughout this book, Revivalist insistence on a unifying aesthetics distracts from poets' contemporary concerns, redirecting attention either to a Saxon past or to the fantasy of an organized, national movement. In Fein's and Lawton's Revivalism-inflected studies, the eyes of alliterative poets are uniformly directed, Janus-like, toward a painful past and a promising but otherworldly future. However lively the joys of such poets, they are for Fein "tainted by the grim knowledge that all earthliness will pass away," with the mitigating hope consisting not of an altered political or cultural future, but the "hope of eternal pleasure to come."[153] The logic of penance directs the thoughts of Lawton's alliterative poets to past sins, in a movement sustained by desire for heavenly reward. Such alliterative poets look simultaneously back to a native literary past, and forward to a spiritual home beyond death—and thus look away from the political and cultural present.

The literary historical influence of Revivalist agonistics seems clear. Such aloof alliterative poets, trapped between morbid reflections on the past and hopes of postmortem joy, seem easy prey for a competing Chaucerian school grounded in contemporary, earthly politics. With nostalgia and apocalypticism overriding current interests, Revivalism's alliterative poets are marginalized, fulfilling Saintsbury's vision of technologically backward, reactionary "alliteratives" rebelling against the "newer" prosody.[154] Imagined as a "backwater" in an English prosodic "stream" that relentlessly assimilates a native four-beat line into the syllabic, proto-iambic style of Chaucer,[155] Revivalism's alliterative verse functions primarily to highlight Chaucer's proto-nationalist triumph. Revivalism's objectification of alliterative unity proves pure fantasy: as we have seen (in the Introduction), little to no clear evidence survives of a metrically self-conscious, nativist alliterative movement. The relentlessly backward gaze of Revivalism artificially isolated a group of alliterative poets as *themselves* backward-gazing. Sustaining an image of a barbaric, native, and ultimately stillborn poetics, Revivalist critics helped create a homogeneous culture by consigning its ethnic civil war to pre-modernity. Much as, according to Robert Crawford, eighteenth-century Scottish critics sought success in Britain by purging Scotticisms that betrayed provincial, if not barbaric, origins,[156] so did Revivalists elevate English identity by exorcising a fatally backward alliterative culture. Such Revivalist fantasy not only centralized English literary history, but also marked its transition to the cosmopolitan, because Continental, literary world inhabited by Chaucer. Forced to serve such a nationalist literary historical agenda, alliterative texts have been regularly distorted by Revivalist frames. Recovering the contemporary concerns and commitments driving alliterative texts requires undoing the nationalist nostalgia embedded in Revivalist editions and literary histories.

Native Wild Men
Recovering Alliterative Irony in *Wynnere and Wastoure*

To demonstrate what is lost through the artificial extraction of texts from the shared terrain of late-medieval British literature, I will consider a passage that is often presented as primary evidence for alliterative self-identification but that in fact proves the product of the totalizing, ethnocentric energies of Revivalism. If Revivalists have manufactured a narrative of failed native rebellion against foreign-influenced poetry, then theorists of the continuity of alliterative practice from the Anglo-Saxon period (e.g., Chambers) and those hypothesizing a sudden re-animation of the meter (e.g., Saintsbury) have only a superficial disagreement, since each camp links the rise of the modern, English-dominated British nation with alliterative culture's death-throes. Revivalism thus evinces a "stagist" vision of literary history,[157] with proponents of continuity and rupture both seeing a pivotal moment of political evolution from pre-modern flux to a metrically monolithic modernity. As we shall see, the nationalist myth of an organized re-animation of a primitive Saxon poetics impels editors and critics to inject stereotypes of native backwardness into texts. Indeed, Revivalists prove especially seduced by the prospect of seeing *themselves* anticipated in the poetry. With his complaints concerning the collapse of traditional poetics, and his anxiety about a provincial space losing its population to a newfangled and inauthentic South, the narrator of the fourteenth-century *Wynnere and Wastoure* is made to look strikingly like a nineteenth-century Alliterative Revivalist.

Wynnere and Wastoure, a fragmentary dream vision uniquely attested in British Library MS Additional 31042, plays a powerful role in Revivalist accounts. Topical references lead some critics to assume a date (c. 1352) at the Revival's very dawn, rendering the poem a privileged window into an alliterative tradition antedating *Piers Plowman.*[158] Turning to *Wynnere and Wastoure* to rehearse the Revivalist fantasy of a traditional, native verse exiled to the provinces, Nevill Coghill portrays a young Langland who heard the spirited satire as it "travelled those hilly Western regions" that were "the last home of our more ancient style of poetry" and its "great tradition."[159] As part of his more general argument for alliterative poetry possessing "certain extra-rational and pre-Christian elements and a certain massive native strength" absent in Chaucer, John Speirs argues that, since *Wynnere and Wastoure* is so "maturely accomplished," there must have been a living and flourishing tradition" of alliterative verse that pre-dated the Revival's written record.[160] *Wynnere and Wastoure* is featured in the first four pages of Turville-Petre's *The Alliterative Revival,* introduced as a poem to which analysts of the "origins and early history of the Revival must pay close attention."[161]

The poem's editorial history illuminates the distortion produced by its prominence in Revivalism's nostalgic, nationalist narrative. Critiquing Gollancz's influential 1920 edition, Trigg urges vigilance concerning the often-invisible products of "editorial politics," since they are difficult to "dislodge from their position of institutional and pedagogical authority."[162] Writing before her own Early English Text Society edition of *Wynnere and Wastoure* effectively dislodged Gollancz's text, Trigg argues that Gollancz's postwar "nationalist fervor" and a "wish to confirm the popular, oral origins of alliterative poetry" produced a "large-scale and heavy-handed" editorial "program" that frequently conflicts with unambiguous manuscript evidence.[163] Reading the poem as merely "topical satire," Gollancz saw this "pamphlet of the day" as intended merely to figure the "outstanding problems of Edward III's reign"; indeed, Gollancz seems disappointed that the poet produced something so "austere" as "a 'social problem' poem."[164] Gollancz's assumption of topicality leads to reductive decoding, as when he uses "wishful argumentation from heraldry" to identify the poem's herald and "wodwyse" [wild man] (71)[165] as Edward the Black Prince.[166] Since so many readers have accepted Gollancz's manipulation of the text according to his "prior interpretation," Trigg concludes, his "literalism" has foreclosed "a full range of critical possibilities for the poem."[167]

Gollancz's reductive historicism is reflected in the discussion of dating that occupies the introduction's largest section, which concludes that *Wynnere and Wastoure* is "probably the earliest extant poem of the alliterative revival."[168] Revivalist obsessions with single, stable origins drive Gollancz away from the poem he is presently editing—both backwards, as he links the *Wynnere*-narrator's calls for refreshment at the end of each *fitt* with "the "Old English 'gleeman' and the Northern 'skald'"; and forwards, as he asserts that "the old man of *Wynnere and Wastoure* inspired Langland, the poet-prophet of England."[169] His Revivalist eyes looking everywhere but in the *Wynnere*-poet's present, Gollancz sees it simultaneously as a relic of antiquated Northernness and as an early action in the alliterative rebellion against metrical modernity.

By resituating *Wynnere and Wastoure* in its cultural moment, I will recover pleasures precluded by such relentlessly literary historicist vision— namely, a playful literary performance that exploited interplay among poet, narrator, and audience. The limitations of Gollancz's Revivalist vision can be seen by considering the "wodewyse" who bears England's arms before the unnamed king (70–80). Gollancz's insistence that this herald is Edward the Black Prince prevents us from appreciating the grotesque playfulness of this figure who welcomes the narrator into the dream. As Susan Crane argues in her analysis of the burning wildmen-performers at Catherine de Fastavarin's 1393 wedding celebrations, the "wodewose" was a sophisticated theatrical symbol: figuring a lack of civilization's constraints on clothing and sexuality, while nevertheless signifying aristocratic culture through the artifice of disguise and ritual context, the wild man reveals the possibility of slippage between courtly culture and the uncannily proximate woods.[170] Similarly, Roger Bartra argues that the medieval wild man, who by *figuring* wildness inhabits the borderlands between nature and culture, is the "realization of a paradox" and "the individual without name."[171] Such a play of possible meanings is arrested by Revivalism's genealogical drive, as Gollancz clumsily punctures the aesthetic veil of the *Wynnere*-poet's "wodewyse," imposing a historical name as his origin and end. As we shall see (in chapter 2), Revivalist assumptions of mere traditionalism often obscure sophisticated uses of cultural figures to serve current needs.

Much as Gollancz's reductive reading of the wild man obscures the figure's ambivalent energy, so does his insistence on a stern and unsophisticated narrator preclude us from appreciating the poet's playful relation to truthfulness. Repeating the Revivalist fantasy of an older, native world being uprooted by a metropolitan Southern culture, Gollancz argues that the *Wynnere*-poet uses an aged narrator to contrast the "simplicity of life" in the provinces with that of "fashionable" London.[172] When the narrator describes himself as a "Western" man and then complains about a world where "nowe alle es wytt and wyles that we with delyn, / Wyse wordes and slee and icheon wryeth othere" [all that we now practice is cunning and deception, crafty, sly words, with each individual deceiving the other] (5–6), we ought to recognize, as Gollancz does not, that the narrator excludes neither himself nor his region from such untrustworthiness.[173] The pre-fabricated Revivalist vision of a solemn, aged, and neo-Saxon narrator inhibits critics from sensing any irony in the narrator's complaint, which is often presented as a mere conduit for the poet's entirely straightforward traditionalism.[174] Delivering damning praise in the manner of ten Brink, for whom a "Teutonic poesy" [*germanischer Poesie*] characterized by "directness" [*Unmittelbarkeit*] has no need for sonic charm or precise imagery, Gollancz reduces this narrator to a medium for the neo-Saxon minstrel-author.[175] Reproducing long-running stereotypes that, in Katie Wales's words, link the "gritty" and "granite" speech of "blunt speaking and straightforward" Northerners with the "harsh and bleak" landscape of the North,[176] Gollancz precludes the *Wynnere*-narrator from delivering any verbal play—for any such frivolities threaten his fantasy of a dying Germanic poesy's stern defense.

The clearest sign of Gollancz's Revivalism lies in his emendation of a line that, despite its improbability, has been cited as primary evidence of alliterative self-identification. After speaking of a past time ["Whylome"] when there were "lordes in londe þat louid in thaire hertis, / To here makers of myrthes þat matirs couthe fynde" [lords in the land that loved in their hearts to hear composers of entertainments who knew how to produce matters of substance] (19–20), the *Wynnere*-narrator says of his own epoch:

Bot now a childe appon chere withowtten chyn-wedys,
Þat neuer wroghte thurgh witt thies wordes togedire,
Fro he can jangle als a jaye and japes telle
He schall be leuede and louede and lett of a while

Wele more þan þe man that made it hymseluen. (24–28)

[But now a beardless youth, who never through his skill worked these
words together, will for a while be believed and loved and esteemed
much more than the man who composed it himself, since he can chatter
like a bird and tell jokes.]

In emending in line 25 to "thre" [three] instead of the paleographically unambiguous manuscript reading "thies" [these], Gollancz writes into the text the same identifying trait by which Chaucer's Parson betokens his non-Southern contemporaries—the three alliterating sounds of the *aa ax* line (Introduction).[177] By literally putting his own reductive view of alliterative composition into the mouth of his editorial creation, Gollancz manufactures "evidence" for a poetics so simplistic as to be content to define itself merely by reference to its meter.

Trigg's "dislodgment" of Gollancz's text through restoration of the manuscript reading in line 25 stands as a crucial revision of Revivalism's literary historical sway. With its insistence upon recovering an authentically Saxon and hence backward alliterative poet, Revivalism impels Gollancz to overlook what Halleck sees as natural to the "nimble-witted" Norman, yet alien to the Saxon "ox" with his store of good, but merely "common," sense—namely, irony.[178] Gollancz's edition prevents us from seeing that the *Wynnere*-poet here craftily embeds the voice of the necessarily absent author within the text, forcing any future performer to mouth his or her own inauthenticity in the very act of performance—to state that the performer did not compose *these* words. What Gollancz influentially interpreted and rewrote as a traditionalist poet's nostalgic complaint about young performers out-earning him obscures what is in fact a sophisticated meditation upon the conditions of publication in manuscript culture, in which the author who publishes necessarily loses all control over the work.[179] Released from reductive, Revivalist editing, the *Wynnere*-poet emerges as anxious about the same unstable book-market into which Chaucer, to whom literary critics such as Gollancz so readily accord a sense of irony and play, anxiously sends his "litel bok" [little book], *Troilus and Criseyde* (V.1786–96). As we shall see (in chapter 5), Revivalist assumptions about alliterative traditionalism blind us to canny engagements with textual culture and writing technologies.

Dislodging *Wynnere and Wastoure* further from Revivalist filters allows us to recover both the poem's factitious archaism and the vibrant, indeed avant-garde, literature that the narrator's pose conceals. When in the prologue, the narrator, presenting himself as a representative "westren wy"

[Western man], bemoans the flight of the younger generation "southewarde" [southward] (7–8), we may suppose that he is complaining about the socioeconomic mobility triggered by the Black Death of 1349 and later outbreaks, which increased demand for labor to such a magnitude that the bonds of *villeinage* tying peasants to specific locales became structurally loosened.[180] With social mobility came instability in reading class from clothing, which led, beginning in 1363, to parliamentary sumptuary legislation regulating certain apparel and cuisine.[181] The *Wynnere*-narrator initially appears to criticize the possibilities for social mobility that have made the younger generation leave the "West," such that the provincial "sone" [son] will not return to care for the father when he "hore eldes" [grows old and gray] (9). Echoing critiques of blurring class divisions in numerous late-medieval political prophecies, the narrator links the coming of "domesdaye" [doomsday] with a world where "boyes of blode with boste and with pryde / Schall wedde ladyes" [young commoners will with boast and pride wed noblewomen] (14–16).[182]

The conservatism and nostalgia that Gollancz and later Revivalists read into the prologue of *Wynnere and Wastoure* proves modern rather than medieval, generated by the critical desire to locate an authentically provincial voice capable of delivering an unfiltered "English" experience.[183] Any claim to the poet's conservatism is undermined by the narrator's endorsing Wastoure's allegorical position in the poem's eponymous debate. Through his regional studies of Cheshire and Lancashire, in which vicinity the *Wynnere*-poet may have worked,[184] Michael J. Bennett depicts the destabilization of social barriers brought about by the prolific getting and spending of wealth in this most important late-medieval English military recruiting ground.[185] The *Wynnere*-narrator, in presenting his dream vision's armies, devotes fifty lines to the description of Wynnere's army of merchants and clergymen, peppering the discourse with conventionally biting anti-fraternal and anti-mercantile satire (143–92).[186] A mere four lines of noticeably non-satirical verse describe Wastoure's literal army. Wastoure's "sadde men of armes" [resolute warriors] (193) include precisely the social climbers whom Bennett sees as stimulating the late-medieval Northwest Midlands economy,[187] for the initial description implies an army consisting exclusively of commoners—"bolde sqwyeres of blode, bowmen many" [bold squires of common stock, and many bowmen] (194). That the narrator is partial to Wastoure's military careerists is made clear when he appropriates one of the insulting words repeatedly used by the dream-disputants in exchanging insults. Shifting from reported speech to the third-person voice, the narrator at one point names the next speaker as "this wrechede Wynnere" [this wretched Winner] (324) and highlights the narrator's insult by having Wynnere retaliate a mere two lines later for Wastoure's having called him a "wriche" [wretche] (309), by calling Wastoure "wrechede" [wretched] (326).

While Nicholas Jacobs reads the narrator's partiality to Wastoure as indicative of an "unfashionable" and "romantic conservative,"[188] I contend that *Wynnere and Wastoure* exposes as a pose the prologue's seeming nostalgia for a traditional Midlands. The narrator appears to embrace the radical socioeconomic changes shaking up the Northwest Midlands, since specific appeals to tradition within the dream debate are voiced consistently by the "wreched" Wynnere. Wynnere claims that the prodigal Wastoure does not "folowe" [follow] his "fadirs" [forebears], who used to store up crops and other provisions for dry times; instead, Wastoure wastes his money on wine, women, clothing for retainers, and indeed whatever his heart "lykes" [desires] (270–83). After noting that the "wyne moste be payed for" [wine must be paid for] (283), Wynnere indicts Wastoure for his involvement in precisely the kind of dynamic economic exchange transforming the Northwest Midlands: Wastoure is said to be compelled to "weddis to laye" [set up mortgages] or his "londe selle" [sell his land] (284). That the men "of blode" [commoners] in Wastoure's army even have lands to sell is powerful evidence for this militarized region's social climbing. Gentrymen and nobles in Wastoure's army who sell their ancestors' lands reveal an economy in flux, since they move capital outside of the direct lines of familial inheritance, allowing new blood into the landowning classes. Insofar as the critique of such socioeconomic change is proclaimed by the "wreched" Wynnere, it follows that the *Wynnere*-poet celebrates the liquidation of tradition in a "West" in which estate sales fuel the consumption of goods by a socially active military class.

Ambiguity concerning the poem's king, who sometimes seems an English monarch and sometimes an emperor of greater sovereign sway, contributes further to an atmosphere of dynamic change.[189] That the king is English is signaled through heraldry, for the "wode-wyse" bears royal arms that signify the English claim to overlordship over France initiated by Edward III in 1337, with two quarters occupied by the "flowres of Fraunse" [flowers of France] and two by the "thre leberdes" [three leopards] of England (75–80). Englishness also enters into the dream vision through translation, with an inscription on the royal pavilion in "fresche lettres" [bright letters] communicating the Order of the Garter's usually French-rendered motto: "Hethyng haue the hathell þat any harme thynkes" [Shame to the person who thinks any harm in this] (65–68).[190] The king's apparent Englishness is undermined by the fact that those paying him allegiance are too numerous and heterogeneous to seem a national body, and indeed include sworn enemies to the English state. The armies who send their representatives, Wynnere and Wastoure, to receive judgment from the king include "alle the folke of Fraunce" [all the people of France], men from Lorraine, Lombardy, Spain, Westphalia, and others of "Inglonde, of Irlonde, Estirlinges" [England, of Ireland, and Hanseatic traders] (138–41). The *Wynnere*-poet leaves artfully ambiguous whether this transnational body of subjects represents the fantasy of a nationalist narrator (a reading that would undermine Revivalist emphasis on regional anti-royalism), or whether this king transcends conventional territorial delimitation. The very proliferation of signs that could be read as indicating nationality precludes any easy assessment of the precise jurisdiction over which the dream-king reigns.

That the figure of the "wode-wyse" is *made* to bear the English arms can also be read as an overdetermined sign indicating anxiety about the price of imperial power. In heraldry, the figure of the wild man of the woods—detached from yet bordering civilization—is often used as an arms-bearer. Signifying the overpowering of a territory's native inhabitants, the heraldic wode-wyse figures conquest as necessarily past, with the tamed wild man forced to hold up his civilizer's sign.[191] Seeing the wode-wyse of *Wynnere and Wastoure* as a "mysterious figure" with "no active role" beyond that of arms-bearing,[192] Trigg points to the essential passivity of this liminal entity, who remains speechless in a poem otherwise overflowing with conversation. In the narrator's fantastic vision, heraldry's allegorical wode-wyse has come to life: the casualty of conquest inhabits—indeed, haunts—the conquering king's space.

This silent service of the *Wynnere*-poet's wode-wyse speaks volumes about a regional reflection on militarism that, as we shall see (in chapters 3 and 4), simultaneously celebrates and undermines Arthurian empire as a figure for the English state. The regional context for such reflections emerges when we resist Revivalist efforts to tie poems such as *Wynnere and Wastoure* to a distant past and a timeless minstrelsy. While inhabitants of the Northwest Midlands region profited from military activities, by the fifteenth century the region was already heading toward decline, having lost "several generations of population" through warfare and plague.[193] Even as the *Wynnere*-poet suggests an English king lording it over all Europe, the text casts an ominous shadow over such success by opening the poem with a reminder of the self-destructive Trojan past that had become part of English self-understanding since Geoffrey of Monmouth: "Sythen that Bretayne was biggede and Bruyttus it aughte / Thurgh the takynge of Troye with treson withinne" [Since Britain was settled and Brutus conquered it, through the taking of Troy by means of treason from within] (1–2).[194] This conjunction of conquest and betrayal is echoed in Arthurian works circulating in and around the Northwest Midlands, revealing an anxious fascination with a war-saturated economy's fragile foundations (see chapter 3).

As much as Turville-Petre assures us that he does not, in isolating an alliterative "school," mean to propose a "sort of fourteenth-century Pre-Raphaelite Brotherhood, with members united by friendship and a common artistic programme and purpose,"[195] it is difficult not to question the value of grouping every alliterative text into a single category, with the dates and provenance of these poems ranging over at least two centuries and all across Britain.[196] While many alliterative texts indeed originated in the Midlands and the North, these regions prove far more diverse than the proverbial province to which Revivalism frequently consigns texts. Moreover, key alliterative works derive from the political culture and book-market of the Greater London area (see chapter 5), a provenance undermining Revivalism's rigidly center-periphery model.[197] By identifying the ways in which generations of Revivalist editions, anthologies, and literary histories have shaped the reception of late-medieval alliterative texts according to racial and national fantasies, I will redirect attention to the local contexts informing these poems. Revivalism's monolithic model and resolutely backward gaze can be critically disengaged. As I did with *Wynnere and Wastoure*, I will work against ethno-historical nostalgia, regaining access to the sophisticated, present-minded literary play obscured by a Revivalism that binds alliterative poems simultaneously to a Teutonic antiquity and a nationalist modernity.

2

Cross-Channel Becomings-Animal

PRIMAL COURTLINESS IN *GUILLAUME DE PALERNE*
AND *WILLIAM OF PALERNE*

NO COMPONENT of Alliterative Revivalist literary history has been more crucial—or more conflicted—than the view that the late-medieval assimilation of formerly hostile Saxons and Normans produced modern English ethnic identity. In his influential argument for the continuity of Anglo-Saxon prose and late-medieval alliterative prosody, R. W. Chambers offers a striking example of Revivalism's racialized historiography. Adopting alarmist language incongruent with the long-pastness of the events that he describes, Chambers asserts that the "national disaster" of the Norman Conquest "robbed us" of possible prose developments in English, through a literary "strangling" that nearly "destroy[ed] the English nationality and the English language."[1] Chambers's Alliterative Revival emerges as a national rescue narrative, with a stable, Saxon Englishness surviving the Norman-French take-over of the channels of power and patronage: alliterative verse moves out of the conquered "Anglo-Saxon hall" and into the "highways," holding out in the shadowy channels of orality until it can reappear in its "full vigour and correctness" in a Revival that takes its place among the "national triumphs" of the "English language."[2]

Chambers's racialized narrative, which conflates language and national identity in its rehearsal of the Norman-Saxon dialectics central to Alliterative Revivalism, reveals the legacy of the nineteenth-century philologies that drove the professionalization of literary studies (see chapter 1).[3] Chambers is exceptional among Revivalists in offering unqualified praise of late-medieval alliterative poets seen as neo-Saxons, and in not emphasizing the movement's inevitable collapse before a Francophile, Chaucerian modernity. However, he reveals a conventional nationalism through his reductive ethno-linguistic historiography. As Anderson argues, the modern vernacular standard, though produced by generations of print-capitalism preying on the death of dialects and competing languages, nevertheless *seems* ancient. Nineteenth-century European nationalists aggressively exploited such factitious antiquity, counting on the emotional power of one's language seeming to "loo[m] up imperceptibly out of a horizonless past," thus linking individuals "affectively to the dead" of a fantastical antiquity.[4] While Revivalist criticism at times appears to stem from an Anglophile, Francophobe nationalism, its primary motivation actually involves a general, rather than partial, nationalism—a defense of the nation in the abstract. The Frenchman Hippolyte Taine, for example, shares Chambers's basic view that language is a battle-ground for national, and indeed ethnic, identity: the "race remains Saxon [*saxonne*]" in part because the "old poetic genius" survives the Conquest, to "flow for a while underground" until the fourteenth-century revival of written alliterative verse.[5] Taine, every bit as much as Chambers, engages in what Geary sees as central to nationalist historiography—the imagination of peoples as "distinct, stable and objectively identifiable social and cultural units" with equally stable linguistic identities.[6]

The fourteenth-century English kingdom presents significant obstacles to nationalist critics straining to conceal the nation's modernity by manufacturing a deeply rooted ethno-linguistic history. With its complex interplay of Latinate culture with English and French dialects,[7] late-medieval English culture resists the post-Romantic conflation of language and national identity.[8] Despite such sociolinguistic heterogeneity, Revivalist critics project a stable English linguistic identity into pre-modernity, isolating a thoroughly English national medium against which ethnic differences can be marked. Building upon the nationalist notion that a language is the private property of a people,[9] Revivalist critics tell a story of attempted ethnic theft, with nativist alliterative poets struggling to preserve a poetics cognate with the English language. As we shall see, ethno-linguistic patriotism such as Chambers's is noticeably absent from a site where Revivalist narrative implies that we should find it—in an alliterative translation of a French work. Rather than a nationalist zealously appropriating foreign material, the poet of *William of Palerne*[10] participates with his French-speaking forebear in a class-based, rather than linguistic, idiom.

Habits of nation-based thinking inflect Revivalism's ethno-linguistic historiography, which imagines Saxon–Norman conflict continuing in a uniformly English-speaking late-medieval culture.[11] Nineteenth-century literary histories regularly present patriotic narratives of linguistic development. As if anticipating Gellner's argument that post-industrial nationalism succeeds in forming nations only after general educational institutions produce the social homogeneity required for constant economic expansion,[12] Thomas B. Shaw argues in his 1849 *History of English Literature* that William I sought to transform his subjects' ethnic status through language policies. Shaw's William enforces "employment of the Norman language in all public acts and pleadings" and "in the schools," using state power to effect "the suppression of the language and nationality of his new kingdom."[13] The Englishman Shaw's romantic vision of ethnic survival, in which Saxonness is kept alive through "the sacred flame of letters" inspiring "patriotic" monks under whose gowns "there often beat the stern Saxon heart,"[14] clearly appealed to his linguistic-nationalist editor and re-writer, the American Truman J. Backus.[15] Arguing that the "national life was not annihilated" at Hastings but survived with its "ineffaceable Teutonic stamp," Backus links the "patriotic spirit of the common people" with resistance to "foreign poesy," and argues that Langland's alliterative tradition seeks to "revive" the prosody of "England" before the Norman Conquest.[16]

Despite such visions of national self-preservation through linguistic resistance, Revivalist criticism installs foreign influence at English literary history's foundation, juxtaposing the collapse of alliterative culture with Chaucer's epochal Englishing of French culture. Warton's seminal argument that Chaucer was not just "the first English versifier who wrote poetically," but also the person who "first taught his countrymen to write English,"[17] required the imagination of barbaric, nativist poets against whom Chaucer differentiated himself. Alliterative poets come to embody the nativist holdouts whom Chaucer had to outshine, with ethnic distinctions concealing the linguistic continuity among the competitors. For Warton, Chaucer is a civilizing force who improved "national manners" that still "retained a great degree of ferocity," using his French-formed poetry to "polish" a rough-hewn England.[18] Applying the supplement of Provençal poetics to his unsophisticated contemporaries, Warton's Chaucer paves the way for the Revivalist view of a backward, neo-Saxon alliterative movement resistant to the Southern importation of French poetic goods.

By isolating alliterative poets as a backward group who pale before an English-speaking but French-influenced Chaucer, Revivalist criticism obscures the transnational complexities of many alliterative works—particularly translations of French literary works. Such limitations follow from the assumption of Chaucer's singular literary historical status as a revolutionary blender of native and Continental traditions who nevertheless remains thoroughly French. The ethno-linguistic incoherence of Revivalist discourse can be seen clearly in William Vaughn Moody and Robert Morss Lovett's 1905 *A History of English Literature*. Moody and Lovett argue that "foreign wars and centuries of domestic intercourse" had "broken down the distinction between men of Norman and men of Saxon blood," producing a "new language" and a "new and vigorous national life."[19] Since Moody and Lovett depict this new culture as a "merging of Saxon and French," we might expect them to present Chaucer, who is this brave new world's "new poet," as a hybrid figure.[20] Quite to the contrary, this "new poet" Chaucer embodies the "Norman-French strain," with his poetry modeled on "the French system," while Langland represents the "other half of the English nature"—the "Germanic strain in the nation," with its "mystical, sombre, spiritually strenuous" qualities expressed in the "old system of native versification."[21] Moody and Lovett stress the weakness of Langland's "rapidly dying verse form," while arguing that "from Chaucer flew the whole stream of later verse, as from a 'well of English undefiled.'"[22] Revivalist criticism again reveals its necessary avoidance of Anglo-Saxonist racism (see chapter 1), since its narrative requires demonstration of an inadequate neo-Saxon culture's collapse before Chaucer's French-hybridized verse. As we shall see, such structural isolation and denigration of the alliterative tradition leads to Revivalism's inability to recover the transnational complexities of translations of French works such as *William of Palerne*.

Revivalism's conflicted portrayal of Chaucer as simultaneously French and yet emblematic of Englishness reveals the literary-historical effect of what Deanne Williams calls the "French fetish."[23] Exploring a dialectics of English attraction and repulsion to Frenchness, Williams describes a late-medieval and early-modern processing of the Norman Conquest as uncannily foreign and yet constitutive of Englishness.[24] Such anxious cultural negotiation of French influences is pronounced in Revivalist discourse. Considering their views of alliterative provinciality and French cultural sway, we might expect Revivalist critics to take a special interest in alliterative translations as acts of aggressive, nativist appropriation. However, this is not the case in the reception of *William of Palerne*, an alliterative translation of the twelfth-century Old French romance *Guillaume de Palerne*,[25] which is often featured in Revivalist narratives due primarily to its date at the alleged dawn of the Alliterative Revival.[26] As a seemingly provincial production appropriating exclusive French material for monolingual English speakers, *William of Palerne* might be expected to attract Revivalists' nationalist attentions. As we shall see, the poem repels such readings, which obscure the cross-Channel ideology of aristocratic exceptionalism that links the Old French and Middle English romances. Nationalist readings conceal the poem's fundamentally transnational motivations.

Rejecting the nation as our unit of analysis allows us to engage with both the European and the global contexts that override parochially "English" concerns.[27] If Andrew Galloway is correct in stating that for a medieval nationalism to "have meaning it must involve a sense of a territorially and culturally unified community exceeding the elite groups of the clergy or aristocracy,"[28] then the poet William's systematic efforts to join with his anonymous French predecessor reveal an emphatically non-nationalist alliance of aristocratic and clerkly privilege.[29] As we shall see, the primacy of late-medieval social status, which Gellner contends is the primary reason that centralizing states such as late-medieval England and France did not produce nationalism's conjunction of polity and culture,[30] renders Revivalism's emphasis on national origin a critical liability. By setting translation and original in dialogue, I will show that William proves to be interested less in a rugged, neo-Saxon Englishness as an antidote to encroaching Gallic culture than in joining with his French predecessor in a transnational project of class consolidation.

Both *Guillaume de Palerne* and *William of Palerne* promote aristocratic exceptionalism through narratives built on the interrelation of animality with sovereign power. For Giorgio Agamben, the figure of the werewolf plays a vital role in instituting sovereignty: revealing the limits of jurisdiction, the banning (and return) of the hybrid demonstrates the continuity of aristocratic privilege between nature and the state.[31] In *Guillaume de Palerne* and *William of Palerne,* narrative animal play functions as part of a ritual engagement with the natural world that extends and enhances the mystery of sovereign power, as noble identity survives submersion into its seeming opposite—the woodland animal's body. Even as William joins his French forebearer in marking the integrity of sovereignty through movement across cultural and natural spheres, the translation process weaves linguistic difference into this romanticization of the stability of aristocratic identity. Negotiating passages both biological and social, *William of Palerne* provides pivotal evidence that late-medieval "chivalric comedy," as Simpson argues, offers a "sophisticated model of human identity" in which the "civilized order survives only by entering into, and having commerce with, all that threatens it."[32]

My focus on *becoming* in these romances stems from recent interest in mapping the complex interplay of unstable agents within shifting environments. Through his study of "identity machines" as "ever-active conglomerations of animated parts that resist constitution" into "bounded" selves, Jeffrey Jerome Cohen steers criticism away from seeing bestial symbolism as merely static and instead tracks the use of animals (or parts thereof) in the active assemblage of social identity.[33] My focus on *ritual,* informed by Bourdieu's sociological analysis of rites of passage, aims to uncover the symbolic work performed by becoming-animal plots that institute class distinctions.[34] Both *Guillaume de Palerne* and *William of Palerne* imagine apparent movement beyond class, with such playful passage serving only to reinforce the social boundaries that the romance marks. Resisting Revivalism's framing of *William of Palerne* as an early expression of alliterative nationalism, I will explore the poem's animalized dialectics of identity and ritual, imagining not national but *trans*national circuits of power. As we shall see, William outdoes his original in the intensity of the violence and humiliation that he inflicts on lower-class bystanders to aristocratic rites of passage; he is driven by anxiety that his homely Middle English will inhibit his French source's elitist conservatism.[35] Both romances stage the violence required for class consolidation, as non-noble victims illuminate an aristocratic class that closes ranks around itself, emerging unscathed from the animalized games played out in the noble idioms of venery and courtly love.

While the conjunction of artificially disguised lovers and an actually transformed werewolf figures a bleeding together of biological and cultural worlds, gender also becomes a crucial element in these romances' identity play.[36] While one would not guess it from the all-male editorial titles *Guillaume de Palerne* and *William of Palerne,* female agency is pivotal to the becoming-animal plots through which aristocratic identity is first pressured and then reconstituted. The poet William works against Revivalist assumptions of a masculinist, neo-Saxon movement by intensifying gendered play, linking Alexandrine's cross-dressing and class-crossing activity with the kitchen origins of the poem's central, virtual metamorphosis. As we shall see, William's fascination with Alexandrine's sophistication and artifice, as well as his intensification of his source's use of elite idioms to allegorize aristocratic privilege, belie Revivalist efforts to read alliterative poets as backward, unsophisticated neo-Saxons. William's translation proves to be driven not by a populist nationalism content merely to make French texts available, but by a desire to collaborate in sustaining an aristocratic exceptionalism shared by its source. Such elitist partisanship and partnership prove decidedly non-global. By rejecting her Greek imperial fiancé, and coupling first with the bear, then the deer, all while being guided by a wolf, Melior chooses the animal over the Eastern other who is banned from the central stage upon which exclusively Western European aristocratic identity is performed.

Telling the Fine from the Filth
Cross-Channel Class Solidarity

If the rise of the nation requires the destruction of feudal class hierarchy in order to enable the socioeconomic mobility required for capitalist culture, then *William of Palerne* offers a uniquely anxious reaction against a dawning modernity. Joining his French predecessor in support of feudal social privileges threatened by economic diversification, William compensates for Middle English's lower status and his socioeconomically mixed working environment by intensifying the ideological material that he recycles. Though the alliterative long lines and mixed Middle English dialect of *William of Palerne*[37] may seem alien to the octosyllabic couplets of the Picard *Guillaume de Palerne,* the English poet often stays close to his French source, enabling critics to pay particular attention to additions, omissions, and transformations.[38] No additions seem more significant than those linked to the poem's patronage and immediate reception. In the first dedicatory passage, at the close of the first "pas" [section] (161), the narrator bids us offer our prayers to the "hend" [noble] Earl of Hereford, Humphrey de Bohun, nephew of King Edward III, "For he of Frensche þis fayre tale ferst dede translate, / in ese of Englysch men in Englysch speche" [for he first ordered the translation of this noble tale from French into English speech, for the pleasure of Englishmen] (161–69). This praise for the patron links access with pleasure, imagining an aristocrat who uses his wealth to make desirable works available to those who do not speak French. That the translation was aimed at making romantic material linguistically accessible to English speakers becomes even clearer in the second dedication, which informs us that the prayer-worthy Humphrey "let make þis mater in þis maner speche / for hem þat knowe no Frensche ne neuer understo[n]" [had this work produced in such speech for those who do not speak French, nor understand it at all] (5528–33).

There has been some dispute as to what this inability to read French suggests about the socioeconomic background to William's translation. According to Turville-Petre, the dedicatory comments disclose Humphrey's intention to patronize material for a non–French-speaking audience "humbler and less sophisticated than the higher nobility," which excludes Humphrey himself from the work's consumption.[39] This "instructive guide" in "the virtues of 'gentilesse' and 'cortaysie'" was intended for Humphrey's "Gloucestershire dependents," among whom, according to Turville-Petre, such elite virtues would surely have been "sadly lacking."[40] For Derek Pearsall, the "banal" quality of *William of Palerne* disqualifies it from being of interest to the Earl; he speculates that this "casual" production was possibly aimed at "some insistent household clerk" or a member of the "kitchen staff."[41] Whether or not we accept Pearsall's dismissive judgment of the poem's quality, as well as his linkage of banality with non-noble status, the very linguistic medium of Middle English may have exposed the poem to similar, contemporary aesthetic bias. According to Williams, medieval England could never entirely escape the "nagging sense that the English language possessed certain barbarous qualities."[42] Bunt, however, asserts that the lack of ability to speak French is no clear marker of class, citing a comment from the narrator of *Of Arthour and Merlin,* that he has seen "mani noble" [many nobles] who "no Freynsche couþe seye" [cannot speak French] (25–26), as evidence that nobles such as Humphrey may have been more comfortable using English than French.[43]

In the case of either the provincial court audience imagined by Turville-Petre[44] or the even more socioeconomically diverse audience theorized by Bunt,[45] anxieties about social class lie at the center of *William of Palerne.* If the "social function of courtly romance" is indeed fundamentally "instructive,"[46] then William's choices in translating *Guillaume de Palerne* make clear that he targets non–French-speaking consumers for literary lessons in the durability and violence of social hierarchy. William clearly separates himself from the class of speakers for whom his work is intended: despite his recourse to the modesty *topos* in stating that he has translated the "Frensche" [French] text as "fully" [completely] as his "febul" [feeble] wit has allowed (5522–23), his very ability to translate French material into English sets him apart from his imagined audience. Probably a clerk in Humphrey's employ,[47] William would have had a material investment in aristocratic dominance as the engine for the patronage of his literary and other clerkly labors. The class of courtiers in twelfth-century France and in fourteenth-century England included both knights and clerks,[48] which suggests that William's use of translation to defend aristocratic dominance was part of a self-interested defense of feudal privileges against socioeconomic pressures from below. The intensity with which William increases his source's classist violence may stem from the very ambivalence of his clerkly status, since such individuals might come as readily from noble families as from upwardly mobile mercantile or peasant families ascending through positions in estate, church, or government administration.[49] Anxious about his own class position within a feudal hierarchy pressured by proto-capitalist forces seeking the socioeconomic mobility required for modern economic exchange,[50] William ramps up his French original's elitist energies in a rear-guard, romantic defense of feudal hierarchy.

The poet's intensification of his source's rhetorical campaign for the maintenance of feudal class boundaries is nowhere clearer than in *William of Palerne*'s treatment of working-class individuals. Exhausted from the rigors of ongoing flight from their seemingly numberless pursuers, the princess Melior reacts with terror at the sudden arrival of workmen. After hearing one of the "choliers" [colliers] (2520) mention the reward offered for her and her lover's capture, Melior quakes at hearing the laborer's double desire—to gain an informant's reward, and to imagine how much the fugitive lovers will "suffre" [suffer] (2528).[51] Melior's terror registers the general unease of the aristocratic and clerkly classes whose feudal privileges were under economic threat. The poet William performs ironic class warfare, reducing all laborers to filth, even as he imbues one collier with a purely ethical nobility:

> Þen was Meliors nei3 mad almost for fere,
> lest þat foule felþe schold have hem founde þere,
> and darked stille in hire den for drede, boute noyse.
> Wi3tly another werkman þat was þerbeside
> gan flite wiþ þat felþe þat formest hadde spoke,
> seide, "Do þi deuer þat þow hast to done!
> What were þe þe better nou3 þei3h þe beris were here,
> to do hem any duresse? Þei misdede þe never.
> Mani hard hape han þei aschapet,
> and so I hope þei schal 3it, for al þi sori wille. (2541–50)

[Then was Melior nearly crazed with fear, lest that foul filth should have found them there, so she lay hidden in her den, silent and afraid. Soon, another workman nearby began to argue with that filth who had just spoken, and said, "do the work that you were assigned. How would you be better off if the bears were here, and you did them harm? They never did you wrong. They have survived many hardships, and I hope that they will continue to do so, despite your ill will."]

Both the vindictive worker, with his *Schadenfreude* at the noble fugitives' plight and his unseemly informant's zeal, and the clearly ethical worker, who sympathizes with the lovers' cause and condemns his colleague's meanness, are categorized as "felþe" [filth]. While the *Middle English Dictionary* registers this term's use as an indicator of low social class, it is a rare use, with *William of Palerne* being only one of five instances reported for definition 3c's conflation of the social and moral: "A sinful or worthless person; a base fellow; a wanton woman, strumpet." The majority of uses simply bring some nuance to the primary meanings linked with the modern "filth": "Anything material that is considered foul, unclean, impure, or defiling; filth, dirt, mud, rubbish, trash, refuse; putrid or decomposed matter, ordure; squalor, vermin" (1a); and "Natural discharges of the body of man or beast" (2a). The distinction between the low- and high-minded individual is invoked in *William of Palerne* only to be leveled, with moral and amoral worker each filtered through a concept of "felþe" that links labor with dirt and discharge.

In categorizing moral and immoral stone-workers as examples of "felþe," William outdoes his source in integrating class prejudice into a narrative endorsement of aristocratic hegemony.[52] The very choice of animal allegory speaks to social conservatism in both romances, for medieval animal fable was frequently concerned with maintaining hierarchical relations.[53] Through conventional stories of the preservation of noble identity despite the trauma of becoming orphaned, and of the heroic defense of the eldest son's inheritance rights, the poets of *Guillaume de Palerne* and *William of Palerne* use animalized allegories to reinforce the aristocratic values and privileges of their respective noble patrons, Countess Yolande (daughter of Baldwin IV) and Humphrey de Bohun, 9th Earl of Hereford.[54] As we shall see, these poets envision noble identity as sustained through violence, as members of the lower classes become subject to brutal rites of passage linked with the resolutely aristocratic process of becoming-animal.

A sketch of these romances' shared story helps illuminate such animalized class conflicts. It all begins with a werewolf abducting the toddler Guillaume [William], heir to the throne of Apulia, in order to save him from nursemaid-assassins hired by his uncle. The werewolf is Alphonse, elder son of the king of Spain, and himself a victim of political intrigue, having been metamorphosed by his Portuguese stepmother, Queen Braunde, who sought to make her own son the heir. The werewolf watches over Guillaume in the woods until a kindly cowherd finds the boy and raises him as his own son. After a chance woodland encounter, the Emperor of Rome insists on removing the remarkable Guillaume to his court, where he becomes a fine warrior-courtier and falls in love with Melior, the Emperor's daughter. Alexandrine, Melior's aristocratic lady-in-waiting, helps Guillaume and Melior overcome their shyness and become lovers. After her father informs Melior that she must marry the Greek emperor's son, Alexandrine convinces the lovers to sew on bearskins and flee. The werewolf re-emerges to assist the lovers, providing them with food and distracting their numerous pursuers throughout their woodland flight. After their bear disguises become too well known, they change into deerskins provided by the werewolf. They make their way to Apulia, the countryside of which has been destroyed by a siege designed to pressure Florence, Guillaume's sister, to marry the Spanish prince. After dreaming that a knight and lady who are simultaneously bear and deer save her realm, the Apulian queen, Felice, approaches the lovers in her own deerskin outfit and recruits Guillaume into military service. No longer disguised, Guillaume leads a rout of the Spanish forces. After the captured Spanish king reveals Alphonse's origins,

Queen Braunde is summoned and compelled to transform the werewolf back into human form. Guillaume knights Alphonse, who reveals Guillaume's noble origins, and then requests and is granted Florence's hand. Braunde sees her son married off to Alexandrine, while the Spanish king agrees to hold his land from Queen Felice and Guillaume. Alphonse eventually becomes king of Spain, while Guillaume and Melior attain first to Apulian and then to imperial Roman sovereignty.

Signs of entrenched attitudes about social hierarchy emerge with considerable clarity in *Guillaume de Palerne* in the forest meeting of the Emperor and Guillaume, then in the cowherd's care. Beauty allows the Emperor to intuit the foundling's nobility from his evidently unbeautiful peasant surroundings: he sees the boy, stops in his tracks, and

> A grant merveille se seigna
> De sa biauté, de sa samblance
> Et de sa noble contenance:
> Merveille soi qui il puet estre
> Ne de quel gent ne de quel estre,
> Cuide chose faëe soit,
> Par ce que seul iluec le voit. (418–24)[55]

[With great wonder he made the sign of the cross / Because of the child's beauty, his appearance, / And because of his noble countenance. / He marvels who the boy might be, / Who his people are and what his situation is. / He believes that the child might be an enchanted creature / Because he sees him alone in that place.]

The Emperor's expectation of rural decrepitude is so strong that the sight of beauty in such a rustic environment stupefies him: he sooner assumes a fairy lineage than that of a peasant. After intimidating the cowherd into revealing William's mysterious woodland origins, the Emperor states that he will remove this beautiful child who had been found with tell-tale beautiful garments (516–29). After Guillaume hears the cowherd deliver a lesson on behavior at court, he says farewell to his companions (544–99). When the Emperor "ot les nons" [hears the names] Huet le nain [the dwarf], Hugenet, Aubelot, Martinet le fil Heugot [son of Hugo], Akarin, Crestiien, and Thumasin le fil Paien [son of the Pagan], "Forment s'en rit et fait grant joie" [He laughs heartily because of them and is very joyous] (600–601). As the majority of the names are standard,[56] the Emperor evidently laughs at the grotesqueness of pretentions to individuality among members of a class that he clearly sees as an undifferentiated (and presumably filthy) mass, alien to the foundling's sublime nobility that shines through his peasant garments.[57]

The English version intensifies the Emperor's elitist behavior, picturing him as having "gaynliche god game" [pleasurable joy] (369) at hearing names linked with peasant faces, and as expressing bemusement concerning the cowherd's heartfelt discussion of proper courtly behavior. The Emperor's "god game" [pleasurable joy] (346) after the cowherd's speech reveals a mocking glee at the grotesquerie of a sophisticated rural worker. It is as if the Emperor is watching what Michael Camille calls the "monkey-business" of manuscript grotesques, in which animals perform human tasks: like a manuscript reader seeing monkeys ape their social superiors, he finds it absurd that lower life forms can master human activities.[58] The origin of the cowherd's knowledge of court—in *Guillaume de Palerne,* the cowherd's father was in a count's "maison" [household] (577), while in *William of Palerne* the father was simply a "kourteour" [courtier] (342)—reveals the threat to aristocratic privilege presented by the shared space of noble courts, which featured individuals of various social ranks, in aristocrats' retinues and among the numerous workers maintaining an estate.[59] The Emperor's overdetermined amusement at the courtly cowherd discloses the aristocrat's anxious awareness, triggered by the very conventionality of his advice, that courtly ethics might govern the behavior of nobles and non-nobles alike.[60]

Such anxiety concerning the permeability of class lines proves crucial to both *Guillaume de Palerne* and *William of Palerne,* and it dictates both the trajectory of and the apparatus involved in the lovers' flight. As we shall see, the animal-skin disguises in which the foundling-turned-warrior and the Emperor's daughter eventually flee serve as paraphernalia in a ritual marking of aristocratic privileges, both social and territorial. The lovers' costumed flight proves to be an allegory of aristocratic identity, with the layering of bestial skins on courtiers' clothes invoking the "sexual restraint" that Crane reads as key to communicating the "superiority of courtly to common loving" in Maying poetry.[61] Much as Maying narratives use ritual movement from the domestic to the natural world (and back again) to territorialize both spaces as aristocratic, so do the animalized lovers ritually enact the continuity of noble power between the natural and cultural worlds.[62]

Doubling the story of the werewolf with that of an aristocratic couple donning animal skins, *Guillaume de Palerne* and *William of Palerne* meditate on the theatrics of medieval political power and in so doing reveal an emphatically pre-national world permeated by class distinctions. Animalized plotlines come to mark an aristocratic exceptionalism that precludes anything resembling a populist alliterative nationalism. The fugitive lovers take on the status of what Agamben calls "bare life," both by becoming the targets of a literal hunt in which animal disguises expose them to potential slaughter by anyone pursuing them, and by attaining "sacred" status as lovers transcending earthly and spiritual laws.[63] Banned from the courtly world, the lovers choose to become animal, intuiting that by appropriating, indeed incorporating, the "state of nature" at the heart of sovereign power, they will survive the imperial hunt with their elite status intact.[64] William and Melior, in wearing the bearskins *above* their everyday clothes (a detail emphasized in the English version's refusal to imagine a nude Melior beneath the skin),[65] fuse the worlds of nature and culture that they will eventually command as imperial Western rulers.

Animalized Rites of Passage
Siting Sovereignty in the Woodlands

While non-nobles are treated with such disdainful glee as displayed by the Emperor, wild animals receive profound respect, as transitions between humanity and animality ritually encode the interrelation of aristocracy and violence. According to Bourdieu, such rites of passage serve to "socially institut[e]" a "pre-existing difference," by separating, not the zones traveled, but those social groups allowed to cross boundaries.[66] The emphatically public performance of becomings-animal in *Guillaume de Palerne* and *William of Palerne,* in which the hunting party tracking the lovers expands as news travels of the reward for their capture, tells us less about differences in species than about the exclusively aristocratic participation in such games. The terror tactics employed by the werewolf in sustaining the lovers' flight reveal the persistence of the nobility's predatory habits in movement between the human and animal worlds. The lovers' thrilling flight discloses the work needed to maintain aristocratic privilege, as well as the significant costs borne by non-nobles made to participate in this performance of exceptionalism.

Alexandrine singles out the procuring of food as her principal worry about the lovers' journey beyond Roman and Greek territories: "De vo mengier ne sai que dire" [I don't know what to say about what you will eat] (3027). Guillaume's youthful idealism about their survivalist skills—"Bien viverons de nos amors, / D'erbes, de fuelles et de flors" [We will live well off our love, / From grass, from leaves and from flowers] (3033–34)—is echoed by Melior, who says, "Souffrerons, / Mengerons glant et sauvechons

/ Et de cest autre fruit boscage" [We will get by; / We will eat acorns and wild apples / And other woodland fruit] (3231–33). Far from proving to be excellent hunters and gatherers, as do Tristan and Iseult during their forest stay,[67] Guillaume and Melior are virtually never even given a chance to fend for themselves. The werewolf follows them from the moment they depart and soon uses the threat of violence to bring them nourishment, by seizing a passing peasant by the teeth and throwing him to the ground, and then despoiling the hapless *villein* of his food (*Guillaume*, 3256–57; *William*, 1848–49).[68] This seizure of goods sets up the pattern for sustaining the lovers' flight, with the three aristocrats joined in an animalized circuit of predation on lower-classed individuals.

Aristocratic violence brings, not the nuts and flowers that the lovers naively thought would sustain them, but *processed* food, in the form of white bread [blanc pain] and boiled meat [char cuite] (3256–57; 1848–49). The werewolf thereby ensures that the fugitive lovers continue to participate in human culture throughout their woodland journey and also reveals the persistence of his own human sensibilities. Having become animal, Alphonse has not lost his aristocratic tastes. As if to make this clear, the werewolf in both versions threatens a passing clerk who is carrying a cask of good wine, apparently sensing that neither of the lovers is prepared to do without the proper beverage to accompany the meal that he so brutally procured (3334–47; 1884–1900). Class solidarity emerges in the differential treatment of peasant and clerk. While in each version the peasant is knocked violently to the ground, the clerk is allowed merely to flee from the menacing werewolf (3341–47; 1892–96). Even as the narratives figure the violence sustaining aristocratic hegemony, they portray the clergy as relatively privileged, insulated from the physical suffering inflicted on those lower on the social scale.

The werewolf's furnishing of the lovers with cultural necessities both furthers the poem's naturalization of aristocratic habits of consumption and demonstrates Alphonse's status as a human–animal hybrid who has avoided total metamorphosis. The English poet emphasizes the werewolf's hybrid nature by foregrounding his intelligence: he inserts a passage detailing Alphonse's retention of human wit (141–44), as well as numerous references to the werewolf as "witty" (e.g., 145; 158). Critics have recently questioned whether Alphonse actually breaches species borderlines. Denying that the entirely wolf-like Alphonse is a hybrid, Caroline Walker Bynum interprets his change as virtual, arguing that when Braunde metamorphoses him with a ritual bath, she merely reveals the "human body" that had been "there under the wolf skin all along."[69] However, hybridity need not be limited to corporeality in romances negotiating humanity and animality. Using gesture to transcend his state of non-linguistic animality and send messages to his human charges, Alphonse demonstrates the communication capacity that in some taxonomies marks the biological passage to humanity.[70] The werewolf humbly delivers his goods to the lovers (3294–95; 1898–1900), and later bows respectfully before his father and the queen of Apulia (7215–17; 4014–16), naturalizing the human concepts of social status through his performance as an animal literally gesturing toward human status.

The lovers join the werewolf in straddling the human and animal worlds, making their way through the wilds by traveling on all fours during the day and on two legs at night, while Alphonse follows and provides goods for them through repeated assaults on peasants and clerks (3384–99; 1912–22). Both versions depict significant violence in the werewolf's supporting actions, yet *William of Palerne* here isolates a particular threat to late-medieval feudal hierarchy. William adds to the description of one attack that the targeted peasant has just come "chepingward" [from the market] (1848), and he also substitutes a "burgeis" [merchant] (1889) for the priest to whom the clerk is bringing the wine in *Guillaume de Palerne*. The werewolf's new targets figure agents involved in money-based exchange systems, suggesting that the aristocrat-animal's violence is directed by the English poet against members of the mercantile class straining to displace feudal with capitalist culture.[71] Class anxieties clearly drive William's translation.

The devastation experienced by non-nobles in *Guillaume de Palerne* and *William of Palerne* is echoed in two other werewolf romances—the anonymous Old French lai *Mélion*, which dates from what Bynum has dubbed "the werewolf renaissance of the twelfth-century,"[72] and the Latin prose tale *Arthur and Gorlagon,* which survives in a fourteenth-century manuscript but which seems to draw on older, Welsh material.[73] In the Old French romance, after Mélion, a baron attached to King Arthur, decides to leave knightly society, he encounters a giant "cerf" [deer] while hunting in the forest (77–79) and soon after meets a splendidly dressed lady who identifies herself only by class and country, stating that she is "de haut parage / e nec de gentil lignage. / D'Yrlande sui a vos venue" [of high estate, and born of noble lineage. I have come from Ireland to you] (107–9).[74] Three years after Mélion marries the lady, he takes a second fateful trip to the forest. After his wife insists that he procure her some meat from a particularly large deer, she transforms him into a wolf by means of his magic ring and then absconds to Ireland with the "escuier" [valet] who had accompanied them (133–72). As with Guillaume and Melior, Mélion and his lady are linked in an overdetermined way with the woods and with animal life, suggesting the symbolic interrelation of the forest and aristocratic identity. Mélion, now become wolf, follows the lady to Ireland and vents his anger by attacking local sheep. He soon expands his reign of rural terror by convincing numerous wolves to join his raiding parties (189–280). That this devastation is absorbed by the lower classes is made clear by the figure of a "paisant" [peasant] who finally locates the wolves and uses this intelligence to pressure the king to assemble a force to end the wolves' rages (281–304). One is left to wonder whether the agrarian underclass's royally sanctioned respite from aristocratic predation is merely temporary.

In *Arthur and Gorlagon,* rural laborers are also made to pay the price for noble love-games. King Gorlagon becomes transformed into a wolf by his adulterous wife, to whom he had fatefully revealed the shape-shifting properties of the branches from his garden's "virgulta virga pulcra" [beautiful slender sapling], which was of his precise age and height.[75] Having become animal, Gorlagon flees into the "interiores silvas" [recesses of the woods] and, after having "se lupe agresti coniunxit" [allied himself with a wild she-wolf], has two "catulos" [cubs] with his new wife (154; 240). Bringing his new wolf family along with him on raids, Gorlagon rampages through the realm, slaughtering his wife's new young sons in one attack (154–55; 240). When his own cubs are killed, he intensifies his campaign of destruction, making "nocturnis excursibus in domesticas pecudes illius prouincie" [nightly forays against the flocks and herds of that province], performing these with "tanta cede" [such great slaughter] that the inhabitants of the countryside pool together resources to combat the rampaging wolves (155; 241). Once again, peasants pay for aristocrats' feuds. The extension of predatory social identity into the forest world reveals these romances' ritualized representation of protagonists being delivered over to their aristocratic selves:[76] Mélion and Gorlagon each pass through a wolf identity and then re-assume their roles as baron (543–68) and king (175; 250), respectively. When nobles become animal in werewolf romances, non-nobles should evidently run for cover.

The lycanthropic and aristocratic violence committed against the lower classes in such medieval romances illuminates the werewolf's special relation to sovereignty. Analyzing an ancient legal trope that figured banned individuals as werewolves, Agamben links both wolf and fugitive with the *homo sacer,* whose special status as one whom all may kill but none may sacrifice is the vital condition for sovereign rule.[77] For Agamben, the "special proximity of werewolf and sovereign" informs Marie de France's *Bisclavret,* in which a baron's temporary but weekly transformation into a predatory werewolf figures the exceptional mode of Hobbes's natural state of war of all against all, upon which violent disposition modern sovereignty is grounded.[78] That the baron and the king are bound together is concretized, as Cohen observes, in Marie's location of the werewolf's return to manhood on his beloved lord's bed.[79] Agamben's political theologization of sovereign animality helps map out the ritual allegory of aristocratic identity in *Guillaume de Palerne* and *William of Palerne*. Alphonse, temporarily a werewolf, and the lovers, banned from the City while they flee in defiance of imperial law, exist in a state of exception—a passionate passage that instantiates the "state of nature" in which "man is a wolf to men."[80] *Guillaume de Palerne* and its English translation deploy the animal violence of a werewolf-noble to naturalize the aggression at the heart of feudal hierarchy, magnifying the endorsement of sovereign power by having the hybrid be not just a helpful agent toiling for the future sovereign couple, but also himself an heir ready to pounce upon the Spanish throne.

Becoming-Bear, Becoming-Food
Aristocratic Play, from the Kitchen to the Wood

Much as criticism has obscured female agency at the heart of *Sir Gawain and the Green Knight,* with critical resistance to Morgan le Fay's centrality revealed in the poem's all-male editorial title (see chapter 3),[81] so has the standard critical title of *William of Palerne* restricted attention to only half of the fugitive pair. Frederic Madden's title for his 1832 Roxburghe Edition, *William and the Werewolf,* goes even further in occluding female participation by pairing William with his male guide.[82] Such editorial bias belies the powerful part played by women in both *Guillaume de Palerne* and *William of Palerne*. The werewolf's role in rescuing William and guiding the fleeing lovers is, of course, crucial. It is two women, however, who initiate each of the becomings-animal: Queen Braunde, who metamorphoses Alphonse into a werewolf; and Alexandrine, who sets William and Melior on their path of becoming-bear. By highlighting Alexandrine's anomalous status as a sorceress, William clarifies this crucial connection between two female characters who create a magic circle of becoming-animal, writing human destinies in distinctly animal ink.[83] In so doing, as we shall see, William presents a romance that severely challenges Revivalism's portrait of a masculinist, neo-Saxon alliterative movement.

Braunde's magical skill is central to both romances, as her transformations of Alphonse into a wolf and back again reveal her supervisory role in the ritual passage instituting her stepson as both aristocrat and Spanish heir. Alexandrine's magical abilities, however, are only evident in *William of Palerne*. In *Guillaume de Palerne,* Guillaume merely dreams by chance of Melior while Alexandrine is deciding how to bring the awkward lovers together (1117–32). In *William of Palerne,* Alexandrine, who was "ful conyng" [very cunning] and "coynt, and couþe fele þinges, / of charmes and of chantemens" [skilled, able to do numerous things by means of charms and enchantments], is able to "set" [cause] a "ful selcouþe swevene" [a very curious dream] (649–60), demonstrating the skills of a sorceress like Morgan le Fay.[84] According Alexandrine magical powers that match those of Braunde, the poet William forges a structural link between the stories of actual and virtual animalization and magnifies the exceptional status of the aristocratic class whose interests drive the romance.

The clear link between Braunde and Alexandrine in *William of Palerne* disallows any simple moral reading of metamorphosis. Not only are Alphonse and the lovers symbolically linked by undergoing human–animal passage; so, too, are the agents responsible for initiating these ritual actions. The conventionally malevolent stepmother and the stereotypically faithful lady-in-waiting become equally complicit in plots that move aristocratic youths into a state of temporary exception, as they pass out of the court and into the wild—ultimately to be delivered back to themselves as nobles with sovereign destinies. The English version's insistence on Alexandrine's magical skill emphasizes the artifice involved in such aristocratic identity maintenance. Clothing proves to be a crucial element in a poetics of aristocratic becoming, as Alexandrine's magical skills call attention to the virtuality of the animal disguises. Noting that William translates with "gusto" the moment when the lovers inspect each other's outfits, Lawrence Warner lingers over this moment of sartorial sleight-of-hand as evidence for the English poet's preference for Alexandrine's sophisticated, superficial design to Braunde's absolute lycanthropic metamorphosis.[85] Much as the *Wynnere*-narrator's sophistication was disclosed by dislodging Revivalist filters (see chapter 1), so does the poet William's preference for virtual over actual transformation undermine Revivalism's vision of a traditionalist, unimaginative, and literalist alliterative movement. Rather than assuming that the lovers' animal skins are traces of an earlier version in which the fugitives were actually transformed into beasts,[86] I will explore the English poet's magnification of Alexandrine's artistry and dwell on William's clear delight in the lovers' costumed enactment of aristocratic identity.

William's intensification of magical agency highlights another element lying dormant in *Guillaume de Palerne*—the otherworldliness of the lovers' initial disguises. The bearskins targeted by Alexandrine are not just of any sort—they are *white* bearskins. If we can safely discount Gaston Paris's speculation that polar bears are intended, as remnants of a hypothetical antecedent Scandinavian version,[87] a more likely conclusion is that these are, like the white deer who returns Guigemar's arrow and sends him on his love-quest in Marie's *Guigemar*,[88] or like the white stag who sends Gawain on his fateful greyhound-killing journey in Malory,[89] otherworldly animals. The bears' conventionally otherworldly white skin signals that the lovers are being brought into a liminal space, crossing over into a purely symbolic world of allegorical instruction. The English poet's fascination with Alexandrine's magical skill thus adds an esoteric charge to the closed circuit of the lovers' aristocratic becoming.

Identity is in play in Alexandrine's plot, both the means and end of the ritual passage she prepares for William and Melior—a fact made clear by Alexandrine's crossing of class and gender lines in procuring the animal skins. In both versions, Alexandrine foregrounds feudal class structure, arguing that the reach of the emperors' hunters will be such that "noþer clerk nor kniȝt nor of cuntre cherle" [neither clerk nor knight nor rural churl] could pass undetected (1675–76; see *Guillaume*, 3003–6). Insisting that no disguise as a member of another social rank could allow them to escape the imperial hunt, Alexandrine prepares them for a passage beyond the classed world of humans into brute animal life. Even as Alexandrine readies the lovers for their ritual travel, she herself proceeds to negotiate socioeconomic boundaries. In order to acquire the animal-skin ingredients for her performative magic, the aristocrat disguises herself as a servant, blending in with the kitchen staff (3056–63; 1704–13). Much like William's own period spent as a peasant youth until the Emperor's aristocratic eye leads to his removal, Alexandrine's becoming-servant is temporary. In each case, the crossing of class lines merely reinforces noble privilege: William's inherent nobility and Alexandrine's pure pragmatism trump the subversive potential of such socioeconomic moves.

Classed identity remains constant in both versions of Alexandrine's plot, with both the werewolf and animal-skin metamorphoses linking aristocratic power with bare life. The lovers mark out the path of future sovereignty by each taking on the status of the *homo sacer*, as they clothe themselves in animality to become subject to a purely mercenary, and hence non-sacrificial, killing by the expanding and unruly search party.[90] The lovers thus join the werewolf, who binds the natural and the political through its status as a "monstrous hybrid," figuring the double existence of the sovereign as brute life in the "forest" and man in the "city."[91] Alexandrine uses her craft to fashion William and Melior into just such hybrids, directing them beyond class and, as bears, into the world of "bare life," even as human culture remains attached to their bodies. Signs of social identity never disappear from the lovers, with each poet keeping the fugitives from becoming truly bare: the skins are sewn, not onto naked bodies lacking traces of class distinction, but onto their "cloþes, þat comly were and rich" [fine and beautiful clothes] (1737; see *Guillaume* 3091).[92] While playing at bare life, the future sovereigns never really take leave of culture.

While both poems destabilize class boundaries by having Alexandrine play servant to obtain the lovers' ritual costumes, *William of Palerne* expands the identity play of Alexandrine's kitchen adventure to breach gender borders as well. When Alexandrine dresses up as a "serjans" [servant] in *Guillaume de Palerne* (3056), she makes a purely class-based descent in the feudal hierarchy. William ups the ante: Alexandrine puts on "boiʒes cloþes" [boy's clothes] (1705), revealing her as a trickster figure capable of coordinating class with gender play. Alexandrine's conflation of sex and status is embedded within the history of the word "boie" itself. The first two definitions of "boie" in the *MED* signal lower-class status: "A servant, attendant, underling, churl" (1a); and "a person of low birth or rank, a commoner" (2a). Definition 3a, "a worthless or wicked fellow; rascal, ruffian, knave; urchin," demonstrates the late-medieval equation of class status and moral character. The *MED* speculates that definition 4, "a male child," may derive from "affectionate use" of the poor character assumed in definition 3a to inhere in the lower classes. Alexandrine discloses the force of such feudal hierarchical logic by simultaneously breaching gender and class boundaries, actions that saturate the lovers' animal disguises with unstable socioeconomic identity.

Class considerations also inform Alexandrine's choice of bear for the lovers' first steps in ritual ascension to aristocratic pre-eminence through animalized self-debasement. Instituting the "pre-existing difference" of their elite social status,[93] Alexandrine supervises the opening phase of a two-pronged process of becoming-animal in which the werewolf later collaborates. She advises the lovers to wear the skin of a fundamentally ambivalent beast: bears straddle the human and animal domains, as both fearsome hunters and, as is clear from their presence in the castle kitchen, as prey in the aristocratic hunt. As natural as such disguises might seem, the bearskins are saturated with culture, drawn from the very site where brute nature is butchered and dressed according to the art of cuisine. The kitchen fuses culture and nature, remaking the material of the bear according to aristocratic gustatory and sartorial use-values. In putting on the skins, the lovers do not just become bear—they become both food and clothing: as they traverse the woods, their stolen wares recall the emphatically cultured kitchen world. Just as the flaying of an animal according to proper procedures figures the transformation of the natural into a work of art, as in oft-cited instances produced by Gottfried von Strassburg's *Tristan* and in *Sir Gawain and the Green Knight*,[94] so does the kitchen activity that Alexandrine witnesses invoke the aristocratic art of reworking animal bodies.

While the bear's status as both prey and product renders it useful for ritual aristocratic passage, the bear's predatory status also serves a crucial role in Alexandrine's design. Commenting on the similitude of bear and human, the English poet presents the lovers' disguise as a first phase in the shedding of their humanity. Alexandrine here adds the striking detail that the bear's ferocious appearance will scare away pursuers:

Miȝt we be coyntise com bi tvo skynnes,
of þe breme beres and bisowe ȝou þerinne,
þer is no liuand lud iliue ȝou knowe schold.
But hold ȝou ouȝt of heie gates for happes, I rede.
rediliche no better red be resun I knowe,
þan to swiche a bold beste best to be disgised,
for þei be alle maners arn man likkest. (1688–94)

[If we could come by two skins of the ferocious bears and sew you two within them, there is no living person who could identify you, but would keep away from you on the highways for fear of misfortune, I suppose. Truthfully, I could give you no wiser counsel than to tell you that it's best to disguise yourselves as such bold beasts, for they are most like man in all forms of behavior.]

Alexandrine links two seemingly disjunct benefits to the bear-disguise: it will produce maximal terror in others, and bears are more proximate to humans than any other animal.[95] Hunting manuals bear out this unsettling likeness: medieval illuminators reveal a sense of the bear's "endearing and anthropomorphic quality," with its quasi-human habit of occasionally walking on two legs.[96]

William's excision of the serpent and goats from the catalogue of kitchen animals in *Guillaume de Palerne*, which ensures that all of the creatures are "alle fair venorye þat falles to metes" [all noble prey of venery proper for the table] (1685), highlights the high status of hunting as courtly art.[97] By restricting the animals to aristocratic prey, the poet ensures that the lovers' flight invokes the noble discourse of courtly love. The animal world can thus serve here as material for an exclusively aristocratic poetics. Carefully selecting the animal costumes for the lovers' initial becoming-animal, Alexandrine seems guided by a courtly conception of the sex life of bears. According to Gaston Phébus, ursine intercourse approximates that of humans, for "when the bear has his way with the she-bear, they do it like man and woman, one stretched on top of the other" [quant l'ours fet sa besoigne aveques la ourse, ilz font a guise d'omme et de femme, touz estenduz l'un sur l'autre].⁹⁸ By fashioning such disguises, Alexandrine eases the lovers in their transition into aristocratic courtship, allowing them to begin their ritual passage on the surer footing of similitude: the lovers become bears, who are quasi-human as much in their bipedal as in their coital habits.

While Alexandrine begins the process of William and Melior's aristocratic becoming-animal, Alphonse initiates the second stage, allowing them to plunge fully into the status of pure passivity—that state of *passio* [suffering] that Andreas Capellanus conceives as essential to the courtly lover's subjectivity.⁹⁹ In making the transition from bears, both active hunters and esteemed quarry, to pure prey, the fugitive lovers move to a state of courtly vulnerability, transcending to the passionate life of "amorous suffering" that is among the fundamental "techniques of living" of Western aristocrats.¹⁰⁰ By becoming-deer, the lovers enter into the world of "befallenness" that, as Fradenburg argues, forges "group prestige" by "cultivating" the "sufferings" of embodied life.¹⁰¹ The lovers leave the dried, otherworldly pelts drawn from the kitchen to take on new warm skins, hot and bloody from the fresh kill that the watchful werewolf performed before their eyes. The werewolf handles the skinning duties in *Guillaume de Palerne* (4393); the English version intensifies the lovers' participation in their ritual passage, as they themselves slice off the skins (2589–90). In leaving the bearskins, the lovers also leave behind the kitchen: dressing themselves in creatures drawn from the very woods in which they move, they now travel on all fours, a signal of their fuller animality. Now become deer, the lovers of *Guillaume de Palerne* and *William of Palerne* ironically ascend in status in the animalized, aristocratic allegory, attaining the summit of Western European venery's symbolic hierarchy.¹⁰²

The English poet's intensification of the lovers' ritual human–animal passage becomes clear in two scenes demonstrating the fugitives' commitment to melding with their borrowed animal identities. Expressing his desire for weapons to defend himself against approaching workmen, Guillaume states that with such war-gear he would make his attackers know "quel beste ceste piax acueuvre" [what beast this skin covers] (4050–54). The English translator removes Guillaume's qualification, eliminating all appeal to a human other beneath the disguise: William is a bear who wishes to take up human arms, with "horse and alle harneys þat behoves to were" [horse and all appropriate war-equipment] (2348–52). Melior in *William of Palerne* signals even more clearly that she is disappearing into her disguise, with her dedication to becoming-bear having transcended mere pragmatism, to become ritual. Guillaume, worried that there is only one way to save his lover from the approaching workers, asks his sweetheart to save her life by revealing the bare body beneath the bearskin: "Car vos metés de la pel fors / Et vos metés em pur le cors" [Please take off the bearskin / And put nothing on your naked body] (4060–64). The English version complicates the simple dichotomy of bearskin and human body in its "pure," nude state, by having William refer to the clothing—and therefore culture—beneath Melior's disguise. William requests that she "dof blive þis bere-skyn and be stille in þi cloþes" [do quickly take off the bearskin and remain motionless in your clothes], after which her attackers will recognize not just her humanity, but her nobility, and will save her "for love of þi fader" [out of respect for her father] (2342–45).[103] After William reiterates his request that she strip (2353), Melior, "wepande wonder sore" [weeping bitterly], makes clear through her vehement refusal that her animal skin has become more than just a convenient disguise and is now part of her identity: "Nay, bi him þat wiþ his blod bouȝt us on þe rode, / þe beres fel schal never fro my bac, siker be þerfore" [No, by him who redeemed us with his blood on the cross, the bear's skin will never leave my back] (2358–61). Melior's emotional excess, with hot tears and a dramatic Christian oath, speaks less to self-preservation than to a passionate commitment to her borrowed bear-identity. Threatened by the assault of laborers, she retreats into the bearskin, the shell in which she has been pursuing the ritual aristocratic passage that will keep her and her lover aloof from those filthy workers' hands.

If the elite idioms of courtly love and venery reveal the lovers' becomings-animal as part of the nobility's ritual self-writing—a symbolic movement charged with the "power of delivering something over to itself"[104]—then a third aristocratic art of self-differentiation, heraldry, is invoked to seal the socializing process. After having shed his deerskin and joined his mother's besieged army, William, still unaware of his noble lineage, is asked to choose his arms. He adopts the "werwolf" (3217), identifying himself via his anomalous animal-world contact, thereby intuitively linking human–animal hybridity with his knightly status. William also links the werewolf's capacity for violence with aristocratic identity, stating that the werewolf is "hidous and huge, to have alle his riȝtes" [huge and menacing, in order to maintain his privileges] (3218). On the battlefield, the Spanish king bemoans that "non miȝt þe werwolf conquere" [no one could defeat the werewolf] (3911), rendering William interchangeable with his heraldic sign. The interrelation of becoming-animal and aristocratic passage is made complete. The former werewolf Alphonse, soon to be sovereign of Spain, forges permanent ties with William, knighting him and binding himself to him by becoming his brother-in-law (8290–96; 4740–47), in an overdetermined display of the "special proximity of werewolf and sovereign."[105] As we shall see, the legal institution of marriage complicates the use of violence in each romance, moving the consolidation of class interests to a transnational frame.

Transnationalizing *William of Palerne*
Romance and Western Exceptionalism

If Williams is correct in assuming a widespread medieval English "sense of linguistic and cultural inferiority" vis-à-vis French culture,[106] then the poet William compensates for his anxiety about Middle English's low status by intensifying both the elitist narrative of ritualized becoming-animal and the classist violence sustaining aristocratic hegemony. Far from acting on nativist impulses sometimes ascribed to late-medieval alliterative poets, William reveals cross-Channel sensibilities in which identity is a function of feudal class rather than nation. Late-medieval French culture, as Michael J. Bennett has shown, was not geographically limited: England in the late 1350s and early 1360s was the virtual "center of the francophone world," with France both militarily and economically depressed.[107] Englishing *Guillaume de Palerne,* William painstakingly preserves the elitist ideology of the French narrative set within a new linguistic skin. His translation is motivated not by a retreat into nationalism, but rather by a desire to collaborate in the maintenance of transnational, Western power.

With its *terminus ad quem* of 1361, *William of Palerne* is often accorded a privileged place as possibly the earliest datable poem of the Alliterative Revival. Such literary historical context places the poem on the margins of an already marginalized movement. According to Hanna, "Old Historicists" fantasizing a Revival render alliterative verse "particularly Other" by imagining a regionalist movement opposed to the Chaucerian South's Francophile culture.[108] *William of Palerne* holds an awkward place in such accounts, insofar as its appropriation of French linguistic and cultural material undermines critical portraits of alliterative poets as resolutely nativist neo-Saxons. Moreover, its poet's passion for sophistication belies the Revivalist refusal to admit gamesmanship and irony in alliterative poems, such as we have seen in the case of ethno-nostalgic readings of *Wynnere and Wastoure* (chapter 1). With its sustained and subtle treatment of courtly love, *William of Palerne* joins *Sir Gawain and the Green Knight* in frustrating critical efforts to restrict alliterative poems to such stern subjects as warfare or penance (see chapter 3).[109]

Faced with the love-saturated *William of Palerne* at the Revival's alleged beginning,[110] critics have held that William deals ineptly with matter alien to an "alliterative" poet. Claiming that William's efforts to reproduce his source's courtly essence are negated by his metrical "medium," Dorothy Everett claims that *William of Palerne* confirms, through its very exceptionality, the correctness of most alliterative poets' "instinct" to eschew "love-romances" in favor of war-related subjects.[111] For Everett, such deficiency in matters of love is linked with alliterative prosody itself: though the English translator follows his French tale closely enough to reproduce its "niceness" and "attractive" characters, the imitator is ultimately "defeated by the essential unsuitability of his medium."[112] Why, precisely, alliterative prosody is "unsuitable" is left unsaid, inviting readers to inject their own regional and literary historical biases. From as early as the sixteenth-century age of antiquarianism, critics have linked alliterative verse with an Anglo-Saxon culture read as fundamentally warlike. William Camden, for example, asserts that the "English tongue" and "nation" are both extracted "from the Germans," whose supreme "moral and martial vertues" were spread throughout England by the Anglo-Saxons' "happy victories."[113] Revivalism inherits such ethno-historical attitudes and routinely assumes that alliterative poets worked not just in the meter but in the spirit of Anglo-Saxon warrior culture. According to Walter S. Hinchman, "our old meter inclines, like our ancestors themselves, to violence";[114] Oakden claims that alliterative poets "inherited" a "heroic spirit" alien to French refinement;[115] and Moorman lists "violence" and "vendetta" as fundamental to "Western alliterative poetry."[116] Such statements make clear why literary critics inured to Alliterative Revivalism might be unprepared for the identity play of a *William of Palerne* that belies, through its extended reflections on love-matters, the fantasy of a uniformly martial, anti-romantic literary school.[117]

Far from being limited by nationalist zeal, *William of Palerne* contributes its narrative of violent identity-formation to a transnational, self-protective aristocratic project. Aligning his work with the elitist values of *Guillaume de Palerne,* William deploys his translation precisely against proto-capitalist values and institutions that would eventually lead to nation-formation: William's becoming-animal narratives thereby reinforce a resolutely pre-capitalist feudal hierarchy.[118] Faced with encroaching proto-capitalism, Humphrey de Bohun patronized the translation of French material not out of national pride, but in the interest of using its violent lessons in aristocratic exceptionalism to stamp out pretensions to socioeconomic mobility on English estates where class distinctions were becoming blurred.

The estates of a magnate such as Humphrey de Bohun consisted of shared space, with non-nobles and nobles occupying a single social world.[119] However much the nobility saw itself as exclusive, the material maintenance of courtly culture required the presence of a diverse range of individuals, from kitchen staff to grooms, notaries to priests. Such diversity-generated fears about class-mixing registered in moments such as the Emperor's disdainful glee at the cowherd's courtesy. Anxiety about such codes produced the need to police them: sumptuary laws reinforced bonds between clothing and class,[120] while poaching laws restricted hunting privileges.[121] While I would agree with Turville-Petre's speculation that Humphrey had "educational motives" in patronizing a *William of Palerne* that featured aristocratic values for an audience significantly below the "higher nobility,"[122] I would argue that such instruction was designed to communicate not the values themselves, but rather the sense of absolute distinction between nobles and non-nobles. *William of Palerne* performs this cultural work through its debasement of non-nobles, demonstrating the violence that sustains the privileges and differences of an aristocracy threatened by socioeconomic mobility. William presents these pre-nationalist values as privileges zealously maintained by a violent elite.

As we have seen, the narratives of becoming-animal in each romance saturate elite youths' stories with the mysteries of courtly love and sovereign violence, in a ritual delivery of aristocrats over to their noble selves. Such aristocratic exceptionalism, alien to the Revivalist vision of a popular nationalism, is made plain in both the translation and the original. The fugitives' re-entry into the aristocratic court is marked as ritual by Queen Felice's decision, unexplained in either version, to approach the lovers while herself sewn up in deerskins (5157–5343; 3059–3201).[123] A representative of the older generation evidently recognizes the completion of an animalized circuit of aristocratic becoming and comes appropriately dressed to welcome them into the noble fold. After the deer-disguised Felice ritually escorts William and Melior back into courtly society, the lovers shed their animal skins and almost immediately pursue the quintessentially aristocratic activities of conducting war and contracting marriages. William takes on the role of elite knight, breaking the Spanish siege, while paving the way for a number of weddings. These marriages come at a significant cost to non-nobles, as is clear not only from those robbed to sustain the lovers' flight, but also from the ravaged towns and fields caught in the crossfire of the Spanish and Sicilian armies warring over William's sister (4400–4437; 2618–61).

Class alone does not determine the magic circle of privilege in the closing marriage series. There is ultimately a limit to which nobles benefit from the aristocratic rites of passage, with Melior's rejection of her Greek fiancé disclosing a transnational, Western solidarity. Though the intended groom who initiates Melior's flight is Christian and had been selected by both the Western and Eastern emperors, he is, as a Byzantine prince, part of a different empire: the ethnic outsider is made to disappear quietly from each romance after the lovers take flight, standing significantly aloof from the central becoming-animal narratives. Much as Western Crusaders during the 1204 sack of Constantinople treated Byzantine Christians as monstrously as they did Saracens during other crusades, so does the Easterner, despite his nobility, come to be abjected.[124] William deliberately intensifies *Guillaume de Palerne*'s exclusionist ethos, removing the very name of the Greek prince and fashioning him into a faceless Eastern other doomed to watch the collapse of his planned marriage to the Western imperial princess. In noting that the prince has heard "how fair, how fetis" [how attractive, how gorgeous] and "how freli schapen" [how nobly shaped] is the "semely" [beautiful] Melior (1446–47), the messenger in *William of Palerne* conveys an Eastern desire for the Western other here aggressively and spectacularly denied.[125]

By excluding Eastern nobles from the productive play of becoming-animal, *Guillaume de Palerne* and *William of Palerne* each link their identity-play narratives to the larger cultural project of Western consolidation. The Greek Other is banned from the closed circuit of reconciliations, as former opponents become bound through the institution of marriage (8763–8942; 4990–5140). Queen Braunde, the seemingly wicked stepmother who metamorphosed Alphonse, is not only forgiven, but sees her son, who had laid waste to Apulia, married off to Alexandrine; Alphonse returns from the animal world to join Florence, William's sister, in wedded life. Melior's flight from marriage to the imperial Greek prince does not come at any personal cost in status, for she ultimately attains the height of Western power, as Roman empress (9352–56; 5341–43). Far from restricting himself to Englishing a text from across the Channel, the poet William both preserves and intensifies the ideological work performed by his French predecessor, deploying the pair of becoming-animal plots to support a transnational ideology of exclusively Western aristocratic hegemony.

3

Destabilizing Arthurian Empire

GENDER AND ANXIETY IN ALLITERATIVE TEXTS OF THE MILITARIZED MIDLANDS

TOWARD THE close of *Sir Gawain and the Green Knight,* a moment designed to bring clarification about identity merely complicates it, as a highly anticipated act of male self-naming leads to the unsettling disclosure of female agency driving the romance. The *Gawain*-poet carefully prepares this moment of identification. Gawain had inquired of the giant, green-hued stranger whom he was about to behead, "howe þou hattes" [what is your name], and received only deferral in response: "Þat is innogh in New 3er; hit nedes no more" [That is enough at New Year; no more is needed right now] (401; 404).[1] When he later learns that the "half etayn" [half-giant] (140) who spares his life and his high-spirited Hautdesert host are identical, and also that his aunt engineered the Beheading Game,[2] Gawain is surely as shocked as first-time readers, who have hitherto had only hints of female power at the heart of the poem:

> 'Bertilak de Hautdesert I hat in þis londe,
> Þur3 my3t of Morgne la Faye, þat in my hous lenges,
> And koyntyse of clergye. Bi craftes wel lerned—
> Þe maystrés of Merlyn—mony ho hatz taken,
> For ho hat3 dalt drwry ful dere sumtyme
> With þat conable klerk; þat knowes alle your kny3te3
>   at hame' (2445–51)

[Bertilak de Hautdesert I am called in this land, / Through the might of Morgan le Fay, who dwells in my house, / And the skill of (i.e., her) education. By crafts well learned—/ The arts of Merlin—many has she taken, / For once she had a most pleasant love affair / With that excellent sage, who knows all your knights / At home] (2445–51).[3]

Even as Bertilak[4] names himself, he complicates the question as to who is in control at Hautdesert, as anxiety over his lordship's limits illuminates Morgan le Fay's superior status. Indeed, Morgan wields power on a level equivalent to Arthur: each proves a regional magnate who commands a network of subordinate agents.

By exploiting expectations concerning alliterative stress patterns, the *Gawain*-poet conveys in a single line the uneasy awareness of magnified female economic power in the Northwest Midlands, the region in which scholars usually situate the poem.[5] Since poets working in alliterative meter tend to avoid placing stress on prepositions and possessive pronouns, editors expecting a regular coincidence of stress and alliteration might suspect failure in the second half-verse of line 2445, "Þurȝ myȝt of Morgne la Faye, þat in my hous lenges," marking "*my*ȝt," "*M*orgne," "*h*ous" and "*l*enges" for stress.[6] By assuming flexibility in stress assignment, and by placing emphasis on "*my*," we uncover the poet's encoding of Bertilak's anxious emphasis that it is *his* house in which Morgan resides. Channeling alliterative prosody's potential to "accommodate a vast range of expression,"[7] the *Gawain*-poet registers a subtly voiced insecurity: even as Bertilak marks his own status as host, he indicates his unease with his political inferiority to Morgan.

As we shall see, the regional lord's telling insistence that it is his house is but one signal of the poem's focus on female participation in the control and consumption of a warrior culture's wealth. The militarist economy centered in the Northwest Midlands was by no means unique in affording late-medieval English women economic opportunities, for English legal custom and economic realities provided considerable freedoms. However, social and economic conditions produced a unique regional perspective. The frequent absences necessitated by careerist soldiering generated more opportunities for spouses and widows to exercise economic power, while the Northwest Midlands' sparsely populated demographics called more attention to such activities.[8] As I shall argue, the *Gawain*-poet presents regionally inflected portraits of the Lady and Morgan as recognizable economic agents negotiating militarist culture's domestic and political spaces. Exposed as the sole source of Bertilak's Green Knight role, Morgan crystallizes anxiety about female power by being figured as a deity capable of humbling any man:

Morgne þe goddes
Þerfore hit is hir name:
Weldeȝ non so hyȝe hawtesse
Þat ho ne con make ful tame. (2452–55)

[Her name is Morgan the Goddess for this reason: no one wields such high power that she could not fully tame him.]

Pursuing the implications of Michael Twomey's hypothesis that Bertilak's subordination to Morgan follows from his "feudal identity,"[9] I will explore both Gawain's and Revivalist literary critics' anxieties about female agency. The *Gawain*-poet's subtle rendering of clashing regional understandings of rank upsets both medieval and medievalist expectations about the gendering of political power. Released from Revivalist filters that strain for a uniformly nativist, conservative movement, *Sir Gawain and the Green Knight* reveals a dynamic social and economic vision. While the poem is no mere historic product reflecting socioeconomic conditions, the *Gawain*-poet's political imagination reveals a fascination with the regional color of a transnational economic zone that resists Revivalism's fantasy of a populist alliterative nationalism.

As we have seen, Revivalist literary history, obsessed with recovering a masculine, Germanic spirit binding the fourteenth century to an Anglo-Saxon past (see chapter 1), often obscures significant female participation in alliterative narratives. Much as with *William of Palerne*, a fascination with female agency undermines Revivalist discourse's hypermasculine portrayal of an alliterative movement (see chapter 2), the *Gawain*-poet's presentation of influential female characters works against Revivalism's gendered biases. Faced with a female power-player demonstrably greater than any male in the poem, critics of *Sir Gawain and the Green Knight* have sometimes sought to preserve their fantasy of a male-dominated Alliterative Revival: such critics hypothesize an originally all-male conflict between Gawain and the Green Knight that is disrupted by an aesthetically flawed, supplementary explanation of Morgan's responsibility for the Beheading Game.[10] Revivalist critics go so far in systematically minimizing Morgan's role as to operate, as Twomey observes, as if the all-male editorial title *Sir Gawain and the Green Knight* were authorial.[11] As we shall see, such occlusion of female agency, both in the case of Morgan and of the Lady, distracts critics from the romance's dialogue with actual sociomaterial conditions.

The socioeconomic context in which the *Gawain*-poet presumably worked has been reconstructed in Michael J. Bennett's studies of Cheshire and South Lancashire, regions teeming with wealth flowing from residents forging military careers in the key theaters of late-medieval English aggression: the French territories targeted in the Hundred Years' War, and Welsh and Scottish lands subjected to English violence.[12] Bertilak's anxiety over his house's ownership stems from unease about women's control and consumption of capital in a militarized, transnational zone stretching well beyond the Northwest Midlands. Female economic power in this region can be demonstrated through legal records. Tracking the local gentry's socioeconomic rise, Bennett examines regional trends in marriage contracts, which were often negotiated to have some portion of an estate held in joint tenure, whereby a widow controlled wealth that otherwise passed on to an heir.[13] Two women (who remain unnamed in Bennett's text) exemplify the complex, gender-inflected status of ownership in the Northwest Midlands: Henry Scarisbrick's widowed mother held onto her third of an estate, which in her absence would have passed on to her son; William Bradshaw's remarried mother brought both her "dower lands" and "effective control of the entire estate" into the hands of her new husband, complicating future negotiations about the inheritance of her children with her first husband.[14] Such women's controlling or collaborating in estate management proves central to *Sir Gawain and the Green Knight*, revealing the strategic unveiling of Morgan as an instance of local color, generated by recognition of the economic potential held by all English women being multiplied by careerist culture's frequent absenteeism and massive wealth.

Both the Lady and Morgan reflect the *Gawain*-poet's desire to highlight landed women's opportunities in the militarized Midlands. Building on critical engagements with female desire structuring *Sir Gawain and the Green Knight*, I will steer investigation toward the economic activities informing the *Gawain*-poet's portrayals. Significant female economic power is evident throughout medieval England. As Rowena E. Archer demonstrates, married women and widows participated in late-medieval estate management, with opportunities for female economic independence enabled both by general English legal custom and by the exigencies of estate control in a social world where class tended to trump gender.[15] Female economic potential is amplified in *Sir Gawain and the Green Knight* due to the frequent flow of careerist soldiers and wealth in and out of the region. The legal power of widows and heiresses has been demonstrated by historians profiting from the names of such *femmes soles* in fiscal records.[16] Wives such as the Lady, largely absent from archival sources, nevertheless exercised considerable social and economic power. Hypothesizing that the *Gawain*-poet's Morgan figures a widow or heiress with full legal independence, and that the Lady participates alongside Bertilak in the management of Hautdesert, I will explore the poem's fascination with the social and economic opportunities for women amplified by late-medieval militarism.

Exploring the unstable nature of the *Gawain*-poet's region proves a necessary first step in recovering this background. Identifying this context requires broadening our understanding of the poem's provenance beyond the Northwest Midlands, while also working against oft-rehearsed assumptions of a remote, rural Revival. As we shall see, there are both cultural and bibliographical links between the Northwest and Northeast Midlands, with militarism proving similarly central to works like *Wynnere and Wastoure* and the Alliterative *Morte Arthure*. Recovering the *Gawain*-poet's milieu also requires abandoning a metropolitan model of England.[17] Revising our understanding of the region as a peripheral English zone illuminates a multiplicity of related urban centers (such as York and Coventry) and transnational channels of war and trade (such as Irish, Manx, and Welsh zones). Such methodological refinements disclose a dynamic, transnational context for the *Gawain*-poet, providing further evidence for the inadequacy of Revivalism's nation-centered model.

Representing as regional the separation of passive and empowered female characters, the *Gawain*-poet structurally foregrounds female agency. The active parts played by the Lady and Morgan signal that the Northwestern Midlands locale to which Gawain travels features radically different possibilities for women. Working against the Revivalist predilection for martial, masculinist narratives, I will analyze the *Gawain*-poet's deployment of scenes of domestic administration and recreation as a reflection of this militarist culture's material dynamism. While the Lady's active role at Hautdesert already calls attention to the ornamentality of women in Guinevere's southerly Camelot (74–84), Morgan increases the stakes, challenging Arthurian empire itself. Morgan proves particularly adept at managing "symbolic capital," asserting her "legitimacy" by aggressively broadcasting her "vision of the world."[18] In her most overtly symbolic construction, Morgan undermines Arthur's claim to ascendancy by manufacturing the Green Knight messenger, who through his very travels expresses the trans-regional reach of her power, as he executes his female lord's blow against Arthurian pride.

Morgan reserves her most powerful symbolic work for self-representation, figuring herself as an old woman to distinguish herself both from the beautiful but innocuous Guinevere, and the beautiful Lady who wields considerable, but considerably less power than Morgan. Morgan's mask of old age communicates that her regional might does not merely derive from sexual attractiveness but follows from dual breaches of gender boundaries, as she appropriates both the status of a political lord, and, by acquiring the "maystrés of Merlyn" [Merlin's expertise] (2448), that of clerk. Much like Geoffrey of Monmouth's Merlin, Morgan demonstrates the superiority of intellectual skill to merely physical strength.[19] Morgan's factitious antiquity also serves to send a political signal. Deploying what Bourdieu calls the "mythico-ritual" trope of the Order of the Ages, Morgan channels a "social structuring of temporality" into an expression of political primacy.[20] She takes up the tripartite model of age also seen in the dream-debate of the alliterative *Parlement of the Thre Ages,* asserting pre-eminence by presenting herself as the Elde [Old Age] who trumps both the middle-aged Bertilak and Gawain as the representative of Arthurian empire in its "firste age" [youth] (54). Speaking through a rhetoric of clothes, Morgan's wise and powerful Elde communicates to a young and fragile Camelot the historical warning in Cicero's *De Senectute* [*On Old Age*], that "you will find that the greatest states have been overthrown by the young and sustained and restored by the old: 'How lost you, pray, your mighty state so soon?'"[21] Instilling anxiety in her Arthurian guest by projecting Elde's sublime decrepitude, Morgan undermines Revivalist assumptions about aged males dominating late-medieval alliterative texts.[22] Much as Morgan's old age is artificial, so too is Revivalism's stereotype of an elderly alliterative poet pining for the old, Anglo-Saxon days.

While the Lady proves powerful in managing Hautdesert's affairs, Morgan maintains a singular sway that nevertheless avoids the hyper-romanticism of Loathly Lady portrayals. While Morgan shares with the hag in *The Wife of Bath's Tale* a magical ability to transform bodily appearances, the *Gawain*-poet's female power-player differs from Chaucer's: Morgan's efforts are not directed toward becoming a pleasing partner to a knight-husband.[23] Morgan remains aloof from potential knightly lovers and is instead presented as maintaining command over lords such as Bertilak. Unlike the Loathly Lady of the *Wedding of Sir Gawain and Dame Ragnell,*[24] Morgan's appearance is not the result of a curse but rather an exercise in self-fashioning. No hag waiting to be transformed by a knight who has succeeded in "conquering his desire for beauty,"[25] Morgan performs an act of territorial aggressiveness, fashioning herself into a sign that communicates her regional sway. The Lady and Morgan ultimately emerge as realistic, regionally inflected figures. Whereas the incalculably wealthy lady of Marie de France's *Lanval,* for example, must ultimately lead her lover away from actuality and into Avalon,[26] the Lady and Morgan remain firmly rooted in a recognizable Northwest Midlands courtly culture enriched by English empire's constant militarism.[27]

As we shall see, Morgan's direct challenge to the legitimacy of Arthurian sovereignty is analogous to other literary acts of female subversion deriving from militarist culture. Such narratives suggest a gendered anxiety concerning war economies that is occluded by Revivalism's privileging of masculinity. Combining the might of Lady Fortune with the cunning of the *Morte*-poet's Guinevere, Morgan poses a challenge both to her political rival, Arthur, and to critics and editors seeking to exorcise her from *Sir*

Gawain and the Green Knight's center. Resisting Revivalist efforts to look away from female agency and toward allegedly ancient Celtic meanings, accomplished both by conflating Morgan and the Lady as doubles and by foregrounding male–male conflict, I will examine a gender-inflicted challenge to Arthurian, and by extension any imperial, ascendancy.

The *Gawain*-poet's portrayal of regional conflict also defies Revivalist insistence on national identity, suggesting empire as the more appropriate political model. As R. R. Davies has argued, Arthurian literature in Middle English always bears an anti-imperialist charge, for English ascendancy is inherently faced with the "chilling challenge" of a Welsh Arthur destined to reconquer Britain.[28] If there is indeed such a "threatening, spectral presence"[29] in *Sir Gawain and the Green Knight,* it is clearly Morgan who haunts Camelot, rendering any simple English–Welsh opposition difficult to maintain. While Arthur is sometimes made to figure English imperial aggression (see chapter 4), it proves difficult to reduce Morgan's role to representing an older, Celtic world resisting English conquest and colonization—particularly as it is Morgan who is the aggressor. Much as, for Ingham, "colonial intimacies" generated by regional and ethnic differences complicate any simple Anglo–Celtic binary,[30] so does the imperial state over which Morgan holds sway prove unsettlingly English, even as it marks itself as other to Arthur's. Centered somewhere in the Northwest Midlands' Wirral Forest, Morgan's sphere of influence signals that regional power overrides national centralization.[31]

By avoiding the projection of distinctly modern views of England's Saxon origins, I will assume an ethnic continuity of Arthur's and Morgan's colliding empires, with gendered differences in politics and culture proving to be the key area of conflict. Over-emphasis on Anglo–Celtic difference follows from a post-Romantic emphasis on race central to Revivalist historiography. As Horsman demonstrates, it is not until Archbishop Matthew Parker's Henry VIII–ordered researches into Anglo-Saxon culture that there emerges any significant break with the Galfridian myth of Britain's generally Trojan origins, while it was only in the seventeenth century that Arthur began to be displaced by Alfred as the favored figure for English origins.[32] Recent archaeological and genetic work also suggests that Anglo-Saxon invader-settlers were never a homogeneous group destined to become "English," and that their numbers were not so great as to displace local Celtic populations throughout England.[33] Rather than using the racial identifications deployed by Revivalist critics, the *Gawain*-poet carves out differences in terms of gender, region, and polity. In the *Gawain*-poet's historical imagination, there are not discrete, ethnically determined nations, but imperial states, to which individuals—such as the Gawain who is ultimately invited back to join Bertilak's commander, Morgan, at Hautdesert (2467–69)—might readily switch allegiance.

Analysis of the *Gawain*-poet's milieu undermines Revivalist efforts to project the English national dawn into the fourteenth century. Working against views of the Northwest Midlands as a self-contained community replicating in miniature a larger nation consolidated by a Middle English standard,[34] I will explore regional identity as a highly unstable, transnational experience, tied to imperial aggression rather than to a static national ideal. For Turville-Petre, the *Gawain*-poet occupies a post-national world: since the "battle for English" as a trans-regional standard had already been "won," Chaucer and the *Gawain*-poet found themselves free to pursue a chivalric "internationalism" that transcended the "conflicts between European nations."[35] Presumably, were their linguistico-nationalist services still needed, they would have become soldiers for vernacular ascendancy.[36] Arguing that the *Gawain*-poet joined Chaucer in disdaining English nationalism by aligning himself with those people of "lore" [learning] who call "pentaungel" [pentangle] what the "Englych" [English] call the "endles knot" [endless knot] (629–30),[37] Turville-Petre adduces evidence that seems rather to undermine the claim for a late-medieval nation. If nationalism involves an ideology according to which one's nation commands an overriding sense of loyalty and identity, then the *Gawain*-poet's divorcing himself from the "Englych" in order to define himself as a member of a transnational intellectual class is a move alien to national identification:[38] Englishness clearly is not an absolute category with which the *Gawain*-poet defines himself. As we shall see, even as English empire informs the *Gawain*-poet's geographical vision, no stable sense of England emerges in a poem that highlights regional discontinuities, shaped by a transnational zone linking the Northern Midlands with English Northern, Welsh, Scottish, Manx, and Irish territories key to militaristic culture.

From Backwater to Network
Expanding Our Sense of the Northwest Midlands

Mapping the network of cultural and political influences informing the *Gawain*-poet requires revising Revivalism's center–periphery model, which arrests, through its insistence on a provincial provenance, the interplay among regional, regnal, and transnational contexts. In his 1932 attempt to name a single author for the poems of British Library MS Cotton Nero A.x (*Pearl, Cleanness, Patience,* and *Sir Gawain and the Green Knight*), Coolidge Otis Chapman worked against growing Revivalist consensus on a

Northwest Midlands–centered alliterative movement, placing the poems in Yorkshire. Chapman's hypothesis was based partly upon material evidence. Tracing the history of the manuscript to its earliest known owner, the Yorkshireman Henry Savile of Banke,[39] Chapman claimed to have found corroborative testimony for his theory that John de Erghome authored the poems. With his quest for origins compelling him to interpret evidence of a manuscript's later location as a secure indication of authorial provenance, Chapman participated in the Revivalist consignment of late-medieval alliterative verse to the provinces—even if the particular provincial locale departed from the standard scheme.

While Chapman is probably wrong in his assessment—most scholars assign *Sir Gawain and the Green Knight* to the Northwest Midlands[40]—his interest in expanding the horizon of investigation to Yorkshire reveals key limitations of Revivalist literary history. As we have seen (chapter 1), Revivalism racializes both temporality and geography, linking alliterative verse with a conservative, neo-Saxon tradition confined to the provincial West and North, and opposing itself to the syllabic verse of the Francophile, London-centered South. What counts as provincial for Revivalism is rarely precise, as seen in Oakden's influential claim that the "Alliterative Revival arose in the west and flourished there."[41] While refining Oakden's hypothesis of an alliterative school that moved north and northeast from its Southwest Midlands origins, Turville-Petre interprets provinciality as separation from London, with alliterative verse maintaining only "slight" connections with the "poetry of the metropolitan, Chaucerian tradition."[42] Revivalism's cultural binarism reveals itself in Everett's confession that she finds it "odd" that "provincial" poems so "far removed from the centers of culture" can have "such a self-assured air."[43] As with Revivalist resistance to alliterative poets' facility with courtly love (see chapter 2), the Revival school is often portrayed as a *culturally* provincial movement, with the *Gawain*-poet the glorious exception to its unsophisticated ways.

The Northwest Midlands was unquestionably a key region for the composition and consumption of late-medieval alliterative poetry, though the paucity of multiply attested works renders arguments about authorial dialect necessarily speculative. Cotton Nero A.x. contains two fully alliterative texts, *Cleanness* (a homiletic exploration of spiritual purity illuminated through Biblical narratives of filth), and *Patience* (a homiletic treatment of the Biblical story of Jonah). Whether these two fully alliterative poems, along with the metrically hybrid *Sir Gawain and the Green Knight* (composed in stanzas fusing a variable number of alliterative long lines with a rhymed, syllabic bob-and-wheel), and the non-alliterative, rhymed, and syllabic *Pearl*,[44] are the product of a single author or evidence of a regional literary community remains controversial.⁴⁵ Two epic alliterative works derive from the Northwest Midlands: *The Wars of Alexander*, consisting of some 5,677 lines devoted to the travels and conquests of Alexander the Great (surviving in two copies), and John Clerk's uniquely attested *Gest Hystoriale of the Destruction of Troy*, a 14,044-line translation of Guido delle Colonne.⁴⁶ While *Saint Erkenwald* has been definitively linked to the Northwest Midlands by dialect, its focus on London has led to speculation that its author was resident there.⁴⁷

Much as Revivalists seek, according to Hanna, to "pack" alliterative works into an artificially condensed timeframe of approximately 1350 to 1415,⁴⁸ so have many critics sought to geographically concentrate the provenance of alliterative poems. Bennett's assumption of an "alliterative revival" in "Cheshire and south Lancashire" demonstrates over-confidence in assigning alliterative works to the Northwest Midlands, which has characterized much work coming in Oakden's wake.⁴⁹ *The Siege of Jerusalem*, which Bennett sees as "categorically assigned to the northwest Midlands," has since been situated in Yorkshire by Hanna and Lawton, while Bennett's placement of *Wynnere and Wastoure* and the *Parlement of the Thre Ages* near Cheshire obfuscates significant contradictory findings.⁵⁰ Revivalism has constructed an artificially provincial context for alliterative verse that accords neither with the trans-regional spread of alliterative texts nor with the dynamic networks of trade and communication that linked provincial regions with cultural and financial centers such as London and York.⁵¹ Such physical marginalization echoes Revivalist insinuations of regional backwardness, ranging from Saintsbury's alliterative "backwater" to Hulbert's vision of provincial, nativist patronage.⁵² Chapman's insistence that the Cotton Nero poems are *either* from the Northwest Midlands or from Yorkshire illuminates a key limitation to overly rigid regional models. The *Gawain*-poet's milieu might in fact best be seen as including the Northwest Midlands *and* Yorkshire.

Chapman's movement beyond the Northwest Midlands to theorize the *Gawain*-poet's background points to the literary historical, bibliographical, and economic links of a transnational network. As Bennett demonstrates, the Northwest Midlands' martial identity was due in large part to its status as a complex borderlands, neighboring North Wales and, up until the twelfth-century stabilization of the Anglo-Scottish border, Southwestern Scotland, while also being connected by sea with Ireland and the Isle of Man.⁵³ The region was a major source of soldiers for Edward I's subjugation of Wales and for the quelling of Welsh resistance throughout the fourteenth century, produced mercenaries for Irish and Manx conflicts, and was the major recruiting ground for the prolonged and often lucrative series of invasions grouped as the Hundred Years' War, as well as the frequent raids and counter-raids into Scotland.[54] Far from being a static province defined by its distance from London, the Northwest Midlands was the heartland of a complex, warfare-stimulated economic zone.

However much critics may focus on courtly sophistication rather than the "conquestes" [conquests] to which the Green Knight ties Camelot's current prestige (311),[55] the poem opens with a suggestive burst of bellicosity.[56] Meditating on Britain's historical foundations in a war-produced Trojan diaspora, the *Gawain*-poet reflects upon his own region's rampant militarism.[57] The narrator catalogues conquests executed by members of the dispossessed Trojan "kynde" [ethnicity] (5), who become "patrounes" [masters] of most of the "provinces" and "wele" [wealth] in the "west" (6–7). Unease with the militarist foundations of such societies is generated by tracing everything back to Aeneas's ambivalent act of "tricherie, þe trewest on erthe" [the truest treachery on earth] (4–5).[58] Presenting "Bretayn" [Britain] (14) as fundamentally unstable, the *Gawain*-poet suggests a background defined by war: the poet envisions the island that Brutus conquered as continuously reproducing its foundational violence, being perennially riven by acts of "were, and wrake, and wonder" [war, revenge, and wonder] (16). Indeed, the warlike Trojan "kynde" live on through a bloodthirsty people who continue its history of violence: "Bolde bredden þerinne, baret þat lofden" [Bold warriors bred therein, who loved battle] (21).

Not only military prospects, but also multiple channels for the flow of labor and capital defined the late-medieval Northwest Midlands. Disdainful of an alliterative school's alleged provinciality, Revivalists often marvel at the *Gawain*-poet's exceptional courtliness. Yet we need look no further than the Northwest Midlands for a transnational framework to sustain a cultural cosmopolitanism. The city of Chester was an important seaport, engaged in trade with Gascony, Ireland, and elsewhere, and it was also part of a network of trade routes linking Wales and the Northern Midlands.[59] The English region of Cumberland to the north, and the thinly populated stretches of land along the Welsh border, offered promising swathes of underdeveloped territory for the taking.[60] Moreover, the military and clerical careerism enriching the region required travel to and from various warzones and economic centers, thus ensuring that the Northwest Midlands could not remain insulated from trans-regional cultural life. Individuals pursuing modest mercantile careers often forged connections with any of the various market-rich urban areas of Britain, and successful military careerists, who often settled wherever they acquired wives, thereby widened the spread of influence—and possible literary patronage—of people hailing from the region.[61] The dynamic economic life of the *Gawain*-poet's milieu thus belies Revivalist arguments that critics should look exclusively to aristocratic households for alliterative poems' patronage.[62]

The case for the importance of including Yorkshire within an alliterative zone encompassing the Northwest Midlands can be made simply by considering the contributions of Robert Thornton, through whose hand and in whose Yorkshire dialect a significant number of alliterative texts survive.[63] As we have seen (chapter 1), *Wynnere and Wastoure,* extant only in Thornton's copy, celebrates the shaking up of provincial culture and economic life through just the sort of dynamic military careerism defining the late-medieval Northwest.[64] The *Siege of Jerusalem* and the Alliterative *Morte Arthure* are other militarist, Thornton-scribed works that Oakden both influentially and overconfidently assigned to the Northwest Midlands.[65] While some scholars trace the *Morte*-poet to the Northwest Midlands,[66] Angus McIntosh makes a powerful case for Lincolnshire,[67] encouraging us further to expand our regional inquiry to the Northeast Midlands. Bibliographical links thus join with cultural affinities in suggesting a Northern Midlands zone that exudes anxieties about militarism and imperialism that also haunt the Anglo-Scottish borderlands (see chapter 4).[68]

Foregrounding the militarist nature of the Northwest Midlands carries the risk of cutting off the *Gawain*-poet's milieu from the broader English background.[69] As we shall see, a militarist regional coloring does not divorce *Sir Gawain and the Green Knight* from a more general English imperialist culture. Focus on regional militarism also brings the risk of suggesting a male-dominated economy. The *Gawain*-poet's gendering of political power works against revivalist visions of alliterative verse as a resurrection of Anglo-Saxon warrior culture, as seen in Hinchman's view of "our old meter" being "all weight, force" and tending, "like our ancestors themselves, to violence."[70] The *Gawain*-poet's alliterative contemporaries are at times represented as militarists, as with Schofield's assertion that the *Morte*-poet was "a thorough-going Englishman" with "simple, sturdy qualities" unadulterated by "foreign sophistications," with "battle his boast" and "his Saxon ideals" the filter through which he would "revivify and naturalize" his works.[71] Such masculinist portraits explain Revivalism's tendency to overlook significant female narrative participation (see chapter 2). Surveying medievalist efforts to minimize Morgan's role in *Sir Gawain and the Green Knight,* I will recover a sense of the economic activities of late-medieval women marginalized in studies that prioritize the male experience of militarism.

Truest Treason
The Gendered Unsettling of Arthurian Empire

In *Sir Gawain and the Green Knight,* the imperial power of King Arthur initially appears to be threatened by a male outsider—the Green Knight who, barging into Arthur's court, prefaces his beheading game proposal with a hypermasculine insult aimed at Camelot's "berdleȝ chylder" [beardless children]: "Here is no mon me to mach, for myȝteȝ so wayke" [No man here can match me; all here are weaklings] (280–82). The silent response to his ludic request instantiates a public shaming of an imperial court made to look very much in its "firste age" [youth] (54). When the laughing Green Knight (316) inquires disdainfully, "where is now your sourquydrye and your conquestes" [where now is your arrogance and all your conquests?] (311), he orally undermines the constitutive martial identity of "Arthures hous" [Arthur's house] (309).

We learn only toward the poem's close that this performance is fundamentally theatrical. If Crane is right in arguing that the Green Knight's staged fusion of wildness and order provides a "model from which Gawain and his fellows might learn a superior courtliness,"[72] then we must also consider that Bertilak is merely a medium for Morgan, who is director and playwright in relation to the male subordinate who communicates her challenge. In supplying the Green Knight with his wondrous appearance and ability to speak with detached head (444–56), Morgan is clearly no mere court magician serving a lord through special skills. Bertilak explains to Gawain that Morgan is his superior, disclosing that "ho wayned me vpon þis wyse to your wynne halle" [she sent me in this disguise to your splendid hall] (2456), and that "ho wayued me þis wonder ȝour wyttez to reue" [she accorded me this wondrous shape to scare you out of your wits] (2459). Forcing us to re-read what originally appeared a male challenge to Arthurian military ascendancy, Bertilak reveals that his message does more than just deliver Morgan's threat: the message *itself* instantiates her transregional influence. Bertilak's Green Knight performance enhances the legitimacy of Morgan's power: no independent male posing a threat from some unknown province, Bertilak is revealed as invested by and expressive of Morgan's regional sway.

Bertilak's willing service to Morgan reveals a powerful female presence on the fissured political field shared by Arthurian empire. Neither under a spell nor held prisoner, the lord Bertilak evidently chooses out of political self-interest to follow the person who he thinks is most likely to prevail—that "goddes" whom he deems capable of making anyone "tame" (2451–55). Considering the tradition of critical resistance to Morgan's centrality in the poem, Lawton argues that the "unwonted respect for a dowager" revealed by Morgan's occupation of the high seat on the dais "presages an unusual power structure at Hautdesert."[73] Such an alternative political scheme is confirmed by the candor with which Bertilak reveals his lower status to Morgan, suggesting that he looks to her just as a knight of Camelot would to King Arthur. Moving beyond the merely playful inversion of lord and lady in courtly love, in which discourse the "fyne fader of nurture" [refined master of courtliness] Gawain is clearly expert (919–27), the *Gawain*-poet uses Bertilak's political self-understanding to differentiate radically the northerly Hautdesert from the Camelot from which Gawain has traveled.

Morgan's pre-eminent status, and the Lady's domestic power at Hautdesert, prove unsurprising in the context of a Northwest Midlands economy in which males pursuing military careers were often, *ipso facto,* elsewhere. The massive wealth flowing through the region ensured that many women occupied positions of great vulnerability, but also of great power, either as war widows or as lone residents on estates during periods of military service by husbands or kin. Such absence left many women free to manage affairs and to ally themselves with rising local powers through marriage.[74] As Mavis E. Mate demonstrates, English legal custom provided married women with considerable rights: when husbands were absent for purposes of war, trade, or diplomacy, wives "were left in charge of the household and property and often enjoyed real power and control over affairs outside the home," while "most women retained complete control over domestic matters" while their husbands were in residence.[75] While such everyday legal realities suggest that the Lady would have been seen as an active participant in estate life in any region, the absenteeism of Northwest Midlands careerist culture magnified the potential for female self-assertion. That Morgan wields the highest concentration of that power suggests anxiety about female control of capital generated by the English war machine, and links Bertilak's female lord with other fictive women who destabilize Arthurian empire.

While the *Gawain*-poet focuses primarily on male founder-figures in the romance's opening stanza, the introduction of the Trojan diaspora's ambivalent origins embeds anxiety concerning female agency into a fatalistic vision of cyclical violence. In another Northwest Midlands alliterative treatment of Troy, the *Gest Hystoriale of the Destruction of Troy,* John Clerk foregrounds female participation in Trojan apocalypse, linking Helen and Paris's fateful "forward" [plan] (3123)[76] with a previous woman-triggered war. Narrating the first Greek destruction of the city, Clerk singles out among the numerous examples of Trojan civilian suffering (1380–84) the giving of Exiona [Hesione] as spoil to Telamon, the first Greek to breach the city walls. Departing from mere reportage of military events, Clerk expostulates on Exiona's responsibility for her city's later destruction: "Bannet worthe the bale tyme þat ho borne was, / ffor the care þat þere come because of hir one" [Cursed be the evil hour in which she was born, because of the grief that she alone caused] (1388–89). Though Exiona does little more than be seized, she and the war become inseparable: "mony boldes" [many men] will "be kylde" [be killed] in battle "for þat bryght" [because of that beautiful woman] (1405). Describing Helen gazing upon Paris in the Temple of Venus, Clerk claims that shameless "wemen dissyre" [female desire] (2920–21) leads to "euyll ende & ernyst" [evil result and sorrow] (2942), and to "treason" that draws "bolde men to batell and biker" [brave men to battle and strife] (2942–44). The "willes of wemen" [women's desires] are portrayed as a force of fundamental, fatal instability (2933–44),[77] with military conflict following from Helen's refusal to follow the poet's apostrophic advice to "holdyn þe at home" [stay at home] (2959). Helen chooses instead to enter the public sphere and thus becomes the destructive "venum" [poison] that "enfecte" [infects] through "loue" [love] (2978–80).

Clerk's misogynistic fervor recalls Gawain's anti-feminist outburst in *Sir Gawain and the Green Knight*. After having learned of Morgan's role and of the Lady's complicity in the Temptation plot, Gawain sends greetings to those "honoured ladyeȝ, / þat þus hor knyȝt wyth hor kest han koyntly bigyled" [esteemed ladies who have so cunningly beguiled their knight through trickery] (2412–13), even as he rejects Bertilak's request to return to "my woneȝ" [my abode], to reach "acorde" [accord] with "my wyf" [my wife] (2400–2406). Refusing to reach a compromise with his "enmy kene" [bitter enemy] (2406), Gawain proceeds to catalogue historical male "sorȝe" [sorrow] produced by the "wyles of wymmen" [women's wiles] (2415), clearly counting himself alongside Adam, David, and others as a "fole" [fool] "bigyled" [beguiled] by women (2413–28). For Sheila Fisher, Gawain, by listing himself in "a noble tradition of Old Testament figures," conspires to join an all-male "Old Order of feudalism" with Bertilak, who destroys all traces of feminine agency by appropriating the green girdle as his giftable property (2395).[78] I would contend that female power actually saturates the exchange. Bertilak claims possession of the girdle by invoking the rules of the Exchange of Winning game, and thus appropriates the item from Gawain, not from the Lady. Gawain's ethical lapse makes sense only if the girdle originally belonged to the Lady, who gifted it to Gawain, who then became obliged to give it to Bertilak. Moreover, regional opportunities for female collaboration in estate management undercut the view that Bertilak's statement that "hit is my wede" [it is my garment] (2358) conflicts with the Lady's property rights. Any pretension to an all-male feudal order is also precluded by Bertilak's unforced revelation of his secondary status to Morgan. In the context of Bertilak's self-aware submission to a woman, Gawain's anti-feminist tirade expresses a juvenile, limited view indicative of Camelot's "firste age" [youth] (54). According to Bertilak's more mature perspective regarding gendered relations, women can and *do* occupy positions of legitimate authority.

Rather than stemming from a generalized medieval misogyny, the toxic depictions of women in the *Gest Hystoriale* and in Gawain's jeremiad reflect regional anxieties about female control of militarist wealth. The Alliterative *Morte Arthure* reveals more such unease, with its stress on Guinevere's complicity in a rebellion organized while Arthur's imperial army is on foreign campaign. The *Morte*-poet departs from the thirteenth-century *La Mort le Roi Artu* [*The Death of King Arthur*], which figures a loyal Guinevere resisting Mordred's entreaties, and instead echoes Geoffrey of Monmouth's report that Guinevere "uiolato iure priorum nuptiarum" [had repudiated her former vows] and "nefando uenere copulatam fuisse" [had united . . . in sinful love] with Mordred.[79] Medieval queenship's liminal status illuminates Guinevere's potential as an agent of instability within the Arthurian empire. Noting that the diplomatic nature of medieval aristocratic marriages ensured that many queens were foreigners, Fradenburg argues that the "mysteriousness" of such "outsiders" was "easily imagined as secret intrigue, witchcraft, hidden poison working its way through the natural or the body politic," and often led to queens' being pressed into the symbolic service of representing "intimate violence" and "internecine strife."[80] In the Alliterative *Morte Arthure,* both the internal instability of civil war and the external threat of foreign agents converge in Guinevere, whose alliance with Mordred brings about the end to Arthur's expansionism.

Like the *Gawain*-poet, the *Morte*-poet cultivates anti-imperialist sentiments by framing Arthurian empire within a history of violence. The "storye" [story] proper (25) opens with a catalogue of Arthur's "conqueste full cruele" [very cruel conquests] (43).[81] Some thirty-two territories are listed as having fallen to Arthur's "swerde kene" [sharp sword], ranging from the Orkney Islands to Greece and including Celtic lands that would contest subjection to late-medieval English empire: Ireland, Scotland, and Wales (30–47).[82] The *Morte*-poet bases the imperial claim both on force and on blood, describing Arthur as of "Ectores kin, the king son of Troy" [the lineage of Hector, Trojan prince] (4343), with his "title" to Rome justified by his British "aunrestres" [ancestors] who were "emperours" [emperors]—Belinus, Brennius, and Constantine (275–85). When Arthur hears Craddok's shocking news that his "warden" Mordred seized his crown and "weddede Waynore" [married Guinevere] (3549–50), he also learns that his own imperial ambitions have facilitated his undoing: Mordred's army is built out of precisely those foreigners peopling the catalogue of Arthur's conquests. Mordred has "sembled a sorte of selcouthe bernes" [made an army out of foreigners], ennobling "Danmarkes" [Danes], "Sarazenes and Sessoynes" [Sarrasins and Saxons], as well as "Peyghtes and paynyms" [Picts and pagans] and knights "of Irelande and Orgaile, owtlawede berynes" [Irish and Scottish outlaws] (3528–34). As we shall see (chapter 4), the *Morte*-poet's catalogue of conquests encodes a tragic poetics of empire that also haunts the militarized Anglo-Scottish marches.

Much as in *Sir Gawain and the Green Knight* Arthur's most active enemy is not the seemingly alien Green Knight but rather his own half-sister, Morgan, so are the *Morte*-poet's "ostes of alynes full horrebill to schewe" [armies of foreigners of frightening appearance] (4061) led not by outsiders but by those closest to him (4061–62).[83] To highlight Guinevere's subversive complicity, the *Morte*-poet has Arthur recognize Mordred by his bearing the sword Clarent, once his own, which had been stowed away at Wallingford in a location known only to Guinevere (4203–5). Unwilling to fulfill Arthur's desire that she be a passive figurehead watched over by Mordred during her husband's absence, Guinevere evidently became a player, commandeering her absent spouse's war-equipment and joining in the civil war machine.[84] Appropriating objects left in her care—goods that would be legally in her control while her husband was off fighting—Guinevere takes an active role in destroying the Arthurian regime. The implosion of the Arthurian empire thereby reveals both the social benefits and costs of militarism, as the increased opportunity for aristocratic women to participate in a war-driven economy accelerates its collapse.

The *Morte*-poet's Guinevere is not the only woman undermining Arthurian empire, for the otherworldly Lady Fortune—even more foreign than Mordred's allies—arrives to confront the acquisitive king. Fortune, who is capable, like the *Gawain*-poet's Morgan, both of elevating and humbling male lords, chastens the empire-building Arthur in a critique tailor-made for war-torn regions.[85] At the height of a continental campaign, readying to take Rome, Arthur dreams of Lady Fortune, who descends from the sky as "a duches dereworthily dyghte in dyaperde wedis" [duchess gorgeously bedecked in finely worked clothes] (3250–51), in a vision that presages the collapse of Arthur's imperial state.[86] In depicting Fortune as a duchess— the "female sovereign of a duchy," according to the *MED*—the *Morte*-poet provides a carefully calibrated image of power, signaling restricted jurisdiction. As Anke Janssen demonstrates, the *Morte*-poet, by linking Fortune only with Arthur's military activities, follows the Boethian tradition of interpreting Fortune as subject to the more powerful Providence.[87] This Duchess Fortune indeed seems a war goddess, asserting that Arthur has "wonnen" [won] all his "wirchip in werre" [glory through war] because she has been "frendely" [friendly] to him and "fremmede" [hostile] to others (3342–43). The militarist Duchess's message is geared toward a culture anxious about its militarist investments, the uncertain status of which is figured in Fortune's vivid crushing of the conqueror on her wheel (3388). By limiting the sphere of her influence, the *Morte*-poet studiously presents Fortune in terms of recognizable political domains.

The *Gawain*-poet adopts a similar strategy with Morgan, choosing to invest her with massive, but not total, power. Bertilak might well be invoking Lady Fortune in describing Morgan as a "goddes" who tames even the proudest man (2454–55),[88] but it is also clear that Morgan requires the aid of vassals such as Bertilak and his Lady, who in turn require their own retinues. Far from descending from the clouds, Morgan is grounded firmly in a feudal power network that would be recognizable in the militarized Midlands. With her hostility to Arthur recalling Duchess Fortune's imperiousness, Morgan points to political fissures that preclude Arthur's Britain being conceived as a proto-national, or even imperial, unity: the *Gawain*-poet's Britain is a fractured, unstable place. If it is indeed through women that Arthur comes to reflect in the Alliterative *Morte Arthure* on the disastrous results of his expansionist policies, then the *Gawain*-poet's indictment of Arthurian empire becomes more complex with the addition of another regionally recognizable power-player—the Lady, who participates, as we shall see, in the control and consumption of wealth within the domestic spaces of militarism.

Dissevering Doubles
Morgan, the Lady, and the Exercise of Militarist Wealth

According to Halleck, late-medieval alliterative verse revives the "love of war" evident in the "songs" of the Anglo-Saxon "race."[89] Turning tellingly to a male metaphor to describe the persistence of the "somber cast of the Teutonic mind" born of the gloomy, battle-soaked North, Halleck argues that "Modern English" verse is a manifestation of Teutonic poetry (including late-medieval alliterative verse) and is "no more unlike Anglo-Saxon than a bearded man is unlike his former childish self."[90] Such vision of a bellicose alliterative spirit is frequent in Revivalist criticism, which often asserts neo-Saxon prosody's predilection for battle-scenes and grim description.[91] As we have seen (chapter 2), Revivalism's ongoing investment in a hypermasculine, neo-Saxon alliterative school leads to a neglect of key female characters in alliterative poems.

Such Revivalist bias reveals itself in a tendency to neutralize the destabilizing socioeconomic presence of the *Gawain*-poet's Lady and Morgan by conceiving them as doubles. Such leveling of two recognizable economic types—the spouse collaborating in estate management, and the widow maintaining sole control of holdings—follows from disparate motives. Some arguments for the Lady and Morgan's doubleness derive from aesthetic claims, in which Morgan's presence is held to be a clumsy and improbable supplement that distracts attention from the poem's central, male conflict. Claiming that those interested in Morgan should refer to Albert B. Friedman, whom he congratulates for having said "about all that needs to be said on the much debated subject of that elusive witch," R. H. Bowers instantiates this tradition with his argument that Morgan "functions solely as a foil to enhance the beauty of Gawain's temptress."[92] The figure before whom Bertilak humbles himself and who is honored above all others at Hautdesert is thus reduced to decorative status, with bedroom proceedings seen from Gawain's perspective clearly more central to Bowers's and Friedman's concerns.[93] Even critics sympathetic to female empowerment in the poem have assumed the aesthetic awkwardness of Morgan's centrality: Fisher, for example, argues that the use of Morgan as *dea ex machina* deliberately risks the narrative's "credibility" in order to "diffuse and marginalize women's power."[94]

Some critics conflate Morgan and the Lady, not on aesthetic grounds, but out of a conviction that Morgan's pre-eminence discloses her identity as a Celtic deity. Asserting Morgan's centrality to the poem, Angela Carson claims that Morgan and the Lady's status as "doublets" would have been recognized by a contemporary audience as readily as Bertilak would have been seen as actually King Urien.[95] Zeal to uncover a Celtic mythical subtext sometimes reduces the Lady to a mere shadow of Morgan. Assuming the *Gawain*-poet's familiarity with a traditional "splitting of Morgain's personality into two selves," Laura Hibbard Loomis contends that the "young beauty" is "at once Morgan's other self and agent, but . . . also has a personality of her own."[96] Such theorists of doubleness at Hautdesert do not explain why knights fulfilling Arthur's orders are unquestionably individuals, while women acting at Morgan's behest—a common-enough occurrence in the Vulgate tradition, in which Morgan often deploys female agents from her network of forest castles[97]—are projections of a fairy's self. In the disclosure of a feminine sub-text to *Sir Gawain and the Green*

Knight, even subtle analysis uncovering the poem's structural contrast of a unidimensional Camelot with a multivalent Hautdesert can arrest Morgan's and the Lady's individual play. Moving beyond merely doubling Morgan and the Lady, Chism groups both under the more general figure of Arthur's queen, arguing that "Gwenore's image will later polarize and split to create the two ladies at Bertilak's court, Morgan and the Lady."[98] Women here become Woman.

Denying some critics' overreaching claims for Morgan's centrality enables recovery of the true magnitude of Morgan's significant, but realistically delimited, jurisdiction in *Sir Gawain and the Green Knight* and also illuminates the Lady's lesser, but still significant, sphere of influence. Arguing that Bertilak, despite his claim that Morgan resides in "my" house (2446), either "owns nothing himself" or owns it only through Morgan's "might," Fisher asserts that Bertilak "becomes the host in name alone," and is the "taken man who is Morgan's token—feminized, as Gawain is, within a world of women."[99] Rather than focusing on Bertilak's lesser power, I would invert such a perspective and observe that Bertilak's lordship over Hautdesert reveals the greater regional power of Morgan, to whose command he eagerly submits. That Bertilak is playing host to Morgan does not conflict with her political superiority: as Morgan's vassal, he would be expected to offer such hospitality. Morgan's honored status as guest is made clear by the parallel seating arrangements in Camelot and Hautdesert, with Morgan recalling the Bishop Bawdewyn by being seated "heȝest" at the dais (1001; 112).[100] Bertilak's impressive lordship over his wealthy court only magnifies Morgan's lordship over so great a man. If Bertilak is indeed, as the text clearly states, a "kyng" [king] (992), his assessment of Morgan as a "goddes" [goddess] discloses her hierarchical superiority— the wider concentric sphere of power within which Bertilak's lordship is situated. Resistance to such a reading by editors such as J. R. R. Tolkien and E. V. Gordon reveals Revivalist anxiety about a woman's pre-eminent political power.[101]

Bertilak's claim of sole responsibility for the Temptation Game stands as further testament to Morgan's greatness. Portraying Bertilak as conflicted about being Morgan's "errand boy," Fisher argues that he transforms himself into a "Father-confessor" and proceeds to "reasser[t] his property rights," claiming the "wife" and the "testing" of Gawain as "his," in order to "deny Morgan's power."[102] While Fisher rightly reads anxiety in Bertilak's claims, his statement, like his nervous insistence that Morgan resides in *his* house, subtly expresses his power's relativity—as both paling in comparison to, and yet depending upon, Morgan's might. In claiming sole responsibility for the original plan (without, it should be noted, his co-conspirator, the Lady, there to qualify his narrative), Bertilak uses language that echoes his own description of Morgan's power over him: just as Morgan "wayned me" [sent me] (2456) to Camelot, he states of the Temptation Game that "I sende hir to asaye þe" [I sent her to test you] (2361–62). If Bertilak speaks of his wife as a subordinate, his language merely underscores his unambiguous description of himself as Morgan's subordinate: far from denying Morgan's power, Bertilak here highlights her preeminence.

In equating Bertilak's lesser power with his being "feminized,"[103] Fisher underestimates the Lady's significant power at Hautdesert, where she would typically have controlled domestic affairs.[104] Equating the Lady's namelessness with powerlessness, Fisher argues that "she comes to represent essentialized womanhood" and "as such, she is so private that she needs no public token by which to identify herself."[105] However, a wealthy household created ample material opportunities for a noble woman. It is not just Bertilak who hosts Morgan and Gawain, but also the Lady, who refers to her management of her household staff in speaking to Gawain of "my burdeȝ" [my ladies] (1232). Besides possessing domestic responsibilities in running the household while her husband is off hunting (or playing Green Knight), the Lady clearly possesses cultural sophistication. In her interactions with Gawain, held to be a master in the "sleȝtes of þewes" [arts of high manners] and of the "teccheles termes of talkyng noble" [flawless expressions of noble conversation] (917–18), the Lady displays clear discursive skill, matching wits with Gawain in a triad of high-stakes courtly conversations (1210–1306; 1476–1555; 1742–1869). Surely such a polished performance in private implies equal skill in her public interactions with her "burdeȝ."

In contrast to the active Lady of Hautdesert, Guinevere plays little role beyond that of beautifying Camelot's hall and being an unwitting object of Morgan's hostility (2460). As critics often note, Arthur's queen blends in with other court adornments as she sits, "dressed on þe dere des, dubbed al aboute" [displayed on the splendid dais, surrounded by adornments] (75), objectified as the "comlokest" [most attractive] among many "gemmes" [gems] (78–81). The Lady of Hautdesert, associated with vibrant conversation and the overseeing of staff and residents hosting both Gawain and Morgan, suggests a more active female life than in southerly, static Camelot. Analyzing the *Gawain*-poet's structural use of Guinevere's Southern passivity, Carolyn Dinshaw argues that the Lady reverses conventional courtly gender roles by figuring Gawain as "the hunted," actively objectifying the knight through her gaze, praise, and offer of service.¹⁰⁶ Far from representing a nameless femininity, the Lady clearly plays a vital role in the management and consumption of a wealthy court's cultural life, with her active role highlighted by her rendering Gawain as passive as Guinevere.¹⁰⁷

English legal custom contributes to some critics' overlooking of the busy lives of women such as the Lady. Medieval wives engaged in numerous practical responsibilities obscured by the English law of the "unity of person" of husband and wife.¹⁰⁸ Reflecting methodologically on this legal fiction, Christopher Cannon urges critics to avoid the literalist interpretation that this doctrine entails a married woman's loss of person through subjection to her husband.¹⁰⁹ Rather, critics should devise methods of indirect retrieval of women's activities from historical records that systematically cloak such information.¹¹⁰ Cannon's critical advice about adjusting methodologies relative to available legal evidence, combined with avoidance of conflating literary characters' narrative prominence with structural significance, aids considerably in recovering female economic agency in the *Gawain*-poet's militarized Midlands.

While Bertilak's and the Lady's power is restricted to the domestic space of the castle and its grounds, Morgan possesses region-wide authority, the wider sphere of which is marked by her sending Bertilak to unsettle Arthur's distant, Southern court. The extent of Morgan's sway is then doubly mapped out by Gawain's journey to and from Hautdesert. In returning, Gawain transports the knowledge of his aunt's power back across the "wylde wayeȝ" [wild ways] (2479) in a geographical journey that Ingham compellingly links with English imperial desire.¹¹¹ Territorial markers such as the Wirral, Anglesey, and North Wales show the reach of Morgan's imperial influence from somewhere in the Northwest Midlands, through wild liminal spaces, to southerly Camelot (691–735).¹¹² Bertilak's literally domestic Temptation game looks small in comparison, indeed. As we shall see, Morgan communicates her greatness through an act of self-fashioning for the Arthurian guest who hand-delivers the message of her power across this hostile British landscape. Morgan's message echoes that of Cicero's Cato, who, responding to the claim that his absence from battlefields detracts from his influence, counters, "and yet I direct the senate as to what wars should be waged and how; at the present time, far in advance of hostilities, I am declaring war on Carthage, for she has long been plotting mischief."¹¹³ While Bertilak and the Lady operate on the immediately apparent field of conflict, Morgan and Cato direct trans-regional games, keeping their eyes on larger imperial concerns, while letting subordinates focus on mere individuals.

Morgan's Mask of Old Age
Of Sublime Decrepitude and Regional Female Power

If the Lady and Morgan each participates in controlling Northwest Midlands wealth, the former seems significantly less threatening to males competing for such resources. Such a discrepancy proves part of Morgan's design. For R. Howard Bloch, the conventional lady of courtly love arises from patriarchal culture's effort to counteract a twelfth-century increase in female access to wealth: through an aggressive idealization of women that is only superficially "empower[ing]," threatened males seek to remove women from material culture altogether.[114] In fashioning herself as an elderly woman—the factitiousness of which is signaled by her over-determined description as an "olde auncian" [elderly old woman] (1001)—Morgan announces that she will not be subject to the courtly gaze that targets women with dangerous economic potential.[115] Morgan's resistance to becoming a courtly object emerges when we counteract scholarly efforts to read Morgan as actually, and not virtually, an "auncian." As Chism aptly argues, Morgan "deliberately veils herself," pursuing a policy of "provincial gamesmanship" that allows her to take "control of her own narration."[116] Indeed, in donning a mask of old age Morgan endeavors to diminish the Arthurian reservoir of symbolic capital, as part of a strategic effort that includes her use of the Green Knight to stage a slap in Arthur's imperial face. Morgan's disguise studiously distinguishes her from women whose narrative significance proves confined to sexual attractiveness, such as Hexione, Helen, and Guinevere. Presenting herself as an elderly woman whose physical grotesqueness she underscores by contrasting herself with the conventionally beautiful Lady who is "wener" [more gorgeous] than "Wenore" [Guinevere] (943–69), Morgan masks her own attractiveness to communicate that it is her clerkly and lordly skills that make her the region's pre-eminent power.[117]

Morgan's donning of a mask of old age links her symbolically with Merlin and his threatening, subversive power. Morgan's shape-shifting abilities recall those of Merlin, who in the Vulgate Cycle inspires fear among the barons assisting in Arthur's consolidation of empire: "for that he chaungeth hym so ofte he is dowted of many a man" [because he alters himself so frequently, he is feared by many men].[118] The "pley" [play] and "connynge" [cunning] that Merlin uses in the *Prose Merlin* (II.312) to fashion himself as a churl or hart was presumably part of the "maystrés" [expertise] that he confers upon the *Gawain*-poet's Morgan (2448): Morgan thus acquires his marginal, unsettling powers of identity-play.[119] Absent from the *Gawain*-poet's world, Merlin gives way to Morgan, who now maintains the uncanny clerkly craft capable of frightening Arthurian imperial agents.

Morgan uses such unsettling shape-shifting power for political purposes that differ strikingly from those motivating only superficially similar Loathly Lady narratives. In the *Weddynge of Sir Gawain and Dame Ragnell,* Ragnelle was "disformyd" [disfigured] by the "nygramancy" [necromancy] of a malicious stepmother, and required rescue by a knight courteous enough to marry her and grant her "sovereynté" (691–99) by deferring to her choice whether to be fair by day and foul by night, or the converse (656–79).[120] By contrast, the *Gawain*-poet's Morgan chooses to become a crone and never alters her appearance to please or reward the knight. While the "olde wyf" [old woman] of Chaucer's *Wife of Bath's Tale* actively chooses to alter her foul appearance for her deferential husband, she ultimately conforms to the knight's conventional notions of youthful female beauty and joins him in domestic bliss (III.998–1000; 1219–58). Working against the Loathly Lady convention she invokes, Morgan never withdraws from her threatening form, and she does not seek to win, but rather to drive away the knight, asserting sole control over her domestic space.

Morgan's symbolic self-fashioning designedly distinguishes her from Loathly Lady figures, who, as Ingham argues, reveal "heterosexist demands" that force female bodies to figure "sovereign control."[121] Analyzing John Gower's "Tale of Florent" from the *Confessio Amantis,* Ingham concludes that the Loathly Lady motif involves male acquisition of territory figured as the female, with the man learning the valuable lesson of "managing his own desire."[122] The *Gawain*-poet depends upon just such a heteronormative and territorialist understanding of the Loathly Lady narrative, highlighting Morgan's counter-move of retaining sovereign right. By having Gawain refuse to join Morgan at Hautdesert (2471), instead to return home empty-handed with the message of Morgan's independent power, the *Gawain*-poet explicitly undermines the Loathly Lady motif's subordination of female interests to the male knight's sexual and territorial desires. Turning a sexist and imperialist story-type to her own advantage, Morgan puts on loathliness to communicate her unassimilation into Arthurian empire.

Age proves even more crucial than loathliness to Morgan's symbolic self-fashioning. A number of critics and editors follow Madden in explaining Morgan's advanced age through reference to a single story from the thirteenth-century Old French *Prophecies de Merlin* cycle, in which Morgan chastises the Lady of the Lake for having exposed her "chair nue et rideé, et mes mamelles pendans, et aussi la peau de mon ventre" [naked and wrinkled flesh, and my sagging breasts, and also the fat of my belly], when people "cuidoit que je fusse de jeune aage" [believed that I was young].[123] Seconding Madden's deduction from this single, ambiguous reference (which may well deploy youthful appearance simply as a metaphor for beauty), Tolkien and Gordon offer added support by citing a claim from the thirteenth-century *Suite du Merlin* that Morgan's use of magic made her "laide" [ugly].[124] Tolkien and Gordon's reliance on this largely irrelevant evidence—for ugliness hardly equates with the elderliness that is the key characteristic of the *Gawain*-poet's "auncian"—suggests a critical anxiety generated by Morgan's masterful management of appearances.[125] Besides the fact that the *Gawain*-poet's insistence that this is the "firste age" [youth] of Arthur's empire renders the advanced age of his sister implausible,[126] audience expectations concerning Morgan argue against her being accepted as an actual "auncian." In the Vulgate Cycle, with which the *Gawain*-poet seems to have been familiar, Morgan's usual appearance is as a zealous participant in courtly love-games.[127] While Morgan is at times depicted as unattractive, her lusts and liaisons are numerous enough to lead to her description in the *Prose Merlin* as a "yonge damsell" [young woman] who was "the moste hotest woman of all Breteigne" [the absolutely most lustful woman of Britain] (II.507). Moreover, the clearly reciprocated love between Morgan and Guyomar is often used to explain Morgan's deep-seated hostility to Guinevere, who is sometimes held to have convinced her cousin to break off his affair with Morgan—and thus to have created the enmity that Bertilak lists among Morgan's motives in sending him to Camelot (2549–52).[128]

In order to signal that "koyntyse of clergye" [cunning in clerkliness] (2447) rather than physical beauty is the basis of her "myght" [power] (2446), Morgan makes use of the structuring trope of the triadic hierarchy of age central to the *Parlement of the Thre Ages*. In this alliterative dream vision, Elde [Old Age] takes discursive control of a debate being waged between Youthe and Meddill Elde [Middle Age]. Elde is largely a comical figure, instantiating what Cicero's Cato concedes is the flaw that "Old Age is naturally inclined to talk too much."[129] Despite his disordered, dubious, and often absurd speech,[130] Elde is at least accorded a respectful silence from his younger interlocutors. It is just such respect that Morgan seeks in taking up Elde's prime position in this temporal hierarchy, while maintaining the dignity of Cato rather than the *Parlement*-poet's garrulous Elde. Appropriating the "social structuring of temporality" of this "mythico-ritual" ordering of "the Ages of Life,"[131] Morgan uses this symbolic capital to signify her superiority both to the youthful Gawain and to Bertilak, described as of "hyghe eldee" [of a distinguished age[132]]

(844). Much as the *Parlement*-poet's Elde silences both the knight-errant Youthe and the land-owning Medill Elde, so does Morgan signal her transcendent power by making herself the third factor in a symbolic *Aufhebung* that reveals the emphatically smaller scale of young Gawain's competition with middle-aged Bertilak (and his Lady). Morgan's aloofness from both the Lady's bedroom temptations and Bertilak's parkland hunting activities, combined with her "auncian" disguise, signal that her honored position (948) is derived not from physical, but from intellectual prowess. In seeming old, Morgan echoes Cato's argument that "it is not by muscle, speed, or physical dexterity that great things are achieved, but by reflection, force of character, and judgement."[133]

Morgan's politically motivated manipulation of appearances also links her to a *Gawain*-poet who displays a clear zest for perspectival play. It is not just Morgan's revered status at table (1001) that speaks against critical complaints about the aesthetically awkward unveiling of her centrality—for the *Gawain*-poet's purposefully skewed presentation is designed to maximize the impact of this revelation. The primacy of "visual poetics" in *Sir Gawain and the Green Knight* has been demonstrated by Sarah Stanbury, who argues that the *Gawain*-poet uses "repeated visual realignments" of "discrete frames" to mark "interpretive change" in a narrative structured by deferral.[134] Stanbury's emphasis on the *Gawain*-poet's visual technique seems to be confirmed by the artful illusion of Morgan's marginality, even as the narrative demonstrates her centrality. After Gawain first arrives at Hautdesert, both Morgan and the Lady approach him and "kallen hym of aquoyntance" [request his companionship] (975). Soon, "þay tan hym bytwene hem, wyth talkyng hym leden / To chambre, to chemné" [they take him between them and lead him, talking as they go, to the room with the fire-place], and then order spices and wine, preparing for much merriment (978–85). The *Gawain*-poet does not report what speech is exchanged, here, but merely *shows* us the fact of speaking, and uses this same technique on each day, to make clear that Gawain spends significant time socializing with *both* Morgan and the Lady. After the first of his boudoir conversations with the Lady, Gawain calls for his chamberlain, changes his clothes, and, after mass and a meal (1309–12), he

> ... made myry al day, til þe mone rysed.
>   with game.
> Watz neuer freke fayrer fonge
> Bitwene so dygne dame,
> þe alder and þe ȝonge;
> Much solace set þay same. (1313–18)

[. . . spent all day in merriness and play, till the moon rose. There was never a man so happily situated between such worthy ladies, that older one and the younger one. They had a wonderful time together.]

This vision of Gawain spending pleasant time with both of the ladies functions as a counterpoint to the mysterious image of Morgan that the *Gawain*-poet cultivates by withholding transcription of Morgan's speech. That Morgan's seeming silence is an artful illusion soon becomes clear, supporting Elizabeth Scala's view that "Morgan's present absence" is an essential component of the poem.[135] We learn that, after the second bedroom conversation, Gawain "wyth þe ladyeȝ layked alle day" [had a good time with those ladies all day] (1560), and that on the third day, Gawain experiences "comlich caroles and alle-kynnes joye" [beautiful carols and all kinds of joy] with those "fre ladyes" [noble ladies] (1885–86). From Gawain's perspective, the *Gawain*-poet makes clear, Morgan is not a shadowy figure at all.

By appropriating the symbolic capital of Elde, Morgan not only fashions herself as a sign, but also transforms Gawain into a message, having frightened him sufficiently to drive him and his story back to Camelot. Gawain's refusal of Bertilak's invitation to rejoin his aunt in Hautdesert speaks less to his feelings of betrayal than to fear generated by Morgan, who clothes herself with Old Age's allegorical force. Standing in proximity to death, Morgan-as-Elde wields the sublime decrepitude of her temporal disguise, which produces in her viewers the state of mind in which we are made to consider "our own destination."[136] Juxtaposing the Lady's stunning beauty with her equally shocking foulness (943–69), Morgan-as-Elde contrasts vitality with signs of future decay, playing the "ȝolȝe" [sallow] to the Lady's "ȝonge" [young] (945–51). Neither a Loathly Lady in need of a hero's transformative gesture, nor a mere double of the Lady in a gendered assault on Gawain, Morgan deploys age as a mask that fuses the *dignitas* and near-deathliness of Elde.[137] Much as Chaucer's Pardoner uses the sublime sign of his "oold man" [old man] who "moot go thider as I have to go" [must of necessity go yonder] to terrorize his audiences, whom he makes think of death with his "belle"-like voice echoing the bells that ring before the plague-struck "cors" [corpse] (I.749; VII.331; 664–65), so does Morgan-as-Elde strike a distancing fear in Gawain. If Morgan had really desired to hold Gawain prisoner, as she does to so many knights in the Vulgate's Valley of No Return, she surely would not have let him depart. Rather, she gains in prestige by having the chastened Arthurian knight tell of the older and mysterious power who occupies a region feared as the wild provinces. Like aged Cato grown from field commander to a senator who orchestrates bodies on a wider scale, Morgan leaves the games of venery and courtly love to her inferior agents, and instead concentrates on fashioning the trans-regional message of her independent power.

Morgan's taunting communication both signifies her supreme status and mocks the child's play of Camelot, speaking through a voice of Elde on another frequency from that through which the young Arthurians typically interpret female agency. Morgan may have a personal motive in masking her true age. Insofar as she is said to have gained her "maystrés" [power] by having "dalt drwry" [had a love-affair] with Merlin (2447–50), she might be zealous to avoid being associated exclusively with the sexually desirable body of women such as Guinevere or the Lady.[138] The Lady of the Lake in the *Prophecies de Merlin* shows just such sensitivity to the diminishment of her accomplishments due to an amorous reputation: just before she entombs Merlin, she cites his having spread rumors about having slept with her as the principal reason for her vengeance.[139] Morgan's use of the Elde disguise to assert her power's intellectual rather than corporal basis confronts both current and future detractors—whether they be contemporary slanderers tying her accomplishments to Merlin's teachings, or later critics vitiating her deeds by declaring them an aesthetic after-thought that distracts attention from a male-centered plot.

With its sophisticated courtly sensibilities and presentation of powerful women pivotal to Hautdesert's political world, *Sir Gawain and the Green Knight* belies Revivalist assumptions that amorous matters are alien to a Francophobic alliterative aesthetic (see chapter 2). The *Gawain*-poet's powerful female characters undermine Revivalism's marginalization of women in portraits of a hypermasculinist alliterative school nostalgic for Anglo-Saxon warrior culture (see chapter 1). By having Morgan literally lord it over Bertilak and the Lady, and by emphasizing the Lady's significant power at Hautdesert, the *Gawain*-poet avoids the fantastical omnipotence of a figure like the *Morte*-poet's Fortune, and instead presents Morgan and the Lady as regionally recognizable female figures participating prominently in the rich material culture of the militarized Midlands. To take up Judith Bennett's terms concerning the control and distribution of wealth, the Lady holds "power" through significant but limited involvement in estate management, while Morgan attains true "authority" in the sense of "recognized and legitimized power."[140] In demonstrating her territorial sway by engineering the Beheading Game and by managing the symbolic capital of the mask of Elde, the *Gawain*-poet's Morgan joins with her active subordinate the Lady in resisting Revivalist efforts to obscure female power in late-medieval courts teeming with the wealth of English empire.

4

Borderland Subversions

ANTI-IMPERIAL ENERGIES IN THE *AWNTYRS OFF ARTHURE* AND *GOLAGROS AND GAWANE*

I F THE MEDIEVAL nation is indeed a medievalist projection of modern political assumptions onto late-medieval texts, then we find ourselves faced with the question of what sorts of political community were actually imagined in the fourteenth and fifteenth centuries. Judging from the perspective of the Anglo-Scottish marches, the primary late-medieval political unit is the imperial state. While the post-industrial nation, with its general education system, fully centralized bureaucracy, and mass-market apparatus, is qualitatively distinct from late-medieval British polities (see chapter 1), modern empire is deeply rooted in the Middle Ages. In rejecting the practice of tracing English nationhood teleologically back to a medieval proto-modernity, I will emphasize that the British Isles hosted a number of imperial aspirants. Analysis of two late-medieval alliterative Arthurian texts, the *Awntyrs off Arthure*[1] and the *Knightly Tale of Golagros and Gawane,*[2] along with continued engagement with the Alliterative *Morte Arthure,* demonstrates that what Davies calls the "First English Empire," while clearly the more aggressive in its expansionist and centralizing policies, was joined by a competing Scottish imperial state.[3]

Territorial instability exposes fundamental differences between medieval imperial and modern national space. As we shall see, regional analysis of the Anglo-Scottish borderlands undermines hypotheses of a late-medieval nation-state, though marcher culture offers key evidence for state centralization and provides continuities with current forms of empire. The expansionist English and Scottish states, which literally bled into one another in a militarized marcher zone, defy analysis as continuous territories with stable borders. According to Anderson, modern, sovereign nations require continuous and clearly delimited territory, with all national possession conforming to a global classification system in which every iota of available land and water is mapped and accounted for by print-capitalist culture's advanced navigational and cartographic technologies.[4] Anderson's genealogy of the nation insists on the unstable nature of "dynastic" late-medieval polities, whose "porous and indistinct" borders generated a fluid political landscape in which "sovereignties faded imperceptibly into one another."[5] Such a dynamic world of blurred borders and intertwining conceptions of legitimacy contrasts sharply with the continuous, homogeneous, and limited nature of modern national territory. As we shall see, late-medieval visions of militarist expansionism direct us away from a progressivist reading of the slowly but linearly forming modern nation, and instead suggest parallels between the fluid power-networks of pre-modern and post-national empires.

Not only shifting notions of territory but also multiple modes of late-medieval loyalty speak against medievalist hypotheses of pre-modern nationalism. While aimed at elaborating the case for a medieval nation, Suzanne Conklin Akbari's differentiation between medieval and modern imaginations of the nation provides crucial support for an alteritist perspective and suggests empire as the more apt model for analyzing late-medieval polities. For Akbari, two forms of "alignment" distinguish a pre-modern nation: the blurring of "national" and religious identities, and the conflation of nation and "race" in the physiological understanding of individuals.[6] Such continuities among medieval modes of identity preclude modern nationalism's demand for pre-eminent loyalty. As Anderson argues, "Christendom" functioned in the pre-modern period as a community that coexisted with secular polities, thereby subjecting medieval individuals to dual jurisdictions in a way alien to modern citizenship, which assumes an overriding national authority in all legal and political contexts.[7] However ethnocentric a modern nation might be, it is a community that, like the linguistic medium in which it is largely conceived, allows one to be "invited" in, or "naturalized," unlike birth-based communities.[8] While there are clearly signs of ethnic "national identity" in medieval English texts, Akbari observes, there is a lack of any "political ideology of nationhood" in "premodern texts."[9] Given such an ideological dearth, medieval English or Scottish individuals would differ sharply from Anderson's modern citizens inhabiting a world where the "national state" is the "overwhelming norm" and for whom "nation-ness is virtually inseparable from political consciousness."[10] If medieval and modern nations differ as fundamentally as Akbari suggests, then we should question the usefulness of extending the nation's genealogy back to the medieval period, and should instead look to alternative forms of political community.

In arguing for an alteritist position regarding medieval nationhood, I do not suggest absolute medieval–modern rupture on all cultural and historical fronts. Indeed, in practicing what Ingham calls the "contrapuntal" historiography that balances differences and alterities in confronting late-medieval texts (see chapter 2),[11] I stress the need to recognize medieval–modern continuity regarding imperialist energies inflecting Anglo-Scottish borderlands culture, even as I emphasize discontinuities in medieval and modern modes of ethnic identification. The borderlands occupied by English and Scottish imperial cultures offer a unique lens through which to investigate the interplay of late-medieval feudal, ethnic, socioeconomic, and imperial loyalties. Modern notions of nation present significant obstacles to analysis of this region. With late-medieval southern Scottish culture having been significantly Anglicized since at least the thirteenth century,[12] and with Northern English militarist culture having more in common with Scottish neighbors than distant southerners, the Anglo-Scottish marches lack the sharp cultural and linguistic differences that anchor many later nationalisms. Interpreting this region as transnational offers a unique perspective on ethnic and imperial identities as factors that destabilize, rather than consolidate, communities.

Even for theorists of the modernity of the nation, it is difficult to escape the powerful hold exerted by logics of ethnic continuity. Arguing that nationalism is both modern and logically prior to the nation, Eric Hobsbawm nevertheless flirts with a continuist historiography through his assumption of "proto-nationalist" identity.[13] Hobsbawm's use of the prefix "proto"—meaning, in the first definition in the *Oxford English Dictionary*, "first in time, earliest, original, primitive"—undermines his argument that the rise of the nation heralds a new epoch: if proto-nationalism involves early expression of national identity, then the nation's origins stretch back into the distant past of ethnic memory. Hobsbawm's inconsistency demonstrates confusions in terminology that perennially plague studies of nationalism (see Introduction)[14] and also reveals the destabilizing role that was played in modern criticism by ethnic identity. Recognizing that "existing symbols and sentiments of proto-national communities" were available for nineteenth-century nationalists, Hobsbawm insists that the use made of such symbolic capital was both artificial and exploitative, with nationalists using the "cement" of emotional attachments to an imagined community to manufacture "a suitable (and suitably impressive) national state in the past."[15] Hobsbawm's recognition of the affective power of ethno-symbolism, even as he insists that its sentimental bonds are materially incapable of generating the centralized, homogeneous nation-state,[16] reveals the difficulty of detaching modern nationalist attachments from the traditional material co-opted by ideologues.

As we shall see, the intense feelings of cultural continuity maintained by modern critics have produced a mass of nationalist Revivalist criticism that too readily assumes discrete ethnic identities such as "Scots" and "Englishmen." Such modern projections obstruct our ability to recover the significance of the transnational borderlands informing the *Awntyrs off Arthure* and *Golagros and Gawane*. As Smith argues, in negotiating between a post-industrial modern nation and the often ancient and deeply held reservoir of ethnic beliefs, the nation as a discursive formation requires the "constant renewal and retelling" of the "mythologies and symbolisms of previous generations."[17] Considering that Revivalist critics project stable ethnic identities such as Saxon, Norman, and Scot into a late-medieval narrative of the modern nation's rise (see chapter 1), I will work against such modern impositions by re-engaging with the fluid identities available in the Anglo-Scottish marches.

In undoing Revivalism's nationalist prejudices, I am motivated both by my own historical moment and by intervening critical desire. My interrogation of Revivalist fantasy steers analysis of Anglo-Scottish borderlands poetics toward current political and cultural parallels: the unstable marcher identity mirrors fluid forms of identification in today's multicultural America, which itself requires a transnational frame in which territorial and ethnic boundaries become increasingly overridden by what Hardt and Negri call Empire.[18] In foregrounding my desire to recover medieval identities caught up in cultural complexes active in my own rapidly deterritorializing world, I am indebted to recent, resolute statements of the historiographical value of channeling current desires—namely, Dinshaw's notion of a "contingent history" in which the literary historian seeks to "touch" the past;[19] and Fradenburg's call to exploit continuities in political desires that bridge past and present.[20] By channeling rather than repressing my own fantasy, I deploy sustained analysis of medieval negotiation of imperial identities to speak to the post-national present in a manner foreclosed by Revivalism's nationalist filters.

Even as I insist on the nation's fundamentally modern nature, and thus also on the absence of the late-medieval Scottish nation-state imagined by Revivalists (see chapter 1), I systematically resist alteritist periodizations that interpret imperialism as exclusively modern.[21] Setting these late-medieval alliterative poems in a pre-modern sociopolitical landscape, I link my analysis with much medievalist work informed by the insights of imperial and postcolonial studies.[22] My focus on continuing empire is balanced with my ongoing rejection of medieval nationhood. Figures like the conquering Arthur and the resolutely independent Golagros may initially suggest English and Scottish stereotypes, for such characters recall the cultural materials out of which later nationalists fashion their fantastically aged national pasts. To read them as proto-nationalist figures, however, requires divorcing them from the shifting political landscapes produced by expansive and discontinuous late-medieval imperial states, in an era devoid of the nation as an inherently limited community. Even if we are to imagine "national fantasy" informing these romances of the war-torn Anglo-Scottish borderlands, we should explore it with Ingham's insistence on balancing the "shared imaginings" of sovereignty and community with the "differential politics" of those involved, while closing off any effort to isolate single communities as lineal ancestors of the modern nation.[23]

As we have seen in the transnational economic zone informing visions of Arthurian empire in the militarized Midlands (chapter 3), and of the cross-Channel consolidation of Western aristocratic power that excludes the Eastern other (chapter 2), the methodological discarding of the medieval nation as an analytical unit discloses alternative forms of medieval political identity. Insisting on a pre-national epoch allows for a fuller engagement with regional identities no longer tethered to a presumed national center and also highlights transnational cultural and economic contexts that inform late-medieval British communities. Turning to late-medieval Arthurian texts that speak to and from a space produced by the collision of expansionist states—the very expansionism of which removes these polities from consideration as nations in Anderson's sense of sovereign, limited territories that accept the territorial limits of other nations[24]—I will emphasize the superior value of empire to nation in political analysis. Late-medieval Anglo-Scottish marcher texts suggest the need to abandon nationalist language in tracing the genealogy of English and Scottish imperial states that mutually constructed each other in this radically localized borderlands. Working to recover what Ingham and Warren describe as "the relevance of premodern dynamics of conquest and settlement to subsequent expansionist projects,"[25] I will explore sustained poetic engagements with British empire-formation. To re-engage with the unstable politics of transnational culture, I will resist the Revivalist nationalism that has inflected reception of the *Awntyrs off Arthure* and *Golagros and Gawane*, filtering the poems through a bipartite model of nascent nationhood alien to the militarized marches in which they were born.

Borderland Identities
The Transnational Anglo-Scottish Marches

A borderland gesture undermines the modern assumption that national identity grounds late-medieval Arthurian political imagination. Before a crowd of eager spectators assembled near Carlisle, Galeron, introduced earlier as the "grettest" [greatest] of Galloway (418), kneels, signaling his submission to the stand-in for the imperial war machine to which he will soon swear allegiance. It is thus through dispossession and repossession that the *Awntyrs off Arthure* stages the centrality of land to power-plays in the Anglo-Scottish marches. The poem does not present an "English" Gawain who defeats a "Scottish" Galeron, winning yet another soldier for the armies of British empire, but rather simultaneously invites and forecloses readings of the poem's territorial conflicts as essentially national or ethnic. In portraying the practice of side-switching key to survival on the militarized Anglo-Scottish border, the *Awntyrs off Arthure* is linked with a text that, though of a more northerly provenance, also defies simple national classification, and is also grounded in the brutal, fluid world of border warfare, where profit regularly trumped patriotism in determining to which magnate marcher lords and their retainers gravitated. *Golagros and Gawane,* though ostensibly of "Scottish" provenance, joins the *Awntyrs off Arthure* in speaking from a marcher perspective of the raids and invasions that wracked the Anglo-Scottish borderlands.

By bracketing our sense of these poems' national origins, I will explore how each romance manages a critique of imperialist expansionism. These critiques register regional reactions to processes of state consolidation that were sweeping away a borderlands culture that fed off the almost continuous armed conflict of the fourteenth and early fifteenth centuries. Even as these texts reveal nostalgia for the bravado and localism of war-torn times, they also speak to the devastation and misery produced by an economic world built upon violence. While the *Awntyrs off Arthure,* set near the border stronghold of Carlisle, ultimately situates the collapse of Arthurian empire at the very edge of its expanding frontier, *Golagros and Gawane* offers the desperate fantasy of a local lord allowed to stand independent of any imperial or proto-national unit imaginable in this violent marcher zone.

Influenced by postcolonial criticism, medievalists have recently shown much interest in destabilizing modern notions of nation as central to the medieval mindset, pursuing the "multiplicity" and "newness" that Cohen sees as opened up by the rejection of progressivist historiography.[26] As early as 1953, K. B. McFarlane isolated armed conflict as a subject particularly plagued by anachronistic emphasis on nationhood, arguing that historians rarely analyze medieval warfare in its own "idiom," having instead "clung obstinately to their own."[27] Speaking of the manner in which the Hundred Years' War was interpreted as a "national" conflict, McFarlane insisted that medieval military activity was essentially local, involving a "speculative" understanding of war as "trade," with participants fighting, not "for love of king or lord, still less for England or for glory, but for gain."[28] While McFarlane presents a useful corrective against the imposition of modern concepts of nationhood in England, R. James Goldstein offers powerful criticism of the manner in which modern nationalist sentiments distort scholarly treatments of late-medieval Scotland. Even as a textual production such as the *Declaration of Arbroath* contributes to the forging of Scottish national identity, Goldstein argues, it speaks only for elite class interests, revealing a "Brucean" ideology that has been wrongly taken as an expression of universal values that transcend local political motives.[29] In both cases, all-too-modern conceptions of the nation as a stable, unitary, and unquestioned monopolizer of legitimate violence obscure essentially local concentrations of aristocratic power.[30]

Such cautionary arguments against the importation of modern concepts of nationhood prove especially valuable in engaging with texts situated in the Anglo-Scottish marches. Edward I's attempt, from 1296, at imperial conquest—his desire to be the *malleus Scottorum* [hammer of the Scots]—sparked centuries of border warfare often conceived in strongly nationalistic terms.[31] As we shall see, it was not until well into the fifteenth century that the Anglo-Scottish marches began to lose their character as a borderlands culture, suggesting that the *Awntyrs off Arthure* dates from the dawn of a significant burst in state consolidation on both sides of the border,[32] while the later *Golagros and Gawane* reveals the more advanced stage of this process.[33] The *Awntyrs*-poet and the *Golagros*-poet reflect on the fluid notions of space and territory in pre-national Britain, setting the politics of the transnational Anglo-Scottish borderlands against the centralizing forces of state-building that haunted the romanticized marches of the imperialist Middle Ages.

I will demonstrate that Gawain's unease with the ethics of militarism voices a regional concern, reflecting a conflicted view of conquest that circulated in late-medieval Britain's most militarized areas. Comparison of the anti-imperialism of the *Awntyrs off Arthure* with similar currents running through *Golagros and Gawane* makes clear the heuristic value of isolating an alliterative zone centered in the Anglo-Scottish borderlands. Such a transnational region might include the Alliterative *Morte Arthure,* which also features a chronicle treatment of King Arthur[34] and which has close textual parallels with the *Awntyrs off Arthure.*[35] While the Alliterative *Morte* illuminates the interpenetration of the militarist zones of the English North and the careerist Northwest Midlands (see chapter 3),[36] it emphasizes civilian suffering to such an extent that it more readily recalls the

Anglo-Scottish borderland that regularly experienced warfare both through aggression and as the site of frequent attacks.[37] As we shall see, the *Awntyrs off Arthure* and *Golagros and Gawane* resist national classification and are read more productively as texts tied to a militarized borderlands, broadly conceived (from Southern Scotland to Yorkshire, in the East, with all of Cumberland in the West).[38] Whereas Blake, in critiquing the monolithic nature of an "Alliterative Revival," suggests that Scotland ought to be seen as having "staged" its "own," I will assert that such a nation-based formulation obscures thematic and metrical affinities that transcend borders.[39] Indeed, the alliterative zone I propose cannot be limited to a single nation, but is rather the product of the difference between Scotland and England— that is, of the militarized zone created by generations of Anglo-Scottish warfare.

Anxiety about a shared culture of militarism is not the only basis for linking the *Awntyrs off Arthure* and *Golagros and Gawane,* for literary historical and codicological evidence connect these texts. The thirteen-line stanza form of the *Awntyrs off Arthure* and *Golagros and Gawane* offers critical evidence of cross-border metrical exchange. Of the two variations of the meter, the form in which the *Awntyrs off Arthure* is written—with the ninth line consisting of four major stresses, unlike the "bob" used in the *Pistill of Swete Susane*—is used in all Middle Scots examples, including *Golagros and Gawane.*[40] By theorizing an alliterative zone that encompasses Southern Scotland and the North of England, I will explore material evidence for Pearsall's literary historical "impression" of an alliterative line "retreating northwards."[41]

Codicological evidence also supports a link between the *Awntyrs off Arthure* and the Alliterative *Morte Arthure*. The Alliterative *Morte* is uniquely attested in Lincoln Cathedral Library MS 91, which also contains a copy of the *Awntyrs off Arthure*.[42] Dialectal evidence also helps link these two texts. While describing the *Awntyrs*-poet's dialect as "almost certainly northern," Hanna suggests the "north" as the most probable site of composition for the Alliterative *Morte Arthure*.[43] In the case of *Golagros and Gawane,* however, we can rely on no such textual or codicological affinities. No manuscript copy of the poem survives, with the sole attestation being the 1508 print made in Edinburgh by Walter Chepman and Andrew Myllar,[44] while the Middle Scots dialect of *Golagros and Gawane* also makes clear verbal parallels rare.

The Edinburgh provenance of our only surviving text of *Golagros and Gawane* need not discount it as a text shaped significantly by the Anglo-Scottish marches, as can be seen by comparing the impact of borderland politics on Richard Holland's *Buke of the Howlat,* which is situated far to the north, in Moray. Though Holland narrates his dream vision of the owl who gains and loses multi-colored plumage from Darnway, the poem itself invokes the border tensions upon which the Black Douglas family—Holland's patrons, whose family arms are reverently expounded upon within the text—built its power.[45] Despite its northerly setting, the *Buke of the Howlat* moves south to foreground Anglo-Scottish conflict, interrupting its avian dream vision to praise the most powerful Scottish house active on the late-medieval marches—the Black Douglases. The distant Moray setting does not stop Holland from using the language of borders, imagining the Douglas family as a fortification. Holland's Douglases are "of Scotland the werwall" [the rampart of Scotland], defending against "our fais force" [our enemies' power] (382–83), with those foes proving to be "sonnis of the Saxons" [sons of the Saxons] coming from south of the border (576–77). While we do not know the provenance of the original *Golagros*-text from which Chepman and Myllar produced their print, the *Golagros*-poet joins Holland in being drawn to the violence of the Anglo-Scottish marches.

It is through anti-imperialist ideology that *Golagros and Gawane* reveals close affinity with the Alliterative *Morte Arthure* and the *Awntyrs off Arthure,* and also shares in the localism that suggests the marches as the region whence the *Awntyrs off Arthure* began to disseminate itself more widely across Britain. In revealing to the ghost his reservations about his career as a military man profiting from the arbitrary dispossession of others, the *Awntyrs*-poet's Gawain gives voice to a regional anxiety generated by the pronounced militarization of borderlands societies. As we have seen, the *Morte*-poet similarly expresses such malaise endemic to war-economics, by figuring Fortune's sudden enmity to the formerly successful conqueror Arthur (see chapter 3). In *Golagros and Gawane,* war-zone angst emerges in the utter arbitrariness of Arthurian aggression: Golagros's rich holdings are attacked for no better reason than that Arthur considers it a "selcouthe" [marvel] that Golagros claims to hold his land from no other man (265–66). Arthur's awareness that the cost of his conquest will be the weeping of many "wedou" [widows] suggests cycles of violence that would be familiar to populations who regularly experienced the ravages of war.[46] Such first-hand experience proves a key factor in distinguishing the Anglo-Scottish marcher zone from the careerist Northern Midlands: while both regions participated in English militarism, the Northern borderlands frequently found *itself* the theater of combat, with Scottish aggression and mercenary raids intensifying the impact of warfare on civilians.

If we can speak of a poetics of empire in the late-medieval Anglo-Scottish marches, then it is crucial to note that the literary grappling with such late-medieval imperialist activity transcends regnal borders. Both England and Scotland had expansionist policies aimed at absorbing regional jurisdictions into a larger body.[47] Insofar as medieval England and Scotland were each fundamentally unstable because aggressive entities, they defy categorization by nation in Anderson's terms. These imperial states did not imagine themselves as sovereign, limited entities, but rather fed off a kind of mobile borderlands that emerged wherever they directed their militaristic attention. As we shall see, the fantasy of Arthur's leaving Golagros alone, aloof from the world of feudal land-holdings, demonstrates that these late-medieval Arthurian contexts differ fundamentally from the modern world of territory-based national sovereignty, in which any piece of land is claimed by one or more nation.[48] Meditation on empire reveals an essentially shifting, unstable medieval notion of land; the poetics of such territorial flux permeates Arthurian marcher romances.

While no clear ethnic or national provenance defines the work of the *Awntyrs*-poet or the *Golagros*-poet, their romances speak to the violent realities of the English and Scottish imperial states, with the former casting the far longer shadow. *Golagros and Gawane* can be read as a response to English attempts to revive imperial conquest, though it can also be seen as a reaction to the various brutal strategies employed by the Stewarts in crushing Scottish magnates.[49] Such readings are enabled by the fact that, as Rhiannon Purdie argues, *Golagros and Gawane* can be dated only generally to the fifteenth century.[50] That the Anglo-Scottish border stands as the key site for literary meditations on the dangers of imperialism stems from the particularly nefarious brand of expansionism practiced by the English. While Scottish imperial policy was indeed active, it was, as Davies argues, "flexible and inclusive," aiming to bring the defeated into "the loose ambit of the authority" of peoples "now, at least formally, ethnically one"; English conquest was a "colonizing, 'external,' and annexing process," institutionalizing a "duality" of peoples.[51] According to Davies, as this "first" phase of English imperialism came to a close in the mid-fourteenth century, the "tensions inherent in such a situation were more likely to be transparent."[52] The *Awntyrs*-poet and *Golagros*-poet speak to the continuing alarm concerning a reversion to an age of unbridled imperialist activity: the *Awntyrs off Arthure* suggests the especially violent marcher wars of the fourteenth century, while *Golagros and Gawane* discloses fears that what Michael Brown and Steve Boardman call the "cold war" of the Anglo-Scottish fifteenth century might heat up and again embroil the region.[53]

Romantic Dispossession
The Negotiation of Lordship in the *Awntyrs off Arthure*

Moving to the other side of the border of the *Awntyrs off Arthure*, in a spatio-temporal transition that is invited by the poem's diptychal structure,[54] I will set Galeron's gesture of submission in the context of an encounter with the Other informed by marcher sensibilities. As if rising out of the very blood-soaked earth of a region wracked by constant warfare, a specter ascends to curse the conqueror Arthur, invoking the violent instability in which his imperial armies deal. This spectral reflection on militarism occurs beside the waters of the Tarne Wathelayne, on the outskirts of the border stronghold of Carlisle, as a ghost claiming to be Guinevere's mother indicts Arthur's expansionist activities:

> 'Your king is to couetous, I warne þe sir kniȝt.
> May no man stere him with strength while þe whele stondes.
> Whan he is in his magesté, moost in his miȝt,
> He shal light ful lower on þe sesondes.
> And ȝour chiualrous king chef shall a chaunce:
> False Fortune in fight,
> That wonderfull whelewright,
> Makes lordes lowe to liȝt.' (265–72)

> ['Your king is too covetous, I warn you, noble knight. No man may physically harm him while the Wheel remains still. When he is in a state of majesty, at the height of his power, he shall fall down very low on the beach. And your chivalrous king will experience a misfortune. Untrustworthy Fortune, that wonderful wheel-worker, makes lords fall to the depths.']

The *Awntyrs*-poet's open criticism of Arthur's thirst for conquest is not unique. The "philosopher" of the Alliterative *Morte Arthure*, asked to interpret Arthur's dream of an avenging Lady Fortune, reminds his king that "Thow has schedde myche blode and schalkes distroyede, / Sakeles, in cirquytrie, in sere kynges landis" [You have shed much blood and have destroyed guiltless people in various realms, out of pride] (3398–99). Such soul-searching in the *Awntyrs off Arthure* does not come from a clerical interpreter, but rather from a key commander of the Arthurian war machine. The ghost's grim telling of empire's collapse immediately follows an imperial warrior's moment of self-reflection, for Gawain had used his moment of contact with the otherworld to inquire as to the spiritual fates of those plying his brutal trade:

'How shal we fare,' quod þe freke, 'þat fonden to fight,
And þus defoulen þe folke on fele kinges londes,
And riches ouer reymes withouten eny right,
Wynnen worshipp and wele þorgh wightnesse of hondes?' (261–64)

['What will happen to us,' said the man, 'who pursue combat, and thus plunder people in many kings' lands, and who unrightfully overrun many realms, and win fame and wealth through physical violence?']

Gawain's ethical question elicits a foretelling of Arthurian empire's collapse: "ye shul lese Bretayn" [you will lose Britain] to a rebel who will crown himself at "Carlele" [Carlisle], and in the violent wars "the boldest of Bretayne" [Britain's heroes] will be "slayne," [slain], with all the Round Table falling on one bloody day (265–312).

The conjunction in the *Awntyrs off Arthure* of the ghost's condemnation of militarism with the later depiction of dispossessed Galeron's absorption into Arthurian empire suggests an audience inured to the shifting allegiances and ceaseless violence of the Anglo-Scottish borderlands. Gawain's duel with this former lord who lost Galloway to Arthurian armies sets up a struggle between regional lordship and the imperial juggernaut, whether Scottish or English. The *Awntyrs*-poet at times appears to side with the Arthurian camp: in all four manuscripts, the poet is pleased that Galeron is limping (615), and Gawain's claim that God will stand with the "riȝt" [just] seems confirmed by the Arthurian knight's decisive victory on the field (471). However, the ghost's indictment of imperial ambition renders any such conquest fraught with ambiguity. In assuring Gawain that the Arthurian regime will return from conquering the Romans to find itself dispossessed (280; 311), the ghost voices anti-imperialist anxieties also registered by the *Morte*-poet and the *Golagros*-poet. The ghost thus joins in a literary reaction to the self-destructive culture of ceaseless warfare in the Anglo-Scottish marches, a region economically connected with the Northwest Midlands that provided soldiers for English military aggression (see chapter 3).

With our retrospective view of the formation of English and Scottish nations within the context of a larger British empire, it is all too tempting to read this narrative of dispossession in nationalistic terms. There is, after all, much to recommend Ingham's argument that this "northern borderlands" text is informed by the metaphor of conflict with Scotland, with Arthur representing the centralizing energy of a territorially acquisitive sovereign.[55] Arguments such as Rosalind Field's—that Arthur in alliterative romances represents the centralizing power of the English Crown—have strong historical support: the English kings who stand out most clearly as empire-builders, Edward I and Edward III, each cultivated associations of King Arthur with their own crown.[56] Moreover, as Nicola Royan argues, Scottish chroniclers perennially worked against the English "chronicle" tradition of Arthur as a "successful imperialist," presenting him as an acquisitive tyrant who achieved nothing like true imperial conquest in Scottish territories.[57] In the *Awntyrs off Arthure,* then, Gawain plays a role well established both in romance and in chronicle, acting as the arm of Arthurian empire and attempting to assimilate the resisting ethnic other into the Arthurian war machine.

Just such a role for Gawain in Arthurian imperialism can be found in a number of texts set in the militarized Anglo-Scottish borderlands. As Thomas Hahn observes, Gawain often plays the part of assimilating the "strange, the threatening and the resistant within the ambit of the Round Table."[58] In the *Avowyng of Arthur,* Gawain comes from the same Tarn Wathelayne to defeat Menealfe of the Mountayne, whom he sends to Carlisle as a gift to the Queen, who in turn gives him to King Arthur, who then officiates over Menealfe's assimilation into the Round Table.[59] And in *Sir Gawain and the Carle of Carlisle,* Gawain succeeds, in his conventional capacity as a diplomat for Arthurian culture, in winning over a fiercely independent giant who has for many years been murdering Arthur's knights; by the text's close, the fierce Carl kneels before Arthur as king, joins his Round Table, and is given, in exchange, the lordship of the country of Carlisle.[60] Gawain's ability to deal with outsiders, either by defeating knights in battle or by impressing them with his impeccable manners, makes him an invaluable imperial agent in a borderlands that featured frequent shifts in military loyalty.

Marcher conflicts often invite medievalist projection of national identity. The *Awntyrs*-poet's depiction of Galeron's assimilation into the Round Table might suggest a nationalist style of warfare associated with Edward I's aggression. The invasion through which Arthur had dispossessed Galeron before the action of the *Awntyrs off Arthure* might recall Edward I's imperialist policies regarding Scotland involved forcing marcher lords into the ambit of English power through destructive raids.[61] Edward III, who sought to conquer Scotland by assimilating those "disinherited" by Robert the Bruce in the 1330s, also aggravated inter-state hostilities in the fourteenth-century Anglo-Scottish borderlands.[62] Galeron, introduced as a "nayre" [an heir] by his lady,[63] might be imagined as moving from the role of the disinherited to that of imperial implant, becoming King Arthur's man in Galloway.

However, even as the *Awntyrs*-poet conceives of territorial conflict in a manner consonant with the late-medieval Anglo-Scottish marches—a zone in which the "currency" of power was land[64]—the poem offers notably little in the way of any clear "national" or "ethnic" identities. It is a very different borderlands from that presented, for example, in John Barbour's *The Bruce,* in which John Balliol "stuffyt" [stuffed] Orkney and Galloway "all with Inglismen" [Englishmen], making his governors those "off Inglis nation" [of English ethnicity], such that "Scottismen" lacked freedom to do things to their "liking."[65] Even such a Revivalist as Amours recognizes the conflicted nature of his claim that the *Awntyrs off Arthure* is a Scottish poem, remarking that "very likely" its author "never gave a thought to national feuds."[66] Despite this awareness, Amours cannot resist the temptation to use national categories in his influential edition, arguing that the contest between Galeron and Gawain is not "between a Scot and an Englishman, but between two Scottish champions."[67]

In choosing champions, the *Awntyrs*-poet complicates the working out of clear national divisions and in so doing presents a text that speaks in the idiom of a marcher zone where the sides to which power-players might switch did not divide neatly into English and Scottish camps. Local identity here trumps the national. For every Robert the Bruce who went from being Edward I's agent to his archenemy, there were far more local lords whose conflicts were with whatever forces threatened their regional power bases, whether Scottish or English.[68] In the continuously militarized late-medieval Anglo-Scottish marches, local lords' first priority was in maintaining control of zones in which profitable raiding monopolies dictated loyalties. The patriotic fervor of poems such as Barbour's *Bruce* or Holland's *Buke of the Howlat* served primarily to harness armed resources for such local lords consolidating their positions.[69]

The most common tactic in late-medieval Anglo-Scottish warfare involved raiding "local communities," which ensured that civilian populations continuously incurred the costs of war.[70] Such costs transcended mere material damage. Analyzing the economic impact of raiding in Northern Britain, J. A. Tuck argues that a "psychological climate" of fear was an even more significant effect than the "actual destruction" wrought by Anglo-Scottish hostilities postdating Edward I's 1296 invasion.[71] Despite such heavy tolls, militarization in the Anglo-Scottish marches brought considerable economic benefits to parties on either side of the border. Marcher life featured the ever-present potential for profits from raiding, ransoms, and the maintenance of garrisons, ensuring a self-sustaining cycle of violence.[72]

Though Amours too readily assumes a Scottish identity for both Galeron and Gawain, there is in fact much to recommend this reading in the case of Gawain. As Madden notes, Gawain was sometimes styled as "the Lord of Galloway"; Gawain's father is usually identified in Arthurian texts as Lot, lord of Lothian and/or Orkney; and Gawain himself is often identified as "of Orkney."[73] Such a pedigree fits better with Robert J. Bartlett's model of multi-ethnic variety surviving in the fringe zones of a centralizing and nationalizing Europe than with a nationalist narrative of unambiguous "Scottishness"—for Orkney was only obtained by the Scottish crown from Christian I of Denmark in 1468,[74] while Galloway is the most politically unstable region in the Scots "nation" imagined by the *Declaration of Arbroath*.[75] As Martin B. Shichtman has shown, a number of fourteenth- and fifteenth-century Scottish chroniclers and romancers, inspired especially by the criticism of the legitimacy of Arthur's sovereignty in John of Fordun's *Chronica gentis Scotorum* (c. 1385), presented Gawain and Mordred as Scottish heroes with powerful claims to British kingship through their mother Anna.[76] As late as in Malory, Gawain is linked clearly with Scotland: the knights allied with Mordred who surprise Lancelot and Guinevere at Carlisle, among whom is found Galeron, are described as all "of Scotland, other of Syr Gawayn's kynne, outher well willers to his brethren" [Scottish, or related to Sir Gawain, or allies to his brothers].[77] Gawain, then, is clearly not an unambiguous ethnic stand-in for the conquering arm of all-mighty England. Much as, according to Royan, "the fluidity of the romance Arthur" allows him to stand in as readily for a Scottish as an English figure, so does the Gawain of Northern romance defy simple nationalist categorization.[78]

It is Amours's claim that Galeron is "Scottish" that appears less self-evident. Galeron describes himself as of "Galwey" [Galloway], and a number of the lands won from him by Arthur's army appear to be territories that might have come under a Galwegian lord's sway.[79] If the poet was interested in competing nationalisms in the contest between Gawain and Galeron, then a more ambiguous area to represent Scotland could not have been chosen than Galloway. Galloway's very name marks its difference from its surroundings—*Gall Ghaidhil*, its Scottish Gaelic name, means "Land of the Stranger Gaels."[80] Analyzing the controversial ethnic origin of Galwegians, A. D. M. Barrell discusses the geographical uniqueness of this region with "closer links with other parts of the Irish Sea world, such as Ireland, Man and north-west England" than with "the kingdom of the Scots."[81] Indeed, Galloway had a perennially complex relationship with Scotland. As Brown notes, even after Anglo-Norman lords in 1234 replaced the rulers of what was "an independent Norse-Celtic realm," the region "was never fully absorbed into Scottish society, retaining its distinct laws, identity and political structure."[82] Galloway maintained traditions of independence throughout the fourteenth and well into the fifteenth century: it was a base of support for the English-backed Balliol cause throughout the Wars of Independence, and it maintained its own legal codes independent of the Scottish Crown as late as 1384.[83]

Both the legendary and the political history of Galloway also undermine the assumption that its lord would be a native. Galloway's legendary romance hero, Fergus of Galloway, was a Norman immigrant.[84] In the fourteenth and fifteenth centuries, the Black Douglases symbolized their conquest of the native Galwegians by depicting tamed wild men as arms-bearers; however, they respected the region as a lordship with a distinct legal and political status, maintaining the region's "traditions of unity" as part of their political management of the Southwest.[85] That Galeron is the "greatest" in Galloway does not immediately signal Scottish ethnic identity: the complex history of Galwegian conflict makes it equally possible to see its lord as one of the Anglo-Normans who displaced the native Norse and Celtic populations, or as a lord linked with the Balliols, originally settlers from Northwest England before becoming regional power-players.

By resisting reading Galeron and Gawain as either "Scottish" or "English," we can better appreciate the social logic of this marcher text.[86] Considering whether the Anglo-Scottish marches constituted a "frontier society," Anthony Goodman stresses that a "multi-faceted process of disengagement," in which these regions self-consciously sought to link themselves with their respective "nations," did not set in until the fifteenth century, with signs of a "hybrid" culture featuring shared techniques of raiding and diplomacy still apparent in the late-medieval period.[87] While I would prefer "state" here to "nation"—for fifteenth-century political centralization, while advanced both in England and Scotland, did not negate the discontinuities in class, religion, and region that prevented the congruence of culture and polity key to modern nationhood—Goodman points to a vital, *regionally* experienced marcher epoch.[88] Moreover, for many lords and their retainers, borders between kingdoms were secondary to membership in the transnational noble class. The Black Douglases, for example, possessed lands across the border, as did the leading family of the English North, the Percies, with both families having made their fortunes through the militarization of the Anglo-Scottish frontier.[89]

The late-medieval Anglo-Scottish marches can indeed be conceived as a unitary zone. In arguing that the borderlands is a "singular society," Goodman analyzes jousting as a key "intercommunal" activity.[90] As late-medieval chivalry became increasingly devoted to pageantry, the bloody brand of jousting called the *mêlée* was pushed to only the most militarized fringes.[91] Such "intercommunal" practice provides vivid local color for the

Awntyrs off Arthure. The struggle between Galeron and Gawain is exquisitely detailed, leading Ingham to describe this "beautiful scene of violent display" as a poetics of "militarism."[92] While individual combats are conventional enough in Arthurian romance, and not unknown historically, the blood-sport in the *Awntyrs off Arthure* recalls the staged duels of marcher culture, further grounding the work in a borderlands culture produced by hostile imperial hosts.

Galeron, assuming the familiar romance role of the challenger visiting Arthur's court, links his identity with lands to the north of the poem's borderland setting. Galeron pronounces a litany of lost possessions seized by Arthur and transferred to another lord's control:

> 'Mi name is Sir Galaron, withouten eny gile,
> Þe grettest of Galwey of greues and gylles,
> Of Connok, of Carrak, of Conyngham, of Kyle,
> Of Lonrik, of Lennex, of Loudan Hilles.
> Þou has wonen hem in werre with a wrange wile
> And geuen hem to Sir Gawayn—þat my hert grylles.' (417–22)

> [My name is Sir Galeron, I tell you truly, the greatest lord of Galloway, of thickets and ravines, of Connock, of Carrick, of Cunningham, and of Kyle, of Lanrik, of Lennox, and of the Lowdon Hills. You have conquered these with unrighteous motivation, and given them to Sir Gawain. This enrages me.]

While the lands listed by Galeron vary somewhat among the manuscripts, and while the precise locations are not always clear, Hahn discloses the frame in which Galeron's catalogue of lost territories sets this violent confrontation, by observing that they are "all presumably in Scotland": Galeron has come south to meet up with the Arthurian armies that conquered and distributed his lands to the north.[93] Galeron and Gawain's bloody struggle, transpiring in a borderland, comes to reflect on lands situated beyond the local arena.

When Arthur later seeks to settle the combat, moved by Guinevere's cry that the ascendant Gawain show mercy to a Galeron whose lady would suffer in seeing his death, he offers Gawain a series of lands (664–76). There is a certain randomness in the catalogue of holdings, with instability both in manuscript readings and in the relations among the territories, which range from Ireland to Wales to England, with some names difficult to decipher.[94] For Hahn, such instability is expressive of empire, with the "vagueness and interchangeability of reference to these fringe territories" revealing their status as "tokens of Arthur's kingly power."⁹⁵ There are, however, clusters among the territories, including the gifting of the "worship of Wales" [lordly honor of Wales] (666) and a series of seemingly Welsh lands.⁹⁶ The *Awntyrs*-poet thereby associates Arthur and his key commander Gawain with territories south of the borderland in which they fight, including lands that in the fourteenth century would be associated with English imperial control over Wales. Poeticizing possession in a landscape destabilized by colliding English and Scottish empires,⁹⁷ the *Awntyrs*-poet foregrounds the liminality of the Carlisle locale in which Gawain and Galeron perform their bloody battle before an assembly of knights and ladies.

That the *Awntyrs off Arthure* dates from the dawn of disengagement from a hybrid frontier culture is explicable in terms of militarism's profitability for marcher lords and their retinues.⁹⁸ Perhaps the *Awntyrs*-poet, in complicating political affiliations, speaks to an armed class that sought to resist sweeping moves toward the consolidation of England and Scotland as centralized, imperial states.⁹⁹ According to Brown, "side-switching" was common in the Anglo-Scottish marches: the defeated would frequently enter the service of powerful lords, regardless of "national" allegiance, in order to continue profiting from raiding.¹⁰⁰ As with mercenaries in the Hundred Years' War, these retainers were not part of "national armies" but served the interests of powerful nobles.¹⁰¹ Questioning the relevance of the concept of "nation" in the "narrow, ethnic sense" of the *Declaration of Arbroath,* Barrell doubts whether many "Scots" in the period "saw their primary loyalty as being to the crown as opposed to their village, burgh or province."¹⁰² The appeal of the *Awntyrs off Arthure* may lie in its response to the concerns of a military class that saw the profitability of its side-switching style of warfare threatened by fifteenth-century efforts to retrench and limit the hybridity of the marcher zone, as seen in legislation aimed at banning intermarriages and the smuggling of goods and coin.¹⁰³

If the *Awntyrs*-poet indeed consciously foregrounds the dynamic interplay of local loyalties key to marcher power, then the poem's patronage may also defy categorization by nation. The power of a family like the Black Douglases depended on continuous Anglo-Scottish tensions; as large-scale border conflict declined, so did the ability of the Douglases to hold and expand their network of influence. The family turned to overt poetic propaganda, patronizing Holland's depiction of the Douglases as Scotland's "werwall" [rampart] at a time when Douglas fortunes were nearly at their nadir.¹⁰⁴ If Hanna's dating of the *Awntyrs off Arthure* from 1400–1430 is correct,¹⁰⁵ then it would fall within the period of general decline in border conflict that threatened Douglas power, but well before the free-fall in the family's fortunes after 1452.¹⁰⁶ Such a contextualization of the poem would also make plausible patronage from an English marcher house such as the Percies, whose borderlands dynasty had much to lose from such efforts to de-militarize the Anglo-Scottish border as those launched by Richard II.[107] By rendering essentially unclear the national affiliations of its major players, the *Awntyrs off Arthure,* which offers few clues about its precise provenance, leaves open the possibility of patrons from either side of the border.

However much we might highlight the hybridity and anti-imperialism of the *Awntyrs off Arthure,* the Arthurian juggernaut that originally dispossessed Galeron emerges unchallenged, despite the ghost's grisly indictment. Far from having his possessions generously restored, Galeron is given back his lands—with a difference: he is "greatest" in Galloway only after having publicly admitted that Arthur is greater. For Robert J. Gates, there is "something amiss" in lines 677–85, in which Gawain responds to Arthur's offer of alternative lands; indeed, these lines have troubled all editors of the poem.[108] But there seems something "amiss" only because the poem here takes up the delicate task of linking the romantic with Realpolitik, invoking chivalric discourse to express the subtleties of feudal land holding. In stanza 53, Gawain releases to Galeron a number of territories, but only after adding a critical condition that is difficult to detect because it is courteously (that is, indirectly) phrased—that Galeron will hold these lands from King Arthur. The Ireland manuscript has Gawain connect the conditional term "withþi" [provided that] to his request that Galeron remain for a while in "oure" lordship: *if* this is the case, then Gawain will "refeff" [re-enfeoff] him.[109] In signaling the condition that Galeron come under the sway of Arthurian lordship, Gawain communicates that the defeated knight must, in marcher fashion, switch sides to survive, becoming again "greatest" in Galloway only by virtue of his attachment to the Arthurian army that has conquered him.

The *Awntyrs*-poet's isolation of Carlisle as the site of the future treason that will bring down Arthur's empire also suggests the poem's provenance from a region ravaged by Anglo-Scottish warfare's raids and counter-raids. Such conflict "arrested agricultural development and further extension of settlement," as the constant threat of invasion caused many to settle within border strongholds such as Carlisle.[110] Carlisle, unlike Berwick or Roxburgh, had been firmly held by England (though not without attack) since the twelfth century and, more than any other border site, would bring to mind Edward I's imperialist efforts to be the *malleus Scottorum.*[111] The ghost of the *Awntyrs off Arthure* asserts that the knight who will bring down Arthur's empire is currently a "barne" [child] playing "balle" at Carlisle (310).[112] Such attributions of political instability to the border city reflect the anxieties of the war-torn marches. Unlike the nearby Hadrian's Wall, which marked the Roman Emperor's intention to mark an end to endless empire and focus instead on administering its holdings,[113] Carlisle, as the key garrison for centuries of English invading forces, marked empire's very front lines.[114]

Perhaps the clearest marcher element of the *Awntyrs off Arthure* is this presentation of Carlisle as the site of future collapse. A pivotal incident in a later Arthurian work suggests an echo of the *Awntyrs*-poet's volatile Carlisle. A Galeron of Galloway is among those who in Thomas Malory's *Morte Darthure* follow Mordred to Carlisle Castle to surprise Lancelot and the Queen—as part of Mordred's plan to destroy Arthur's realm through a civil war which, in versions such as the Alliterative *Morte Arthure*, transpires while the king is off conquering elsewhere.[115] The *Awntyrs off Arthure*, with its borderland sensibility to the frequency of dispossession—so often followed by re-enfeoffment to further future dispossessions, in a borderlands cycle of violence—suggests that the assimilation of other Galerons into an ever-swelling empire ultimately brings only the seeds of self-destruction.

Widening the Marches
Resistance to Nationalism and *Golagros and Gawane*

Turning to *Golagros and Gawane*, we might expect a counter-example to the resistance to state centralization in the *Awntyrs off Arthure*. We would expect Scottish nationalism not only because of the *Golagros*-poet's Middle Scots dialect, but also because of the fiercely independent spirit of its local lord holding fast to his freedom—a concept key to romanticized narratives of late-medieval Scottish nationhood. The 1320 *Declaration of Arbroath*, although designed for communication with the papacy and of only limited circulation, indelibly inflected later Scottish historical works through its linkage of zeal for liberty and Scottish identity.[116] Despite the disjunction between its ideological statement and its propagation by an elitist regime,[117] the *Declaration of Arbroath* produced a seminal portrait of freedom-loving Scots vowing "Non enim propter gloriam, diuicias aut honores pugnamus sed propter libertatem" [It is in truth not for glory, nor riches, nor honors that we are fighting, but for freedom].[118] Perhaps the most influential statement of the value of freedom in late-medieval Scotland lies in the opening of *The Bruce*, with its description of Edward I's theft of Scots' "fredome" [freedom]: freedom is a "noble thing," to all men's "liking," and a "solace," contrasting such liberty with the "thyrldome" [slavery] initiated by English imperialism (I.220–27; 228–74). When in *Golagros and Gawane* the lord Golagros, faced with an invading Arthurian army, insists,

> Bot nowthir for his senyeoury nor for his summoun
> Na for dreid of na dede na for na distance,
> I will noghth bow me ane-bak for berne that is borne,
> Quhill I may my wit wald.
> I think my fredome to hald,
> As my eldaris of ald
> Has done me beforne (449–53)

[But neither due to his authority nor due to his command, nor out of fear of some action or of hostility, I will not bow down backwards for any earthly man, so long as I am of sound mind. I intend to maintain my freedom, as my elders have perennially done before me]

we might be inclined to see Golagros as quintessentially Scottish and situate this text within a long-running Scottish project of separation from English overlordship. The poem adds further, tantalizing evidence for such a view, ultimately leaving Golagros free as Arthur had originally found him, unassimilated into what looks like an arbitrarily expanding English empire.

However, much as the *Declaration of Arbroath* is "primarily a piece of propaganda" originating more from factional power-plays than from true nationalist "unanimity,"[119] a clearer picture of *Golagros and Gawane*'s provenance emerges when we resist the temptation to read it as nationalist. While *Golagros and Gawane* is composed in a "formidable" Scots dialect, this language speaks across borders, sharing "vocabulary and forms" with "northern Middle English alliterative poems."[120] Such trans-march continuity in language, overriding ethnic or regnal distinctions, has become increasingly evident. Linguistic historians have critiqued overly precise conceptions of discrete northern dialectal areas, suggesting instead a model of continuum, with both English and Scottish standards inflecting local variations.[121] Narrative events offer further evidence of such a transnational background. While "descriptions of landscapes and fortifications," as Hahn asserts, "conform strikingly to the border areas between Scotland and England, where the poem originates,"[122] the action of *Golagros and Gawane* takes place on a transnational plane. In the poem's opening, Arthur moves his army toward "Tuskane" [Tuscany] (2),[123] encounters Golagros's holdings near the "Ro[n]e" [Rhone] (311), and journeys to and from Jerusalem (302–5).[124]

In tracking Arthur's continental adventures, the *Golagros*-poet focuses on imperialist activities key to chronicle romances such as the Alliterative *Morte Arthure,* the better part of which is devoted to Arthur's many and brutal conquests on the European mainland. As we have seen, the Alliterative *Morte* resists precise localization, and its sustained reflections on the costs of imperial aggression resonated throughout the militarized zones of the Northern Midlands and the English North to which it has also been traced (see chapter 3).[125] The *Morte*-poet works within Geoffrey of Monmouth's narrative of Arthur's final foreign campaign being triggered by the Roman Emperor Lucius's demand for tribute, which leads to Arthur's counter-claim that he is the legitimate "ouerlyng" [overlord] of the "Empire of Rome" (520). The ad hoc nature of Arthur's assertions, as well as the bloody swathe that his armies cut as they make their way across the Continent to Rome, argue against Kenneth Hodges' view that, insofar as Arthur justifies taking Rome by imagining it as a sovereign and limited territory formerly possessed by his ancestors Belinus and Brennius, the invasion is a medieval example of modern nation-building.[126] Far from merely seeking to reclaim a lost piece of a stable and continuous territory,[127] Arthur betrays, both through his hot-headed response to Lucius's demand and through his initiation of a roving Continental campaign, that he is acting according to the impulses of expansionist empire. An Andersonian sense of the nation as both sovereign and *limited* would have saved Arthur, whose outward aggression reveals not just his sense of territory as unstable, but also the discontinuities in his holdings revealed by Mordred's heterogeneous rebel army (see chapter 3).

In narrating the response of Arthurian empire to another empire's overlordship claim, the *Morte*-poet manages a multi-ethnic portrait of imperial consolidation that undermines visions of medieval proto-nationalism. The Arthurian war machine, systematically pursuing the imperial goal of making Arthur "ouerlynge of all þat on erthe lengez" [overlord of everything on earth] (3211), is presented as an English-led force that requires the assimilation of non-English others. That Arthur is an English overlord is made clear by the *Morte*-poet in a council convened at Carlisle (64) to discuss how to "answer the alienes" [respond to the foreigners] (306).[128] As we have seen (chapter 3), representatives of Celtic regions here rehearse and endorse their own conquest and absorption in a public display of submission. King Aungers, speaking "fore Scottlande" [for Scotland] (292), tells Arthur, "thow aughte to be ouerlynge ouer all oþer kinges" [you ought to be overlord over all other kings] (289), while the "Walsche kyng" [Welsh king] Valyant, not to be outdone in praising Arthur's empire, announces,

"Now schalle we wre full wele þe wrethe of oure elders!" [Now shall we well avenge the anger of our ancestors!] (321). The image of a submissive Scottish king would surely have been welcome in the war-torn English North. Welsh warriors might also have readily represented English expansionism, since they often fought as mercenaries in English imperial armies.[129] The Welsh king's words offer some evidence suggesting that the *Morte*-poet envisions a Northern rather than Northwest Midlands, insofar as a Welshman's rage against Romans might be read as a thinly veiled reference to remembrance of English imperial atrocities. Valyant's vendetta would be chilling to a Northwest Midlands audience just across the border and only a few generations removed from Edward I's brutal conquest of Wales, and it would be especially unsettling during the period of Owain Glyn Dŵr's uprising.[130]

Imagining the *Morte*-poet's conquest-catalogue from an Anglo-Scottish borderlands rather than Northwest Midlands perspective magnifies its anti-imperialist energies. If, as Ingham argues, the opening rehearsal of Arthur's conquests involves the *Morte*-poet's strategic move from Continental gains to a pleasurable "insular return" to exclusively British holdings, then the chorus of Celtic rulers voicing submission to Arthur reveals such wholeness to be a purely imperial production.[131] When the *Morte*-poet refers to Arthur's aggressive knights as "our" warriors (e.g., 1820, 1880), we can make no clear judgment on this ethnic self-identification, insofar as Welsh, Bretons, Scots, French, and others form a body that suggests, but cannot be reduced to, the late-medieval English imperial state.[132] While the *Morte*-poet's vision of various Celtic commanders cooperating with a single overlord may seem a hopeful one for insular peace, it is of course precisely this continental military campaign with which the *Awntyrs*-poet's ghost links the collapse of Arthur's empire. The *Morte*-poet's meditations on the Arthurian war-state disclose anxiety about the costs of aggression that, while relevant to the Northwest Midlands' careerist culture (see chapter 3), speak even more directly to inhabitants of the Anglo-Scottish war zone that continually bore the brunt of clashing empires.

By focusing on a mobile imperial Arthurian army traversing the Continent and beyond, the *Golagros*-poet signals that any "Scottish" affinities are subordinated to interest in just such transnational aggression as the *Morte*-poet envisions. Though *Golagros and Gawane,* like the *Awntyrs off Arthure,* is constructed as a diptych,[133] it clearly takes a central interest in territorial dispossession. The poem's focus on land issues close to home is made eminently, indeed comically, clear by the merely four lines (in a poem of nearly fourteen hundred) devoted to Arthur's trip to Jerusalem (302–5); the poet's interest is clearly drawn, like Arthur's, back to the lands of Golagros that have allured the conqueror's eye.[134] The opening action involves a famished Arthurian army that injudiciously sends the tactless Kay to request provisions from the lord of a nearby town. After Kay, having struck and stolen a fowl from a dwarf-servant, is himself beaten by the castle's "grym sire" [frightening lord], the impeccably courteous Gawain is sent in his traditional diplomatic role to repair any damage (79–135). After the lord refuses to sell provisions to Arthur's army, Gawain politely replies that "that is at youre avne will" [it is at your discretion], and that it is "grete skill" [very reasonable] to "mak you lord of youre avne" [consider yourself the master of what is yours] (146–47).[135] The "grym sire" then explains that he had merely been testing Gawain, and sends him back to Arthur with an invitation to his troops, making "yow of myne maister of myght" [you the commanding lord of all that is mine], and imploring him to "ressaue" [receive] all his "wyis and welth" [servants and goods] as "your awin" [your own] (185–95). The first ethical instruction offered to Arthur in *Golagros and Gawane,* then, has to do with consideration for local lords: through mutual respect and diplomacy, rather than warfare or pillage, all parties can benefit.[136]

The desire for conquest soon causes Arthur to forget this lesson in diplomacy—and the remainder of the poem focuses on his decidedly arbitrary attempt to dispossess a lord who has in no way threatened his own person or holdings. While on his way to fulfill a vow to visit Jerusalem, Arthur encounters a castle, the legal status of which is more stunning for him than its "riche river," numerous ships, and very sightly exterior (244–53). The impressive appearance of this property, held by Arthur to be "þe semyliast sicht þat euer cou[t]h I se" [the most gorgeous sight that I might ever see], initiates an inquiry into "quha is lord of yone land" [who is lord of that land] and "quham of is he haldand" [from whom does he hold it] (255–60). Arthur's request to know the precise feudal chain of tenure leads to Spynagros's revelation that this lord seems to stand outside lordship's norms, in an anomalous legal situation that catches Arthur's imperialist attention:

Yone lord haldis of nane leid that yone land aw
Bot euerlesting but legiance to his leving
As his eldaris has done, enduring his daw. (262–64)

[That lord holds his land of no man who owns that land, but rather possesses it in perpetuity without any allegiance to anyone, as his ancestors have always done, up until this day.]

Arthur is clearly unnerved by this report of a lord who lordlessly holds land. Stunned, Arthur exclaims, "Hevinly God . . . how happynis this thing?" [My God! How can such a thing happen?] (265). The very incomprehensibility for Arthur of such a hold-out from feudal lines of sovereignty illuminates his imperial view of possession and dispossession as the norm in the marches.

The brutal nature of medieval warfare is highlighted by Arthur's hotheaded vow and heated military planning: he swears that he will, if need be, make "mony wedou" [many widows] in forcing Golagros to "mak homage and oblissing" [do homage and obeisance] (267–99) and later asserts that he will "reve thame thair rentis with routis full ride" [rob them of their possessions by means of fully ferocious raids], even if it takes nine years (502–3). Such "routis" involved "pillaging and scorched earth policy" used by the English armies first in the Hundred Years' War and then in the Anglo-Scottish border wars.[137] Arthur apparently did not learn lessons of mercy in his journey to Jerusalem, a city whose infamously brutal first-century siege was widely narrated in the late-medieval North through texts such as the alliterative *Siege of Jerusalem*.[138] Arthur responds to Golagros's claim to independent lordship with a savage style of warfare that brings misery to soldiers and civilians alike, echoing both the impetuosity and the viciousness of Arthur's campaigning in the Alliterative *Morte Arthure*. Whatever the imperial threat, Golagros refuses to have his "senyeoury" [lordship] be under "subjecioun" [subjection], nor to have "legiance" [allegiance] to another, insisting that he will hold his ancestral "fredome" [freedom] (447–53). Despite the lesson Arthur received about letting the other be lord of his own, and despite his adviser Spynagros's insistence that the wise should avoid a foolish war, Arthur encamps outside Golagros's lands (274–314). An extended battle ensues—though it seems more like the controlled environment of a tournament than the brutal brand of warfare that Arthur has promised, with matched numbers of knights engaging in combat before spectating citizens, in an atmosphere of artificiality generated by the fact that matched foes have alliterating names.[139] However stylized, Arthur's widow-making siege aestheticizes the brutal reality of the borderlands.

His army having sustained heavy casualties, a desperate Golagros finally takes the field in a match with Gawain, who ultimately has a felled Golagros at his mercy.[140] It is here that the *Golagros*-poet introduces a crisis of wills in which Gawain's courtesy is put to an emphatically public test. Insisting that Gawain kill him, Golagros is dissuaded only by Gawain's generous request that Golagros inform him how he might "succour" [aid] him without loss of "pris" [honor] (1095–96) "before thise pepill" [before these people]. Sharing Gawain's sensitivity to the struggle's spectacular nature, Golagros makes an extraordinary request that he insists he will "quyte" [repay]: Gawain is to act as if Golagros defeated him, and allow himself to be led as prisoner to Golagros's "castel quhare I haue maist cure" [castle, where I have supreme authority], in a performance that Golagros insists will "saif me fra syte" [save me from shame] (1097–1105). Noting that to entrust his life to the "gentrice" [courtesy] of a stranger is "hard" and "wounder peralous" [marvelously dangerous], Gawain nevertheless accedes, saying, "I do me in thi gentrice" [I entrust myself to your courtesy] (1106–14).

With this critical compact between two lords, the *Golagros*-poet moves us very far from anything resembling proto-nationalist love of freedom and instead displays the sort of solidarity based upon transnational identities of class and religion that we have seen uniting seeming opposites in *William of Palerne* (chapter 2). Besides emphasizing honor and trustworthiness as key chivalric values that transcend feudal loyalties, the *Golagros*-poet highlights the general Christian identity that each shares: Golagros insists that because he has been "cristynit parfite" [baptized properly], he will "quyte" [repay] Gawain's "kyndnes" [generosity] and save his "honoure" [honor] (1103–5), thus linking his courtesy with his co-citizenship in Christendom. The arbitrariness of such solidarity is highlighted by the figuring of self-identification as performance, as Golagros and Gawain enter into a *pas de deux* of Christian-aristocratic exceptionalism: they act on their "note new" [recent compact], "fenyeand" [feigning] to fight so fiercely that no one knew of their "quentance" [agreement], for "it semyt be thair contenance þat kendillit wes care" [it seemed from their faces that anger had been aroused] (1119–24). Through the staged hostilities and the drama of the inwardly "murnand" [mourning] Golagros leading his fellow thespian Gawain captive to his tent (1125–31), the *Golagros*-poet shows the intense labor required to maintain feudal privilege, as aristocracy is performed before a "pepill" [people] susceptible to the self-interested compacts of an aristocratic class protecting its privilege.

The very spectacularity of Golagros and Gawain's performance, which stages the Christian knight's trust that his social equal's promise overrides physical control in a combat situation, undermines the view that the *Golagros*-poet thinks in the absolutist terms of nationalism, in which a "Scottish" Golagros faces an "English" Arthurian war-machine. It is, rather, a theatrics of class, with Golagros demonstrating that elite lords are zealous to protect the interests (and lives) of fellow aristocrats, whatever their regnal loyalties.[141] Golagros, after all, has already concocted his plan of showing Gawain's willingness to put himself in another *lord*'s control as a sign of his civility. Such behavior signals that the residents of Golagros's holdings would experience merely the replacement of one chivalrous lord for another, in defeat. Golagros, then, stages a rite of passage—a formalized, highly visible ceremony that, though it calls attention to transition (from Golagros's to Arthur's rule via the ethical intermediary, Gawain), actually naturalizes the line separating those who can from those who cannot make such a passage. This drama thus institutes the "pre-existing difference" that marks aristocrats as those who take the lives of others into their consideration and control.[142] Golagros and Gawain perform a ritual marking their interchangeability, differentiating themselves from the "pepill" [people] who watch them from a *social,* rather than merely physical, distance.

Far from taking the absolute stand of preferring death to loss of liberty voiced in the *Declaration of Arbroath,* Golagros reveals that he is concerned primarily with personal honor, along with the well-being of his holdings' occupants. Golagros proves an inherently noble figure, in both the class-based and moral senses of the word. To emphasize this, the *Golagros*-poet shifts the focus away from the Arthurian army and its expansionist war and toward Golagros's concerns for the fate of those under his "cure" [authority] (1101). Golagros submits to Arthur only after consultation with his people and after testing Gawain's submission to the chivalrous code that consolidates Western aristocracy. Had Gawain, as an agent of Arthur, acted dishonorably—namely, by refusing to accept the personal word of a fellow Christian knight—Golagros would presumably have concluded that Arthur's armies would be uncivilized in conquest, and thus he would have fought to the very last. Only through negotiation with his fellow lord Gawain does Golagros submit to (and hence agree to switch to the side of) King Arthur, making "obeising / As liege lord of landis" [obeisance, as to the land's liege lord]: "Yone bald berne" [that bold fellow] Gawain has convinced Golagros that socioeconomic hierarchy will not be threatened by releasing his land-claims to his conqueror (1319–26).

In a gesture as extraordinary as Gawain's agreeing to play prisoner to a defeated knight, Arthur then makes "releisching" [release] of Golagros's "allegiance," leaving him "fre" [free] as he first found him (1357–66). Although Arthur's restoration of Golagros's lordship further emphasizes the arbitrariness of his imperial power, the gesture would strike Anglo-Scottish marchers inured to the politics of military consolidation as indeed marvelous. Recall that in the *Awntyrs off Arthure,* Galeron is given back his lands, but only at the cost of his own subjection—a price that Golagros, due to Arthur's assessment of his honorable behavior, does not have to pay. Perhaps the clearest evidence that *Golagros and Gawane* dates from a later period than either the *Awntyrs off Arthure* or the Alliterative *Morte Arthure* lies in a conquering king's return of lands without cost—something too idealized for romances firmly rooted in an era of ceaseless marcher side-switching.

The *Awntyrs off Arthure,* the Alliterative *Morte Arthure,* and *Golagros and Gawane* share more than just alliterative meter and vocabulary; each also features critiques of arbitrary dispossession consonant with the militarized Anglo-Scottish borderlands. In response to Gawain's query about the destiny of the unrighteous plunderers of others' lands, the ghost of the *Awntyrs off Arthure* turns to the traditional medieval symbol of arbitrary change, "False Fortune," to present a world of recurring conquest in which conquerors themselves are displaced. The Arthurian armies of the Alliterative *Morte Arthure* and *Golagros and Gawane* traverse territory just as treacherous as the political landscape of the *Awntyrs off Arthure,* where the "lordes" of today are suddenly and terribly made "lowe" [low] tomorrow (272). These texts speak not from national perspectives, but from a culture of constant militarism driven by feudal lords, in which always-local acts of violence are linked to King Arthur as an agent of a more general imperialist activity transcending Englishness or Scottishness. While the careerist military culture of the Northwest Midlands contributes to a larger poetics of empire (see chapter 3), the Anglo-Scottish zone indicates a more intense experience of war produced by the local visitation of imperial warfare. As the marches were experiencing pressure from the rapidly centralizing Scottish and English states, the *Awntyrs off Arthure* and *Golagros and Gawane* voiced a conflicted regional reaction that simultaneously yearns for the era of unchecked militarism and yet dwells on the misery and violence upon which that militarism feeds. Arthur's gift to Golagros of his conquered lands stands as a uniquely romanticized incident, the very unlikelihood of which highlights the vicious cycles of possession and dispossession haunting the Anglo-Scottish borderlands.

5

Bags of Books and Books as Bags

POLITICAL PROTEST, COMMUNICATIONS TECHNOLOGIES, AND THE *PIERS PLOWMAN* TRADITION

DESCRIBING THE Anglo-Saxons as "illiterate, without social culture, given to coarse dissipation," Shaw and Backus illuminate the Saxon primitivism at the heart of Revivalist literary historiography.[1] Barbaric Saxons prove easy prey to Normans with superior weapons and culture. According to Shaw and Backus, Langland inherited the roughness of his Anglo-Saxon forebears, acquiring a vulgar "national character" that precludes him from generating the "sparkle of lyric verse."[2] Saxons and neo-Saxons can deploy only "rude alliteration," a literary technique decidedly inferior to rhyme's sparklingly advanced literary technology.[3] Langland's literary backwardness represents for Revivalism a significant counter-current to England's national progress, which was set in motion only when Saxon ancestors received the cultural supplement of Norman conquest (see chapter 1). In Revivalism's evolutionary literary history, alliterative verse proves essentially atavistic. Halleck, it will be recalled, encodes alliterative prosody's throwback nature by deploying the language of breeding: the English are unique because the Saxon "ox," which possessed "common sense," was injected with the "nimble witted, highly imaginative" spirit of the Norman "eagle."[4] Far from glorifying Saxon blood in the infamous, racist fashion of a Thomas Carlyle or Josiah C. Nott,[5] Revivalists insist on a primitive Saxon race incapable of withstanding Norman-French military and cultural might. Insofar as Revivalism's alliterative poets are pure Saxons, they are marked for extinction, not global supremacy.

Even when Normans are grouped ethnically with Saxons in a larger "German-Norse" identity, Revivalist narrative emphasizes the primitivism of a native culture requiring the invasive aid of culturally superior cousins.[6] In his 1909 textbook *English Literature*, William J. Long imagines the Normans' Scandinavian ancestors as "big, blond fearless men" who, after conquering what would become Normandy, are literally transformed by the civilizing power of French culture. Rather than imitating the Danes by "blotting out a superior civilization," these conquerors willingly "abando[n] their own" culture.[7] Long figures such acculturation in racial terms: Norse "power" is joined with the "eager curiosity and vivid imagination" of the French, generating the Norman people.[8] Long's hybrid Normans present an uncanny other to the Saxons, fusing shared Germanic strength with foreign French wit. In Revivalism's teleological vision, alliterative poets reject the brilliant advances of a hybrid culture and choose to reanimate the "rude" poetry of the Saxons, a primitive people long ago forcibly exposed to the "cultured and progressive" Norman-French civilization.[9]

Whereas Chaucer maximizes the potential of assimilating Continental wit with native common sense, Langland represents for Revivalism the fundamentally "retrograde" nature of the alliterative "rebellion" against progress.[10] As we have seen (chapter 1), Saintsbury, in depicting alliterative poets as inadequately armed rebels, turns to technology to represent rhymed, syllabic verse's transcendence of a neo-Saxon cultural backwater. By portraying alliterative poets as reactionary "bowmen" confronting the "gunpowder" devices of rhyme, Saintsbury interprets exclusive composition in alliterative meter as rejection of the superior technologies of the Southern "foreigner."[11] While Chaucer moves on to modernity, Saintsbury's alliterative poets look back to the distant, oral past of the pre-Conquest warrior culture disdained in Warton's and Taine's foundational histories (see chapter 1).

If literary production is indeed technology in the sense of the "deployment of mechanical power" that "magnifie[s] human strength and reach,"[12] then the poems of the *Piers Plowman* tradition reveal both a fascination and facility with mechanical and cultural innovation that belie the Revivalist fantasy of an ancient, regressive tradition. Complex concepts of authorship, audience, and communications media inform Langlandian poems, which join *Wynnere and Wastoure* in undermining the Revivalist assumption of a retrograde, conservative alliterative school linked with an oral past rather than a written present (see chapter 1). *Pierce the Ploughman's Crede* reveals the importance of writing technologies for Langlandian poets, whose turn to Langland is nothing like the resolutely backward gaze of Revivalism's neo-Saxons. Co-inhabiting the bureaucratic and bibliographical world connecting the Midlands with Greater London, the anonymous poets of *Richard the Redeless* and *Mum and the Sothsegger* bring material textual self-reflection to the center of technologically and politically experimental poems, exploding Revivalist myths of alliterative nostalgia. Traditional anti-fraternalism and critiques of flattery emerge alongside sophisticated approaches to manuscript dissemination that saturate political allegories. Such innovations, however, do not prevent Langlandian poets from providing further evidence against hypotheses of late-medieval nationhood. However avant-garde Langlandian poets seem in theorizing communications, and however attentive they may be to individual suffering, commitments to class hierarchy, and to religious rather than regnal loyalty, ensure that, as in the case of *William of Palerne* (chapter 2), transnational interests overwhelm anything resembling proto-nationalism.

The poems of the *Piers Plowman* tradition enable further critique of Revivalism's narrative of a provincial movement limited to the sparsely populated Midlands. Much as the contextualization of alliterative Arthurian romances requires expanding our view beyond the Northwest Midlands (chapter 3), and beyond merely national frames (chapter 4), so do Langlandian poems require us to resist Revivalism's perennial insistence on peripheral provenance. To contextualize the *Piers Plowman* tradition necessitates a systematic interrelation of urban and rural economies, exploring a cultural nexus that linked the greater London area with the Southwest Midlands, including Bristol, Southampton, and other urban sites. Of all proposals for a localized alliterative movement, the *Piers Plowman* tradition offers the clearest evidence for a zone of activity, in a simultaneously rural and metropolitan culture that belies Revivalism's center–periphery logic.

The material legacy of *Piers Plowman* itself undermines Revivalism's portrait of a remote, rural, alliterative school. Not only have the sheer number and range of *Piers Plowman* manuscripts led some critics to declare it England's first "national" poem,[13] but also the crucial role of London in terms of both internal and external evidence undercuts Revivalist views of alliterative poetry as exclusively provincial. Movement between the Southwest Midlands and London is key to *Piers Plowman*'s opening: after falling asleep in Worcestershire's Malvern Hills, Langland's narrator Will dreams of legal corruption bringing him to London (II.148), where Mede is to be married at Westminster (II.174). The debate about Mede that initiates this trans-regional movement,[14] featuring topics such as legal malfeasance, regnal budgets, and mercantile economics (III.155–327), suggests the interests and expertise of an unbeneficed clerk with legal training, which many scholars assume Langland to have been.[15] Such a clerical position enabled economic and physical mobility, and Will's movements between Midlands and metropole are indeed not confined to dreams. Like many other post-Plague Midlands residents, Will moves to London, where he describes himself in the C-text as a clerk living among "lollares" [idlers] and "lewede eremytes" [lay hermits] (V.4).[16] *Piers Plowman* also provides ample external evidence of a Southwest Midlands–London nexus. Besides manuscript productions and clerkly coterie reading circles connected with the London book trade, a large number of manuscripts have been traced to the Southwest Midlands, including a concentration of C-Text manuscripts suggesting that Langland's movement from the Midlands to London was not unidirectional.[17]

The geographical contexts of Langlandian poems also suggest a Southwest Midlands–London regional backdrop for the *Piers Plowman* tradition. The opening scene of *Richard the Redeless* takes place in Bristol, the most important Southwest Midlands town,[18] while the poem frequently considers affairs in the Westminster Parliament and Richard II's London court. *The Crowned King* situates its bureaucratic dream narrative between Bristol and London, on a hill outside of Southampton (20), where the narrator envisions a king negotiating with parliament to raise a "soleyn subsidie to susteyne his werres" [large subsidy to finance his wars] (36).[19] *Pierce the Ploughman's Crede* also reveals internal and external London connections, complementing the rural identity of its plowman protagonist. Architectural references show the *Crede*-poet's familiarity with London, while the fragmentary text in British Library MS Harley 78 was produced by a "prolific London scribe" of the late-fifteenth-century London book trade.[20]

Tracing the spread of manuscripts of Langland's and Langlandian work in coterie "reading circles," Kathryn Kerby-Fulton and Steven Justice have reconstructed a nexus between the administrative center of Greater London and the Southwest Midlands, linking literary culture with "bureaucratic service."[21] Far from a workaday world separate from the aesthetic realm, these civil-service circles provide the "first home" of late-medieval literature.[22] Exploring the intersection of aesthetic and political interests at the heart of the "documentary poetics" shaping *Piers Plowman* and its reception,[23] I will investigate the *Piers Plowman* tradition as a communications-focused "community of response"[24] to Langland's poetic inspiration. Through a facility and fascination with material textuality tied to the bureaucratic world that they inhabit, Langlandian poets approach book production as a cutting-edge technology allowing them to navigate late-medieval English politics.

Langland's Ambivalent Legacy
Subversion, Containment, and Recursive Writing

Langland often plays an exceptional role in Revivalist narrative, alternately grounding and contesting images of alliterative unity. Editions of the various texts of *Piers Plowman,* along with controversy over the poem's possibly multiple authorship, played a vital role in the shaping of an alliterative corpus in Revivalism's foundational years. Skeat's seminal series of Early English Text Society editions, begun in 1868 and including separate volumes for texts and critical notes, established the A-B-C sequence as the standard view of Langland's individual authorship and contributed to Revivalist efforts to filter a vast and heterogeneous set of manuscript data through a unitary model.[25] Some critical resistance to such monolithic visions has often characterized Langland scholarship. Anxiety concerning the authorship of *Piers Plowman* inspired the Early English Text Society in 1906 to produce a special volume dedicated to John Manly's insistence on five authors' responsibility for *Piers Plowman.*[26] The commitment to a single model for Langland's single authorship of three discrete versions of one poem has proved a powerful force, as witnessed by the devaluation of scribal labor in George Kane and E. T. Donaldson's controversial Athlone B-Text,[27] and by the ferocious reaction to A. G. Rigg and Charlotte Brewer's hypothesis of a Z-Text authorial draft.[28]

Langland's singular status illuminates the ongoing impact of Revivalist discourse. Lawton's crucial statement of the need to work against Revivalist efforts to restrict alliterative works to a single provenance is (advisedly) at odds with his own insistence on a Langland-introduced, penitential aesthetic unifying alliterative poems.[29] Moreover, it is telling that Duggan's argument for a "shared grammar of composition" necessitates his exclusion of Langland—and, thus, with the fifty-odd manuscripts and prints of *Piers Plowman,* much of the very corpus that Duggan's theory is meant to explain.[30] In invoking Langland as a "ghost"—no "real," historical person, but rather a critical construct to which the editor must be "committed"—Donaldson provides a powerful insight into the practical effects of editorial fantasy.[31] Clearly committed to the author's function as a "principle of thrift in the proliferation of meaning,"[32] Donaldson presents the assumption of single authorship as an enabling fiction that allows the editor to "work profitably" in the highly variant world of Langlandian textuality.[33] Donaldson's critical candor concerning this fundamental methodological artifice, which allows the editor to "recognize the influence that the ghost is having on the interpretation of the text,"[34] illuminates the highly unstable centrality that Langland holds not just in the *Piers Plowman* corpus but also in the ongoing Alliterative Revivalist project.

With *Piers Plowman* having produced such crucial editorial and literary historical debates, it is unsurprising that texts tied to Langland's legacy display ambiguous textual status and suggest collaborative composition. Controversy has shadowed Langlandian work since its inception, with the "literary heritage" of *Piers Plowman* having been launched "ominously" by the 1381 rebels,[35] and with Langlandian work emerging in the "hothouse atmosphere" of late-fourteenth and early-fifteenth-century politics.[36] Facing sociocultural landscapes destabilized by the Crown-noble tensions of Richard II's tumultuous reign, by the anxious Lancastrian propaganda in the uncertain early years of Henry IV's regime, and by censorious legislation such as the 1401 *De Haeretico Comburendo* and the 1409 Arundel Constitutions,[37] the poets of the *Piers Plowman* tradition put a range of scribal skills to work in navigating an environment hostile to the dissemination of politically and theologically suspect material.

The political ends for which Langlandian authors deploy authorial multiplicity prove as ambivalent as those fueling the Rising. Even as the 1381 rebels appear revolutionary in some of their aims, such as the redistribution of clerical wealth and the abolition of class distinctions, they seem in other ways deeply reactionary: the insurgents looked with authoritarian eyes to a king whom they saw as their natural protector and whom they excepted from class warfare, while anti-immigrant assaults following the taking of London besmirched the rebels' campaign.[38] In exploring strategic uses of multiplicity in the *Piers Plowman* tradition, I will avoid uncritically embracing the self-differentiating tactics employed by the anonymous participants in Langlandian productions. I here take heed to Fradenburg's reminder that multiplicity is not in and of itself to be desired, with both subversion and containment being modes of enjoyment;[39] and to Hardt and Negri's caution against joining global capitalism's fetishization of difference as an end in itself.[40] The critical conundrum faced by literary historians assessing such seemingly subversive techniques within otherwise socially conservative discourses is captured by Simpson, who cautions that "claims to represent an alternative voice" in "early Lancastrian policy texts" may have "merely offered the appearance of alterity, while they really served the interests of the status quo."[41] In engaging with the textually radical poetics of the *Piers Plowman* tradition, I will take care not to justify the often-authoritarian orders of which these subversive texts dream. However, insofar as the uncertain status of authorship in manuscript culture bears uncanny similarities to the unstable textual environments of the digital age, I will explore recursive textual techniques deployed by Langlandian poets that suggest powerful tactics for navigating book culture in the electronic age.[42]

Contemporary criticism has generally portrayed a socially conservative Langland revising the C-text in alarmed response to anxieties about religious heresy and rebel appropriation of his work.[43] However reactionary Langland may seem to us, his poetry clearly had a powerful appeal to radical elements rising up in violent opposition to standing late-medieval socioeconomic policies.[44] *Richard the Redeless* and *Mum and the Sothsegger* reveal similarly ambivalent political programs. Much as *Piers Plowman* both undermines class hierarchy by looking to a plowman as a spiritual paragon and yet reinforces class boundaries by rejecting a knight's desire to engage in agricultural labor,[45] so do Langlandian poets present powerful strategies for negotiating institutional strictures on political communication, even as they reveal authoritarian social and economic visions. Abstracted from such motivations, Langlandian poets present instructive techniques for politicizing manuscript culture. As we shall see, in re-processing the cultural capital of *Piers Plowman,* the poets of the *Piers Plowman* tradition turn particularly to communications: single voices become transformed into virtual networks, as books facilitate the circumnavigation of precarious social and political conditions.

Langlandian poets continue Langland's ambivalent textual legacy, applying the alternately radical and conservative energy of *Piers Plowman* to social and theological problems. *Pierce the Ploughman's Crede,* a relatively popular satire dating from the close of the fourteenth century,[46] demonstrates Langlandian poetry's simultaneous oppositionality and traditionalism. Presenting Piers Plowman as the sole source of enlightenment for a narrator questing to learn the Apostle's Creed, the *Crede*-poet subverts class hierarchy by joining Langland in conferring supreme politico-theological authority upon a rural laborer. As we shall see, the *Crede*-poet's socioeconomic radicalism is echoed by the *Mum*-poet, who introduces a "gardyner" [gardener] (976) as the poem's highest spiritual (and textual) authority.[47] The *Crede*-poet launches radical social critique by foregrounding rural poverty, moving beyond Langland's sporadic comments concerning post-Plague socioeconomic conditions[48] while highlighting the conflict between peasants and absentee landlords that destabilized the post-Rising Southwest Midlands.[49] Poverty is incorporated into the very name of the *Crede*-poet's hero: asked to identify himself, Piers says "Peres . . . the pore man, the plowe man y hatte" [I am called Piers the Poor-Man, the Plowman] (472–73). "Beslombered in fen" [splattered with mud], Piers works while wearing tattered mittens, a coat made of "cloute" [rags], a hood "full of holes," and shoes "clouted full thykke" [covered with patches]; Piers's wife, wearing a "cutted" [torn] coat and a "wynwe schete" [winding sheet] to ward off the rain, walks "barefote on the bare ijs that the blod folwede" [barefoot on the bare ice, bloodying her feet] (422–36). The peasant couple's "litell childe" [infant] lies "lapped in cloutes" [wrapped in rags], while two-year old twins sing a "careful note" [miserable tune] that "sorwe was to heren" [was painful to hear] (438–41). This vivid portrait of peasant poverty transcends merely theological allegory, dwelling on the actual conditions of a socioeconomically depressed rural England.

While the *Crede*-poet is concerned with the injustice of rural poverty, he proves as zealous as Langland to police class boundaries. The *Crede*-poet joins the C-Text Langland in railing against laborers who seek to rise in rank.[50] Noting that "now mot ich soutere his sone setten to schol, / And ich a beggers brol on the booke lerne" [now must each cobbler send his son to school, and each beggar's offspring learns from books], the *Crede*-poet reveals his anxiety concerning such children's social ascent to the level of a "writere" [clerk] or a "frere" [friar] (744–46). For the *Crede*-poet, social hierarchy's rigid structure has come undone, as poor children rise to the rank of "bychop" [bishop], to sit among "peres" [peers] and be bowed to by "lordes sones" [sons of lords] and "knyghtes" [knights] (748–51). As we shall see, Langlandian radicalism is often coupled with a reactionary politics bent upon reinforcing class hierarchy and monarchical pre-eminence, and is thus in sharp contrast with Revivalism's fantasy of a populist nationalism.

While Revivalist criticism imagines alliterative texts as nostalgic participants in a predominantly oral, minstrel tradition (see chapter 1), the *Crede*-poet reveals self-conscious immersion in manuscript culture. Setting *Pierce the Ploughman's Crede* in the context of anti-academic Lollard pedagogy,[51] John Scattergood argues that the poem appropriates its poet's favored form of instruction—the primer, or "elementary schoolbook," designed to teach lay-folk the "rudiments of Christian belief and literacy."[52] The *Crede*-poet's allegorical frame exemplifies the textual imagination driving Langlandian poetics. "Attending to the materiality of the medium," the *Crede*-poet appropriates the primer's layout in a critical mode that N. Katherine Hayles calls Media Specific Analysis.[53] The *Crede*-poet embeds a virtual instructional manual within the text: after a capital A that begins an ABC, the poem continues with *paternoster* and *ave* prayers and then uses the absence of the prayer expected next in the format to launch the narrator's quest for a guide who can instruct him in the "CREDO" (794a); the poem closes with this achieved prayer, followed by an "AMEN" (850).[54] Picturing itself as a hybrid textual construction, consisting of a quest narrative situated within the literal space of a primer ready for circulation, *Pierce the Ploughman's Crede* reveals a familiarity with book culture that permeates the *Piers Plowman* tradition.

Langlandian poets demonstrate such self-reflexive treatment of material textuality, cultivating what Hayles calls "recursive" analysis, whereby texts "incorporat[e] aspects of competing media into themselves while simultaneously claiming the advantages their own forms of media offer."[55] Such recursive documentary strategies speak against the Revivalist reading of alliterative verse as turned away from writing technologies and toward the oral, Saxon past. Rather than fleeing from technology, Langlandian poems prove firmly rooted in their political present. As we shall see, two Langlandian poems once thought to be one—*Richard the Redeless* and *Mum and the Sothsegger*—reveal a recursive relationship with late-medieval bureaucratic culture.[56] Examining moments such as the *Richard*-poet's invitation to handlers of the manuscript to collaborate in composition, and the *Mum*-poet's aestheticization of book-production, I will move from consideration of what Ethan Knapp calls the "procedural habitus" of bureaucratically influenced writers[57] to the application of such textual practices in complex sociopolitical environments. As Frank Grady asserts, the *Piers Plowman* tradition makes a general move from the conventional dream vision of *Piers Plowman* to a documentary world, which leads to *Mum and the Sothsegger*'s effort to fashion itself as a legal text.[58] Grady's vision points to the self-reflexive nature of Langlandian textuality. While *Richard the Redeless* adopts the recursive strategy of incorporating within itself the practice of maintenance that it critiques,[59] *Mum and the Sothsegger* goes even further in dissolving the distinction between text and context. Presenting itself as a narrative of a legal matter being pursued in a non-localizable juridical space, *Mum and the Sothsegger* invokes and yet forecloses the utopic vision of a discursive space in which one might receive a single truth to communicate to those in power. With a structural shift from a single voice of authority to an unstable assemblage of disparate documents, the *Mum*-poet presents the world as a legal arena in which effective spokespersons need to master the art of manipulating media to compete in the communication of political truths.

Making Meaning Out of Multiplicity
Decomposing *Mum and the Sothsegger*

In *The Piers Plowman Tradition,* Helen Barr makes a key intervention in Revivalist literary history, editing what Mabel Day and Robert Steele argue in their Early English Text Society edition is a single "composition," *Mum and the Sothsegger,*[60] as the separate poems *Richard the Redeless* and *Mum and the Sothsegger.* For Barr, however, the two poems are works of the "same author."[61] Considering these texts' circulation within a Southwest Midlands–London nexus, I will question not only whether both, but *each* of these works is best conceived as the product of a single hand. Internal references to manuscript culture within each poem unsettle editorial assertions concerning authorship, multiplying the number of hands at work in the *Piers Plowman* tradition. As we shall see, *Richard the Redeless* invites handlers of manuscripts to join in the process of composition, while *Mum and the Sothsegger* imagines books as inherently multiple phenomena, before itself decomposing in a recursive figuring of the "bisynes" [business] of "boke-making" [book-making] (1281). The *Richard*-poet and the *Mum*-poet reveal a regional reception of Langland's work as an unstable monument that authorized collaborative composition in a politicized literary enterprise.[62]

Day and Steele assert that the fragmentary poem contained in what is now British Library Additional MS 41666, which they call "M," is the second "part" of "one longer composition," the first part of which is attested by the fragmentary poem from Cambridge University Library MS L1.4.14, which they call "R."[63] According to Day and Steele, both internal and external evidence supports their decision to edit the fragments as portions of one "author's text."[64] Their assertion of an "identity of language and form" between the poems[65] is unconvincing, however. While Simon Horobin has argued for a Bristol dialect as the original form for both *Richard the Redeless* and *Mum and the Sothsegger,* previous studies have been less sure about such localization,[66] and prosodic evidence offers only general similarities.[67] Day and Steele's assertion of identical form proves more problematic. *Richard the Redeless,* unlike *Mum and the Sothsegger,* is divided into *passus* (though such layout may be purely scribal).[68] The narrative voice of each text differs strikingly as well. Besides his opening description of witnessing political events from Bristol and a brief dialogue with Reason, the narrator of *Richard the Redeless* fashions a static, monological discourse, merely reporting on past political events and advising Richard II. The narrator of *Mum and the Sothsegger,* on the other hand, is actively involved in events, engaging in a running dispute with Mum and going on a quest for advice concerning the "matere" [matter] of "Mum" versus the "soeth-segger" [truth-teller] (396–7). The *Richard*-narrator never departs from the pretense of advising Richard II, whereas the *Mum*-poet's only reference to a king is to Henry IV.[69] The fragments are thus both formally and narratively incongruous.

It is in considering the material circumstances of "M" that Day and Steele provide their most compelling evidence for identifying it with "R." Describing the "dilapidated" manuscript BL Additional MS 41666, the editors argue from the stiffening of its back that the nineteen leaves were formerly part of a "fairly substantial volume" that was "7/8 inches thick."[70]

They assert that the manuscript, collated "in 8's," is missing all of its first quire ("a"), the first four folios of quire "b," and folios 2 to 8 of the final quire, "e."[71] Assuming that all five quires of the manuscript were devoted to the single "composition" they posit, Day and Steele use an average of forty-six lines per page to estimate the loss of 1,104 lines at the poem's beginning and as many as 552 at its close.[72] As *Mum and the Sothsegger* clearly lacks its opening lines (whatever their precise number), the editors have material and textual grounds for asserting that a version of *Richard the Redeless* was the opening part of a single poem.

Noting that Nicholas Brigham provided a catalogue entry for "Mum, Sothsegger" that includes a Latin translation of *Richard the Redeless*'s opening two lines, Day and Steele adduce reception evidence to bolster their case for a single poem.[73] As neither "Mum" nor "Sothsegger" appears in *Richard the Redeless*—nor anywhere else, as a pair, in Middle English—it seems likely that Brigham identified "M" and "R" as a single work. According to Day and Steele, further codicological evidence supports their assertion of a conflated version: an "early owner" of the *Mum*-manuscript added in a fifteenth-century hand on the "last cover" the inscription "The lyff off kyng Rychard the ij."[74] As *Mum and the Sothsegger* never mentions Richard II, this bibliographical evidence suggests that BL Additional MS 41666 contained enough poetic material concerning Richard II to invite such an inscription. Since each poem can be reasonably dated to the early fifteenth century,[75] the bibliographic evidence and Brigham's mid-sixteenth-century note support the hypothesis of a single composition.

Criticizing Day and Steele's use of Bale's "single second-hand note" as "the only real piece of evidence" for the editors' "association of the two texts," Dan Embree speculates that the poems shared manuscript space due merely to common authorship or similar themes.[76] The bibliographical environment of *Richard the Redeless* supports Embree's "case of mistaken identity."[77] The untitled poem in CUL MS L1.4.14 immediately follows a B-text of *Piers Plowman* and is written in the same hand and in similar layout (with red capitals dividing up the text and Latin quotations placed in the margin). As the last folio of the *Piers Plowman* text runs nearly to the bottom of the page and features only a small-sized "Amen" for an *Explicit*, a careless reader of the manuscript could easily have taken the untitled text of *Richard the Redeless* to be part of *Piers Plowman*. Brigham's misidentification of *Mum and the Sothsegger* and *Richard the Redeless* may stem from a similar codicological context, or it could be due simply to his unfamiliarity with the texts' Midlands dialects or fifteenth-century diction.

Day and Steele's edition of a unitary *Mum and the Sothsegger* is thus unsettled by reference to the material circumstances of attestation and reception. That numerous scholars have grounded their assessments of the fragments on Day and Steele's influential edition supports Charlotte Brewer's observation that the "physical characteristics of the edition in which a work is read" powerfully influence critics' perceptions of texts.[78] Just as critics of *Piers Plowman* reading in the "wake" of Skeat's editions uncritically reproduce interpretations generated by "the modern editing and publishing process," many scholars have more or less assumed the unity of Day and Steele's "M" and "R," either as a single narrative or as works of single authorship.[79] As we have seen (chapter 1), such a tendency toward singularity is central to the Revivalist model that continues to inflect the reception of alliterative texts. However, internal references to the status of written material within each fragment undermine such assumptions about common authorship and suggest that these works derive instead from a textual environment peopled by copyists frequently engaged in collaborative authorship.[80] Both the *Richard*-narrator's invitation to "corette" [correct] and "amende" [improve] his text (I.59–60) and the presence of numerous corrections and insertions in the *Mum*-manuscript suggest the possibility of a culture of collaborative composition as the medium for Langlandian verse.

The narrator of *Richard the Redeless* claims that his "tretis" [treatise] is still "secrette" [private], and will remain so until "wyser wittis" [wiser minds] have "waytid it ouere" [perused it] (I.61–62). The narrator clearly targets his text, intending it for readers with the political wisdom to "amende" it such that it be "lore laweffull and lusty to here" [lawful teaching and pleasant to hear] (I.63). The targeting of such "wyser wittis" suggests a coterie audience privy to works in restricted circulation.[81] The narrator shows a clear concern with the practicalities of political communication, repeatedly foregrounding what Gabrielle Spiegel calls a text's "moment of inscription," whereby the material, historical world informing the work is recursively represented.[82] The narrator expresses anxiety about making his king "wrothe" [angry] (I.76–77): he claims "it longith no liegeman his lord to anoye" [it is wrong for a liege to offend his lord], unless his "wit faile" [wit fails] (II. 67–68) and urges us to "blame not the berne that the book made" [blame not the person who composed the book], but rather the "wickyd will and the werkis" [wicked desires and actions] that it critiques (I.86–87). Working to ensure that his text is not just "lusty," but "lawefull," the *Richard*-poet recognizes the risky nature of disseminating political discourse and so packages his text for a "secrette" circulation that will minimize the threat of surveillance by hostile authorities.[83] The poet insulates himself further from blame by having Reason offer an ethical justification for his work as a selfless contribution to the state: if God has given one "grace for to knowe / Ony manere mysscheff that myghtte be amendyd" [grace to know of any sort of mischief that could be corrected], Reason reasons, one should "schewe that to thi souereyne to schelde him from harmes" [show it to one's king, to protect him from harm] (I.72–74).

Adding a twist to the *Fürstenspiegel* form by addressing an already-deposed Richard II, *Richard the Redeless* presents itself as an "advice-to-former-princes" text.[84] While much of the narration is in the form of direct address, the poet clearly directs his material text to other eyes—and hands—than those of the freshly deposed monarch. The narrator initially describes his work as having begun in a period of uncertainty as to whether Richard II might be given "grace" to again be "oure gioure" [our ruler] (I.27–29). Reflection upon the monarch's shortcomings has led the narrator to "written" [write] Richard a "writte to wissen him better" [a text to teach him better] and to "meue him of mysse rewle" [dissuade him from misrule] (I.31–32). Continuing to refer to Richard in the third person, the narrator states his desire that the work will "mende him of his myssededis" [make him amend his misdeeds] and that "his gost myghte glade be my wordis" [his spirit might be comforted by my words] (I.38–40). It would certainly be curious for the narrator to refer to the former king in the third person if the text were intended exclusively for Richard. Indeed, the narrator explicitly extends the range of his intended audience, claiming that his "tretis" [treatise] might offer "conseil" [advice] to the "kyng and the lordis" and "teche men ther-after" [teach common men afterwards] (I.47–52).

In the first direct address to the reader—or, rather, handler—of *Richard the Redeless,* the narrator invites the audience to participate in the collaborative composition of this "secrette" work (I.161). Conflating the tactile and visual channels, the narrator states, "And if it happe to youre honde beholde the book onys" [And if it happens that your hands sometime behold the book] and if, in perusing it "ye finde fables or folly" [you find fables or folly] or "fantasie" [fantasy] therein, then "lete youre conceil corette it and clerkis to-gedyr, / And amende that ys amysse and make it more better" [let your wisdom correct it, along with clerks, and correct and improve that which is wrong] (I.50–60). The invitation to participate in revising such a "secrette" text suggests the narrator's expectation that sufficient "conceil" would entail some familiarity with the poem's dense legal language and numerous topical allusions. Many critics follow Skeat's editorial view that "youre" intends the "king's hand."[85] However, it seems more likely that the narrator here engages his audience.[86] The narrator has heretofore referred to Richard exclusively in the third person and does not unambiguously address him until after his discussion of the circumstances of composition, when the advice proper begins: "Now, Richard the redeles, rewith on you-self" [Now, Richard-without-advice, have pity on yourself] (l.88).[87] Skeat's assertion that "youre honde" reflects formal address to a sovereign is undermined by reading it either as a plural form addressing the various "men therafter" who might benefit from the text's wisdom or as a purely formulaic, formal address to the audience.[88]

The narrator's invitation to his audience to improve upon the text makes uncertain even the individual authorship of *Richard the Redeless*. Insofar as the poem is uniquely attested, we have no evidence to discount the possibility that a number of readers may have accepted the narrator's request to "amende" and thus become re-writers of the poem, thereby recirculating fresh texts that include the invitation to further collaboration. Such "cumulative composition"[89] would be facilitated by medieval "modes of publication," whereby a medieval text "became very rapidly the property of its users and beneficiaries":[90] once a text would "happe" to "honde," a reader might offer it to others to be transcribed. Quite differently from the Chaucer who fears the fate of *Troilus and Criseyde* in the destabilizing hands of scribes,[91] the *Richard*-narrator literally invites readers to transform the work during its dissemination, thereby inscribing in the text the very transference of authority fundamental to medieval publication.[92] The narrator of *Richard the Redeless* invites precisely the kind of collaborative composition evidenced in Langland's reception, as seen in the work of the scribe John But and of numerous readers of *Piers Plowman* C-texts.[93]

Such strategic weaving of the possibility of multiple authors into the text seems a sound tactic in the censorious and politically volatile atmosphere of Lancastrian England, making it less likely that the "berne that the boke made" might suffer physical "blame" (86).[94] If the *Richard*-poet included the ongoing invitation to collaborate as a means of rendering it impossible to trace the work to a single origin, then the poet takes up what Simpson calls *Piers Plowman*'s "communal authorial position," which resists localization and thus impedes surveillance.[95] Such obfuscation of authorship in *Richard the Redeless* also supports Kerby-Fulton's argument that pre-print English book culture was an era of "failed censorship," with various "techniques of indirection" in manuscript production rendering it difficult to gather the intelligence on authorial identity necessary for textual regulation.[96] Possible multiplicity works against surveillance, with the text's artfully modulated circulation protecting the anonymity of political discourse.

Such blurring of authorial identity reveals a concept of textuality that privileges communal participation over a rigid author–scribe distinction. Appealing to a pool of agents capable of playing the dual roles of readers and writers,[97] the *Richard*-narrator envisages readers who would be at home in the civil-service circles key to Langlandian literature.[98] The view of a text as a collaboratively produced, anonymous document was indeed a product of the "bureaucratic muse" informing much Lancastrian verse.[99] As Knapp demonstrates, Thomas Hoccleve's training in the Privy Seal office impelled him to conceive of a text as a "collage or palimpsest of all the writs and letters that had preceded it in interdepartmental correspondence."[100] Such a professionally and regionally disseminated understanding of textual instability and multiplicity informs *Richard the Redeless,* which imagines multiple participants in order to obfuscate the precise authorial attribution that censors need to transform a *Fürstenspiegel* into actionable intelligence.

Besides reflecting on bureaucratic modes of collaborative composition, the *Richard*-poet makes further use of writing technology, subsuming other media according to the recursive practice of Media Specific Analysis. In exploring the bonds between power-players and their agents in maintenance, the bastard feudalist system in which retainers wore their lords' badges, the *Richard*-narrator moves beyond formal description to material manifestation, literally animating the signs that form maintenance's currency. Richard II's followers, bearing the king's personal white hart badge, become "herrtis y-heedyd" [harts with antlers] who "ronne youre rewme thorou-oute" [travel throughout your realm], discouraging complaints about corruption, until the "egle" [eagle], apotheosizing Henry Bolingbroke's personal sign, brings "oure helpe" [our help] (II.1–9). Showing the political power of symbolic media by vivifying the "signes" [signs] that materially instantiate social and economic bonds, the narrator chastises Richard II for thinking himself "myghtier" because his retainers "so thikke sowid" [disseminated so profusely] the "priuy printe" [personal badge] (II.100–108). The narrator's disingenuousness highlights the inescapability of symbolic media: even as he indicts Richard's use of retainers, he reinforces the maintenance system by praising Henry IV under his personal eagle sign.

Such recursive writing practice is echoed elsewhere in the *Piers Plowman* tradition. The *Mum*-poet not only enlivens maintenance by reporting the nightmarish detail that all those whom he meets on his travels are "of oon lyuraye and looke so to-gedre" [wear one livery and so all look alike] (801–3), but he also enfolds a "raggeman rolle" [accusatory roll] containing complaints concerning "mayntennance" into a literal bag of books (1565–66). *Mum and the Sothsegger* may also stand testament to just the sort of diffusion of authorial responsibility imagined in *Richard the Redeless.* At least twenty-seven alliterative long lines have been inserted throughout the fragmentary text in British Library Additional MS 41666, in the same

Secretary hand that provided numerous marginal corrections.[101] The scribe may have felt that he or she had sufficient "conseil" to "amende" and add to the text of *Mum and the Sothsegger* that had come to "honde" [hand], accepting an invitation to collaborative composition such as offered by the *Richard*-narrator. As we shall see, the *Mum*-poet pushes Media Specific Analysis to such an extreme that the text threatens to disappear into the array of documents it deploys, in an aestheticization of Langlandian political communication.

The Sounds of Silence
Material Dreams and Mum as the Principle of Pragmatic Noise

Like *Richard the Redeless*, *Mum and the Sothsegger* presents itself as a discourse that benefits the state, with the narrator imagining political crisis as fundamentally informational. The fragment's first lines feature the narrator's observation that "the king ne his cunseil" [king and his advisers] do not "knowe / What is the comune clamour ne the crye nother" [know the subjects of popular complaint nor outcry] (157). The narrator reasons that the realm suffers because "no man of the meynee" [no retainer] is foolish enough to "wisse thaym any worde" [let them know a single word], nor "telle thaym the trouthe ne the texte nothir" [tell them the truth nor the story] (158–60). Such miserable social conditions set the *Mum*-narrator on a quest that recalls Langland's Will's wanderings in search of political and spiritual enlightenment. The *Mum*-narrator's goal is to find a "Sothsegger" [truth-teller] (48), a "fabuler" [communicator] who can inform the clueless king of "mischief" [societal ills] (140–41).

The *Mum*-narrator argues that there are two causes for the informational abyss between suffering subjects and the ruling classes: the fiscal benefits of flattery, and the physical risks assumed by truth-tellers. The longed-for "fabuler" might as well be named "[S]aunder the seruiselees" [Sanders the Serviceless] (44), insofar as flatterers—the men of Mum—reap all material benefits of patronage. Mum urges the narrator to navigate this mercenary world and tries to convince him to say only what the well-heeled wish to hear, citing his own material success to the art of "oyle" [flattery]: "Thus leede I my life in lust of my herte, / And for my wisedame and witte wone I with the beste" [Thus I lead my life according to my heart's desire, and through my wisdom and wit inhabit elite social circles] (248–49). Seeming confirmation of Mum's mantra about the power of obsequiousness comes with the questing narrator's first sight of an actual "Sothsegger" in his natural habitat: absent from a "halle" [hall] in which Mum, the "mayre" [mayor], and numerous hangers-on all feast, the truth-teller dines with a single companion, "Dreede" [Dread] (821–38).

The *Mum*-narrator stresses that a would-be "soth-segger" risks physical threats along with poverty. Mum and his men practice both intimidation and surveillance, seeking to prevent the king and his "cunseil" [advisers] from acquiring a truth-teller's services. Those capable of communicating truths about the state of the realm "kepe thaym cloos for caicching of wordes" [keep things to themselves, for fear of being overheard] and "shony forto shewe what the shire meneth" [avoid conveying the common opinion in the county], since they know that a person who will "bolde hym to bable the soth" [risks speaking the truth] escapes neither "scorne other scathe" [scorn nor injury] (158–72). The narrator reports on the material risks of truth-telling in Lancastrian England: a person can be "a-frountid" [accosted] and "y-[ferked] vnder foote" [trampled] for a "feithful tale" [honest report] (54–55), and even killed for discussing "mischief" [corruption] stemming from "misse-reule" [misrule] (165–67). Collapsing the distinction between truth and truth-telling in order to prioritize communication over content, the narrator presents "trouthe" [Truth] itself as "doun y-troode" [downtrodden] and "Y-bete and y-bounde in bourghes and in shires" [beaten and bound in towns and in counties] (171–72).[102]

The figure of Mum is often read as a representative of silence, following from both the poem's political allegory and modern usage. Modern "mum" often intends silence, as with the *OED*'s definition A2 ("Refusal to speak, silence"), the early modern "mummer" as an actor in a dumb show, or the modern idiom of keeping "mum."[103] Indeed, the *OED* suggests a significant tradition of perceiving Mum as an apotheosis of quiet, tracing back to 1399 (via Bale's 1562 catalogue entry) the earliest recorded use of definition B ("A command to be silent or secret").[104] Such modern linkage of Mum and silence might seem to mesh well with the *Mum*-poet's criticism that lack of communication enables social corruption.

However, to link Mum with silence is to confuse the character's ontological status with his activities and effects. The only silence associated with Mum is that which he brings about through the pragmatic deployment of noise. Indeed, the most basic meaning of "mum" signals the fundamentally sonic nature of Mum's allegorical identity. As the *MED*'s definition of "mum" ("an inarticulate vocal sound, a mumble") makes clear, "mum" is a word that means precisely what it sounds: it signifies the sound one makes when one's lips are pursed together, in an anatomical position that produces noise but disallows any articulation.[105] This primarily sonic sense of "mum" is also the first definition in the *OED*, which cites Langland's recourse to Midlands meteorology to communicate the material power of voice: "Thow myghtest betre meten myst on Maluerne hulles / Than gete a mum of here mouth ar moneye were hem shewed" [You'd sooner see mist on Malvern Hills than get a sound out of their mouth before money is offered] (Prol. 163–64).[106] Mum may make silence, though he effects this only through the manipulation of his essential element, noise.

While Mum embodies the purely sonic substrate "prior to meaning,"[107] his noisy genealogy does not prevent him from providing vital training to a narrator struggling to advance his truth-telling project. It is through dialogue with Mum that the narrator learns to abandon his idealizing monologues and instead study the concrete, political world for which he must fashion speech. To develop a counter-discourse to the corrupt world ruled by Mum, the narrator must first learn to compete with the noisy flatterer who continually presents obstacles to the communication of political truths.[108] The consummate chatterbox, Mum is seemingly ubiquitous in the poem's social world, conversing with various people in positions of power, both lay and religious. When Mum tells the narrator, "I am Mum thy maister [master]" in "alle maniere places" [everywhere] (243), he makes clear that the informational abyss from which the realm suffers is not produced by silence, but by the superabundance of speech—the endless noise of Mum.

While the *Mum*-poet highlights this difference between noisy flattery and earnest truthfulness, the distinction between Mum and the narrator nevertheless proves unstable. In his first appearance, Mum suggests the continuity between his own and the narrator's methods:

'Nomore of this matiere,' cothe Mum thenne,
'For I meruaile of thy momeling more thenne thou wenys.
Saides [not] thou thyself, and sothe as me thoughte,
That thees sothe-siggers seruen noon thankes?" (232–35)

[Then, Mum said, 'No more of this subject matter, for I marvel at your mumbling more than you might believe. Didn't you just say yourself (and truthfully, in my opinion), that these truth-tellers perform thankless service?]

Having just listened to the narrator's minimally 233-line speech[109] on the need for political truth-telling, Mum weaves his own name into his reduction of the narrator's arguments to a single stream of noise—to "*momelynge.*" After aggressively transforming the narrator's discourse into its raw material of sound, Mum co-opts the narrator's logic through his question-begging argument that a truth-teller's scant recompense demonstrates

Mum's primacy. As we shall see, the narrator learns well this lesson of appropriating the materials of one's opponents—for the truth-teller soon becomes the apprentice of the flatterer.

If Mum is indeed the narrator's "maister" [master] in the art of speech, then the narrator occasionally proves to be a diligent student in the transnational art of flattery. In order to show how he has attained ascendancy over truth-tellers "in alle maniere places," Mum multiplies heads of state, stating that he spends time with "souuerauns and seruyd with greete" [sovereigns, catered to along with nobles] (243–44). Revealing that he acts according to aristocratic class interests, Mum notes that he leads a materially rich life among the "beste" [elite] by choosing never to "withseye" [contradict], but rather to "folowe thaym" [follow them], attaching himself to the monied class through "oyle" [flattery] (243–49). Speech, Mum insists, is the means through which one can attain power. Mum counsels the narrator to learn to control himself, for his "wilde wordes" [wild speech] often "maken wretthe" [cause anger], when he should instead "parle for thy profit and plaise more here-aftre" [speak for your own profit and so please more people, from now on] (249–57).

If Mum had been listening more carefully, he would have recognized that the narrator had already demonstrated skill in the art of "oyle." After having described the sorry state of truth-telling in the realm (165–72), the narrator praises the "hovs" [household] of Henry IV, and then proceeds to paint an obsequious portrait of the "soorayn" [sovereign]:

> the graciousist guyer goyng vppon erthe,
> Witti and wise, worthy of dedes,
> Y-kidde and y-knowe and cunnyng of werre
> Feers forto fighte, the felde euer kepith
> And trusteth on the Trinite that trouthe shal hym helpe;
> A doughtful doer in deedes of armes
> And a comely knight y-come of the grettist,
> Ful of al vertue that to a king longeth,
> Of age and of al thing as hym best semeth (211–20)

[the most gracious leader living upon earth, witty and wise, performing worthy deeds, famous and well-regarded and knowledgeable in war, fierce in battle, always keeping the field, while trusting in the Trinity that truth will aid him; a brave fighter in battle, and a handsome knight born of the noblest lineage, full of all the virtues that are proper to a king, in age and in all respects of the noblest appearance]

The narrator's prose here is oily, indeed. The narrator deploys two tactics that Paul Strohm links with Lancastrian poetics: the attempt to supply legitimacy to a king vulnerable to charges of forceful usurpation, and an emphasis on the sovereign's ability to bring order to an unstable realm.[110] Seeking to pre-empt any doubts about Henry IV's nobility, the narrator describes his lineage as "grettist" [noblest], while praising Henry's martial skill and bravery as qualities of a king who might "stable" [stabilize] a realm that will then "stonde stille for oure dayes" [be at peace in our time] (225–26).

The *Mum*-narrator's endorsement of the aristocratic ideology in which legitimate rule is restricted to those of "grettist" blood is not confined to such conventional flattery of the king. Despite a late-medieval literature of peasant complaint informed by legal speech enabled by legal reforms,[111] *Mum and the Sothsegger* actively closes off the right of legal complaint from peasants, limiting it to clerks and nobles. The narrator claims he cannot think of a "kindely cause why the comun shuld / Contre the king-is wil ne construe his werkes" [natural cause whereby the commons should oppose the king's will or ponder his deeds] (1458–59). He clarifies that he does not mean by "comun" the "knightz that cometh for the shires" [knightly parliamentary representatives], but the lower classes, for "hit longeth to no laborier" [it is not proper for a laborer] to participate in the legal process, since the "lawe is agayne thaym" [law is against them] (1460–62). With its stringent support of class boundaries, going so far as to speak against commoners even thinking about kingly actions (1459), *Mum and the Sothsegger* recalls the reactionary energy of aristocratic exceptionalism in *William of Palerne* (see chapter 2). Much as Revivalist insistence on nativist nationalism is undermined by transnational culture and economics (see chapter 4), any suggestion of national unity in *Mum and the Sothsegger* is trumped by overriding class interests that shape its political imagination.

Richard the Redeless demonstrates a similarly pre-national investment in class hierarchy, further undermining Revivalism's view that English nationalism drives late-medieval alliterative verse. In one instance, the narrator cloaks class contempt by opening with a conventional complaint concerning the youth of Richard II's chosen advisers (I.175–76), before proceeding to rail against Richard, stating that "hobbis ye hadden of Hurlewaynis kynne, / Reffusynge the reule of realles kynde" [you brought in Jacks of Goblin race, refusing to be governed by royal nature] (I.177–78). The non-noble and non-clerkly status of Richard's favorites is figured under the rubric of monstrosity: the *MED* cites Hob as a "generic proper name for one of the common class," derived from its basic meaning as the "familiar form of the name Robert," while the Hurlewain to whom the commoner is bound by blood is a "mischievous sprite or goblin." Reinforcing what Gellner calls the "entropy-resistance" central to pre-modern culture, such grotesque images of commoners militate against socioeconomic mobility.[112] The narrator later links poor advice given to Richard II with the social pretensions and inadequacies of favorites, saying that advisers urged him to engage in oppressive policy moves because they wanted to be "sure of hem-self and siris to ben y-callid" [in secure positions and to be called "Sir"] (l.191). The *Richard*-narrator joins Piers Plowman, who refuses to allow a knight to plow, in policing class boundaries: he condemns Richard II for having "cleued to knavis" [cleaved to knaves] in forming his government, and blames Richard's non-elitism for having emboldened these advisers to "belde vppon sorowe" [add to the misery] in the realm (l.199–200). Both the *Richard*-poet and the *Mum*-poet insist on a class-striated realm in contrast with the homogeneous, horizontally conceived modern nation that Revivalism projects into late-medieval England.

The *Mum*-narrator's desire to restrict the lower classes from communicating their displeasure with current affairs, and the *Richard*-narrator's insistence on limiting which classes can provide advisers to the king, reveal an openly hierarchical social vision that belies Revivalism's assumption of a populist alliterative nationalism. The *Mum*-poet injects further classism into the narrative, presenting the narrator's ethical pursuit as an exclusively clerkly quest. Despite his travels involving a series of conversations with secular and religious clerks, the narrator presents his wanderings as dramatic and difficult. Such clerkly labors lead to physical strain on the narrator and, as we shall see, to a crucial identity crisis for Mum. The pivotal confrontation comes as the narrator nears his breaking point: feeling constantly "manachid" [menaced] by Mum, the narrator becomes "full woo" [utterly sorrowful], worried that his obsession with the matter of Mum versus the Sothsegger has made all deem him "mad for my wordes" [insane, because of my speech] (570–81). Having sought in vain for a priestly explanation of why tithing does not indict all its practitioners as Mum's followers, the narrator discovers to his horror that all the clerks have a "memoire of Mvm" [mental image of Mum] rather than of "martires of heuene" [spiritual martyrs] (630–31). When Mum suddenly appears, it is unsurprising to see the panopticon-like figure respond; however, Mum's sudden concern for the narrator's well-being is something new. Mum warns the narrator that his verbal excess exposes him to physical risk (674) and urges him to "be stille" [be quiet], for "suche maniere wordes" [such kinds of speech] as his anti-tithing tirade are "holsum" [wholesome] neither for his "heed" [head] nor "herte" [heart] (674–78). Mum calls the narrator "mad" to believe that Mum could have a "maister" [master] among wealthy men, noting that Mum "maketh mo men" [brings more men into his service] in a month than the truth-teller does in seven-score winters (680–83).

While offering the narrator a practical lesson in speech,[113] Mum suddenly and strikingly steps outside of himself. Such instability comes even as he takes up the topic of self-control. Imagining a social gathering in one of those "priuy places there peeris assemblen" [private places where peers congregate], charged with tension by the introduction of a "matier" [subject], Mum reports that "Mvm musith there-on and maketh many cautelles, / With a locke on his lippe" [Mum considers the matter, and deploys many tricks with a lock on his lip] (687–90). Mum observes that Mum knows to refrain from speaking until he can determine what sort of political speech will appeal to "the beste" [the elite] (687–94). The narrator is at first resistant. After Mum urges him to consider "with whom that thou mellys" [with whom you are speaking] and recognize that clerks are capable of physical retaliation, the narrator denies the possibility that ecclesiasts could commit violence (698–709). Mum can only shake his allegorical head at such idealism. Scoffing at the narrator's "a-dasid" [blurred] vision that associates the clergy with "the sothe" [the truth], Mum imagines a ruthless political world where one must always be "ware of wiles and waite wel aboute" [be wary of deceit, and be on your guard] (710–15).

Mum's indictment of clerks leads to his curious and fateful defense of truth-telling, which provides the narrator with the key information about communication that he does not yet "perceipues" [perceive] (719). Mum considers Pontius Pilate's public request for water to wash his hands as a "signe" [sign] that his conscience is "clensid as clene as his handes" [cleansed as fully as his hands] regarding Jesus's killing (719–25). Mum draws an uncharacteristic conclusion from this incident, castigating Pilate in terms that mirror the narrator's own conviction that the truth-teller is ethically obliged to inform his ruler of misdeeds:

> Yit was he ground of the grame and moste guilty eeke,
> For euery man that mynde hath may wel wite,
> That prelatz aughten haue pite when princz bee moeued,
> And reede thaym so that rancune roote not in hert,
> And ere the grame growe ferre the ground so to wede
> And amende that were mysse ere any more caicche
> Of man-slaughter or mourdre, as hath many dayes. (726–32)

[Nevertheless, he was the cause of the evil, and most guilty indeed, for anyone with the capacity for thought can clearly see that prelates ought to have pity when princes are emotionally disturbed, and counsel them, lest rage take root in their heart and evil expand to form weeds in the ground, and correct that which was amiss before any other evils take root, such as man-slaughter or murder, as has often happened]

While Mum may here refer to insurrectionary acts in the early years of Henry IV's reign,[114] he seems less concerned with topicality than with truth-telling itself, for he soon takes up the self-referential subject of sound. Mum endorses as a "trewe lawe" [true law] the custom that a defendant capable of speech will be found guilty if he or she remains silent after having been accused of a felony (751–57). For Mum, the silent defendant deserves censure *ipso facto*—for he has not mastered the basic skill of knowing when one must speak.

Mum proceeds to speak like a truth-teller, asserting that the failure to speak honestly to the powerful increases societal problems and that political corruption is a disease for which the truth-teller offers verbal healing. In figuring truth-telling as medicinal, the *Mum*-poet makes use, as Matthew Giancarlo has shown, of legal rhetoric shaping contemporary parliamentary petitions.[115] He shows a concern for societal order, seconding the narrator's praise of the "conseil of clergie" [clerkly counsel] as a means of preventing the "grucching of grete that shuld vs gouuerne" [fighting of nobles, who should instead be governing us] (759–62),[116] and he expresses his desire for the state's corporal health, hoping its "lymes" [limbs] do not "pynen" [suffer] because of the woes of the "heed" [head] (763–64). The thrilled narrator tells Mum that now "thy talking me plesith" [your words please me], for he has "saide as sothe" [spoken as truly] as anyone (767–69). The narrator, whose ambition as a truth-teller Mum marks as medicinal by calling him "Lucas" (775),[117] works within Mum's conceit of truth-telling as medical practice: he urges Mum, who has shown skill in identifying and treating societal "woundz" [wounds], to go to those in power and "telle the same tale that thou has told here" [tell the same story you told here] (770–73).

If the flattering narrator earlier seemed like Mum, then Mum further muddies the waters, coming to embody the truth-teller. Such identity instability is highlighted by yet another moment of self-differentiation. In a moment of allegorical confusion, Mum literally breaks down, referring to himself as his own disciple: "So taughte me the trusty techer on erthe, / My maister and maker, Mvm that I serue" [So taught me that trusty teacher in worldly matters, my master and creator, Mum whom I serve] (778–79). While Day and Steele assume that "the author has forgotten that it is Mum who is speaking,"¹¹⁸ I maintain that the *Mum*-poet here figures identity crisis. As Mum's self splits into master and student, the poet reveals Mum as the apotheosis of practical speech. Resistance to Revivalist nostalgia aids criticism in recognizing the *Mum*-poet's theatrical ambition. Much as the *Wynnere*-poet's sophisticated identity play emerges only through disruption of Revivalist assumptions of alliterative traditionalism (chapter 1), so does rejection of Revivalist efforts to see Langlandian poetry as merely imitative of *Piers Plowman* disclose a sophisticated meditation on rhetoric in the *Mum*-poet's adventurous allegories of political communication.¹¹⁹

Mum's sudden shift to the discourse of truth-telling is due neither to the over-burdened conscience of a momentarily regretful flatterer nor to the poet's aesthetic lapse. The *Mum*-poet here systematically destroys the Mum–Sothsegger binary. By having the dislocated Mum refer to himself as he takes up the truth-telling position, the narrator undoes the very distinction between flattery and truth, revealing practical reason as the more fundamental mode of language grounding these seeming opposites. Mum's practical concerns prove key to the very survival and shape of the text. As Simpson demonstrates, when the narrative ventures into the only "really dangerous complaint in the poem, against the Council of Henry IV," this potentially censurable discourse is "suppressed by Mum as soon as it is about to become explicit."¹²⁰ While Mum may be superficially opposed to the Sothsegger, he is more clearly aligned with the poet, whose business it is to circulate texts in a political world marked by the physical risks of truth-telling. Mum's self-control in speech proves an indispensable component of the truth-telling poet's work.

Gardening Tips for Subversives
Multiplicity and the Blessed Business of Book Making

Through his deconstruction of the Mum–Sothsegger opposition, the *Mum*-poet makes clear that effective political counsel requires both Mum's sonic persuasiveness and the truth-teller's spiritual rectitude. The *Mum*-poet uses the elaborate opening frame to concentrate the oneiric authority of Langlandian discourse in the single character encountered in the fragment's dream vision. Having conducted throughout the poem's opening a kind of conversational travel narrative, the narrator eventually despairs of finding clarity as to the case of Mum versus the Sothsegger. In the dystopic, urban, transnational information quest,¹²¹ the narrator converses with individuals of influence in towns, monasteries, and churches, shuddering to hear all of them speak of Mum's supremacy. Mirroring the trajectory of *Piers*

Plowman, which many scholars see as figuring movement from the social world of the *Visio* to the interior world of the *Vita,*[122] *Mum and the Sothsegger* makes a sudden shift from the public sphere of corruption to the private space of dreams. Wincing at the painful "sothe" [truth] that Mum leads a "myrier" [merrier] life than the Sothsegger (848–49), the narrator, exhausted from his inquisitive "rennyng aboute" [running about] (858), falls asleep. He is transported to the idyllic terrain of a "frankeleyn-is freholde" [land-owner's free-holding] (946), where he meets the Gardener,[123] engaged in killing weeds and worms that harm his plants, and drones that steal honey from his hives (976–85). The Gardener soon becomes the unlikely spokesperson for the poem's radical political and paleographical agenda.

The Gardener sheds some light on the quest-weary narrator's "matiere": he explains that Mum is indeed the "maker" of "al the mischief and mysse-reule" [all corruption and misrule] in the realm (1115–16) and insists that the "soth-segger" is most sorely needed in a "parlement" [parliament] (1118) filled with Mum's men. Despite his criticism of Mum, the Gardener comes to sound strikingly like his nemesis. In a lengthy monologue, he echoes Mum by imagining a volatile political world in which pragmatism trumps Truth. Seeking, as did Mum, to bring order to the narrator's wild speech, the Gardener counsels his new disciple to be "soft of thy sawys" [gentle in your speech] (1249–50), and to avoid speaking in "tirant-is wise" [like a tyrant] (1270–74). The Gardener also shares Mum's pragmatic, paranoiac view of society as a legal forum fissured by competing discourses. He urges the narrator to be "ware of wiles" [aware of tricks] and "mases" [deceits] in a world where Mum's men "debateth" [debate] each day with the Langlandian ethical figure of "Do-welle" [Do-well], always threatening to take the "maistrie" [mastery] and win the "mote" [lawsuit] (1252–61).

The Gardener's political vision proves no more comforting than Mum's dystopic portrait of an agonistic world ruled by power and patronage. He presents an authoritarian solution to the communication problem driving the narrator's quest, offering a political allegory that reads chillingly like a guide to targeting political enemies (982–1086). Drawing from Bartholomaeus Anglicus's popular bestial allegory *De Proprietaribus Rerum,* the Gardener compares a well-run state with the cooperative world of bees. Drones who steal the honey of those laboring for the common good should be exterminated (1086), just as earthworms who trouble gardeners should be killed for the greater good (979–81).[124] Much as *William of Palerne* sustains aristocratic privilege through a naturalization of aristocratic ideology (chapter 2), *Mum and the Sothsegger* maps monarchical rule onto the insect world. The *Mum*-poet's biologization of state power is grounded in a fundamentally conservative understanding of justice, which in late-medieval political theory interrelated public order, the sanctification of property, and the stabilization of morality.[125] Moving from moral condemnation to the killing of the selfish drones who steal others' honey, the Gardener stresses proactive violence in his model for running a state.

If the Gardener's apiary social allegory is unsettling, his political analysis proves to be an even more troubling legitimation of state violence. Describing Genghis Khan's unification of the state through his demand that each of his noble subjects sacrifice his eldest son (1414–56), the Gardener outdoes Mum in imagining aggression as the political solution for nonconformism.[126] By opening and closing the discussion with the comment that Genghis was a successful conqueror (1415; 1455), the Gardener emphasizes that the basis of the Khan's ability to silence competing voices was his monopoly on force.[127] This view of an ordered state recalls Mum's programmatic deference to the great. While Mum advises that one say only that which pleases powerful people, the Gardener praises Genghis for having cultivated such an intimidating reputation that "his wil was not encountrid" [his desire was not questioned], freeing him to do "alle with oon wil" [everything according to one desire] (1449–52). Whether it be Mum or the Gardener, instructive authorities offer rigidly hierarchical views of culture in *Mum and the Sothsegger,* in contrast to the populist, proto-modern nation that Revivalism projects onto the Middle Ages.

After his authoritarian political monologue, the Gardener moves to Mum's favored subject of practical communication, shifting attention away from speech and toward writing. Much as the *Richard*-narrator conceives of his text materially, as something that can "happe" into a reader's "honde" (I.59), the Gardener reveals Langlandian poetics' recursive interest in writing technologies. He conceives the wisdom of his "sothe tale" [true tale] (1058) as merely the first step of a textual process that requires execution by someone willing to "sue to th'ende" [pursue to completion] of a politico-textual project: since "I have infourmed the faire" [I have given you excellent information], says the Gardener, the narrator must now "make vp thy matiere" [compose your case] (1277–82).[128] Not content to provide timeless truths from his idealized state, the Gardener gives precise instructions as to how the "matire" [case] of Mum is to be "made" [composed] (1306) in the political world outside of the dream. The Gardener thereby confers oneiric authority on the "blised bisynes" [blessed business] of "book-making" [book-production] (1281).

The Gardener's specific instructions for publication show deep familiarity with such codicological "bisynes." He advises the narrator, "furst feoffe thou therwith the freyst of the royaulme, / for yf thy lord liege allone hit begynne" [first, enfeoff yourself with the most noble ones in the realm, for if the liege lord by himself begins it], then surely "knyghtz" [nobles] will "copie hit echone, / And do write eche worde" [each copy it, transcribing each word] (1284–86). Such advice makes eminent sense in late-medieval book culture: by sending advance copies to the most prominent patron possible, he will generate maximum demand for a new text in a world where fashion was "set at the top."[129] However utopic the Gardener's freehold might seem, it still features social class as a factor to be exploited in negotiating the market conditions that await the narrator's ethical treatise.

Through a radical disjunction between the Gardener's political discourse and its transmission in the material world, the *Mum*-poet deploys Media Specific Analysis in a poeticization of book production that prioritizes legal documents. The Gardener leads us to expect transcription as his discursive mode, for he insists that the narrator "write" his "wordes echone" [each word], so that "hit wol be exemple to sum men" [it will be an example to people] (1268–69). That the Gardener's unitary discourse becomes multiple in the dissemination process forces us to rethink the meaning of transcription in this "blised bisynes" of "boke-making" (1281). Having urged the narrator to copy his speech until "hit" [it] is "complete to clapsyng" [finished and ready to be clasped] (1282), the Gardener suggests a single, stable volume. However, the narrator launches suddenly into a description of a "bagge" [bag] of books, composed of disparate, variously sourced documents (1343–47), with which assemblage the narrator plans to counsel the king. As Richard Firth Green has shown, the *Mum*-poet's recourse to the legal documents that dominate the bag's contents is rooted in Langland's poetic practice,[130] suggesting a recursive tradition of documentary imagination in the Southwest Midlands–London nexus. By means of such bureaucratically modulated discourse, the *Mum*-poet prioritizes communication over content, with the Gardener's unitary discourse becoming transformed into a mobile archive.[131] For Andrew Wawn, the unveiling of this bag of books captures the recursive essence of *Mum and the Sothsegger* as "not a satiric poem or a poem of complaint," but rather a "poem *about* poems of satire and complaint," in which book-production itself is "dramatize[d]."[132]

By creating the expectation that the narrator's "boke-making" (1281) will involve transcribing the Gardener's speech, and yet proceeding to describe the narrator's deployment of a heterogeneous set of documents, the *Mum*-poet presents the medieval book as a multiplex phenomenon. Such codicological inconsistency seems strategic. By becoming the "bibliographer of other people's writing" rather than the communicator of a single political tract, the narrator insulates himself, Barr argues, from authorial attribution.[133] The mutation of the single text into a bag of them thus figures the poet's negotiation of the social risks of truth-telling. Though the narrator describes the bag's contents as "many a pryue poyse" [many private poetic works] (1343), most of the items prove quite different from either a medieval or modern understanding of "poesy." For example, the first two items, a "quayer of quitances of quethyn goodes" [quire of receipts of bequeathed goods] bound "al newe" [afresh] by bishops (1348–49), and their "penyworth of papir of penys" (1350), are a receipt and "an IOU," respectively,[134] while the "rolle of religion, how thay their rentz hadde" [religious administrative rolls, enumerating profits from rents] (1364) and a "writte of high wil" [will] (1498) are everyday documents in striking contrast with the Gardener's moral and political treatise. The Gardener's seemingly straightforward instruction to transcribe his "wordes" leads to a bewildering array of sources that the narrator "unknitte" [exposed] before the king, such as a "copie for comunes" [copy for the Commons] containing political rumors (1388), a "scrowe for squyers" [scroll regarding squires] detailing maintenance-related corruption (1489), a "librarie of lordes" [nobleman's library] revealing magnates' desire for "lordship that to the coroune longeth" [power belonging to the crown] (1626–27), and a "poynte of prophecie" [prophetic treatise] that "museth on the meruailles that Merlyn did deuyse" [meditates on Merlin's marvels] (1724–25). Legitimizing the Sothsegger-narrator's voice by appropriating the authority of others' discourses, the *Mum*-poet uses the bag of books to figure political composition as a communal, multi-voiced practice.

Much as *Richard the Redeless* inscribes within itself the possibility that numerous authors have collaborated in its production, *Mum and the Sothsegger* uses the mutation of the single "boke" into a multiplex "bagge" to call into question its own authorial status. Ascribing to the *Mum*-poet the goal of appropriating the legal force of the bag's assorted documents, Grady argues that *Mum and the Sothsegger* desires "to be one of the 'books' in the bag."[135] I would suggest that the recursive practice of Langlandian poetics invites us to theorize the converse of Grady's canny formulation: by incorporating the bag of books into itself and making ambiguous whether its multifarious contents are indeed the "boke" commissioned by the Gardener, the *Mum*-poet shows that a book is inherently multiple, becoming invariably a bag of them. Navigating the risky environment for Lancastrian political communication, the narrator has learned from the mystical Gardener the strategic value of multiplicity, both in terms of incorporated media and of the possibility of corporate authorship.

Such a corporate conception of authorship suggests Langlandian poets' independence in engaging with Langland's authorial legacy. While Langland, according to Kerby-Fulton, uses tactics of authorial self-presentation to "control the reception of his text" in a volatile political environment,[136] the *Richard*-poet and *Mum*-poet appear to have proceeded in opposite fashion, using invitations to collaborative writing and multiplication of authorities to destabilize textual unity. Langland's legacy as an assertive, yet ambiguous, authorial presence[137] suggested the strategy of circumventing censorious eyes by making fundamentally unclear how many hands are responsible for the propagation of texts. Allowing their authorial voices to be multiplied through invitations to readers to become rewriters, the writers of *Richard the Redeless* and *Mum and the Sothsegger* strategically forewent authorial control in order to fashion narratives channeling both Mum's pragmatic noise and the Gardener's moral and political publishing program. Both Mum and the Gardener offer key communications advice about negotiating the volatile discursive environment of early Lancastrian England.

Much recent criticism seeks to move beyond trans-historical notions of authorship that denigrate scribal participation as inherently inferior to originary authorial work.[138] The many hands at work in Langlandian poems invite just such a materialist focus on late-medieval book culture. Analysis of collaborative composition as structurally woven into the texts of *Richard the Redeless* and *Mum and the Sothsegger* undermines efforts to stabilize the poems of the *Piers Plowman* tradition as discrete, merely topical responses to Langland's work. Focus on bibliographical habits generated by the bureaucratic culture of the Southwest Midlands–London nexus suggests a network of unstable, codiocologically sophisticated texts negotiating the treacherous Lancastrian world. While their classist motives and transnational religious loyalties prove alien to Revivalist dreams of a populist, alliterative nationalism, Langlandian poets seem strikingly modern in their systematic engagement with writing technology. Undermining Revivalist visions of a neo-Saxon nativism that strains to revivify an outmoded oral past, Langlandian poets present through their politicization of manuscript culture uncanny parallels to the dynamic modes of anonymous, collaborative composition in the unstable textual networks of the digital age.

EPILOGUE

Epochal Historiography and Re-Engagement with Alliterative Poems

IN HIS REVIEW of Turville-Petre's *The Alliterative Revival,* Blake suggests that "it might not be too much of a paradox to say that the best book on the alliterative revival is likely to be the one which takes as its theme that such a book is unnecessary because it organizes Middle English poetry in the wrong way."[1] Such a book would at least "allow the author to dwell fairly on the differences as well as the similarities among alliterative poems."[2] In critiquing Alliterative Revivalism's monolithic vision, while exploring contexts foreclosed by nationalist literary historiography, I have intended the simultaneously destructive and creative response envisaged by Blake. The Revivalist portrait of a unified, nativist, provincial alliterative movement proves rooted in nationalist, ethno-historical discourses that evolved along with the Western discipline of literary studies. However fantastical Revivalism appears, it continues to shape our reception of late-medieval alliterative texts, suggesting images of nostalgia, ethnic pride, and, above all, its master narrative of cultural death followed by revival followed by second death.

My assumption of the nation's nineteenth-century origins might suggest an epochal literary historiography predicated upon the absolute alterity of the Middle Ages. However, it is only regarding national identity and race that I stress medieval–modern difference. As I have shown through my engagement with classism and Western consolidation (chapter 2), female participation in a transnational economy (chapter 3), marcher culture and empire (chapter 4), and the politicization of book culture (chapter 5), alliterative texts are variously caught up in cultural practices of continuing significance. By systematically undoing the layers of Revivalist fantasy that have accreted to alliterative works, I aim to recover the medieval desires and commitments obscured by the literary-historical yoking of poems to an allegedly native Saxon past.

My insistence on the nation's modernity takes place in the context of a vigorous historiographical debate. Medievalist scholars have offered powerful criticism of modernist theories of nationhood, particularly Anderson's view of a decisive shift from a dynastic Middle Ages with a transnational religious structure and "sacral" sense of time, to secular, socially horizontal communities, each imagined in the "homogeneous empty time" of print-capitalist culture.[3] Ingham, for example, has powerfully interrogated Anderson's evolutionary argument that continuously developing capitalist pressures cause the "passing away" of dynasticism and typology, which disappear in the past of a linear model of history.[4] In emphasizing the continuities of pre-modern and current imperial identities, I submit that alternative approaches such as Ingham's "dialectical" method are vital adjustments required for the application of modernist theories such as Anderson's.[5] I have sought to isolate the precise aspects of Anderson's (and Gellner's) models that contribute to my critique of Revivalism, not the least of which is the discursive coincidence of the nationalist age with the professionalization of literary studies (chapter 1).

I would urge medievalist critics to recognize the epochal, rather than binary, potential of Anderson's and Gellner's historiographies. In tracing European national modernity only as far back as the nineteenth century, I adopt a version of modernity that undermines the marginalization of the Middle Ages in periodizations that assume a decisive sixteenth-century shift. Timelines such as Gellner's post-industrialist rise of nationalism remove the medieval era from isolation, joining it with the early-modern and eighteenth-century periods in a reconfigured, pre-national epoch.[6] Insofar as periodization, as Davis argues, is a "political technique" that always serves current interests,[7] it is unsurprising that the concept of modernity is as ambiguous as it is historiographically inevitable. As we have seen, some medievalist scholars trace a progressively developing English national identity as far back as the Anglo-Saxon period;[8] other critics, using criteria such as Reformation culture or cartography, argue for a sixteenth-century dawn;[9] while others, examining anti-French literary culture or British political union, assert eighteenth-century beginnings.[10] Considering such a variety of narratives of national growth, it seems an oversimplification to view Anderson as unique in constructing Western modernity on the basis of a medieval other. Unless one assumes primordial ethno-national identities that stretch continuously beyond historical memory, one must draw an exclusionary line at some historical point. Anderson's late-eighteenth-century Creole print-capitalism is no less arbitrary in its explanatory force than Hastings's argument for Anglo-Saxon religious identity or Greenfeld's prioritization of the English Reformation.¹¹ Moreover, Anderson's historiography accommodates non-linear readings. By foregrounding technological developments and the cultural effects of the mass migrations that produced Creole consciousness, Anderson identifies a nationalist age while simultaneously implying that decisive shifts in technology and demographics can produce alternative epochs.¹²

With its emphasis on political and technological ruptures in cultural history, epochal historiography can bring *post*modern criticism into proximity with the medieval period. Two of the topics I pursue demonstrate how an epochal historiography of nationalism works against alteritist tendencies. When I turn to Anderson to explore the unstable nature of borders in the Anglo-Scottish marches, insisting that the assumption of nation inhibits us from seeing the identity play within such communities (chapter 4), I am motivated in part by a desire to theorize radical return to pre-modern territorial instability. As Hardt and Negri argue concerning the "new *physiology*" of global politics, the notion that power can be contained within limited sovereign territorial states is already being undermined, with transnational power networks preying upon the very belief in fixed national borders.¹³ The dynamic imperial states of the late-medieval period bear uncanny similarities to such post-national entities. When I focus on the political use of anonymity and multiplicity in Langlandian book culture (chapter 5), probing the "manuscript matrix" that often eludes a print-centered critical tradition,¹⁴ I am driven by a fascination with the similarly unstable nature of manuscript and digital textuality. Tracking the multiplication of texts and the obfuscation of authorial responsibility in Langlandian poems, I hope here to open up theoretical lines of communication between the age of the manuscript and the electronic epoch.¹⁵

In applying Gellner's argument that industrial modernity requires a homogeneous society capable of being efficiently mobilized for capitalist production, I highlight both class loyalties and regional distinctions that prove incompatible with the Revivalist fantasy of medieval nationalism. While it would be naïve to claim that modern capitalism utterly levels class distinctions, Gellner's modernist model offers the crucial insight that post-industrial society organizes itself *as if* pre-national social hierarchies have been destroyed, with general education programs, nationalist political rhetoric, and nation-wide bureaucracy assimilating all localities into a single market system.¹⁶ Gellner's insistence on industrialism's systematic production of socioeconomic entropy highlights the qualitatively different status of medieval classism, thus exposing Revivalism's imagination of a populist nationalism as a distracting fantasy.

Arguing for a late-thirteenth-century rise of an English nation, Turville-Petre asserts that nationalist loyalties existed alongside both local and transnational identities, such as the Church, with the trans-regional growth of English as the vernacular standard producing a national perspective.[17] I would advance two criticisms of this view. While patriotism concerning the English realm has presumably existed as long as has the kingdom, such emotional attachments require a systematic and self-sustaining ideology to rise to the level of nationalism.[18] Moreover, considering the lack of late-medieval mass media and general education institutions to disseminate such an ideology uniformly, I join Pearsall in asserting that medieval invocations of English identity invariably prove local, serving merely to rhetorically reinforce class or regional interests.[19] As seen in *William of Palerne* (chapter 2), the notion of a nationalist ideology transcending class interests is a medievalist projection: William "Englishes" French material not out of patriotism, but in the service of aristocratic exceptionalism. Besides such overriding class interests, the entities that inspire loyalties in the poems that I explore in this book, such as the imperial war machines of Arthurian romance (chapters 3 and 4), bear little resemblance to the modern nation. Much as the *Mum*-narrator slips seamlessly from Orléans back to London (chapter 5), much as Galeron of Galloway switches unflinchingly from one side to a stronger (chapter 4), and much as the monarch of *Wynnere and Wastoure* unproblematically bears the arms of England and yet rules over French and Germans (chapter 1), late-medieval Middle English poets prove unconcerned with the exclusive loyalties required by modern national identity.

My reflection on regional perspectives also aims to release select alliterative poems from subjection to Revivalism's fantasy of nationalist nativism and ethno-poetic nostalgia. Convinced that the identification of Revivalist discourse facilitates re-engagement with alliterative texts deracinated by generations of nationalist reception, I investigate contexts that speak to current critical priorities. I propose alliterative zones flexible enough to accommodate social and cultural cross-connections, while simultaneously elucidating regional identities obscured by nationalist models. Analysis of the fissured nature of pre-national political identity proves vital in recovering such local contexts. Rejecting Revivalism's monolithic contextualization of alliterative poetry, I adopt what Jacques Derrida calls that "interpretations of interpretation" that affirms the ludic potential for manipulating elements, acquired through recognition of the non-totalizable nature of the literary historical field.[20] I advisedly make no effort to provide exhaustive coverage of an alliterative movement or movements. Indeed, I highlight the partiality of my selections of texts and regions because it is central to my argument that the Revivalist vision of a single alliterative school that *could* be reconstructed is a limiting fantasy. It is not fantasy itself that I indict—or claim to transcend. In foregrounding the heuristic nature of my regional contextualizations and the arbitrariness of my choices of poems for analysis, I seek to illuminate medieval–modern continuities in alliterative poems, in order to encourage further *interested* reconfigurations of social and political contexts informing alliterative works.

In insisting on the modernity of nationalist literary history, I assert that nineteenth-century racialist logic, rather than medieval ethnic identity, produces the Alliterative Revival. As we have seen (chapter 1), while Revivalism depends upon a modern, pseudo-scientific taxonomy of discrete races, its most immediate, Anglo-nationalist goal prevents it from participating fully in the Anglo-Saxonist racism of nineteenth- and early-twentieth-century America and Britain. In order to construct its narrative of English exceptionalism, Revivalist theory presents neo-Saxon culture as retrograde, technically inferior, and doomed to fall before a Chaucerian school that embraces and assimilates an imported French culture. Far from idealizing Saxons as a uniquely gifted and indomitable race, Revivalists portray them as second-rate provincials, with limited, if purist, talents. Revivalists aestheticize ethno-historical material to produce a literary history that, while Anglo-centric, appeals through its nationalist rhetoric to various British, American, and Continental critics committed to post-Romantic ethno national paradigms.[21] That American critics were among the first and most virulent Revivalists (chapter 1) supports Anderson's hypothesis that the first nations derived from Creole cultures linked by print technologies with imperial ethnic homelands,[22] and also highlights the modern nexus of nationalism and imperialism. Much as a shared sense of Germanic origins and imperial destiny drove both American and English nationalist literary histories, so does the participation of Scottish critics alongside English scholars sustain imperialist visions of an Anglo-centric British antiquity.

In his description of nationalism's historiographical sleight of hand, namely, that "it preaches and defends continuity, but owes everything to a decisive and unutterably profound break in human history,"[23] Gellner offers what could stand as a summary of Revivalist practice. The Saxon–Norman binary out of which Revivalism constructs its modern England is a fantasy produced by forgetting, performed in the mode of "thinking nationally" that, as D. Vance Smith argues, "obliviate[s]" differences "in memorializing the nation."[24] Revivalism invokes Saxon–Norman difference only to kill it off, with its primary motivation being the installation of a modern Englishness that postdates the alliterative movement's defeat by a Chaucer who epochally blended native vigor and Norman style.[25] If Smith is correct in maintaining that modern nations require an ethnic core (even if factitious) to survive,[26] then Alliterative Revivalism's post-industrial production of medieval ethnic homogeneity aims to anchor modern national identity. The identification of Revivalist discourse facilitates resistance to such nationalist leveling of the ethnic, regional, and class differences informing individual alliterative poems.

Through his analysis of the diversity of audiences, composers, and traditions of late-medieval alliterative verse, Lawton deems it necessary to note that he does not intend to imply that "there is no such thing as alliterative poetry."[27] For the polemical purpose of revising the Revivalist model that continues to inflect our reception of alliterative verse, I would suggest that criticism benefits from acting *as if* there were no such thing as alliterative poetry. A fixation on prosodic identity is the driving force of Revivalism's nationalist narrative of neo-Saxon nativists collapsing before a successful, because hybrid, Chaucerian poetics. While critics understandably relish the metrical skills of a Chaucer or a Dunbar, they rarely insist on linking such poets with their prosodies, which is precisely what Revivalist scholars do when fashioning monolithic narratives that foreground the choice of alliterative meter. While alliterative prosody is, of course, a recognizable meter, whether used exclusively or in combination with rhyme, I would suggest that scholars have not often enough considered how transparently this verse-form was used. Given the near absence of primary evidence of alliterative self-consciousness (Introduction), it is clear that Revivalism's prioritization of prosodic difference is a gross imposition of modern literary-historical taxonomy. Much as the notion of a single rhythmic standard for alliterative verse is an anachronistic, post-print production (chapter 1), so does Revivalism's single alliterative movement provide an influentially reductive frame. By disrupting Revivalism's nationalist story of a futile reanimation of the Old English past, I have endeavored not only to negate the ongoing impact of such totalization, but also to suggest reconfigured sociohistorical contexts. I have selected poems that figure transnational identities, regional politics, and writing technologies, deliberately replacing Revivalist fantasy with my own set of informing desires, in an effort to re-engage with the current energies animating late-medieval alliterative poems.

NOTES

Introduction

1. Walter W. Skeat, "An Essay on Alliterative Poetry," in *Bishop Percy's Folio Manuscript: Ballads and Romances,* vol. 3., ed. John W. Hales and Frederick J. Furnivall (London: N. Trübner and Co., 1868), xi–xxxix [xii].

2. Ibid., xi. By "temporal" and "accentual," Skeat refers to quantitative and stress-based prosodies, respectively.

3. Ibid., xii.

4. Ibid.

5. Ibid., xii–xiv. For a definitive analysis of alliterative prosody, see Ralph Hanna III, "Defining Middle English Alliterative Poetry," in *The Endless Knot: Essays on Old and Middle English in Honor of Marie Borroff,* ed. Teresa M. Tavormina and R. F. Yeager (Cambridge: D. S. Brewer, 1995), 43–63 [44–46].

6. On the New Medievalism's disciplinary self-interrogation, see Stephen G. Nichols, "Introduction: Philology in a Manuscript Culture," *Speculum* 65 (1990): 1–10. See Sylvia Federico and Elizabeth Scala's call for a "profession-wide interrogation of contemporary critical practices," in "Getting Post-Historical," in *The Post-Historical Middle Ages,* ed. Elizabeth Scala and Sylvia Federico (New York: Palgrave Macmillan, 2009), 1–12 [1].

7. R. Howard Bloch and Stephen G. Nichols, "Introduction," in *Medievalism and the Modernist Temper,* ed. R. Howard Bloch and Stephen G. Nichols (Baltimore: Johns Hopkins University Press, 1996), 1–22 [2].

8. Sarah Kay, "Analytical Survey 3: The New Philology," in *New Medieval Literatures* 3, ed. Wendy Scase, Rita Copeland, and David Lawton (Oxford: Clarendon Press, 1999), 295–326 [309–11].

9. I take the notion of a medievalist "family romance" from Lee Patterson's study of the disciplinary inheritance of the nineteenth-century medieval "revival," read as the necessary starting point for the politico-historical question of "what it means to be a medievalist," in *Negotiating the Past: The Historical Understanding of Medieval Literature* (Madison: University of Wisconsin Press, 1988), 3–9.

10. See David Matthews's "material history" of the development of Middle English studies from its origins in eighteenth-century antiquarianism, to its central role in F. J.

Furnivall's nationalist publication projects, and finally to its nineteenth-century professionalization in universities, in *The Making of Middle English, 1765–1910* (Minneapolis: University of Minnesota Press, 1999), xxxiv–xxxv.

11. To avoid a rhetoric of rupture, Derek Pearsall utilizes the term "efflorescence" to describe the mid-fourteenth-century burst in manuscript evidence of alliterative verse, in "The Origins of the Alliterative Revival," in *The Alliterative Tradition in the Fourteenth Century,* ed. Bernard S. Levy and Paul E. Szarmach (Kent, OH: Kent State University Press, 1982), 1–24 [1–7]. Thorlac Turville-Petre posits a single late-medieval alliterative "school," in *The Alliterative Revival* (Cambridge: Cambridge University Press, 1977), 27.

12. James Simpson, *Reform and Cultural Revolution: The Oxford English Literary History, Vol. 2: 1350–1547* (Oxford: Oxford University Press, 2002), 11–12. Simpson argues that John Bale's and John Leland's antiquarian programs are the "first attempts to shape a British, or even an English tradition as an identifiable national tradition of letters" (11).

13. On prejudice as determining interpretive horizons, and on the hermeneutic method of adjusting one's assumptions as objects of study present alternative limits of meaning, see Hans-Georg Gadamer, *Truth and Method,* 2nd ed., rev. ed., trans. Joel Weinsheimer and Donald G. Marshall (London: Continuum, 2004), 278–306.

14. Kathleen Biddick, *The Shock of Medievalism* (Durham, NC: Duke University Press, 1998), 1. See David Perkins' argument that literary histories are recyclical, always "made out of literary histories," in *Is Literary History Possible?* (Baltimore: Johns Hopkins University Press, 1992), 73.

15. Ralph Hanna, "Alliterative Poetry," in *The Cambridge History of Medieval English Literature,* ed. David Wallace (Cambridge: Cambridge University Press, 1999), 488–512 [497]. Hanna provides a crucial revision of temporal "Othering" by Revivalist critics, who "pack" alliterative poems into the "second half of the fourteenth century, to construct a deep and integrated model of Revival," despite the fact that numerous poems clearly date from well into the fifteenth century (495–97).

16. Ibid., 511; 504; 512.

17. Ibid., 511.

18. Christine Chism, *Alliterative Revivals* (Philadelphia: University of Pennsylvania Press, 2002), 1.

19. On medievalist fantasy and social welfare programs, see L. O. Aranye Fradenburg, *Sacrifice Your Love: Psychoanalysis, Historicism, Chaucer* (Minneapolis: University of Minnesota Press, 2002), 248; on medievalist "complicity" in nationalist historiography, see Fradenburg, "'So That We May Speak of Them': Enjoying the Middle Ages," *New Literary History* 28.2 (1997): 205–30 [218–19].

20. Stephen G. Nichols, "Writing the New Middle Ages," *PMLA* 120.2 (2005): 422–41 [423]. On nationalist ideology and the German Romantic view of nations as natural entities whose particular cultures need to be preserved through state development, see Elie Kedourie, *Nationalism,* 3rd ed. (London: Hutchinson, 1966), 55–68.

21. See Reginald Horsman's anlysis of Enlightenment universalism and Romantic particularism, in *Race and Manifest Destiny: The Origins of American Racial Anglo-Saxonism* (Cambridge, MA: Harvard University Press, 1981), 98–138.

22. On Saxon-Norman struggle in Victorian literary historiography, see Clare A.

Simmons, *Reversing the Conquest: History and Myth in Nineteenth-Century British Literature* (New Brunswick, NJ: Rutgers University Press, 1990), 43–73.

23. Horsman links the development of American racialism with efforts to justify dispossessions of Indians understood as savages. According to Horsman, a majority of Americans maintained an Anglo-Saxonist self-perception by the 1848 close of the U.S.-Mexican War (see *Race*, 189–228). I follow Horsman in restricting the term "Anglo-Saxonist" to the sense of medievalist, ethno-historical myths about Germanic origins. I do not use the word to mean a "self-conscious national and racial identity" that "came into being among the early peoples of the region that we now call England," as do Allen J. Frantzen and John D. Niles in "Anglo-Saxonism and Medievalism," their introduction to *Anglo-Saxonism and the Construction of Social Identity* (Gainesville: University Press of Florida, 1997), 1–14 [1].

24. John Guillory, *Cultural Capital: The Problem of Literary Canon Formation* (Chicago: University of Chicago Press, 1993), 42.

25. Dipesh Chakrabarty, *Provincializing Europe: Postcolonial Thought and Historical Difference* (Princeton, NJ: Princeton University Press, 2008), 7–8.

26. See Walker Connor's study of shifting terminology in nation studies, particularly regarding conflations of nation and state, in *Ethnonationalism: The Quest for Understanding* (Princeton, NJ: Princeton University Press, 1994), 90–117. See also Susan Reynolds's discussion of the difficulties of mapping modern nationalism onto medieval political theory, for which reason Reynolds avoids the terms "nation" and "national," preferring "kingdom" and "regnal" to describe lay collective identities, in *Kingdoms and Communities in Western Europe, 900–1300* (Oxford: Oxford University Press, 1984), 250–54.

27. Kathy Lavezzo, "Introduction," in *Imagining a Medieval English Nation*, ed. Kathy Lavezzo (Minneapolis: University of Minnesota Press, 2004), vii–xxxiv [xvi–xvii].

28. Charlton T. Lewis, *An Elementary Latin Dictionary* (1890; Oxford: Oxford University Press, 1998), 527.

29. In the *Vulgate*, the catalogues of each of the three sons' descendants, each enumerating various ethnic groups called alternately *nationes* and *gentes*, are followed by the summary statement that it is from the *nationes* of Noah's three sons that all post-diluvium *gentes* are derived (Gen.10:32). Isidore of Seville follows his definition of "gentes," which he equates with "nationes" (IX.2.1), with an account of nearly all ethnic genealogies, as traceable to Japheth, Shem, and Ham, in *Isidori Hispalensis episcopi Etymologiarum sive Originum*, ed. William Lindsay (Oxford: Oxford University Press, 1911), IX.2.2–127. On the early modern spread of medieval genealogies of Noah's sons, see Benjamin Braude, "The Sons of Noah and the Construction of Ethnic and Geographical Identities in the Medieval and Early Modern Periods," *William and Mary Quarterly* 54 (1997): 103–42. On the confluence of geographic, ethnic, corporal, legal, and other forms of differentiation in the hybrid, fluid collective identities of the medieval West, see Jeffrey Jerome Cohen, *Hybridity, Identity, and Monstrosity in Medieval Britain: On Difficult Middles* (New York: Palgrave Macmillan, 2006), 11–42.

30. On the post-Romantic legacy of linguistic nationalism, see Kedourie, *Nationalism*, 62–73.

31. Anthony D. Smith, *The Ethnic Origins of Nations* (Oxford: Blackwell, 1986),

13–15. While discrete, stable, (pseudo-)scientifically endorsed races are post-Romantic products, there were clearly medieval modes of ethnic identification that made use of differences in culture and appearance; Smith's work helps avoid an alteritism that would erase ethnic difference from pre-modernity. On clear cases of ethnic differentiation in Anglo-Norman legislation and in Gerald of Wales's "area studies" (5–8), along with a critical introduction to a collection of articles theorizing pre-modern race, see Thomas Hahn, "The Difference the Middle Ages Makes: Color and Race before the Modern World," *Journal of Medieval and Early Modern Studies* 31.1 (2001): 1–37.

32. Smith, *Ethnic Origins,* 212; 175.

33. See Alfred P. Smyth's critique of teleological historiographies that seek out "signs of constitutional and political sophistication" to be interpreted as early stages of developing English, Irish, Welsh, or Scottish nations, in his preface to *Medieval Europeans: Studies in Ethnic Identity and National Perspectives in Medieval Europe,* ed. Alfred P. Smyth (New York: St. Martin's Press, 1998), xii–xiii.

34. On narratives of British national community that defy a progressivist historiography, see Patricia Clare Ingham, *Sovereign Fantasies: Arthurian Romance and the Making of Britain* (Philadelphia: University of Pennsylvania Press, 2001), 9–10.

35. On the late-eighteenth-century Creole production of the nation, with European imitations appearing around 1820, see Benedict Anderson, *Imagined Communities: Reflections on the Origin and Spread of Nationalism,* rev. ed. (London: Verso, 1991), 47–81.

36. Ibid., 47–65; 45.

37. Ibid., 45.

38. Ibid., 144–45.

39. On the nation's rise relative to industrial-capitalist growth, which requires population homogenization effected through a confluence of general education, mass communications systems, and bureaucratic centralization, see Ernest Gellner, *Nations and Nationalism* (Ithaca, NY: Cornell University Press, 1983), 19–52. For a general analysis of the global economic transformation brought about by industrialization, a process begun in Britain, see Eric Hobsbawm, *Industry and Empire: The Birth of the Industrial Revolution,* rev. ed., ed. Chris Wrigley (New York: New Press, 1999), 34–111.

40. Ibid., 48.

41. Ibid. See Connor's argument that ethnic identification underwrites the nation, a fundamentally psychological entity, in *Ethnonationalism,* 90–117.

42. Jeffrey Jerome Cohen, "Introduction," in *The Postcolonial Middle Ages,* ed. Jeffrey Jerome Cohen (New York: St. Martin's Press, 2000), 1–17 [5].

43. On Edward I having achieved imperial sway in Britain, see R. R. Davies, *The First English Empire: Power and Identities in the British Isles, 1093–1343* (Oxford: Oxford University Press, 2000), 22–30.

44. Michael Hardt and Antonio Negri, *Empire* (Cambridge, MA: Harvard University Press, 2000), xiv–xv.

45. On the transnational as a methodological concept replacing "fixed and exclusionist" identities with a "relation identity" generated by multi-cultural influences, see Carine M. Mardorossian, *Reclaiming Difference: Caribbean Women Rewrite Postcolonialism* (Charlottesville: University of Virginia Press, 2005), 3–7.

46. Kathleen Davis, "National Writing in the Ninth Century: A Reminder for Post-

colonial Thinking about the Nation," *Journal of Medieval and Early Modern Studies* 28 (1998): 612–37 [612–13].

47. See Geoffrey of Monmouth's widely disseminated *The History of the Kings of Britain* (c.1136), ed. Michael D. Reeve, trans. Neil Wright (Woodbridge: Boydell, 2007), 30–33; 34–35; 84–85.

48. Liah Greenfeld not only locates the "birth of the English nation" in the sixteenth century, but also attributes the "birth of nationalism" to the English example, in *Nationalism: Five Roads to Modernity* (Cambridge, MA: Harvard University Press, 1992), 23; 29–87.

49. Pierre Bourdieu, "Rethinking the State: Genesis and Structure of the Bureaucratic Field," in *Practical Reason*, trans. Loïc Wacquant and Samar Farage (1994; Stanford, CA: Stanford University Press, 1998), 35–63 [46].

50. Ibid.

51. Derek Pearsall, "Chaucer and Englishness," in *Chaucer's Cultural Geography*, ed. Kathryn L. Lynch (New York: Routledge, 2002), 281–301 [294–96].

52. See N. F. Blake's criticism that the Alliterative Revival theory departs from standard literary historical practice by isolating alliterative poems according to meter, in "Middle English Alliterative Revivals," *Review* 1 (1979): 205–14 [205].

53. On Chaucer's exclusive use of rhyme and regular syllable patterns in his poetry, see Norman Davis, "Language and Versification," in *The Riverside Chaucer*, 3rd ed., gen. ed. Larry D. Benson (Boston: Houghton Mifflin, 1987), xxix-xlv [xlii-xlv].

54. Chaucer, *The Canterbury Tales*, in *Riverside Chaucer*, ed. Benson, X.41–42. All citations from Chaucer are from the *Riverside;* my translations. I translate "fe fi fo" to indicate the barbaric sounds in which the Parson encodes non-Southern verse.

55. Most critics believe Chaucer's Parson alludes to the *aa ax* alliterative long line (with *a* marking alliterating stresses, and *x* marking non-alliterating stresses). However, Blake asserts that the Parson refers only generally to alliterative patterns, which are also found in rhythmical prose, in "Chaucer and the Alliterative Romances," *Chaucer Review* 3 (1969): 163–69 [165]. John Bowers argues that the singleness of Chaucer's mention of alliterative verse was not due to unfamiliarity, since alliterative poets competed alongside him in the London book-trade, in *Chaucer and Langland: The Antagonistic Tradition* (Notre Dame, IN: University of Notre Dame Press, 2007), 15–17.

56. Chaucer, *Troilus and Criseyde*, ed. Benson, V.1793–96.

57. Chaucer's gesture may be repeated by Philip Sidney, whose singing out of Chaucer for praise in that otherwise "misty time" of medieval English poetry suggests willful occlusion of alliterative (and, of course, all other non-Chaucerian) verse, in the *Defence of Poesy*, in *Sir Philip Sidney*, ed. Katherine Duncan-Jones (Oxford: Oxford University Press, 1994), 134. That Sidney would have had no knowledge of alliterative verse seems unlikely, considering the fascination with metrical variety that he reveals throughout the *Eclogues* of *The Old Arcadia*. George Puttenham suggests significant literary historical appreciation of alliterative verse in Sidney's day, listing "that nameles" writer of "Piers Plowman" among the "most commended writers in our English Poesie," in *The Arte of English Poesie* (1589; Menston, UK: Scolar Press, 1968), 74.

58. Richard Helgerson, *Forms of Nationhood: The Elizabethan Writing of England* (Chicago: University of Chicago Press, 1992), 25. In arguing for an early modern English nation that legitimized itself by appeals to transcendent notions of "order and

civility," even as it "enforced boundaries of class" (10–11), Helgerson asserts that the "nation-state" can only "constitute" itself by distinguishing itself from its "former self or selves" (22). Helgerson's class-striated, literarily self-conscious England is not a nation in the modernist sense, for it lacks a leveling of socioeconomic ranks, and would require generations of governmental centralization enabled by print-capitalism to thoroughly disseminate a uniform culture; see Eric Hobsbawm, *Nations and Nationalism since 1780: Programme, Myth, Reality,* 2nd ed. (Cambridge: Cambridge University Press, 1992), 9–12. On medievalist debate concerning English nationhood, and for an argument that medieval, proto-nationalist imaginings were sharpened by self-perception as a uniquely marginal community, see Kathy Lavezzo, *Angels on the Edge of the World: Geography, Literature, and English Community, 1000–1534* (Ithaca, NY: Cornell University Press, 2006), 8–11.

59. William Dunbar, *The Goldyn Targe,* in *Selected Poems,* ed. Priscilla Bawcutt (London: Longman, 1996), 231–45. On the reception of Chaucer in Scotland, see L. O. Aranye Fradenburg, "The Scottish Chaucer," in *Writing After Chaucer,* ed. Daniel J. Pinti (New York: Garland, 1998), 167–77. On the competition between alliterative and "Chaucerian" styles in fifteenth-century Scotland, see William Craigie, "The Scottish Alliterative Poems," *Proceedings of the British Academy* 28 (London: Humphrey Milford, 1942), 1–20.

60. Bawcutt, ed., in Dunbar, *Selected Poems,* 33–57 [33].

61. Critics sometimes argue that the *Gawain*-poet refers to the alliterative long line by describing his verse as "wyth lel letters loken" [bound together with loyal letters] (35), though this seems vague enough to refer to any metrically composed—and hence memorable—work (*Sir Gawain and the Green Knight,* ed. William Vantuono, rev. ed. [Notre Dame, IN: University of Notre Dame Press, 1999]; my translation). William offers a more suggestive reference with his worry in *William of Palerne* that his "metur" is not to everyone's delight; see G. H. V. Bunt's edition (Groningen, Netherlands: Bouma's Boekhuis, 1985), 5524; Turville-Petre reads this as anxiety concerning audience resistance to a newly revived prosody, in *Alliterative Revival,* 24–25.

62. See Ronald J. Deibert, *Parchment, Printing, and Hypermedia: Communication in World Order Transformation* (New York: Columbia University Press, 1997), 105; N. F. Blake, *The English Language in Medieval Literature* (London: Methuen, 1977), 42–50; Paula Blank, *Broken English: Dialects and the Politics of Language in Renaissance Writings* (London: Routledge, 1996), 7–32; and Anderson, *Imagined Communities,* 41–46.

63. George Saintsbury, *A History of English Prosody, from the Twelfth Century to the Present Day,* 3 vols. (London: Macmillan, 1906–10), I.110.

64. Alice Chandler, *A Dream of Order: The Medieval Ideal in Nineteenth-Century English Literature* (Lincoln: University of Nebraska Press, 1970), 195–96; 7–10. Chandler argues that "naturalist" medievalists (e.g., William Morris) looked to a Middle Ages that was more attuned to nature, emotion, and heroism, while "feudalist" medievalists (e.g., Walter Scott) looked to the medieval political order for social harmony and stability missing from modernity (195–96). For a survey of nineteenth-century British applications of medievalism in educational, recreational, social, and political practices, see Mark Girouard, *The Return to Camelot: Chivalry and the English Gentleman* (New Haven, CT: Yale University Press, 1981), 130–293.

65. See Chandler, *Dream*, 184–230.

66. F. V. N. Painter, *Introduction to English Literature, Including a Number of Classic Works with Notes* (Boston: Leach, Shewell, and Sanborn, 1894), 3.

67. On the participation of nineteenth-century American and Scottish critics alongside English Anglo-Saxonists, see Horsman, *Race*, 62–76; 158–86. On Virginia-born Franklin Verzelius Newton Painter (1852–1931), see Richard Henry Hudnall's biography in *Library of Southern Literature*, ed. Edwin Anderson Alderman and Joel Chandler Harris, vol. 9 (New Orleans: Martin & Hoyt, 1917), 3889–94.

68. My formulation here depends on Friedrich Nietzsche's evolutionary view that "what does not kill me makes me stronger," in *The Twilight of the Idols* (1889), trans. R. J. Hollingdale (New York: Penguin, 1968), 23. See also Perkins' speculation that "literary histories are shaped by the pleasures of aggression" (*Is Literary History*, 33).

69. On racist views of Anglo-Saxon purity in Britain and America, see Horsman, *Race*, 61–77; 116–38. While many nineteenth-century Anglo-Saxonists saw the Normans as part of a larger Germanic-Norse family (ibid., 62–68; 162–64), Revivalist discourse typically insists on French-speaking Normans as introducing a foreign culture into Saxon England.

70. Reuben Post Halleck, *History of English Literature* (New York: American Book Company, 1900), 47.

71. See Simmons, *Reversing the Conquest*, 201–2. Ralph Waldo Emerson shares with Revivalists an alternative, evolutionary view of hybridity, arguing that the English are "collectively a better race than any from which they are derived," in *English Traits* (Boston: Phillips, Sampson, and Company, 1857), 56–58.

72. Blake, "Middle English," 207. Blake's specific target for criticism is Turville-Petre's *The Alliterative Revival*.

73. Hanna argues that "north Yorkshire" is a "generative provincial culture" often "ignored" in analyses of alliterative meter, in "Defining Middle English Alliterative Poetry," 55.

74. On the alliterative line in the York mysteries, see Jesse Byers Reese, "Alliterative Verse in the York Cycle," *Studies in Philology* 48 (1951): 639–68. On urban context as essential to the York pageants, see Sarah Beckwith, *Signifying God: Social Relation and Symbolic Act in the York Corpus Christi Plays* (Chicago: University of Chicago Press, 2001), 31–41. Robert Thornton's two miscellanies, British Library Additional MS 31042 and Lincoln Cathedral MS 91, provide unique texts of the Alliterative *Morte Arthure*, *Wynnere and Wastoure*, the *Parlement of the Thre Ages*, and *Cheuelere Assigne*, as well as texts of the *Siege of Jerusalem*, the *Awntyrs off Arthure*, and the *Quatrefoil of Love*. On Thornton's life and work, see George Keiser's studies, "Lincoln Cathedral Library MS 91: Life and Milieu of the Scribe," *Studies in Bibliography* 32 (1979): 158–79; and "More Light on the Life of Robert Thornton," *Studies in Bibliography* 36 (1983): 11–19.

75. Adrian Hastings, *The Construction of Nationhood: Ethnicity, Religion and Nationalism* (Cambridge: Cambridge University Press, 1997), 4; 22–39.

76. M. T. Clanchy, *England and Its Rulers, 1066–1272,* 2nd ed. (Oxford: Blackwell, 1998), 173–89.

77. On the fluid nature of political loyalties in medieval regions, and on scholars' projection of current geographical understanding of British nations onto medieval po-

litical communities, see Davies, *First English Empire*, 54–88.

78. See Smith's argument that class and regional differences precluded medieval English nationhood, with policies and communications technologies unable to generate fully "standardized conditions" of bureaucracy and labor, in *Ethnic Origins*, 175. On the perception of a social gulf between the English North and South, see Katie Wales, *Northern English: A Cultural and Social History* (Cambridge: Cambridge University Press, 2006), 1–31; 64–115; and Helen M. Jewell, *The North-South Divide: The Origins of Northern Consciousness in England* (Manchester: Manchester University Press, 1994), 119–51. Robert W. Barrett, Jr., urges scholars to coordinate analyses of regional perspectives with studies of medieval English national identity, in *Against All England: Regional Identity and Cheshire Writing, 1195–1656* (Notre Dame, IN: University of Notre Dame Press, 2009), 1–23.

79. On scholarly claims for a late-medieval "revival" of a defunct alliterative line, as against arguments for the meter's "survival" through oral channels, see David Lawton, "Middle English Alliterative Poetry: An Introduction," in *Middle English Alliterative Poetry and Its Literary Background*, ed. David Lawton (Cambridge: D. S. Brewer, 1982), 1–19; 125–29. Pearsall assumes multiple generations of (now lost) manuscript survival of alliterative texts in Worcestershire, in "Origins," 6–17.

80. On the Greater Westminster area as an administrative center that significantly shaped late-medieval literary culture, see Kathryn Kerby-Fulton and Steven Justice, "Langlandian Reading Circles and the Civil Service in London and Dublin, 1380–1427," in *New Medieval Literatures*, ed. Wendy Scase, Rita Copeland, and David Lawton (Oxford: Clarendon Press, 1997), 59–83; and Ethan Knapp, *The Bureaucratic Muse: Thomas Hoccleve and the Literature of Late Medieval England* (University Park: Pennsylvania State University Press, 2001), 4–9; 20–36.

81. Gabrielle M. Spiegel, "History, Historicism, and the Social Logic of the Text in the Middle Ages," *Speculum* 65 (1990): 79–86 [77].

82. In interrelating desires in medieval texts with my own critical concerns, I am indebted to much medievalist reflection on negotiating alterity. Carolyn Dinshaw, in critiquing conceptions of the Middle Ages as an utterly pre-modern totality, urges critical vigilance in identifying potential allies in the political work of "coalition building," in *Getting Medieval: Sexualities and Communities, Pre- and Postmodern* (Durham, NC: Duke University Press, 1999), 12–21; David Aers reflects on the recovery of medieval labor history erased by New Historicism's reductive genealogy of modern individualism, in "A Whisper in the Ear of Early Modernists; or, Reflections on Literary Critics Writing the 'History of the Subject,'" in *Culture and History, 1350–1600: Essays on English Communities, Identities and Writing*, ed. David Aers (Detroit: Wayne State University Press, 1992), 177–202 [178–79]; and Lee Patterson asserts the "political" nature of all forms of historicism, suggesting that modern desires could never be fully extracted from the interpretation of medieval texts, in *Negotiating*, ix–xi.

Chapter 1

1. Turville-Petre, *Alliterative Revival*, 27.
2. William Henry Schofield, *English Literature from the Norman Conquest to*

Chaucer (New York: Macmillan, 1906), 372.

3. Saintsbury, *History,* I.100–101.

4. J. P. Oakden, *Alliterative Poetry in Middle English,* 2 vols. (Manchester: Manchester University Press, 1930–35), II.86–87; I.153. Oakden sees the alliterative "school" originating in the "west," and being displaced as "shorter and more popular" poems appeared in the "north" (II.87).

5. Dorothy Everett, "The Alliterative Revival," in *Essays on Middle English Literature,* ed. Patricia Kean (London: Oxford University Press, 1959), 46–96 [46].

6. Pearsall, "Origins," 2.

7. Hanna, "Alliterative Poetry," 488; 508; 504.

8. On Percy's *Reliques* as a foundational text for a professionalizing, nineteenth-century literary criticism, see Matthews, *The Making of Middle English,* 3–24; and Arthur Johnston, *Enchanted Ground: The Study of Medieval Romance in the Eighteenth Century* (London: Athlone Press, 1964), 75–99.

9. Thomas Percy, ed., *Reliques of Ancient English Poetry* (1765; rpt. Philadelphia: Porter & Coates, 1869), 266. Percy assumes the unrevivable death of alliterative meter, stating that "the ravages of time will not suffer us now to produce a regular series of poems entirely written in it" (266).

10. Ibid., 270. On the criteria for alliterative meter, see Hanna, "Defining Middle English Alliterative Poetry," 43–63. Angus McIntosh differentiates alliterative meter from "homomorphic" prosodies, in which lines consist of regular dispositions of stressed and unstressed syllables (i.e., feet); "heteromorphic" lines (such as the alliterative long line) have varying feet and hence variant rhythms; see "Early English Alliterative Verse," in *Middle English Alliterative Poetry,* ed. Lawton, 20–33 [21–22]. Alliterative verse was not unknown before Percy: some scholars have recognized the strong-stress nature of Old English meter since the mid-sixteenth-century development of Anglo-Saxon studies; see Allen J. Frantzen, *Desire for Origins: New Language, Old English, and Teaching the Tradition* (New Brunswick, NJ: Rutgers University Press, 1990), 35–50. However, a number of key critics either ignore or misunderstand strong-stress meter: Sidney makes no mention of alliterative verse in his *Defence* (c. 1580), while Puttenham dismisses *Piers Plowman*'s prosody as "but loose meetre," in *Arte,* 74.

11. Later editions reveal the seminal status of Warton's work for a slowly professionalizing literary criticism. Matthews memorably describes Warton's text after having passed through editions by Richard Price (1824), Richard Taylor (1840), and William Carew Hazlitt (1871) as "a bloated compendium encrusted with all the quarrelsome learning of a century of antiquarian dispute and fact-grubbing" (*The Making of Middle English,* 31). On the foundational status of Warton's literary historiography, see Johnston, *Enchanted Ground,* 100–119; and Trevor Ross, *The Making of the English Literary Canon: From the Middle Ages to the Late Eighteenth Century* (Montreal: McGill-Queen's University Press, 1998), 261–67. On Warton-era literary histories joining with novels in a new historiographical reflection on continuity that had escaped empiricist historical treatises, see Ruth Mack, *Literary Historicity: Literature and Historical Change in Eighteenth-Century Britain* (Stanford, CA: Stanford University Press, 2009), 3–5.

12. Thomas Warton, *The History of English Poetry, from the Close of the Eleventh to the Commencement of the Eighteenth Century,* 3 vols. (London: J. Dodsley, 1774–81), I.i.

13. Ibid., I.ii; I.vi.

14. Ibid., I.vi. See Simpson's argument that Warton's narrative of the sixteenth-century humanist break with barbaric medieval romance appropriates the "terms of romance" (*Reform,* 262).

15. Warton, *History,* I.ii.

16. In commentary on *Piers Plowman* chosen to replace Warton's analysis, Skeat directly attacks Warton, arguing that "it is untrue that Langland adopts the style of the Anglo-Saxon poets," and that Langland chose the meter because it was recognizably and "thoroughly English," in Thomas Warton, *History of English Poetry from the Twelfth to the Close of the Sixteenth Century,* 4 vols., rev. ed., ed. W. Carew Hazlitt (1871; rpt., New York: Haskell House, 1970), 250. Skeat here cites George Perkins Marsh, who argues that Langland's work is utterly un-Saxon, instead "exhibit[ing] the characteristic moral and mental traits of the Englishman, as clearly and unequivocally as the most national portions of the works of Chaucer or of any other native writer," in *The Origin and History of the English Language* (London: Sampson Low, 1862), 303.

17. Warton, *History* (1774–81), I.266.

18. On British national identity as having developed after the 1707 Act of Union between England and Scotland, with empire, warfare, and Protestantism binding formerly distinct communal identities, see Linda Colley, *Britons: Forging the Nation, 1707–1837* (New Haven, CT: Yale University Press, 1992), 364–75.

19. Anderson, *Imagined Communities,* 47–65.

20. Gellner, *Nations and Nationalism,* 53–62.

21. Anderson, *Imagined Communities,* 201.

22. Ibid.

23. Eric Hobsbawm, "Inventing Traditions," in *The Invention of Tradition,* ed. Eric Hobsbawm and Terence Ranger (Cambridge: Cambridge University Press, 1983), 1–14 [13–14].

24. Anderson, *Imagined Communities,* 195–96.

25. Gellner, *Nations and Nationalism,* 55.

26. Deanne Williams, *The French Fetish from Chaucer to Shakespeare* (Cambridge: Cambridge University Press, 2004), 3. On the evidence for ethnic diversity within English culture, and on resistance to such views being based on notions of separate races in Victorian pseudo-science, see David Miles, *The Tribes of Britain: Who Are We? And Where Do We Come From?,* rev. ed. (London: Phoenix, 2005), 7–34.

27. On the rise of the Norman Yoke theory among scholars of the Society of Antiquaries, and on its prominent place among English Radicals, particularly the Levellers, see Christopher Hill, "The Norman Yoke," in *Puritanism and Revolution: Studies in Interpretation of the English Revolution of the Seventeenth Century* (1958; Harmondsworth: Penguin, 1986), 58–125; see also Horsman, *Race and Manifest Destiny,* 11–24; and Gerald Newman, *The Rise of English Nationalism: A Cultural History, 1740–1830,* rev. ed. (New York: St. Martin's Press, 1997), 189–91. On Saxon and Norman stereotypes from the sixteenth to the nineteenth century, see Simmons, *Reversing the Conquest,* 13–41.

28. Krishan Kumar, *The Making of English National Identity* (Cambridge: Cambridge University Press, 2003), 48–49.

29. I take this description from Suzanne Conklin Akbari's analysis of distinct local

communities formed by assimilative Norman conquerors, in "Between Diaspora and Conquest: Norman Assimilation in Petrus Alfonsi's *Disciplina Clericalis* and Marie de France's *Fables*," in *Cultural Diversity in the British Middle Ages: Archipelago, Island, England*, ed. Jeffrey Jerome Cohen (New York: Palgrave Macmillan, 2008), 17–37 [19–23].

30. On William the Conqueror's pragmatic self-presentation as king of the English, and on continuity of loyalties and traditions between Anglo-Saxon and Anglo-Norman England, see David C. Douglas, *William the Conqueror: The Norman Impact upon England* (Berkeley: University of California Press, 1964), 271–75; and Kumar, *The Making of English National Identity*, 49.

31. On nationalism in nineteenth-century philologies, see the essays collected in Bloch and Nichols, eds., *Medievalism;* Horsman, *Race and Manifest Destiny*, 29–38; and Patrick J. Geary, *The Myth of Nations: The Medieval Origins of Europe* (Princeton, NJ: Princeton University Press, 2002), 29–36.

32. On the nineteenth-century development of racist Anglo-Saxonism, which shifts from general praise of liberty-loving Anglo-Saxons to a pseudo-scientific doctrine of racial superiority in which Anglo-Saxons are an elite sub-group within an allegedly superior "Germanic" branch of a "Caucasian" race, see Horsman, *Race and Manifest Destiny*, 25–61.

33. Defining the nation as a community imagined as "inherently limited and sovereign," Anderson insists that every nation sees its borders as "finite" and its place as situated on a plane with "other nations" (*Imagined Communities*, 6–7).

34. Marsh writes that "Early English poetry divided itself into two schools," with one "follow[ing] Continental models in literature," while "the other sought to recommend itself to the taste and character of the more numerous part of the population, by reviving the laws of Saxon verse, some remains of which still lingered in the memory of the common people" (*Origin and History*, 276).

35. Horsman, *Race and Manifest Destiny*, 180–82.

36. On ten Brink's background, see A. H. Tolman, "Obituary: Bernhard ten Brink," *Modern Language Notes* 7 (1892): 191–92.

37. Henry Louis Gates, Jr., "Writing 'Race' and the Difference It Makes," *Critical Inquiry* 12.1 (1985): 1–21 [3].

38. Hippolyte Taine, *L'Histoire de la littérature anglaise*, 4 vols. (Paris: Librairie Hachette, 1863–64), I.xxii. As Taine's tripartite literary historical scheme is well known, I leave the terms untranslated. All English translations derive from Taine, *History of English Literature*, trans. H. van Laun (New York: Grosset & Dunlap, 1908). I incorporate the original French in brackets where significant alternatives might be imagined.

39. Taine, *History*, I.17.

40. On the "invader thesis" in nineteenth-century Victorian archaeology, according to which "waves" of invading Saxons, Vikings, and Normans merely "calmed down" enough to become "proto-English," until the "Norman Conquest" enabled truly permanent settlement, enabling national "progress," see Robert Colls, *Identity of England* (Oxford: Oxford University Press, 2002), 133. Despite the Normans' singular role, Colls shows, the "invader thesis" inspired much Victorian Anglo-Saxonism, which resurfaces as an anti-immigrant reaction in England, beginning in the 1940s (133–39).

41. Geary, *Myth of Nations*, 12.
42. David Wallace, *Premodern Places: Calais to Surinam, Chaucer to Aphra Behn* (Madden: Blackwell, 2004), 26–27.
43. Taine, *History*, I.81 [*Histoire* I.60].
44. The Reformation is accorded a foundational role for a precocious English nationalism, in Greenfeld, *Nationalism*, 51–53; and Hastings, *Construction of Nationhood*, 57–60.
45. Gellner, *Nations and Nationalism*, 29–38.
46. Taine, *History*, I.117–18 [I. 105].
47. Ibid., I.108 [I.120].
48. Ibid., I.120 [I.108].
49. Ibid.
50. Ibid., I. 140–41 [I.134].
51. Ibid., I. 134 [140–41].
52. Warner Brothers' 1938 *The Adventures of Robin Hood* (directed by Michael Curtiz and William Keighley; written by Norman Reilly Raine and Seton I. Miller) stages explicit Saxon-Norman conflict in 1191, with simply dressed, hard-working "Saxons" oppressed by "Norman" nobles prone to feasting and armed tax collection. Resistance to the Norman juggernaut is played out in the forest-zones beyond the reach of the Norman war machine, with Robin Hood highlighting the national nature of his insurgency: "I'll organize a revolt. . . . And I'll never rest until every Saxon in this shire can stand up free men and strike a blow for Richard and England." That Revivalist formulations parallel such cinematic story-telling supports Fradenburg's view of the profound interrelation of fantasy and scholarship—that "philology also dreams" ("'So That We May Speak of Them,'" 210).
53. Taine, *History*, I.161 [I.160].
54. Ibid., I.161–62 [I.161].
55. Ibid.
56. Ibid., I. 165; 169 [I.166; 170].
57. Bernhard ten Brink, *Early English Literature (to Wiclif)*, trans. Horace M. Kennedy, 2 vols. (London: George Bell & Sons, 1891), I.329; Bernhard ten Brink, *Geschichte der Englischen Litteratur*, ed. Alois Brandl, 2 vol. (Berlin: Robert Oppenheim, 1877), I.411. For all citations from ten Brink, I utilize Horace M. Kennedy's translation, which was revised by ten Brink (vii–viii), and is a key source for Revivalist use of the term "Revival"; I incorporate bracketed translations from the original German when helpful. *Wiederaufblühen* could be more literally rendered as "reflowering."
58. Ibid., I.329–30 [I.412].
59. Ibid., I.330 [I.413].
60. Ibid.
61. Ibid.
62. Ibid., I.330 [I.413].
63. Ibid., I.332 [I.415].
64. Saintsbury, *History*, I.179.
65. On variations of the thirteen-line stanza form, see Thorlac Turville-Petre, 'Summer Sunday,' 'De Tribus Regibus Mortuis,' and 'The Awntyrs off Arthure': Three Poems in the Thirteen-Line Stanza.' *Review of English Studies* 25 (1970): 1–14; and

David Lawton, "The Diversity of Middle English Alliterative Poetry," *Leeds Studies in English* 20 (1989): 143–72 [151–64].

66. Saintsbury, *History*, I.110.
67. Ibid.
68. Ibid., I.179–80.
69. Halleck, *History*, 47.
70. Ibid.
71. Saintsbury, *History*, I.179–80.
72. Ibid.
73. Ibid., I.100–101.
74. Ibid., I.191.
75. Ibid., I.290–92.
76. Ibid.
77. On the Southampton-born Englishman Saintsbury (1845–1933), see A. Blyth Webster's "A Biographical Memoir," in *A Saintsbury Miscellany*, ed. Augustus Muir et al. (New York: Oxford University Press, 1947), 27–73.
78. Saintsbury, *History*, I.290–92.
79. On nationalist teleology and the organization of the past, see Gellner, *Nations and Nationalism*, 55–56.
80. On the idealization of a Middle Ages "home" by nineteenth-century British medievalist scholars and artists, see Chandler, *Dream of Order*, 10.
81. Gellner, *Nations and Nationalism*, 57.
82. Ibid., 55.
83. Insisting on the provincial nature of Scottish poet Huchown's verse, such critics work against what Robert Crawford analyzes as the tendency among modernizing Scottish critics to favor Southern English, in *Devolving English Literature*, 2nd ed. (Edinburgh: Edinburgh University Press, 2000), 16–44.
84. See Horsman's argument that the politico-religious histories of England and America predisposed these societies toward racialized historiography, in *Race and Manifest Destiny*, 22–28. If Anderson is correct in locating the nation's origins in Creole communities, then American Revivalist criticism had the longest nationalist gestation (see *Imagined Communities*, 50–65). Such American interventions may be motivated by what Biddick calls the "lingering magic power" of "English America," according to which American educational institutions prioritize English history in a joint Anglo-Saxonist imperialism (*Shock of Medievalism*, 59).
85. Derek Pearsall, "The Alliterative Revival: Origins and Social Backgrounds," in *Middle English Alliterative Poetry*, ed. Lawton, 34–53 [35].
86. Andrew of Wyntoun, *The Original Chronicle of Andrew of Wyntoun*, ed. F. J. Amours, 6 vols. (Edinburgh: W. Blackwood and Sons, 1903–14); my translations. The "Gest Hystoryalle" and the "Gest of Brutis aulde story" may simply be alternative titles for either of the Arthurian texts attributed to Huchown. F. J. Amours, strongly committed to a Scottish "Huchown," interprets the latter two texts as variant titles of the Alliterative *Morte Arthure*, in *Scottish Alliterative Poems in Riming Stanzas*, The Scottish Text Society 27; 38, 1897 (London: Johnson Reprint Corporation, 1966), lvi–lvii.
87. Amours, after describing the poet's dialect as of a "Northern" origin that could be either English or Scottish, cites external evidence in placing the *Pistill* in Scotland

(ibid., lxx; lxxxii). Alice Miskimin discusses the practical necessity of treating the *Pistill*-dialect as only generally "Northern," in her edition, *Susannah: An Alliterative Poem of the Fourteenth Century* (New Haven, CT: Yale University Press, 1969), 67–79. For arguments that *Pistill* can be attributed to Huchown, see Henry Noble MacCracken, "Concerning Huchown," *PMLA* 25 (1910): 507–34 [507–8]; ten Brink, *Geschichte*, II.402–3 [*History*, II.50–51]; and Pearsall, *Old English*, 321n.

88. Frederic Madden, ed., *Syr Gawayne: A Collection of Ancient Romance Poems, by Scottish and English Authors* (1839; New York: AMS, 1971), 301–4; italics in original. In his catalogue of dead poets, "The Lament for the Makaris," William Dunbar claims that Clerk of Tranent composed the "anteris of Gawane" [adventures of Gawain] (ed. Bawcutt, 65–66)

89. Richard Morris, ed., *Early English Alliterative Poems* (EETS o.s. 1, 1864), viii–ix; xviii–xxv.

90. F. J. Furnivall, ed., *The Stacions of Rome* (EETS o.s. 24, 1867). On Furnivall and the populist, patriotic foundations of the Early English Text Society, of which Furnivall was the driving force and primary director from 1864 until his 1910 death (and replacement by Israel Gollancz), see Matthews, *Making of Middle English*, 138–61; and William Benzie, *Dr. F. J. Furnivall: A Victorian Scholar Adventurer* (Norman, OK: Pilgrim, 1983), 117–56. On the relative strengths of Furnivall's passion and scholarship, see Richard J. Utz, "Enthusiast or Philologist? Professional Discourse and the Medievalism of Fredrick James Furnivall," in *Studies in Medievalism XI—Appropriating the Middle Ages: Scholarship, Politics, Fraud*, ed. Tom Shippey and Martin Arnold (Woodbridge: Boydell and Brewer, 2001), 188–212.

91. F. J. Furnivall, *Early English Text Society Annual Report*, February 1871, 1–2 [cited in Benzie, *Dr. F. J. Furnivall*, 131–32]. See also John Robert Seeley, "English in Schools," in *Lectures and Essays* (London: Macmillan, 1870), 217–44 [238–39].

92. On the EETS's early years, and on Furnivall's nationalist publishing aims, see Matthews, *Making of Middle English*, 151–57.

93. MacCracken, "Concerning Huchown," 507.

94. Ibid., 515–16. Neilson speaks dramatically of the "heroic extreme" to which his opponents Bradley and Gollancz went in "claiming Huchown as English," in *Huchown of the Awle Ryale, the Alliterative Poet: A Historical Criticism of Fourteenth Century Poems Ascribed to Sir Hew of Eglintoun* (Glasgow: James MacLehose and Son, 1902), 6.

95. MacCracken, "Concerning Huchown," 517–18; 519.

96. Neilson, *Huchown*, 14.

97. Ibid., viii.

98. On Francis Joseph Amours, see the anonymous obituary in *Scottish Historical Review* 8 (1911): 101–4.

99. Amours, ed., *Scottish Alliterative Poems*, lxxi. See also Moritz Trautmann, who restricts Huchown's authorship to the *Morte* and *Pistill*, in "Der Dichter Huchown und seine Werke," *Anglia* 1 (1878): 109–49.

100. Amours, ed., *Scottish Alliterative Poems*, lxxi. Amours cites as examples of Huchown's alleged identification with the Arthurian forces references to "oure seggez" [our men] (1422), "oure men" [our men] (1428), "oure rerwarde" [our rear guard] (1430), and "oure syde" [our side] (2802); see *The Alliterative 'Morte Arthure,'* ed. Valerie Krishna (New York: Burt Franklin, 1976).

101. Amours, ed., *Scottish Alliterative Poems*, lxxi.

102. Ibid., lxxxii.

103. For Chambers's biography, see Janet Percival, ed., *The Papers of Raymond Wilson Chambers (1874–1942)* (London: Library of University College, London, 1978). On Hulbert, see the Biographical Note to the James R. Hulbert Papers, Special Collections Research Center, University of Chicago Library.

104. Gates, "Writing 'Race,'" 4. See Gates's analysis of the post-Romantic, post-nationalist use of race as the "ultimate trope of difference" in literary historiography (5).

105. On late-nineteenth- and early-twentieth-century conflation of ethnicity and language in European nationalisms, see Hobsbawm, *Nations*, 102–3.

106. R. W. Chambers, *On the Continuity of English Prose from Alfred to More and his School* (EETS o.s. 191, 1932), lxv.

107. Ibid., lxvi–lxvii.

108. Ibid., lxvii. Chambers presumably means Langland and the *Gawain*-poet.

109. The interchangeability of "Saxon" and "English" in Chambers's Revivalist criticism recalls Anglo-Norman strategies of containment. See Robert M. Stein's argument that Norman cultural policing led William of Malmesbury to reduce Anglo-Saxon tribal and regnal differences to being "simply English," in "Making History English: Cultural Identity and Historical Explanation in William of Malmesbury and Laʒamon's *Brut*," in *Text and Territory: Geographical Imagination in the European Middle Ages*, ed. Sylvia Tomasch and Sealy Gilles (Philadelphia: University of Pennsylvania Press, 1998), 97–115 [98].

110. Chambers, *Continuity*, lxvi.

111. James R. Hulbert, "A Hypothesis Concerning the Alliterative Revival," *Modern Philology* 28 (1931): 405–22 [406–7].

112. Ibid., 409; 412.

113. Oakden situates alliterative verse primarily in the "west," with "some activity" in the equally provincial "north," in *Alliterative Poetry*, II.87.

114. Elizabeth Salter, "The Alliterative Revival," *Modern Philology* 64 (1966–67): 146–49; 233–37 [233–34].

115. Ibid., 147–49.

116. Turville-Petre, *Alliterative Revival*, 43. Turville-Petre notes that the key exception is *Alexander and Dindimus*, which entered into the "de-luxe" manuscript MS Digby 202 due to a scribe's mistaken belief that it supplied missing text in the French romance that occupies most of the illuminated manuscript (43). See also John Burrow's argument that the numerous and materially heterogeneous manuscripts of *Piers Plowman* were marketed for the fifteenth-century "bourgeoisie," in "The Audience of Piers Plowman," *Anglia* 75 (1957): 373–84 [377].

117. Turville-Petre, *Alliterative Revival*, 27.

118. Gellner, *Nations and Nationalism*, 1.

119. Hulbert, "Hypothesis," 412–13.

120. Gellner, *Nations and Nationalism*, 128.

121. On the material links among aristocratic libraries throughout England, see Salter, "Alliterative Revival," 146–50.

122. On Southerners' movement away from identification with a Norman feudal culture whose serf-holding justified slavery, to a post–Civil War identification with An-

glo-Saxons as the victims of conquest, see Gregory A. VanHoosier-Carey, "Byrthnoth in Dixie: The Emergence of Anglo-Saxon Studies in the Postbellum South," in *Anglo-Saxonism*, ed. Frantzen and Niles, 157–72 [161–67]. On Southern Anglo-Saxonism and the justification of slavery, see Horsman, *Race and Manifest Destiny*, 116–38.

123. Anderson, *Imagined Communities*, 200–201.

124. Ibid., 199–200; see Ernest Renan, "What is a Nation?," trans. Martin Thom, in *Nation and Narration*, ed. Homi K. Bhabha (1882; London: Routledge, 1990), 8–22 [11]; Renan, *Qu'est-ce Qu'une Nation?* (1882; Paris: R. Helleu, 1934), 30. Renan argues that "forgetting" [*l'oubli*] is a vital component of nation formation, insofar as it must consign to the shadows the violent foundations of the state—for "unity is always effected by means of brutality" [*l'unité se fait toujours brutalement*], in "What is a Nation?", 11; Renan, *Qu'est-ce Qu'une Nation?*, 25–26. On the violence against Huguenots in the 1572 massacres, see Barbara B. Diefendorf, *The St. Bartholomew's Day Massacre: A Brief History with Documents* (New York: Bedford/St. Martin's, 2009). On the military suppression of the Cathar movement, see Joseph R. Strayer, *The Albigensian Crusades*, with epilogue by Carol Lansing (1971; Ann Arbor: University of Michigan Press, 1992), 55–142.

125. Renan argues, "No French citizen knows whether he is a Burgundian, an Alan, a Taïfale, or a Visigoth" [*Aucun citoyen français ne sait s'il est Burgonde, Alain, Taifale, Visigoth*], while each such citizen shares the constitutive forgetting of pre-modern traumas; see "What is a Nation?", 11"; *Qu'est-ce Qu'une Nation?*, 30.

126. Anderson, *Imagined Communities*, 201.

127. Charles Moorman, "The English Alliterative Revival and the Literature of Defeat," *Chaucer Review* 16.1 (1981): 85–100 [96].

128. Ibid., 90.

129. Ibid.

130. See Michelle R. Warren's analysis of the genealogical critical practice of "strategically deploying ethnic and family resemblance as well as difference" to forge "continuities across time," in *History on the Edge: Excalibur and the Borders of Britain* (Minneapolis: University of Minnesota Press, 2000), 11.

131. Geoffrey Shepherd, "The Nature of Alliterative Poetry in Late Medieval England," *Proceedings of the British Academy* 56 (1970): 57–76 [180].

132. Ibid., 179; 183.

133. W. P. Ker, *The Dark Ages* (1904; rpt. New York: Mentor, 1958), 15; 14. Ker's book was originally the first volume of the George Saintsbury-edited series, *Periods of European Literature* (1897–1907). On Ker's distinction of an "English, [N]ordic, and primitive" medieval "traditionalism" and a romantic "medieval modernity," see John Ganim, "The Myth of Medieval Romance," in *Medievalism*, ed. Bloch and Nichols, 148–66 [156–58].

134. Ker, *Dark Ages*, 20.

135. Though there have been debates concerning the possibility of a half-verse with three major stresses, most scholars accept Marie Borroff's resolution of such stresses as "secondary," in *Sir Gawain and the Green Knight: A Stylistic and Metrical Study* (New Haven, CT: Yale University Press, 1962), 198–203. To my knowledge, only Robert William Sapora, Jr., denies the caesura's essential role in alliterative verse, in *A Theory of Middle English Alliterative Meter with Critical Applications* (Cambridge, MA: Me-

dieval Academy of America, 1977), 17–18. Besides the counter-evidence that caesurae are often marked in late-medieval manuscripts, see the criticisms put forth by Stephen A. Barney, "Langland's Prosody: The State of Study," in *Endless Knot*, ed. Tavormina and Yeager, 65–85 [74–75]; and Hoyt N. Duggan, "Alliterative Patterning as a Basis for Emendation in Middle English Alliterative Poetry," *Studies in the Age of Chaucer* 8 (1986): 73–105 [77n].

136. Thomas Cable, *The English Alliterative Tradition* (Philadelphia: University of Pennsylvania Press, 1991), 63–65.

137. Standard scansion marks alliterating stresses with the same letter, non-alliterating stresses with an *x*, and the caesura by a space.

138. Skeat, "Essay on Alliterative Poetry," xi–xxxix [xviii]; italics in original.

139. Ibid.; italics in original.

140. McIntosh, "Early English Alliterative Verse," 21–22.

141. Hanna, "Defining Middle English Alliterative Poetry," 50–51.

142. Duggan, "Alliterative Patterning," 76–77.

143. Stephanie Trigg, "Israel Gollancz's *Wynnere and Wastoure*: Political Satire or Editorial Politics?" in *Medieval English Religious and Ethical Literature*, ed. Gregory Kratzmann and James Simpson (Cambridge: D. S. Brewer, 1987), 115–27 [121]. In his review of Gollancz's edition, John Steadman argues that "the poem is boldly rewritten," in *Modern Language Notes* 36 (1921): 103–10 [105].

144. While he does not discuss Duggan's database, Barney argues that the "corpus" of late-medieval alliterative poetic material should be "defined precisely" and its "textual status" (including "editorial interventions") made clear, in "Langland's Prosody," 69; 81–82.

145. Texts in alliterative meter typically display variation in stress-patterns. The notable exception is the *Gest Hystoriale of the Destruction of Troy*, a late (possibly sixteenth-century) and very lengthy text (Hanna, "Alliterative Poetry," 497), which has been scanned as consisting of 99 percent *aa ax* lines (Oakden, *Alliterative Poetry*, I.169).

146. Duggan, "Alliterative Patterning," 82.

147. Susanna G. Fein, "The Ghoulish and the Ghastly: A Moral Aesthetic in Middle English Alliterative Verse," *Modern Language Quarterly* 48 (1987): 3–19 [3; 5–6].

148. Ibid., 16; 18.

149. See Lawton's survey of literary historical theories of alliterative verse, and his analysis of key evidence for regionalist alliterative movements, in "Diversity of Middle English Alliterative Poetry," 143–72.

150. David A. Lawton, "The Unity of Middle English Alliterative Poetry," *Speculum* 58 (1983): 72–94 [74]. Lawton cites the "challenge" of N. F. Blake's doubts concerning a single alliterative school as inspiring his argument for unity (73).

151. Ibid., 73; 92.

152. Ibid., 76.

153. Fein, "Ghoulish and the Ghastly," 19.

154. Saintsbury, *History*, I.101–2.

155. Ibid., I.100–101.

156. Crawford, *Devolving English Literature*, 18–38.

157. See Chakrabarty, *Provincializing Europe*, 8–9.

158. Citing topical references to the 1352 Statute of Treasons and to Chief Justice

William Shareshull's tenure, as well as heraldic references to Edward III and the Black Prince, Gollancz dates the poem to c. 1352–53, in his edition, *A Good Short Debate Between Winner and Waster* (London: Humphrey Milford, 1920). Gollancz's dating was seconded by J. M. Steadman, in "The Date of 'Winnere and Wastoure,'" *Modern Philology* 19 (1921): 211–19, and again by Oakden, in *Alliterative Poetry*, II.51. Hulbert, in "The Problems of Authorship and Date of *Wynnere and Wastoure*," *Modern Philology* 18 (1920–21): 31–40, argues for extending the dating to 1366 (the end of Shareshull's term), while Salter undermines earlier critics' assumptions of topicality, in "The Timeliness of *Wynnere and Wastoure*," *Medium Ævum* 47 (1978): 40–65. On critics' desire for antiquity leading to a reductive use of topicality in trying to identify a pre-Langland alliterative text, see Thomas H. Bestul, *Satire and Allegory in Wynnere and Wastoure* (Lincoln: University of Nebraska Press, 1974), 1–23. On the dating of *Wynnere*, including an argument for a range from 1352–c. 1370, see Stephanie Trigg, ed., *Wynnere and Wastoure* (EETS o.s. 297, 1990), xxii–xxvii.

159. Nevill Coghill, *The Pardon of Piers Plowman, Proceedings of the British Academy* 30 (London: Humphrey Milford, 1945), 2.

160. John Speirs, *Medieval English Poetry: The Non-Chaucerian Tradition* (London: Faber and Faber, 1957), 30; 264.

161. Turville-Petre, *Alliterative Revival*, 1.

162. Trigg, "Israel Gollancz's *Wynnere and Wastoure*," 115.

163. Ibid., 118; 120; 119.

164. Gollancz, *Good Short Debate between Winner and Waster,* xv; xxiii.

165. All citations from *Wynnere and Wastoure* are from Trigg's edition; my translations.

166. Trigg, "Israel Gollancz's *Wynnere and Wastoure*," 116; 117; 120–21.

167. Ibid., 119; 123.

168. Ibid., viii–xiii; xxiii.

169. Ibid., xxiii–xiv.

170. Susan Crane, *The Performance of Self: Ritual, Clothing, and Identity During the Hundred Years War* (Philadelphia: University of Pennsylvania Press, 2002), 155–62. On the theatrical significance of the wild man, see Richard Bernheimer, *Wild Men in the Middle Ages: A Study in Art, Sentiment and Demonology* (Cambridge, MA: Harvard University Press, 1952), 49–84; and Samuel Kinser, "Wildmen in Festival, 1300–1550," in *Oral Tradition in the Middle Ages,* ed. W. F. H. Nicolaisen (Binghamton, NY: Center for Medieval and Early Renaissance Studies, 1995), 145–60. Maura Nolan analyzes the crucial role of theatricality in a *Wynnere and Wastoure* shaped by chivalric pageants and treason trials, in "'With Tresone Withinne': *Wynnere and Wastoure,* Chivalric Self-Representation, and the Law," *Journal of Medieval and Early Modern Studies* 26.1 (1996): 1–28 [11–16].

171. Roger Bartra, *Wild Men in the Looking Glass: The Mythic Origins of European Otherness,* trans. Carl T. Berrisford (Ann Arbor: University of Michigan Press, 1994), 117.

172. Gollancz, ed., *Good Short Debate,* xxii.

173. See Jerry D. James, who links the *Wynnere*-poet with Chaucer as members of a "mocking brotherhood," in "The Undercutting of Conventions in *Wynnere and Wastoure*," *Modern Language Quarterly* 25 (1964): 243–58 [245].

174. Charles Moorman links the *Wynnere*-narrator's "moral earnestness and high seriousness" with "the alliterative tradition" and insists that "nothing frivolous" appears in the text, in "The Origins of the Alliterative Revival," *Southern Quarterly* 7 (1969): 345–72 [370]. Turville-Petre reads the opening section as a "series of linked commonplaces," in "The Prologue of *Winner and Waster,*" *Leeds Studies in English* 18 (1987): 19–29 [20]. Derek Traversi reveals extreme regionalism, arguing that provincial poets such as Langland, uniquely affected by two centuries of "reversal and foreign domination," were "divorced" from "healthy contact with important sources of self-consciousness and intelligence," in "Langland's *Piers Plowman,*" in *The Pelican Guide to English Literature, vol.1: The Age of Chaucer,* ed. Boris Ford (Harmondsworth: Penguin, 1959), 127–45 [131].

175. Ten Brink, *Early English Literature,* I.354 [I.454].

176. Wales, *Northern English,* 25–28.

177. In their editions of *Wynnere and Wastoure,* Turville-Petre (in *Alliterative Poetry of the Later Middle Ages: An Anthology* [Washington, DC: Catholic University of America Press, 1989], 38–66) and John W. Conlee (in *Middle English Debate Poetry* [East Lansing, MI: Colleagues Press, 1991], 63–98) join Gollancz in emending to "thre." Warren Ginsberg rightly retains the manuscript "thies" in his edition (Kalamazoo: Medieval Institute Publications, 1992), 1–42. Reviewing Gollancz's edition, Dorothy Everett criticizes Gollancz's emendations based on unquestioned faith in an *aa ax* standard, in *Review of English Studies* 9 (1933): 213–18 [214–15].

178. Halleck, *History,* 47.

179. On strategies for maintaining authorial identity within pre-copyright culture, see Kathryn Kerby-Fulton, "Langland and the Bibliographic Ego," in *Written Work: Langland, Labor, and Authorship,* ed. Steven Justice and Kathryn Kerby-Fulton (Philadelphia: University of Pennsylvania Press, 1997), 67–143 [78–82].

180. On the late-medieval desertion of villages, a phenomenon most frequently found in the Midlands, see Nigel Saul, "Medieval Britain," in *The National Trust Historical Atlas of Britain: Prehistoric to Medieval,* ed. Nigel Saul (Phoenix Mill, Gloucestershire: Alan Sutton, 1994), 115–204 [137–42]; and Colin Platt, *King Death: The Black Death and its Aftermath in Late-Medieval England* (Toronto: University of Toronto Press, 1997), 33–47.

181. Scott L. Waugh, *England in the Reign of Edward III* (Cambridge: Cambridge University Press, 1991), 118. For a general study of sumptuary laws, see Alan Hunt, *Governance of the Consuming Passions: A History of Sumptuary Law* (New York: St. Martin's Press, 1996).

182. The Harley MS 2253 version of "Thomas of Erceldoune's Prophecy" lists "when laddes weddeth lovedis" [when commoners marry ladies] (15) among the signs of coming apocalypse; see *Medieval English Political Writings,* ed. James Dean (Kalamazoo: Medieval Institute Publications, 1996), 11. The largely alliterative *When Rome is Removed into England,* extant in twenty-one manuscripts (ed. Reinhard Haferkorn [Leipzig: Verlag von Bernhard Tauchnitz, 1932], 23–39), links class-blurring with misfortune, speaking in the A-version of "knyghtys and knauys" [knights and churls] wearing "one clothing" [the same clothes] (8).

183. Speirs sees *Wynnere* as among the "last English masterpieces of the oral tradition of early Northern poetry," composed by a poet whose "old-fashionedness" indi-

cates his "belonging to a dying culture" (*Medieval English Poetry,* 266–67). Nicholas Jacobs echoes Gollancz in calling the narrator a "romantic conservative" who has "social reality" and even "the language against him," in "The Typology of Debate and the Interpretation of *Wynnere and Wastoure,*" *Review of English Studies* n.s. 36 (1985): 481–500 [497]. Revivalist disdain for the alliterative poet is clear in David V. Harrington's listing of the *Wynnere*-narrator among those "inadequate spokesmen for one-sided positions"; despite his interest in the poem's "indeterminacy," Harrington locates all sophistication in *readers'* interpretations, in "Indeterminacy in *Winner and Waster* and *The Parliament of the Three Ages,*" *Chaucer Review* 20.3 (1986): 246–57 [257].

184. On the dialect of *Wynnere,* with localizations ranging from the Northwest Midlands to the Northeast Midlands, see Trigg's edition, xviii–xxi.

185. Michael J. Bennett, *Community, Class and Careerism: Cheshire and Lancashire Society in the Age of 'Sir Gawain and the Green Knight'* (Cambridge: Cambridge University Press, 1983), 162–91.

186. On the satirical traditions informing the allegorical figures of Wynnere and Wastoure, see Bestul, *Satire and Allegory,* 1–23.

187. See Bennett, *Community, Class and Careerism,* 108–33.

188. Jacobs, "Typology of Debate," 497.

189. On the transnational nature of Northwest Midlands military culture, see Bennett, *Community, Class and Careerism,* 162–91; and see chapter 3 (below).

190. The Garter motto is traditionally phrased as "Honi soit qui mal y pense."

191. On heraldic representations of the wild man, see Timothy Husband, ed., *The Wild Man: Medieval Myth and Symbolism* (New York: Metropolitan Museum of Art, 1980), 179–95.

192. Trigg, ed., *Wynnere and Wastoure,* 22n.

193. Bennett, *Community, Class and Careerism,* 248.

194. On Geoffrey of Monmouth's role in promoting a secularized historiography authorized by Virgil, and on Geoffrey's grounding of British history in ambivalent Trojan–British origins, see Patterson, *Negotiating the Past,* 157–70; 197–206; and Francis Ingledew, "The Book of Troy and the Genealogical Construction of History: The Case of Geoffrey of Monmouth's *Historia regum Britanniae,*" *Speculum* 69 (1994): 665–704 [669–80]. On the prominent role of literary myths of Trojan ancestry shaping post-Roman European ethnic identity, see Geary, *Myth of Nations,* 60–62; and Richard Waswo, "The History that Literature Makes," *New Literary History* 19 (1988): 541–64.

195. Turville-Petre, *Alliterative Revival,* 27.

196. For a survey of manuscripts attesting alliterative texts, see A. I. Doyle, "The Manuscripts," in *Middle English Alliterative Poetry,* ed. Lawton, 88–100.

197. Salter argues against viewing the "revival" as a "local affair," noting that "clerkly poets were probably as well traveled as their noble patrons," in "Alliterative Revival," 233.

Chapter 2

1. Chambers, *Continuity,* lxxxi; lxxxii–iii.

2. Ibid., lxxxi; lxvi–vii. For criticism of efforts to assume continuity of Old Eng-

lish metrical practice with either Laȝamon's twelfth-century poetics or with fourteenth-century poetry, see Cable, *English Alliterative Tradition,* 41–65; and Daniel Donoghue, "Laȝamon's Ambivalence," *Speculum* 65 (1990): 537–63 [538–39].

3. Nineteenth-century philological influences link early literary studies with a number of racialized political movements, ranging from French chauvinism to pan-Germanism. On German Romanticism's influence on nationalist philologies in France and Germany, see three essays in *Medievalism,* ed. Bloch and Nichols: Stephen G. Nichols, "Modernism and the Politics of Medieval Studies," 25–56 [34–40]; John M. Graham, "National Politics and the Publishing of the Troubadours," 57–94 [60–80]; and Jeffrey M. Peck, "'In the Beginning Was the Word': Germany and the Origins of German Studies" (127–47). On the Nazi legacy of such philology, see Bryan Sykes's discussion of "the Aryan myth" that originated in the work of German linguist Max Müller, who posited an "original Aryan people" linked with an originary Indo-European language, in *Saxons, Vikings, and Celts: The Genetic Roots of Britain and Ireland* (New York: W. W. Norton, 2006), 42–43.

4. Anderson, *Imagined Communities,* 44–45; 144–45.

5. Taine, *History,* I.94; *L'Histoire,* I.75–76. Taine's vision of racialized struggle for cultural ascendancy anticipates modern views concerning the instability of ethnic boundaries. See Fredrik Barth's seminal discussion of ethnic boundary maintenance, in which social and economic changes enable movement across ethnic lines, in his introduction to *Ethnic Groups and Boundaries: The Social Organization of Cultural Difference,* ed. Fredrik Barth (1969; Long Grove, IL: Waveland Press, 1998), 9–38.

6. Geary, *Myth of Nations,* 11. For Taine, Anglo-Saxon stability is in sharp contrast with Norman identity: Norman "conquerors themselves were conquered" as "their speech became English" see *History,* I.94; *L'Histoire,* I.75–76.

7. For analysis of fourteenth-century monastic culture that links Latinate writing with proto-national identity, see Andrew Galloway, "Latin England," in *Imagining a Medieval English Nation,* ed. Lavezzo, 41–91 [45–73]. Ardis Butterfield critiques reductive views of late-medieval linguistic complexity, noting that a "mixed" language was often deployed in mercantile documents, while "English" and "French" often varied as cultural markers depending upon one's class and place of origin, in "French Culture and the Ricardian Court," in *Essays on Ricardian Literature in Honour of J. A. Burrow,* ed. A. J. Minnis, Charlotte C. Morse, and Thorlac Turville-Petre (Oxford: Clarendon Press, 1997), 82–120 [82–85]. For a survey of self-consciously English-speaking statements from the early fourteenth century, see Turville-Petre, *England the Nation: Language, Literature, and National Identity, 1290–1340* (Oxford: Oxford University Press, 1996), 11–22.

8. Building upon Anderson's argument that the fixity of languages produced by print-capitalism is a precondition to the nation's eighteenth-century rise (*Imagined Communities,* 37–46), Hobsbawm asserts that a national standard can be constructed only through a post-print hierarchizing of dialect differences, in *Nations,* 51–63. Susan Crane's dialect-based view that the English language only begins to suggest "national identity" well into the Lancastrian fifteenth century also challenges Revivalist assumptions of a fourteenth-century nationalism; see "Anglo-Norman Cultures in England, 1066–1460," in *Cambridge History,* ed. Wallace, 35–60 [55–56]. Turville-Petre exposes the anachronism of linking discrete languages and ethnicities, critiquing "patriotic"

efforts to associate English with "the people," and Latin and French with the clergy and the "noble descendants of the Norman oppressors"; these languages actually mingled in a single "culture in three voices" (*England the Nation,* 181).

9. On the nineteenth-century "lexicographic revolution" and the reification of languages as the "personal property" of national entities, see Anderson, *Imagined Communities,* 83–84.

10. *William of Palerne,* uniquely attested in King's College Cambridge MS 13 (dated 1350–75; for a full description, see Bunt, ed., 1–10; 14–19), is a translation of the twelfth-century Old French romance, *Guillaume de Palerne,* which is uniquely attested in the thirteenth-century manuscript Paris, Arsenal Fr. 6565, ff. 77–157 (Alexandre Micha, ed. [Geneva: Librairie Droz, 1990], 7–8).

11. On nationalists' efforts to conceal the nation's modernity by presenting languages as "the primordial foundations of national culture and the matrices of the national mind," see Hobsbawm, *Nations,* 54. V. C. Galbraith critiques the Saxon-Norman myth by analyzing Saxons' rapid transference of loyalty to an accommodating Norman elite, with each group sharing Latin as an administrative language, in "Nationality and Language in Medieval England," *Transactions of the Royal Historical Society,* 4th ser., 23 (1941): 113–28 [120–24]. Considering the complexities produced by class, language, and ethnicity, Galbraith qualifies his view of medieval national identity by adopting a deliberately broad definition of the nation as "any considerable group of people who believe they *are* one" (113; emphasis in original).

12. Gellner, *Nations and Nationalism,* 20–38.

13. Thomas B. Shaw, *Outlines of English Literature* (Philadelphia: Lea and Blanchard, 1849), 25. As Galbraith shows, there were indeed medieval efforts to portray the Norman conquerors as zealous to eradicate the English language, though such patriotic accounts begin only in the fourteenth century ("Nationality and Language," 120–24). William Camden provides an early-modern instance, claiming that Edward III enabled the ascendancy of "our language" by releasing legal scholars from the "bondage" of French, in *Remains Concerning Britain* (1605; rpt. London: John Russel Smith, 1870), 34–35.

14. Shaw, *Outlines,* 25.

15. Truman J. Backus and Thomas B. Shaw, *Shaw's New History of English Literature together with A History of English Literature in America,* rev. ed. (1874; New York: Sheldon and Company, 1884), 25. For Backus's racialized vision of the survival of Englishness after the Norman Conquest, and of late-medieval attempts to "reviv[e]" the "ancient English style of poetry," see 35–36; 58–59. Backus, listed as co-author with the deceased Shaw, provides further evidence of Anglo-American linguistico-nationalist collaboration. Backus's 1884 edition opens with the claim that "in their literary inheritance, the readers of the English language are the richest people that the sun shines on" (17). On Thomas Budd Shaw (1813–62), and on his work's popularity in America, see Franklin E. Court, *The Scottish Connection: The Rise of English Literary Study in Early America* (Syracuse, NY: Syracuse University Press, 2001), 155–59. For Backus's biography, see William S. Pelletreau, *A History of Long Island,* vol. 3 (New York: Lewis Publishing), 1903, 288–89.

16. Backus and Shaw, *Shaw's New History,* 35; 38; 58.

17. Warton, *History* (1774–81), I.344. Warton merely continues a traditional view

of Chaucer as the "Father of English poetry," the Lancastrian and Tudor origins of which are analyzed by Seth Lerer, in *Chaucer and His Readers: Imagining the Author in Late-Medieval England* (Princeton, NJ: Princeton University Press, 1993), especially 3–21.

18. Warton, *History* (1784–81), I.344. Warton's instructive Chaucer forms "a style by naturalizing words from the Provencial [sic], at that time the most polished dialect of any in Europe" (I.339).

19. William Vaughn Moody and Robert Morss Lovett, *A History of English Literature* (New York: Charles Scribner's Sons, 1905), 34.

20. Ibid.

21. Ibid., 51–55. Moody and Lovett reveal Revivalism's Norman-Saxon obsession by speaking only to Chaucer's French influences while disregarding the massive influence of Italian poetry.

22. See also J. J. Jusserand, who turns to Chaucer and Langland to represent the "two races" forming the English "nation." Though Jusserand speaks of a national metrical "compromise" that produced modern English verse, he has a distinctly one-sided view: Langland, who "rejected" French "rime" and remained with the "past of his kin" by writing in alliterative meter, disappears from the narrative, while Chaucer evolves beyond alliteration to a higher, strictly syllabic modernity, in *A Literary History of the English People from the Origins to the End of the Middle Ages* (New York: G. P. Putnam's Sons, 1893), 245; 401–2.

23. Williams, *French Fetish*, 1–3.

24. Ibid., 19–20.

25. The narrator of *Guillaume* claims to be translating from a Latin source (Micha, ed., 9659–60). For the evidence that the Irish *Eachtra Uilliam* is a translation of *William*, see Cecile O'Rahilly's edition (Dublin: Dublin Institute for Advanced Studies, 1949), xi–xii. There survive two sixteenth-century editions of an English prose version of the story printed by Wynkyn de Worde, as well as four early modern editions of Pierre Durand's French prose redaction of *Guillaume;* see Bunt, ed., *William of Palerne*, 21–26.

26. Noting *William*'s status as "possibly the earliest of the alliterative romances," Oakden offers fairly typical Revivalist disdain, questioning "whether the alliterative meter was a suitable medium for the French original," since it seems "beyond the power of the English translator to copy" the original's "polish and grace" and "elaborate play" (*Alliterative Poetry*, II.38–40). See also Everett, "Alliterative Revival," 53–54; and Derek Pearsall, *Old English and Middle English Poetry* (London: Routledge & Kegan Paul, 1977), 156–57.

27. On balancing local contexts with a view to the broader consolidation of Europe, which itself transpired within a global frame, see Patricia Clare Ingham, "Contrapuntal Histories," in *Postcolonial Moves: Medieval through Modern*, ed. Patricia Clare Ingham and Michelle Warren (New York: Palgrave Macmillan, 2003), 47–70 [55]. Ingham's "contrapuntal" historiography, which seeks out "distinction" on a fluid field featuring the "complex dynamics of 'here' and 'there,' 'then' and 'now'" (48), informs my own efforts to balance findings of medieval–modern continuities and alterities.

28. Galloway, "Latin England," 42.

29. Lawrence Warner speculates that William, otherwise unknown outside of *Wil-*

liam, is William Langland, citing dialectal (and first-name) similarity (397), while arguing that a past engagement with animal-skin disguises would explain Langland's penchant for disguise imagery (401–5; 410), in "Langland and the Problem of *William of Palerne,*" *Viator* 37 (2006): 397–415.

30. Gellner argues that late-medieval culture, part of the "agrarian" phase of economic development, is fundamentally concerned with reinforcing and illuminating social rank, with this differentiating function preventing nationalism's use of culture to "mark the boundaries of the polity" (*Nationalism,* 20).

31. Giorgio Agamben, *Homo Sacer: Sovereign Power and Bare Life,* trans. Daniel Heller-Roazen (Stanford, CA: Stanford University Press, 1998), 5–8; 104–11. Agamben here seeks to recover a biopolitical history that pre-dates the eighteenth-century epochal shift proposed by Michel Foucault, who restricts the era of "biopower" to a French "classical" period post-dating demography and innovations in physical subjugation techniques. On biopolitics involving capitalist states' bringing of subjects' bodies to the center of political calculation, see Foucault, *The History of Sexuality,* vol. 1, trans. Robert Hurley (New York: Vintage, 1978), 139–45.

32. Simpson, *Reform and Cultural Revolution,* 271–73.

33. Jeffrey Jerome Cohen, *Medieval Identity Machines* (Minneapolis: University of Minnesota Press, 2003), 3; 42–44. See also Gilles Deleuze and Félix Guattari's analysis of "machinic assemblages" as identities under constant construction, in *A Thousand Plateaus: Capitalism and Schizophrenia,* trans. Brian Massumi (Minneapolis: University of Minnesota Press, 1987), 3–13.

34. Bourdieu argues that the "social function" of rites of passage is to "*consecrat[e]*" the line that differentiates elite participants from those barred from making such crossings, in *Language and Symbolic Power,* ed. John B. Thompson, trans. Gino Raymond and Matthew Adamson (Cambridge, MA: Harvard University Press, 1991), 117–18.

35. On English self-consciousness concerning the epoch-making Norman Conquest, see Williams, *French Fetish,* 20.

36. On the "attraction and terror of shape-shifting" to twelfth-century audiences fascinated with the metaphysics of change, see Caroline Walker Bynum, *Metamorphosis and Identity* (New York: Zone Books, 2005), 109.

37. For an extended discussion of dialectal evidence in the unique text of *William,* see Bunt's "Introduction" to *William of Palerne: An Electronic Edition,* Society for Early English & Norse Texts A:3 (Ann Arbor: University of Michigan Press, 2002), 6.1–10. While Bunt has tentatively suggested a place of origin for the poem in southern Worcestershire or Warwickshire (in "Localizing *William of Palerne,*" in *Historical Linguistics and Philology,* ed. Jacek Fisiak [Berlin: Mouton de Gruyter, 1990], 73–86 [82]), he still maintains that multiple stages of transmission and mixed (Southwest Midland and Eastern) forms render the dialects of both poet and scribe uncertain (Bunt, "Patron, Author and Audience in a Fourteenth-century English Alliterative Poem," in *Non Nova, sed Nove: Mélanges de civilisation médiévale dédiés à Willem Noomen,* ed. Martin Grosman and Jaap van Os (Groningen, Netherlands: Bouma's Boekhuis, 1984), 25–36 [31–32]).

38. On translation in *William,* see W. R. J. Barron, "Alliterative Romance and the French Tradition," in *Middle English Alliterative Poetry,* ed. Lawton, 70–87 [75–80]; and Bunt, ed., *William of Palerne,* 30–36.

39. Turville-Petre, *Alliterative Revival*, 41.
40. Ibid. See also Turville-Petre, "Humphrey de Bohun and *William of Palerne*," *Neuphilologische Mitteilungen* 75 (1974): 260–62.
41. Pearsall, *Old English and Middle English Poetry*, 157. For similar criticism, see Warner, "Langland," 407.
42. Williams, *French Fetish*, 20.
43. Bunt, ed., *William of Palerne*, 18–19. On linguistic identity and late-medieval English noble self-consciousness, see Chris Given-Wilson, *The English Nobility in the Late Middle Ages: The Fourteenth-Century Political Community* (London: Routledge & Kegan Paul, 1987), 9.
44. Turville-Petre, "Humphrey de Bohun," 262.
45. Bunt, "Patron, Author and Audience," 32.
46. Ad Putter, *'Sir Gawain and the Green Knight' and French Arthurian Romance* (Oxford: Clarendon Press, 1995), 209–10.
47. Turville-Petre, "Humphrey de Bohun," 262.
48. Putter, *'Sir Gawain,'* 200–201.
49. W. M. Ormrod, *The Reign of Edward III*, rev. ed. (Charleston: Tempus, 2000), 116–36.
50. On the activities of proto-capitalist agents before capitalism's post-1500 rise in fully urbanized European economies, see Charles Tilly, *Coercion, Capital, and European States, A.D. 990–1992*, rev. ed. (Oxford: Blackwell, 1992), 17–19.
51. All citations from *William* are from Bunt's edition; my translations.
52. On "excremental discourse" as a "social control" mechanism deployed against medieval "others," see Susan Signe Morrison, *Excrement in the Late Middle Ages: Sacred Filth and Chaucer's Fecopoetics* (New York: Palgrave Macmillan, 2008), 33–36.
53. On late-medieval animal fable's promotion of a conservative social order, see Joyce E. Salisbury, *The Beast Within: Animals in the Middle Ages* (New York: Routledge, 1994), 118–31.
54. Micha, ed., *Guillaume de Palerne*, 23; Bunt, ed., *William of Palerne*, 14–15.
55. All citations of *Guillaume* are from Micha's edition; all translations are from *Guillaume de Palerne*, trans. Leslie A. Sconduto (Jefferson, NC: McFarland, 2004). Sconduto's lineation follows Micha's.
56. Charles W. Dunn, *The Foundling and the Werwolf: A Literary-Historical Study of 'Guillaume de Palerne'* (Toronto: University of Toronto Press, 1960), 70–71.
57. Dunn (ibid.) regards "Aubelot" as relatively unusual and notes that Akarin has links with Saracen culture.
58. Michael Camille, *Image on the Edge: The Margins of Medieval Art* (Cambridge, MA: Harvard University Press, 1992), 12–13; 33.
59. Given-Wilson, *English Nobility*, 87–103.
60. The comical deployment of grotesque images of peasants in both *Guillaume* and *William* serves to reinforce hierarchical social visions. For analysis of the use of stereotypical images to provide the "comfort of confirming an audience's prejudices" and so consolidate class privileges, see Andrew Stott, *Comedy* (New York: Routledge, 2005), 43–44. On the cultivation of identifiable features as a means of "entropy-resistance," countering socioeconomic mobility in the agrarian world, see Gellner, *Nationalism*, 65.
61. Crane, *Performance of Self*, 55; 49.

62. Ibid., 39–72.

63. Agamben, *Homo Sacer*, 81–86.

64. Ibid., 35.

65. In *Guillaume*, Guillaume bids Melior remove the bearskin and so display her "pur" [naked] body (4061–62); William's translation emphasizes the clothing beneath the skins (2417).

66. Bourdieu, *Language and Symbolic Power*, 119.

67. On the sylvan lives led by the fugitive Tristan and Iseult, see Corinne J. Saunders, *The Forest of Medieval Romance: Avernus, Broceliande, Arden* (Cambridge: D. S. Brewer, 1993), 81–94.

68. Hereafter, when citing both versions, I cite first from *Guillaume* and then from *William*.

69. Bynum, *Metamorphosis*, 109. Bynum argues that hybrids, necessarily conjoining different characteristics in a single visual plane, fuse incompatible categories that "comment" on one another, while metamorphosed figures instantiate a breakdown of categories (29–31). See also Doryjane Birrer, who argues that Alphonse is a "humane" wolf whose wolf-body is as factitious as the lovers' disguises, merely covering over a reasonable and sympathetic self, in "A New Species of Humanities: The Marvelous Progeny of Humanism and Postmodern Theory," *Journal of Narrative Theory* 37.2 (2007): 217–45 [218; 229].

70. See Giorgio Agamben, *The Open: Man and Animal*, trans. Kevin Attell (Stanford, CA: Stanford University Press, 2004), 34–38.

71. Gary Day, *Class* (London: Routledge, 2001), 19–23.

72. Bynum, *Metamorphosis*, 94

73. On the possibly Welsh context for *Arthur and Gorlagon*, see George L. Kittredge, ed., *Arthur and Gorlagon, Studies and Notes in Philology and Literature* 8 (1903): 149–275 [176–209].

74. *Mélion*, in *Les Lais anonymes des XIIe et XIIIe siècles*, ed. Prudence Mary O'Hara Tobin (Geneva: Librairie Droz, 1976), 38–110; my translations.

75. *Arthur and Gorlagon*, ed. Kittredge, 153. All citations from the original are from Kittredge's edition; all translations are from Frank A. Milne's version, in *A Lycanthropy Reader: Werewolves in Western Culture*, ed. Charlotte F. Otten (Syracuse, NY: Syracuse University Press, 1986), 234–55 [238].

76. On the ritual ends of animalized aristocratic violence, see Agamben's analysis of the symbolic "power of delivering something over to itself," in *Homo Sacer*, 106.

77. Ibid., 104–6.

78. Ibid., 107–8; Thomas Hobbes, *Leviathan*, 1651; ed. Richard E. Flathman and David Johnston (New York: Norton, 1997), 76.

79. Marie de France, *Bisclavret*, in *Lais*, ed. Karl Warnke, trans. Laurence Harf-Lancner (Paris: Librairie Générale Française, 1990),11. 25–27; 63–66; 298–99. Jeffrey Jerome Cohen argues that Bisclavret, by becoming his king's hunting dog and intimate, if servile, companion, internalizes the "superiority of the bond that ties him to the king over that which had joined him to his spouse," in *Of Giants: Sex, Monsters, and the Middle Ages* (Minneapolis: University of Minnesota Press, 1999), 129.

80. Agamben, *Homo Sacer*, 105–6.

81. See Sheila Fisher, "Taken Men and Token Women in *Sir Gawain and the Green*

Knight," in *Seeking the Woman in Late Medieval and Renaissance Writings,* ed. Sheila Fisher and Janet E. Halley (Knoxville: University of Tennessee Press, 1984), 71–105 [71–72]; and Michael W. Twomey, "Morgain la Fée in *Sir Gawain and the Green Knight,*" in *Text and Intertext in Medieval Arthurian Literature,* ed. Norris J. Lacy (New York: Garland, 1996), 91–115 [93].

82. Frederic Madden, ed. *William and the Werewolf* (1832, rpt.; New York: Burt Franklin, 1970). Madden offers no explanation for his use of only two of the three protagonists in his title, and he even notes that the "original" title, the "*Roman de Guillaume de Palerne,*" offers no justification for adding the werewolf (vii). Helen Cooper points to one revision of this gender bias, noting that Richard Hyrd entitled the work "Wyllyam and Milior" in a 1529 list of romances; see *The English Romance in Time: Transforming Motifs from Geoffrey of Monmouth to the Death of Shakespeare* (Oxford: Oxford University Press, 2004), 235; 37–38.

83. For Deleuze and Guattari, an anomalous agent always functions as the bridge to the process of becoming-animal that shatters static identity (*Thousand Plateaus,* 243–44).

84. Morgan in the Vulgate *Lancelot* manipulates a lover's mind-set, using a potion to make Lancelot dream of Guinevere; see *Lancelot-Grail: The Old French Arthurian Vulgate and Post-Vulgate in Translation,* vol. 2., ed. Norris J. Lacy, trans. Samuel N. Rosenberg and Carleton W. Carroll (New York: Garland, 1993), 328.

85. Warner, "Langland," 402.

86. Kate Watkins Tibbals, "Elements of Magic in the Romance of William of Palerne," *Modern Philology* 1 (1903–4): 355–71 [358].

87. Gaston Paris, "La Sicile dans la littérature française du moyen âge," *Romania* V (1876): 108–13 [109].

88. Marie de France, *Guigemar,* in *Lais,* ed. Warnke, 90–102.

89. Thomas Malory, *Le Morte Darthure,* ed. Stephen H. A. Shepherd (New York: W. W. Norton, 2004), 66–70.

90. Agamben defines "bare life" as "the life of *homo sacer* (sacred man), who *may be killed and yet not sacrificed,*" in *Homo Sacer,* 8 (emphasis in original).

91. Ibid., 106–7.

92. In *Guillaume,* Guillaume, overstimulated by the erotic charge of the disguises, momentarily forgets that Melior is not nude beneath her bearskin (4060–64).

93. Bourdieu, *Language and Symbolic Power,* 119.

94. After returning to his native Cornwall, Tristan gains entry into the Cornish royal court by instructing a noble hunting party in the art of flaying and presenting a deer, in Gottfried's *Tristan,* ed. and trans. A. T. Hatto (Baltimore: Penguin, 1960), 78–86. The *Gawain*-poet describes at grisly length the flayings of a deer and a boar, in *Sir Gawain,* ed. Vantuono, 1324–61; 1605–18.

95. The lovers' putting on the skins of aggressive animals that are also prey ritually sexualizes their bodies in courtly terms. On aggression as key to the "social reproduction of the body" in the self's "social institution" through orchestrated corporal activities, see Graham L. Hammill, *Sexuality and Form: Caravaggio, Marlowe, and Bacon* (Chicago: University of Chicago Press, 2000), 4–9.

96. John Cummins, *The Hound and the Hawk: The Medieval Art of Hunting* (London: Phoenix Press, 1988), 121. Hunting manuals, like the story of *Guillaume,* cross

the Channel that both binds and separates medieval English and French culture. On the Englishing and expansion of Gaston Phébus's *Livre de la chasse* into Edward, Duke of York's *The Master of the Game*, see William Perry Marvin, *Hunting Law and Ritual in Medieval English Literature* (Cambridge: D. S. Brewer, 2006), 114–31.

97. In *Guillaume*, Alexandrine reports that "chevrex" [goats] are among the beasts in the kitchen (3014). The "bukkes" [bucks] catalogued in *William* (1684) could be goats or deer, according to the *MED*. That deer are intended is suggested by the qualification that they are of "fair venorye." In *Guillaume*, Alexandrine inexplicably acquires the skin of a "serpent" (3063) along with the bearskins. The English poet's omission of the serpent excises a creature alien to venery's symbolic world.

98. I take the translation from Cummins, *Hound and the Hawk*, 121; the original text is from Gaston Phébus, *Livre de Chasse*, ed. Gunnar Tilander (Cynegetica 18. Karlshamn, Sweden: E. G. Johanssons, 1971), 85.

99. Andreas Capellanus, *On Love*, ed. and trans. P. G. Walsh (London: Duckworth, 1982), 33.

100. Fradenburg, *Sacrifice Your Love*, 40–41.

101. Ibid., 97–99. Fradenburg here connects the corporal risks and pleasures in the medieval hunt with the courtly life constructed from lovers' physical sufferings in Chaucer's *Book of the Duchess* (79–112).

102. See Cummins, *Hound and the Hawk*, 32–83.

103. The blurriness of species borderlines seems evident in William's supposition that the workmen would take Melior's choice of a bear as a traveling and sleeping companion in stride.

104. Agamben, *Homo Sacer*, 109.

105. Ibid., 108.

106. Williams, *French Fetish*, 20.

107. Michael J. Bennett, "*Mandeville's Travels* and the Anglo-French Moment," *Medium Aevum* 75 (2006): 273–92 [282–83].

108. Hanna, "Alliterative Poetry," 497.

109. See, for example, Everett, "Alliterative Revival," 53; Pearsall, "Origins," 16; and Lawton, "Unity," 80.

110. See Turville-Petre, *Alliterative Revival*, 27.

111. Everett, "Alliterative Revival," 53.

112. Ibid., 54.

113. Camden, *Remains Concerning Britain*, 25. On Anglo-Saxonism's rise, see Hugh MacDougall, *Racial Myth in English History: Trojans, Teutons, and Anglo-Saxons* (Hanover, NH: University Press of New England, 1982), 31–50; and Frantzen, *Desire for Origins*, 35–50.

114. Walter S. Hinchman, *A History of English Literature* (New York: Century, 1916), 22.

115. Oakden, *Alliterative Poetry*, II.87.

116. Moorman, "English Alliterative Revival," 91.

117. Chism aptly argues that the more critics produce disciplinary histories of literary criticism, the "less shrill" will sound the nationalist antiquarians who have insisted on an alliterative English "archaism," in *Alliterative Revivals*, 39.

118. On the contestation among national fantasies competing for communal defini-

tion in medieval Britain, see Ingham, *Sovereign Fantasies,* 7–15. Whether or not we assume that the nation is a modern, post-capitalist formation (see Anderson, *Imagined Communities,* 37–46; and Gellner, *Nations and Nationalism,* 139–43), it is clear, as Lavezzo has shown, that fantasies of constitutive sameness and otherness were at work throughout medieval English history, providing material out of which a future nation-state could be constructed; see "Introduction," vii–xxxiv.

119. Given-Wilson, *English Nobility,* 87–103.

120. On the cultural work performed by sumptuary legislation to render clothing a stable indicator of class, see Crane, *Performance of Self,* 11–15.

121. On the rise of foresters as a police force that protected aristocratic recreative privilege, see Barbara A. Hanawalt, "Men's Games, King's Deer: Poaching in Medieval England," *Journal of Medieval and Renaissance Studies* 18 (1988): 175–93.

122. Turville-Petre, *Alliterative Revival,* 41.

123. Micha supplies from a sixteenth-century prose version a passage, missing from *Guillaume*'s manuscript text, in which Felice's clerk, Moysant, advises her to dress as a deer (*Guillaume,* 191n-92n). Moysant's rationale—that Felice should be "vestue tout ainsi quilz sont" [dressed just like they are] and so can lie near them and speak "a vostre ayse" [at ease] (191n–92n)—is nearly as opaque as the lack of explanation in earlier versions and suggests reception of the romance's becoming-animal narrative as ritual.

124. On atrocities during the sack of Constantinople, see Donald E. Queller and Thomas F. Madden, *The Fourth Crusade: The Conquest of Constantinople,* 2nd ed. (Philadelphia: University of Pennsylvania Press, 1997), 193–203.

125. The Greek prince is named Leternidon in *Guillaume* (3362).

Chapter 3

1. Unless otherwise noted, all citations from *Sir Gawain* are taken from Vantuono's edition; my translations.

2. Scholars typically deploy George Lyman Kittredge's division of *Sir Gawain* into the Beheading Game (in which Gawain allows the Green Knight to strike at his head with an axe, after having dealt the Green Knight himself one such blow), and the Temptation (according to which each player agrees to give the other each day's winnings, with Bertilak going hunting on each of three days, while Gawain spends significant time with his host's wife); see *A Study of 'Gawain and the Green Knight'* (Cambridge, MA: Harvard University Press, 1916), 7–9.

3. I here replace both Vantuono's text and my translation with Twomey's insightful redaction, in "Morgan le Fay at Hautdesert," in *On Arthurian Women: Essays in Memory of Maureen Fries,* ed. Bonnie Wheeler and Fiona Tolhurst (Dallas: Scriptorium, 2001), 103–19 [111]. Twomey's punctuation captures Bertilak's linkage of his lordly status with subjection to Morgan and suggests that Bertilak is just one of a number of knights in her service.

4. Whereas Vantuono reads "Bercilak," I prefer "Bertilak," as it leaves open the possibility that the regional lord of *Sir Gawain* evokes the Vulgate *Lancelot* cycle's Berthelai, who engineers the False Guinevere plot whereby Arthur is convinced that his current queen has usurped the rightful place of Berthelai's mistress, Guinevere's

half-sister. Since it is difficult to distinguish "c" from "t" in the hand of Cotton Nero A.x, both readings are possible; see Vantuono, ed., *Sir Gawain,* 241–42n. For the False Guinevere plot, see *The Vulgate Version of the Arthurian Romances,* ed. H. Oskar Sommer, vol. 4.ii; rpt. (New York: AMS Press, 1979), 44–80; and see *Lancelot-Grail: The Old French Arthurian and Post-Vulgate in Translation,* ed. and trans. Norris J. Lacy et al., vol. 4 (New York, Garland, 1993–96), 245–78. On the *Gawain*-poet's immersion in French Arthurian tradition, see Putter, *'Sir Gawain,'* 1–9.

5. Most scholars accept Angus McIntosh's narrowing of the dialect of the Cotton Nero poems to northeast Staffordshire or southeast Cheshire, in "A New Approach to Middle English Dialectology," *English Studies* 44 (1963): 1–11 [5–6].

6. One could also stress "*Faye*" rather than "*my3t*," which would deliver a perfectly acceptable *ax ax* line, assuming that we place stress on "*my*" rather than "*hous.*" Even hypotheses of strict rules governing the disposition of stressed and unstressed syllables in alliterative verse acknowledge some flexibility in stress assignment. Asserting that a "hierarchy of word classes determines which words may appear in metrically prominent positions," Duggan argues that words from "open classes," meaning "nouns, adjectives, most verb forms, adverbs ending in -ly or of 2 syllables, pronouns ending in -*self*," take "precedence over" words from "closed classes," identified as "prepositions, some verbs, auxiliaries, pronouns, monosyllabic adverbs" ("Alliterative Patterning," 77–78). Duggan (77), like Skeat ("Essay," xvi), insists that stress and alliteration must coincide.

7. Turville-Petre, *Alliterative Revival,* 48–50.

8. On the Northwest Midlands' sparse population due both to its remoteness and to military service, see Bennett, *Community, Class and Careerism,* 8–10; 190–91. On the trend toward depopulation in the late-medieval Midlands, see Saul, "Medieval Britain," 137–42.

9. Twomey, "Morgan le Fay," 113.

10. On anxiety concerning female power in criticism of the poem, see Geraldine Heng, "Feminine Knots and the Other: *Sir Gawain and the Green Knight,*" *PMLA* 106 (1991): 500–514; and Twomey, "Morgain la Fée," 91–115.

11. Twomey, "Morgain la Fée," 92–93

12. Bennett, *Community, Class and Careerism,* 162–91.

13. Ibid., 29.

14. Ibid.

15. See Rowena E. Archer's extraction of such social realities from the anonymous women inhabiting fifteenth-century records, in "'How ladies . . . who live on their manors ought to manage their households and estates': Women as Landholders and Administrators in the Later Middle Ages," in *Woman is a Worthy Wight: Women in English Society,* ed. P. J. P. Goldberg (Phoenix Mill, Gloucestershire: Alan Sutton, 1992), 149–81 [150–62].

16. On late-medieval estate management by women, see Archer, "'How ladies,'" 149–81. On the significant social and economic power held by widows in late-medieval England, see Peter Coss, *The Lady in Medieval England, 1000–1500* (Phoenix Mill, Gloucestershire: Sutton, 1998), 56–72. On female economic power in the distribution of wealth in European feudal society, see Jerold C. Frakes, *Brides and Doom: Gender, Property, and Power in Medieval German Women's Epic* (Philadelphia: University of

Pennsylvania Press, 1994), 47–95.

17. See Salter's urging of the reintegration of alliterative works with a national culture centered in metropolitan London and spread through aristocratic households, in "Alliterative Revival," 146–49; 233–37.

18. On legitimacy and symbolic communication, see Bourdieu, *Language and Symbolic Power,* 230; 234.

19. In supervising the removal of the "chorea gigantum" [Giants' Ring (Stonehenge)] from its location on Mt. Killaraus in Ireland, Geoffrey of Monmouth's Merlin challenges Utherpendragon's men, "Employ your might, men, to take down the stones and we shall see whether your brains yield to brawn or vice versa" [Vtimini uiribus uestris, iuuenes, ut in deponendo lapides istos appareat utrum ingenium uirtuti an uirtus ingenio cedat]. After laughing at their failure, Merlin easily moves the structure to Britain; see Geoffrey of Monmouth, *History of the Kings of Britain,* 172–75. All citations and translations from Geoffrey are from Reeve and Wright.

20. Pierre Bourdieu, *Outline of a Theory of Practice,* trans. Richard Nice (Cambridge: Cambridge University Press, 1977), 165.

21. Cicero, *De Senectute,* ed. and trans. William Armistead Falconer (Cambridge, MA: Harvard University Press, 1923), vi.20 [maximas res publicas ab adulescentibus labefactatas, a senibus austentatas et restitutas reperietis: 'Cedo qui vestram rem publicam tantam amisistis tam cito?']. Cato here asserts the superiority of senators' mental talents to young soldiers' physical skills (vi.18–19). On Cicero as a late-medieval authority on old age, see Joel T. Rosenthal, *Old Age in Late Medieval England* (Philadelphia: University of Pennsylvania Press, 1991), 178–80. On *De Senectute*'s classical and medieval popularity, see J. G. F. Powell, ed., *Cicero: Cato Maior, De Senectute* (Cambridge: Cambridge University Press, 1988), 30–51.

22. For Revivalist insistence that the alliterative poet is essentially old, see Shepherd, "Nature of Alliterative Poetry," 64–65; and Hanna, "Alliterative Poetry," 501.

23. See Chaucer, *Canterbury Tales,* ed. Benson, X.1048–66; 1239–57.

24. *The Wedding of Sir Gawain and Dame Ragnelle,* in *Sir Gawain: Eleven Romances and Tales,* ed. Thomas Hahn (Kalamazoo: Medieval Institute Publications, 1995), 47–70.

25. Ingham, *Sovereign Fantasies,* 182.

26. In *Lanval,* Marie states that neither Octavian nor Semiramis could pay for a single flap of the Lady's pavilion tent (80–86); the Lady demonstrates superiority to Arthur by providing Lanval with seemingly limitless wealth (135–42). That Lanval can only live publicly with the Lady in the otherworldly Avalon (641–45) marginalizes her power as geographically exceptional; see Marie de France, *The Lais,* ed. and trans. Glynn S. Burgess and Keith S. Busby, 2nd ed. (New York: Penguin, 1999), 73–81; 139–55. For a thoroughgoing study of otherworldly female figures in Arthurian romance, see Lucy Allen Paton, *Studies in the Fairy Mythology of Arthurian Romance* (1903; rev. ed., ed. Roger Sherman Loomis; New York: Burt Franklin, 1970). For analysis of Morgan's magic involving craft rather than otherworldliness, see Carolyne Larrington, *King Arthur's Enchantresses: Morgan and Her Sisters in Arthurian Tradition* (London: I. B. Tauris, 2006), 7–96.

27. On the *Gawain*-poet's use of geographical detail to figure multiple regional, ethnic, and gender loyalties, see Ingham, *Sovereign Fantasies,* 114–24.

28. Davies, *First English Empire*, 39–40. On the subversive potential of Geoffrey of Monmouth's Merlin and the prophetic tradition that appropriates his "oppositional discourse," see Ingham, *Sovereign Fantasies*, 31–50. On the medieval English appropriation of the Celtic King Arthur, see MacDougall, *Racial Myth*, 7–27; and R. R. Davies, *Domination and Conquest: The Experience of Ireland, Scotland and Wales, 1100–1300* (Cambridge: Cambridge University Press, 1990), 125–28.

29. Davies, *First English Empire*, 39–40.

30. See Ingham's analysis of Gawain's journey as reflecting both English desire to colonize Welsh territory and the complexity of late-medieval ethnic identity, in *Sovereign Fantasies*, 116–21.

31. See Barrett's analysis of Wirral as a unique region within a larger English imperial frame, in *Against All England*, 137–38.

32. Horsman, *Race and Manifest Destiny*, 10–13.

33. On the arbitrariness of modern concepts of Anglo-Saxons, and on post-Romantic notions of racial classification, see Horsman, *Race and Manifest Destiny*, 4–5; 25–42; and Geary, *Myth*, 115–18. On recent archaeological work examining the ethnic diversity of "Anglo-Saxon" cultures in post-Roman Britain, see Miles, *Tribes of Britain*, 156–91. On recent genetic studies suggesting significant continuity of native "Celtic" populations from pre-Roman to post-Saxon times throughout Britain, see Sykes, *Saxons*, 277–88.

34. See Hastings, *Construction of Nationhood*, 36–48.

35. Turville-Petre, "The Brutus Prologue to *Sir Gawain and the Green Knight*," in *Imagining a Medieval English Nation*, ed. Lavezzo, 340–46 [341].

36. Ibid., 341. See Turville-Petre's argument that late-medieval poets and chroniclers sought to make English the language of a medieval nation, in *England the Nation*, 1–26.

37. Turville-Petre, "Brutus Prologue," 345. Turville-Petre here concedes Pearsall's claim that Chaucer evinces no signs of nationalism (Pearsall, "Chaucer and Englishness").

38. On nationalism involving primacy in tests of loyalties with competing forms of identity, see Connor, *Ethnonationalism*, 102.

39. See Chapman, "Authorship," 353. On the contents and history of Henry Savile's library, see Andrew G. Watson, *The Manuscripts of Henry Savile of Banke* (London: The Bibliographical Society, 1969). There is little certainty as to how Savile (1568–1617) acquired the manuscript, which was obtained by the antiquary Robert Cotton (1571–1631), joined the Cotton Collection in 1700, and passed to the British Museum in 1753 (Vantuono, ed., *Sir Gawain*, xiv). William Crashaw, Savile's contemporary, claims that Savile's grandfather acquired a large collection of manuscripts "plundered" from "mostly northern" libraries (Watson, *Manuscripts*, 6). For a full description of the manuscript, see A. S. G. Edwards, "The Manuscript: British Library MS Cotton Nero A.x," in *A Companion to the 'Gawain'-poet*, ed. Derek Brewer and Jonathan Gibson (Cambridge: D. S. Brewer, 1997), 197–219.

40. While most scholars situate the *Gawain*-poet in the Northwest Midlands dialect area, John Bowers argues that a single poet responsible for the Cotton Nero poems resided in London, in *The Politics of 'Pearl': Court Poetry in the Age of Richard II* (Cambridge: D. S. Brewer, 2001), 12–16. Carter Revard assumes a mobile, trilingual

author moving among Northwest Midlands, London, and French locales due to attachment to a noble court participating in Hundred Years' War activities, in "Was the *Pearl* Poet in Aquitaine with Chaucer? A Note on *Fade,* L. 149 of *Sir Gawain and the Green Knight,*" *SELIM* 11 (2001–2): 5–26.

41. Oakden, *Alliterative Poetry,* I.135. Oakden's sense of the "west" excludes northern English and Scottish works, which he holds to be both later and inferior to West Midlands poems (I.153). On the "extremely vague frontiers" of the West Midlands region, see R. H. Hilton, *A Medieval Society: The West Midlands at the End of the Thirteenth Century* (New York: John Wiley & Sons, 1966), 7–23 [8].

42. Turville-Petre, *Alliterative Revival,* 35.

43. Everett, "Alliterative Revival," 48.

44. Though *Pearl* features frequent alliteration as an ornamental device, and though alliteration often binds stanzas through concatenation, it is not composed in alliterative meter. On the distinction between "heteromorphic" meters, which feature variant feet (as with alliterative prosody), and "homomorphic" poems with relatively regular foot patterns, as in *Pearl,* see McIntosh, "Early English Alliterative Verse," 21–22; and Hanna, "Defining Middle English Alliterative Poetry," 43–63.

45. The notion that the manuscript's four poems were produced by a single author has not been decisively established, though many scholars operate under this assumption. Much of the evidence used to argue for common authorship, such as common themes, linguistic usage, and poetic technique, could be due either to a single redacting hand, or to contemporary poets sharing language and literary taste. On efforts to determine the authorship of the Cotton Nero poems, see Malcolm Andrew, "Theories of Authorship," in *Companion to the 'Gawain'-poet,* ed. Brewer and Gibson, 23–33. Much as Revivalism insists on a single frame for alliterative verse, so do single-author hypotheses risk functioning as what Michel Foucault calls the "principle of thrift" that reduces multiplicity by filtering data according to post-Enlightenment, bourgeois individualism; see "What Is an Author?" trans. Josué V. Harari, in *Textual Strategies: Perspectives in Post-Structuralist Criticism* (Ithaca, NY: Cornell University Press, 1979), 141–60 [159]).

46. Hoyt N. Duggan and Thorlac Turville-Petre argue for a Northwest Midlands origin for *The Wars of Alexander* in their edition, EETS s.s. 10 (1989). Walter W. Skeat hypothesizes an originally Northumbrian dialect in his edition, EETS e.s. 47 (1886), xxiii. On *Wars* as expressing both the chivalric ethos of the martial Northwest Midlands and a conflicted transnational reaction to rising Eastern powers, see Chism, *Alliterative Revivals,* 111–54 (updating her "Too Close for Comfort: Dis-Orienting Chivalry in the *Wars of Alexander,*" in *Text and Territory,* ed. Tomasch and Gilles, 116–39). Turville-Petre identifies John Clerk as the author of the *Gest Hystoriale of the Destruction of Troy* (hereafter, *Gest Hystoriale*) and situates him in Whalley, Lancashire, in "The Author of *the Destruction of Troy,*" *Medium Aevum* 57 (1988): 264–69. On the dialect of the *Gest Hystoriale* and its unique attestation in Glasgow University Library MS Hunterian 388, see George A. Panton and David Donaldson's edition (EETS o.s. 39, 86), liii–lxii.

47. On the dialect and manuscript of *Saint Erkenwald,* see Clifford Peterson's edition (Philadelphia: University of Pennsylvania Press, 1977), 1–11; 23–26. Bennett speculates that the author of *Erkenwald* was a native of the Northwest who moved to

London as a clerical careerist (*Community, Class and Careerism,* 233). If the *Erkenwald*-poet indeed operated from London, he joins Langland in providing evidence that knowledge of an author's regional origin must often be supplemented by research into relocations throughout a literary career.

48. Hanna, "Alliterative Poetry," 495.

49. Oakden traces the "bulk" of late-medieval alliterative verse to the Northwest, in *Alliterative Poetry,* II.87.

50. On the "veritable flowering of literary culture" in the Northwest Midlands, see Bennett, *Community, Class and Careerism,* 231–32. For Hanna and Lawton's arguments for a West Riding (Yorkshire) dialect of the *Siege of Jerusalem,* see their edition, EETS o.s 320 (2003), xxvii–lxxiv. While Bennett cites M. Y. Offord and J. P. Oakden in support of a Northwest Midlands origin for *Wynnere* and *Parlement,* Angus McIntosh places both poems in the Northeast Midlands, "not very far from where the counties of Yorkshire, Lincolnshire, and Nottinghamshire meet," in "The Textual Transmission of the Alliterative *Morte Arthure,*" in *English and Medieval Studies Presented to J. R. R. Tolkien,* ed. Norman Davis and C. L. Wrenn (London: Allen & Unwin, 1962), 231–40 [231–32]. On the provenance of *Wynnere,* see Trigg, ed., xvii–xxi.

51. On the Northwest Midlands as part of a transnational economic zone that included England, Wales, the Isle of Man, and Ireland, see Bennett, *Community, Class and Careerism,* 108–33.

52. Saintsbury, *History of English Prosody,* III. 101; Hulbert, "Hypothesis," 405. Hulbert's aristocratic bias can be seen in his inferring the noble status of *Sir Gawain* and the *Awntyrs* from their being "condensed and allusive in style" and "developed artistically" (412).

53. On the late-medieval North (including the Northwest Midlands) as a militarized borderlands that grew increasingly important in English politics after Edward I's 1296 invasion of Scotland, see Frank Musgrove, *The North of England: A History from Roman Times to the Present* (Oxford: Basil Blackwell, 1990), 118–54. The North's status as a militarized frontier may explain the region's frequent production of Arthurian romances. Warren analyzes Arthurian literature as a practice of "border writing," reading Arthur as a locus for political contestation among Welsh, Scottish, and English communities each dealing with the Norman Conquest's legacy (*History on the Edge,* 1–16).

54. On the Hundred Years' War's political and administrative background, see Anthony Tuck, *Crown and Nobility: England 1272–1461,* 2nd ed. (Oxford: Blackwell, 1999), 93–287. On tactics in Anglo-Scottish warfare and their impact on the English North, see Michael Prestwich, *Plantagenet England: 1225–1360* (Oxford: Oxford University Press, 2005), 250–65. On Northwest Midlands careerist soldiers' activities on the Continent, in Scotland, and in Wales, see Bennett, *Community, Class and Careerism,* 162–91.

55. Turville-Petre suggests that we focus on the constructive energies of the Trojans who as "patrounes" become patrons of a Western culture translated from Troy's ruins, in "Brutus Prologue," 344.

56. The *Wynnere*-poet also foregrounds late-medieval militarist culture (see chapter 1). On distinguishing "chronicle" texts that intend military realism from more fanciful Arthurian "romances," see Rosalind Field, "Romance in England, 1066–1400," in *Cambridge History,* ed. Wallace, 153–76 [170–72].

57. For a survey of anti-militarist anxieties in late-medieval Troy narratives, see Simpson, *Reform,* 68–103; 116–20. The Trojan past features prominently in *Saint Erkenwald,* in which the miraculously preserved body of an upright inhabitant of "New Troie" (25) is uncovered during work on London's "New Werke" (38; ed. Peterson).

58. The medieval reception of Trojan myth highlighted the treasonous acts of Aeneas and Antenor, who pursued self-interested negotiations with the Greeks. For a Northwest Midlands alliterative version of Aeneas's treachery, see *Gest Hystoriale,* ed. Panton and Donaldson, 11192–350. Theodore Silverstein analyzes the complex Trojan legacy processed by the *Gawain*-poet, in "*Sir Gawain,* Dear Brutus, and Britain's Fortunate Founding: A Study in Comedy and Convention," *Modern Philology* 62 (1965): 189–206 [192–94].

59. Bennett, *Community, Class and Careerism,* 12. On the need to resist land-based assumptions and to recognize the political, economic, and military connections produced by maritime proximity, see Connor, *Ethnonationalism,* 119–43. For a thoroughgoing analysis of Chester, see Barrett, *Against All England,* especially 2–23.

60. On fourteenth-century opportunities for frontier-like "expansion into the Celtic fringe," see Bennett, *Community, Class and Careerism,* 248; and David Walker, *Medieval Wales* (Cambridge: Cambridge University Press, 1990), 139–64.

61. On the settlement patterns of Northwest Midlands merchants and military careerists, see Bennett, *Community, Class and Careerism,* 123–33; 188.

62. Everett reveals Revivalist bias against Northwest Midlands culture, arguing that critics must assume an aristocratic household as the immediate context for such a "self-assured" and courtly *Gawain*-poet ("Alliterative Revival," 48). Salter calls for a broadening of patronage research to include the numerous individuals in multiplex, mobile aristocratic networks ("Alliterative Revival," 237). Besides neglecting households lower on the social scale, Salter focuses primarily on London. See Turville-Petre's argument that the gentry should be seen as the primary consumers of late-medieval alliterative texts, in *Alliterative Revival,* 46–47. Bennett discusses the importance of gentry residents in the Northwest Midlands, in *Community, Class and Careerism,* 75–77.

63. On cultural and economic links between Yorkshire and surrounding areas, including the Northwest Midlands, see David Hey, *A History of Yorkshire: 'County of the Broad Acres'* (Lancaster: Carnegie, 2005), 174–76.

64. On the manuscript context for *Wynnere,* see John J. Thompson, *Robert Thornton and the London Thornton Manuscript* (Cambridge: D. S. Brewer, 1987).

65. Cable indicates Oakden's seminal influence by explaining that the "empirical" genesis of his study of alliterative meter was "Revise Oakden" (*English Alliterative Tradition,* 1; 87–89). On Oakden's metrical principles, see Barney, "Langland's Prosody," 71–72. Thornton's redaction in Lincoln Cathedral MS 91 provides the sole copy of the Alliterative *Morte.*

66. See S. O. Andrew, "The Dialect of *Morte Arthure,*" *Review of English Studies* 4 (1928): 418–23; and Oakden, *Alliterative Poetry,* II.87–88.

67. McIntosh's localization of the *Morte*-poet's dialect, based on his argument that Thornton's working copy derives ultimately from southwest Lincolnshire, has been widely accepted, though McIntosh does not discount the possibility of an originally West Midlands provenance ("Textual Transmission," 240). The provenance of the Alliterative *Morte* may yet be determined through analysis of the base-text used by Malory,

who apparently used a different text than Thornton did; see Eugène Vinaver's notes to his edition of Malory, *Works,* 3 vols. (Oxford: Clarendon, 1947), III.1360–97.

68. The Alliterative *Morte* connects northern Midlands alliterative texts with works composed in the Anglo-Scottish marches, as it features textual links with the *Awntyrs, Sir Gawain,* and *Golagros;* see William Matthews, *The Tragedy of King Arthur: A Study of the Alliterative Morte Arthure* (Berkeley: University of California Press, 1960), 151–77. On the late-medieval association of Gawain with the northerly regions of Britain, see Hahn, ed., *Sir Gawain: Eleven Romances,* 29–33.

69. Davies excludes the militarized regions of the Northwest Midlands from the essentially southern English zone of "sweet civility," in *First English Empire,* 114–17. On the socioeconomic distinctiveness of the North, see Jewell, *North-South Divide,* 77–118; 119–52.

70. Hinchman, *History of English Literature,* 22.

71. Schofield, *English Literature,* 254. On now-discredited nineteenth-century historiographical idealism about Saxon origins, see MacDougall, *Racial Myth,* 73–86; 127–30; and Horsman, *Race and Manifest Destiny,* 25–43.

72. Crane, *Performance of Self,* 169. Crane argues that the Green Knight's actions take the form of a "staged interlude" (168).

73. Lawton, "Unity," 90.

74. On the economic opportunities opened to women by widowhood and military service, see Waugh, *England,* 133–35. On the economic risks and opportunities for widows created by plague outbreaks, see Platt, *King Death,* 49–62.

75. Mavis E. Mate, *Women in Medieval English Society* (Cambridge: Cambridge University Press, 1999), 61–62. Bertilak's trip to Arthur's foreign court is a form of diplomatic travel.

76. All citations from the *Gest Hystoriale* are from Panton and Donaldson's edition; my translations.

77. The *Gest Hystoriale* should be included among the "bokes" [texts] that Chaucer's Criseyde proclaims will "shende" [slander] her for her having "falsed" [betrayed] Troilus (*Troilus,* V.1060). After her father Calchas, asked why he is "trewly" a "traitour" (*Gest,* 8109), states that it is better to join the winning side than be "murthert" [killed] (8157), Breisaid [Criseyde], lavished with gifts from Greeks, "lightly ho left of hir loue hote" [lightly she left from her passionate love] and "now is Troiell, hir trew luff, tynt of hir thoght" [now her true love Troilus is forgotten] (8174–77).

78. Fisher, "Taken Men," 92–93. The green girdle that Gawain accepts in the hope of avoiding decapitation represents Gawain's single ethical lapse in the Temptation game, for which breach he receives a slight neck-wound (2309–14). On Gawain's adoption of the green girdle as his personal sign revealing his transition from absolutism to relativism, see R. A. Shoaf, *The Poem as Green Girdle: Commercium in Sir Gawain and the Green Knight* (Gainesville: University Presses of Florida, 1984), 7.

79. Geoffrey of Monmouth, *History of the Kings of Britain,* 248–49. In *La Mort le Roi Artu,* Guinevere sees through Mordred's forged letter claiming that Arthur has died; she resists Mordred's advances to the last, locking herself up in the fortified Tower of London, in Jean Frappier, ed. (Geneva: Librairie Droz, 1964), 171–81; and *The Death of King Arthur,* ed. and trans. James Cable (London: Penguin, 1971), 161–68. On the *Morte*-poet's sources, see Matthews, *Tragedy of Arthur,* 3–31.

80. L. O. Aranye Fradenburg, *City, Marriage, Tournament: Arts of Rule in Late Medieval Scotland* (Madison: University of Wisconsin Press, 1991), 252–53. Fradenburg here analyzes the conjunction of sovereignty and menace in the "Loathly Lady," examining dangerous, anomalous figures like Guinevere's mother in the *Awntyrs* and the alternately fair and foul female prophetess of *Thomas off Erceldoune* (253–54).

81. All citations from the Alliterative *Morte* are from Krishna's edition; my translations.

82. See Ingham's analysis of the imperial nature of Arthur's holdings in the Alliterative *Morte*, particularly her discussion of the "pleasures" of "insular return" in the catalogue of British holdings that figure an idealized insular unity later undone by imperial ambitions, in *Sovereign Fantasies*, 87–94. Laurie A. Finke and Martin B. Shichtman argue that an analogous catalogue of Arthur's conquests in Laʒamon's *Brut* illuminates the multiplex and discontinuous nature of the political landscape in Arthur's emphatically pre-national Britain, in *King Arthur and the Myth of History* (Gainesville: University Press of Florida, 2004), 112–15.

83. The internal nature of Arthurian civil war is doubled by the rebellion's leaders being Arthur's wife and Mordred. Though Mordred's "sibreden" [kinship] with Arthur is that of a nephew (*Morte*, 688–91), the fourteenth-century understanding of Mordred was haunted by even more intimate relations. As Elizabeth Archibald shows, Mordred's intimacy relative to Arthur increased over the Arthurian legendary history, with an incestuous story becoming attached to his birth from the thirteenth century, moving him from Arthur's nephew to his son; see *Incest and the Medieval Imagination* (Oxford: Oxford University Press, 2001), 132–33.

84. Geoffrey of Monmouth offers a precedent for such a dangerous Guinevere, if Fiona Tolhurst is correct in holding that Geoffrey, in support of Matilda's regnal claims against Stephen (r.1135–54), highlights Guinevere's Roman lineage and portrays her as a potential British empress, in "The Britons as Hebrews, Romans, and Normans: Geoffrey of Monmouth's British Epic and Reflections on Matilda," *Arthuriana* 8.4 (1998): 69–87 [73–75].

85. On the *Morte*-poet's integration of Fortune within an anti-imperialist poetics, see Matthews, *Tragedy of Arthur*, 115–50.

86. Guinevere's mother similarly indicts the agents of Arthurian expansionism in the *Awntyrs*, suggesting that the female voices marginalized in Bennett's Northwest Midlands military history find an accusatory voice in the more northerly (and materially vulnerable) Anglo-Scottish borderlands (see chapter 4). On the anti-imperialist focus on civilian suffering in the *Awntyrs*, see Ingham, *Sovereign Fantasies*, 186–88.

87. Anke Janssen, "The Dream of the Wheel of Fortune," in *The Alliterative Morte Arthure: A Reassessment of the Poem*, ed. Karl Heinz Göller (Cambridge: D. S. Brewer, 1981), 140–52 [140–41]. On the pan-European influence of the Boethian Fortune, see Jerold C. Frakes, *The Fate of Fortune in the Middle Ages: The Boethian Tradition, Studien und Texte zur Geistesgeschichte des Mittelalters* 23 (Leiden: E. J. Brill, 1987), 1–10.

88. The same marker of power used by the *Morte*-poet to figure Fortune's female sovereignty is connected with Morgan's blood even as she is named the "*duches* doʒter of Tyntagel" [*Duchess* of Tintagel's daughter] (2465, my emphasis).

89. Halleck, *History*, 22.

90. Ibid., 14–15; 68.

91. For examples, see Hinchman's argument that alliterative meter is "at its best in describing the din of war, the uncertain swaying of warriors in battle" (*History,* 22); Schofield's assertion that "the old alliteration seemed appropriate to patriotic poets for the recounting of their warlike deeds" (*English Literature,* 253); Everett's influential view that "poets of the tradition" are "most impressive when describing violent action—battles and storms at sea in particular" ("Alliterative Revival," 58); and Moorman's claim that late-medieval alliterative verse is distinctive in exuding ancestral sensitivity to "violence, the deep-seated violence of nature," the "eye-for-an-eye, tooth-for-a-tooth pagan ethos," the "vendetta," and the "comitatus code" ("English Alliterative," 91).

92. R. H. Bowers, "*Gawain and the Green Knight* as Entertainment," *Modern Language Quarterly* 24 (1963): 333–41 [336n]. Albert B. Friedman speaks for a number of critics in arguing that the poem's sole flaw is the Green Knight's explanation of Morgan's responsibility for much of the plot, in "Morgan le Fay in *Sir Gawain and the Green Knight*," *Speculum* 35 (1960): 260–74 [260]. For similar aesthetic critiques, see Kittredge, *Study of 'Gawain and the Green Knight,'* 154; and J. R. Hulbert, "Syr Gawayn and the Grene Knyȝt," *Modern Philology* 13 (1915): 433–62; 689–730 [454].

93. See Lawton's indictment of "a modern criticism" that "mostly refuses to accept the poet's own explanation of his plot," in "Unity," 89.

94. Fisher, "Taken Men," 98. While Fisher argues cogently for a "deliberate marginalization" of Morgan (71–72), her contention that the poem undermines the significance of Morgan's role reproduces previous assumptions of aesthetic faultiness. The *Gawain*-poet's careful foreshadowing of Morgan's pre-eminence undermines such assumptions. See Elisa Marie Narin's examination of rhetorical techniques that signal Morgan's supremacy from her first appearance, in "'Þat on . . . þat oþer': Rhetorical Description and Morgan le Fay in *Sir Gawain and the Green Knight*," *Pacific Coast Philology* 23 (1988): 60–66. For an alternative perspective, see Elizabeth Scala's argument that Morgan's absence structures the poem, with attempts to resituate Morgan's centrality at the poem's opening misrecognizing the narrative's fundamental "reconfiguration" that follows the revelation of Morgan's role, in *Absent Narratives, Manuscript Textuality, and Literary Structure in Late Medieval England* (New York: Palgrave Macmillan, 2002), 62–68.

95. Angela Carson, "Morgain la Fée as the Principle of Unity in *Gawain and the Green Knight*," *Modern Language Quarterly* 23 (1962): 3–16. Urien is sometimes described as Morgan's husband.

96. Laura Hibbard Loomis, "*Gawain and the Green Knight*," in *Arthurian Literature in the Middle Ages: A Collaborative History,* ed. Roger Sherman Loomis (Oxford: Clarendon Press, 1959), 528–40 [535]. Edith Whitehurst Williams also conflates the Lady and Morgan, referring to the former as Morgan's "guise as temptress," in "Morgan la Fée as Trickster in *Sir Gawain and the Green Knight*," *Folklore* 96 (1985): 38–56 [49]. Maureen Fries counters claims that the Lady is Morgan's double, arguing that she is Morgan's instrument, not her "other," in "The Characterization of Women in the Alliterative Tradition," in *Alliterative Tradition,* ed. Levy and Szarmach, 25–45 [36].

97. See Morgan's deployment of both a messenger-maiden and a maiden tasked with testing her hostage Lancelot's loyalty, while operating from her woodland holding,

the Val Sanz Retour, in *Lancelot-Grail,* ed. Lacy, trans. Rosenberg and Carroll, 314–25.

98. Chism, *Alliterative Revivals,* 90.

99. Fisher, "Taken Men," 80.

100. See ibid., 79–80.

101. Tolkien and Gordon emend the *Gawain*-poet's description of Bertilak as "kyng" to "lord" (992), arguing that "kyng" is "an error, and not a mysterious vestige of a mythological analogue," in *Sir Gawain and the Green Knight,* ed. J. R. R. Tolkien, E. V. Gordon, and Norman Davis, 2nd ed. (Oxford: Oxford University Press, 1967), 103n. Malcolm Andrew and Ronald Waldron also make this emendation in their edition, in *The Poems of the 'Pearl' Manuscript,* 4th ed. (Exeter: University of Exeter Press, 2002).

102. Fisher, "Taken Men," 89.

103. Ibid., 80.

104. Mate, *Women,* 61–62.

105. Fisher, "Taken Men," 80.

106. Carolyn Dinshaw, "A Kiss is Just a Kiss: Heterosexuality and its Consolations in *Sir Gawain and the Green Knight,*" *Diacritics* (1994): 205–25 [211–13].

107. Ibid., 211.

108. On the circumstances in which a woman might assume full control of an estate in her husband's absence, see Archer, "'How ladies,'" 150–51; and Mate, *Women,* 61–66. On the legal implications of women's classification as either married or unmarried, see Cordelia Beattie, *Medieval Single Women: The Politics of Social Classification in Late Medieval England* (Oxford: Oxford University Press, 2007), 13–38.

109. Christopher Cannon, "The Rights of Medieval English Women: Crime and the Issue of Representation," in *Medieval Crime and Social Control,* ed. Barbara A. Hanawalt and David Wallace (Minneapolis: University of Minnesota Press, 1998), 156–85 [160].

110. Ibid.

111. See Ingham, *Sovereign Fantasies,* 114–21.

112. Barrett argues that geographical markers invite a regionalist reading of the poem, in *Against All England,* 136–38.

113. Cicero, *De Senectute,* vi.18 [At senatui quae sint gerenda praescribo et quo modo; Carthagini male iam diu cogitanti bellum multo ante denuntio].

114. R. Howard Bloch, *Medieval Misogyny and the Invention of Western Romantic Love* (Chicago: University of Chicago Press, 1991), 165–97 [196].

115. Ibid., 196.

116. Chism, *Alliterative Revivals,* 103.

117. Morgan may also seek to highlight her unmarried status, channeling the anxiety-producing singleness that Karma Lochrie sees as triggering Lollard insistence on marriage and critiques of female sexual aloofness, in *Heterosyncrasies: Female Sexuality When Normal Wasn't* (Minneapolis: University of Minnesota Press, 2005), 49–51.

118. *Merlin,* ed. Henry B. Wheatley, 2 vols. (EETS o.s. 10; 21; 36; 112 [1865–69]), I.168. All citations from the *Prose Merlin* are from Wheatley; my translations. The *Prose Merlin* is a fifteenth-century rendering of the thirteenth-century, Old French Vulgate Cycle, which features Merlin as both prophet and war-adviser; see John Conlee, ed., *The Prose Merlin* (Kalamazoo: Medieval Institute Publications, 1998), 8–10.

119. On the relation of Merlin's shape-shifting to Celtic analogues, see Paton, *Studies in the Fairy Mythology,* 23–24.

120. "The Wedding of Sir Gawain and Dame Ragnelle," ed. Hahn, 41–80; my translation.

121. Ingham, *Sovereign Fantasies,* 183. Ingham refers to Fradenburg's study of the Loathly Lady as figuring idealized sovereignty transformed by the "right" form of rule (*City, Marriage, Tournament,* 253–54).

122. Ingham, *Sovereign Fantasies,* 181–84.

123. Madden, ed., *Syr Gawayne,* 325–26n.

124. Tolkien, Gordon, and Davis, eds., 130n. In the passage upon which Tolkien and Gordon lean, Merlin argues that Morgan "fu bele damoisele jusques a celui terme que elle commencha a aprendre des enchantemens et des charroies. Mais puis que li anemis fu dedens li mis et elle fu aspiree et de luxure et de dyable, elle pierdi si otreement sa biauté que trop devint laide" [was a beautiful woman up until the point when she began to learn spells and tricks. But since the enemy had installed himself within her and she was inspired both by luxury and deviltry, she lost so utterly her beauty that she soon became ugly], in *La Suite du Roman Merlin,* ed. Gilles Roussineau, 2 vols. (Geneva: Librairie Droz, 1996), I.19–20; my translation. Fries assumes that Morgan's foul appearance would be known from this "French anecdote" and argues that the Lady is destined to become like Morgan, in "Characterization," 34.

125. See Heng's argument that a "masculine" criticism's desire for mastery leads to a "fantasy of textual closure and command," in "Feminine Knots," 500.

126. On various interpretations of Morgan, see Twomey, "Morgain la Fée," 91–115.

127. Marjory Rigby compares temptations of Lancelot and Gawain, arguing for the *Gawain*-poet's familiarity with the Vulgate tradition, in "*Sir Gawain and the Green Knight* and the Vulgate *Lancelot,*" *Modern Language Review* 78.2 (1983): 357–66.

128. On Morgan's ill-fated affair with Guiomar, see Paton, *Studies in the Fairy Mythology,* 60–73.

129. Cicero, *De Senectute,* xv.55 [et senectus est natura loquacior].

130. Elde's lengthy speech, aimed at undermining earthly interests by showing the inevitability of death, is a study in overkill, with its rambling religious message shutting down Youthe and Medill-Elde's social and economic debate. On Elde's idiosyncratic and bloated speech, see Lisa Kiser, "Elde and His Teaching in *The Parlement of the Thre Ages,*" *Philological Quarterly* 66 (1987): 303–14. On the primacy of economic issues over religious authority in the *Parlement,* see Randy P. Schiff, "The Loneness of the Stalker: Poaching and Subjectivity in *The Parlement of the Thre Ages,*" *Texas Studies in Literature and Language* 51.3 (2009): 263–93 [267–74].

131. Bourdieu, *Outline,* 165.

132. Most editors of *Sir Gawain* take this phrase as signifying middle age, interpreting as supporting evidence Bertilak's "bright" and "bever-hwed" [beaver-colored] beard (845) and energetic hunting activity. Eiichi Suzuki, however, argues that Bertilak is elderly, in "A Note on the Age of the Green Knight," *Neuphilologische Mitteilungen* 78 (1977): 27–30. On interpretations of this description, see Vantuono, ed., *Sir Gawain,* 193n. Even if the *Vulgate Lancelot*'s Berthelai the Old is intended by Bertilak, we can imagine that this is some years before his acquiring the moniker.

133. Cicero, *De Senectute,* vi.17 [Non viribus aut velocitate aut celeritate corporum

res magnae geruntur, sed consilio auctoritate sententia].

134. Sarah Stanbury, *Seeing the 'Gawain'-Poet: Description and the Act of Perception* (Philadelphia: University of Pennsylvania Press, 1991), 107–11.

135. Scala, *Absent Narratives,* 66. Scala steers criticism away from merely "retrospective" readings of Morgan's absence from early portions in the narrative, reading her ongoing absence as figuring the "text's unconscious" (65–66).

136. Immanuel Kant, *Critique of Judgement,* trans. J. H. Bernard (New York: Hafner Press, 1951), 96. For Kant's definition of the sublime, see 86–89.

137. Morgan's appearance, while grotesque, differs from the "loathly dame" figure analyzed by Whitehurst, in "Morgan la Fée," 49. While Morgan's disguised Elde is unsightly, with "sellyly blered" [wondrously bleary] and "soure" [sour] facial features (961–63), the overall description is restrained in comparison with such extreme loathsomeness as depicted in the *Wedding* (231–45), or in the hag's description in Chaucer's *Wife* as "fouler" than anyone could imagine (III.999).

138. Bertilak's story of Morgan's love-affair may well be a tale designed to deal with the anxiety of Morgan's unsettling female power, with such gossip explaining Morgan's need to manage her reputation.

139. In the thirteenth-century *Prophecies de Merlin,* the Lady of the Lake traps Merlin in a magical tomb (167–68), explaining to him, "Saches vraiement que je t'ai mis ici dedens pour ce que tu aloies disant en tous les lieus ou tu aloies que tu avoies jeu a moi, dont je en fui pute clamee par la bouche meisme(s) Morgein" [Know for certain that I have put you in here because you were going around saying everywhere you went that you had your fun with me, because of which I am proclaimed a whore by the very mouth of Morgan], in *Les Prophecies de Merlin,* ed. Lucy Allen Paton, vol. 1; 1926 (New York: Kraus Reprint Corporation, 1966), 169; my translation.

140. Judith Bennett, "Public Power and Authority in the Medieval English Countryside," in *Women and Power in the Middle Ages,* ed. Mary Erler and Maryanne Kowaleski (Athens: University of Georgia Press, 1988), 18–36 [19].

Chapter 4

1. *The Awntyrs off Arthure at the Terne Wathelyn,* ed. Ralph Hanna (Manchester: Manchester University Press, 1974), 418; my translations. For manuscript variants, see Robert J. Gates's edition, *The Awntyrs off Arthure at the Terne Wathelyne* (Philadelphia: University of Pennsylvania Press, 1969), 86–195.

2. All citations from *The Knightly Tale of Golagros and Gawane* (hereafter, *Golagros and Gawane*) are from Ralph Hanna's edition (produced with material by W. R. J. Barron), Scottish Text Society Fifth Series 7 (Woodbridge: Boydell, 2008); my translations.

3. Davies, *First English Empire,* 79–81; 203.

4. Anderson, *Imagined Communities,* 19–21; 171–73; 188.

5. Ibid., 19.

6. Suzanne Conklin Akbari, "Orientation and Nation in Chaucer's *Canterbury Tales,*" in *Chaucer's Cultural Geography,* ed. Lynch, 102–34 [117–18].

7. On modern nations' appropriation of political legitimacy formerly dominated by

religious authorities, see Anderson, *Imagined Communities,* 10–11.

8. Ibid., 145.

9. Akbari, "Orientation," 117.

10. Anderson, *Imagined Communities,* 135.

11. Ingham, "Contrapuntal Histories," 48.

12. See Davies, *First English Empire,* 160–62.

13. Hobsbawm, *Nations,* 46–78.

14. See Connor, *Ethnonationalism,* 90–117

15. Ibid., 10; 76–77.

16. Ibid., 76.

17. Smith, *Ethnic Origins,* 206–8.

18. Hardt and Negri define Empire as an overarching "concept" defined "fundamentally by a lack of boundaries," aimed at dealing with a globalized economy in which national and ethnic boundaries give way to transnational corporate interests, in *Empire,* xiv–xv.

19. See Dinshaw, *Getting Medieval,* 38–40

20. See Fradenburg, *Sacrifice Your Love,* 43–78.

21. While some post-colonial critics insist that imperialism post-dates the mercantilist capitalism of the sixteenth-century age of European expansion, some emphasize Enlightenment ideologies, and some argue that imperialism is a product of nineteenth-century industrial expansion, post-colonial theorists generally assign imperialism to the modern era. On debates concerning the timeframe for imperialism in post-colonial theory, see Bill Ashcroft, Gareth Griffiths, and Helen Tiffin, *Post-Colonial Studies: The Key Concepts* (London: Routledge, 2000), 122–27.

22. On the critical possibilities enabled by replacing a progressivist vision of history with a systematic sensitivity to "difficult similarity conjoined to complex difference," see Cohen's introduction to *Postcolonial Middle Ages,* 8; see also Ingham and Warren's methodological discussion in "Introduction: Postcolonial Modernity and the Rest of History," in *Postcolonial Moves,* 1–15. See also Bruce W. Holsinger's analysis of the foundational influence of medieval studies in postcolonial theory, traced in the impact of *Annales* historiography on the Subaltern Studies group, in "Medieval Studies, Postcolonial Studies, and the Genealogies of Critique," *Speculum* 77 (2002): 1195–1227. For a historiographical justification of medieval empire as an object of study, see Davies, *First English Empire,* 191–203. Kathy Lavezzo usefully urges caution in linking post-coloniality with "any type of social oppression," suggesting our need to justify our recourse to models of empire, in her review of Cohen's *Postcolonial Middle Ages,* in *Journal of Colonialism and Colonial History* 3.1 (2002).

23. Ingham, *Sovereign Fantasies,* 10. Ingham's rejection of the goal of locating the modern nation's "teleological ancestor" renders her methodology particularly powerful for marcher zones. See especially Ingham's discussion of negotiating common cultural characteristics with political differences in the analysis of "antagonistic intimacies" in the fourteenth-century Anglo-Welsh borderlands (232–33n).

24. Ibid., 5–6.

25. Ingham and Warren, introduction to *Postcolonial Moves,* 1.

26. Cohen, introduction to *Postcolonial Middle Ages,* 8. For analysis of the critical possibilities for medievalist literary history opened up by postcolonial criticism, see

Finke and Shichtman, *King Arthur,* 6–8. On recent postcolonial scholarship on empire building in the medieval West, see Barbara Fuchs, "Imperium Studies," in *Postcolonial Moves,* ed. Ingham and Warren, 71–90. For strategies for rethinking modern concepts of nationhood within a British context, see Jeffrey Jerome Cohen, "Introduction: Infinite Realms," in *Cultural Diversity,* ed. Cohen, 1–16.

27. K. B. McFarlane, "The English Nobility, 1290–1536," in *The Nobility of Later Medieval England: The Ford Lectures for 1953 and Related Studies* (Oxford: Oxford University Press, 1973), 1–141 [19–20].

28. Ibid., 21.

29. R. James Goldstein, *The Matter of Scotland: Historical Narrative in Medieval Scotland* (Lincoln: University of Nebraska Press, 1993), 79–103.

30. On the rise of the modern nation being tied directly to the diminishment of feudal privileges through the concentration of physical force capital in national armies, see Bourdieu, "Rethinking the State," in *Practical Reason,* 1–18.

31. On Edward I's empire-building efforts, see Michael Prestwich, *Edward I,* rev. ed. (New Haven, CT: Yale University Press, 1997), 42–52. For a thoroughgoing study of late-medieval Anglo-Scottish marcher culture, see Cynthia J. Neville, *Violence, Custom and Law: The Anglo-Scottish Border Lands in the Later Middle Ages* (Edinburgh: Edinburgh University Press, 1998). On medieval Scotland as decentralized, largely splintered into local lordships, see Michael Brown, *The Black Douglases: War and Lordship in Late Medieval Scotland, 1300–1455* (East Linton, East Lothian: Tuckwell Press, 1998), 4–5. On the persistence of identification with local lords rather than an overarching national identity in fifteenth-century Scotland, see Anthony Goodman, "The Anglo-Scottish Marches in the Fifteenth Century: A Frontier Society?" in *Scotland and England: 1286–1815,* ed. Roger A. Mason (Edinburgh: John Donald, 1988), 18–33 [19]. For an alternative view, see Robin Frame, who, while recognizing the marginal political and economic status of Anglo-Scottish border culture, nevertheless insists that such regional uniqueness was developed within larger regnal and national frames, in *The Political Development of the British Isles, 1100–1400* (Oxford: Oxford University Press, 1990), 202–3.

32. Although there is no secure means for dating the composition of the *Awntyrs,* Hanna's rough estimate of 1400–1430 seems sound (*Awntyrs,* 52). Many scholars' earlier assessments derive from the presence of early fourteenth-century manorial records in the Ireland MS, to which a copy of the *Awntyrs* was, Hanna explains, only much later appended (50–51; 51n).

33. Rhiannon Purdie dates *Golagros* from between the "early fifteenth century" (when the *Awntyrs* and the Alliterative *Morte* begin to circulate) and 1508 (the date of Walter Chepman and Andrew Myllar's print), in "The Search for Scottishness in *Golagros and Gawane*," in *The Scots and Medieval Arthurian Legend,* ed. Rhiannon Purdie and Nicola Royan (Cambridge: D. S. Brewer, 2005), 95–107 [95n].

34. On "chronicle" Arthurian works, see Field, "Romance in England," 171. For a rejection of the chronicle–romance distinction in the Alliterative *Morte,* and for analysis of the poem's dialectics of history and poetry, see Ingham, *Sovereign Fantasies,* 79–82.

35. Matthews lists textual links among these poems, in *Tragedy of Arthur,* 156–61. Although Matthews's evidence for textual parallels is unassailable, his argument that the *Awntyrs*-poet borrowed from the Alliterative *Morte Arthure* rests on slim grounds

(159), since these poems resist certain dating. The Alliterative *Morte* also resists precise localization and is best conceived within a generally militarized zone including the northern Midlands and the English North (see chapter 3).

36. For Musgrove, the Northwest Midlands are part of the North (see *North of England,* 118–54).

37. On civilian suffering in the Alliterative *Morte,* see Matthews, *Tragedy of Arthur,* 115–50; and Ingham, *Sovereign Fantasies,* 87–100.

38. On postcolonial theorists' recent attempts to "dislodge" the "national geographies" inflecting medievalist criticism, see Ingham and Warren's introduction to *Postcolonial Moves,* 1–15.

39. Blake, "Middle English Alliterative Revivals," 207.

40. On the Scottish adoption of the meter of the *Awntyrs,* see Craigie, "Scottish Alliterative Poems," 221–22. Turville-Petre theorizes a single "school" of poets working within the thirteen-line stanza, in "'Summer Sunday,'" 12. Lawton offers a searching analysis of the evidence for a thirteen-line stanza movement, in "Diversity of Middle English Alliterative Poetry," 151–64. Oakden posits two "Revivals" in his commentary on the stanzaic meter of *Sir Gawain,* which he sees as a "compromise" between the syllabic and alliterative prosodies of "antagonistic" literary schools, in *Alliterative Poetry,* I.218.

41. Pearsall, "Alliterative Revival," 37–38.

42. The *Awntyrs* survives in three other manuscripts. The Lincoln Cathedral Library MS 91 text of the *Awntyrs* comes from the West Riding of Yorkshire, while the Ireland Blackburn MS version was copied in the Lancashire area. The provenance of the Bodley MS Douce 324 copy has been traced to the "south-eastern counties" by Doyle ("Manuscripts," 97), while Gates describes the Lambeth Palace 491 copy as of the "southernmost" origin (*Awntyrs,* 15). For full manuscript descriptions, see Gates, ed., *Awntyrs,* 6–16. Hanna's claim that the *Awntyrs* is a composite of two poems ("*The Awntyrs off Arthure:* An Interpretation," *Modern Language Quarterly* 31 [1970]: 275–97) is largely irrelevant to tracing the poem's codicological history, since all copies present roughly the same text. Hanna's evidence does not strike me as decisive, since the relatively short length of the text exaggerates the significance of statistical variations (see especially 292–93), while his view of "poetic incompetence" in the latter part of the poem is too subjective (293). Even if one grants Hanna's arguments for the *Awntyrs*'s composite origin, the version that has survived was clearly fashioned as a single poem—and, as far as manuscript evidence informs us, it is only as a single poem that the *Awntyrs* was presented to medieval audiences.

43. For Hanna's dialectal localization, see *Awntyrs,* 49. Hanna has recently expressed uncertainty about the Northern English origins of the Awntyrs and has suggested Scotland as a possible origin, in *Knightly Tale of Golagaros and Gawane.* For Hanna's regionalization of the Alliterative *Morte,* see "Alliterative Poetry," 509.

44. *Golagros* was among the first works printed by Chepman and Myllar (see Hahn, ed., *Golagros,* 232).

45. Richard Holland, *The Buke of the Howlat,* in Priscilla Bawcutt and Felicity Riddy, eds., *Longer Scottish Poems, Volume One: 1375–1650* (Edinburgh: Scottish Academic Press, 1987), 43–84; 323–40. On the Black Douglas patronage of Holland's *Howlat,* see Michael Brown, "'Rejoice to hear of Douglas': The House of Douglas and

the Presentation of Magnate Power in Late Medieval Scotland," *Scottish Historical Review* 76.2 (1997): 161–84. On the *Howlat* as a text informed by Anglo-Scottish marcher militarism, see Randy P. Schiff, "Holland as Howlat: Shadow Self and Borderland Homage in *The Buke of the Howlat*," *Mediaevalia* 29.2 (2008): 91–116.

46. *Golagros,* 297–98. Compare *Alliterative 'Morte,'* 3342–44.

47. For a comparison of Scottish expansion into the Isles and the Highlands as "the best parallel for the English conquests in Wales and Ireland," see Alexander Grant, "Scotland's 'Celtic Fringe' in the Late Middle Ages: The Macdonald Lords of the Isles and the Kingdom of Scotland," in *The British Isles, 1100–1500: Comparisons, Contrasts and Connections,* ed. R. R. Davies (Edinburgh: John Donald, 1988), 118–41. Goldstein marks Edward I's subjugation of Wales as the beginning of the "history of English imperialism," in *Matter of Scotland,* 31.

48. Each of these empires differs from the modern nation in granting the church jurisdictional authority that overlaps with secular power. However militaristic these empires appear, neither ever questions the status of "Christendom" as a second "imagined community," with individuals subject to an ecclesiastical jurisdiction. On the diminishing power of Christendom as an "imagined community" within expanding vernacular bureaucracies, and on the absence of independent secular communities before the eighteenth century, see Anderson, *Imagined Communities,* 41–42.

49. On Stewart tactics against noble families linked to a programmatic cultivation of transnational cultural and political prestige for a centralized Scotland, see Michael Brown and Steve Boardman, "Survival and Revival: Late Medieval Scotland," in *Scotland: A History,* ed. Jenny Wormald (Oxford: Oxford University Press, 2005), 77–106 [93–103].

50. Purdie contends that the oft-cited approximate date of 1470 reflects "the tendency of scholars to assign any undated Scottish text with a political slant to the troubled reign of James III," in "Search for Scottishness," 95n.

51. Davies, *First English Empire,* 189–90.

52. Ibid., 190.

53. Brown and Boardman, "Survival and Revival," 93. See Elizabeth Walsh's argument for a pacifist *Golagros,* in "*Golagros and Gawane:* A Word for Peace," in *Bryght Lanternis: Essays on the Language and Literature of Medieval and Renaissance Scotland,* ed. J. Derrick McClure and Michael R. G. Spiller (Aberdeen: Aberdeen University Press, 1989), 90–103.

54. See A. C. Spearing, "*The Awntyrs off Arthure,*" in *Alliterative Tradition,* ed. Levy and Szarmach, 183–202 [186].

55. Ingham, *Sovereign Fantasies,* 188. Ingham, while aligning Arthur with England (162), still leaves the "national" provenance of the *Awntyrs* open to question (184).

56. Rosalind Field, "The Anglo-Norman Background to Alliterative Romance," in *Middle English Alliterative Poetry and Its Literary Background,* ed. Lawton, 54–69. On the cultivation of the Arthurian legend by Edward I and Edward III, see Prestwich, *Edward I,* 37; 204–5; and MacDougall, *Racial Myth,* 13–15. On a "royal cult" of Arthur maintained by English kings exploiting the Galfridian concept of a pan-British monarch, see N. J. Higham, *King Arthur: Myth-Making and History* (London: Routledge, 2002), 226–35. Daniel Birkholz links Edward I's appropriation of Arthurian territorial models with the politics of English imperial geography, in *The King's Two Maps: Car-*

tography and Culture in Thirteenth-Century England (New York: Routledge, 2004), 95–98.

57. Nicola Royan, "The Fine Art of Faint Praise in Older Scots Historiography," in *Scots,* ed. Purdie and Royan, 43–54 [43–44]. On competing late-medieval English and Scottish claims in a "war of historiography," see Goldstein, *Matter of Scotland,* 57–103. On the Scottish chronicle tradition and transnational marcher politics, see Katherine H. Terrell, "Subversive Histories: Strategies of Identity in Scottish Historiography," in *Cultural Diversity,* ed. Cohen, 153–72.

58. Hahn, ed., *Sir Gawain: Eleven Romances,* 83. On the concentration of Gawain romances in the North; and for the geographical settings of *Avowyng* and *Carlisle,* see Hahn, ed., *Sir Gawain: Eleven Romances,* 29–33; 81–84; 113–17.

59. See the *Avowyng of Arthur,* ed. Hahn, in *Sir Gawain: Eleven Romances,* 119–50.

60. See *Sir Gawain and the Carle of Carlisle,* ed. Hahn, in *Sir Gawain: Eleven Romances,* 85–103. For a fuller list of Arthurian works circulating in the North of England, see Jewell, *North-South Divide,* 188–90.

61. Such raiding was common in the Anglo-Scottish marches well into the fifteenth century and involved allegiance to local lords rather than national armies; see Brown, *Black Douglases,* 3–6.

62. On Edward III and Scotland, see Michael Brown, *The Wars of Scotland: 1214–1371* (Edinburgh: Edinburgh University Press, 2004), 232–54; see also Michael Prestwich, *The Three Edwards: War and State in England, 1272–1377,* 2nd ed. (New York: Routledge, 2003), 57–62. On the "disinherited" and the conflicted nature of marcher land claims, see Brown, *Black Douglases,* 24–26.

63. This reading is derived from the Ireland manuscript; the other manuscripts offer "errant" [D], "armed" [T], and an omission [L]; see Gates, ed., *Awntyrs,* 138. Hanna's text has Galeron described as an "errant" knighte (349).

64. Brown, *Black Douglases,* 160.

65. John Barbour, *The Bruce,* ed. and trans. A. A. M. Duncan (Edinburgh: Canongate, 1997), i.183–98. All Barbour citations are from Duncan's edition.

66. Amours, ed., *Scottish Alliterative Poems,* lxxii. The very title of Amours's collection silently argues his nationalist view of the *Awntyrs.* Amours's claim for a Scottish *Awntyrs* (which, to my knowledge, no recent scholars accept) contributed significantly to debate about Huchown (li-lxxxii).

67. Ibid., lxxii.

68. On the historiographical need to resist exaggerating the scope of rarefied legal discourses about constitutional change or monarchical centrality, given the overwhelming importance of "personal" relationships in medieval political life, see Smyth's preface to *Medieval Europeans,* xii–xiii.

69. On class-based interests in Barbour's *Bruce,* see Goldstein, *Matter of Scotland,* 133–214. Goldstein observes of "heroic poetry" that among its basic ideological functions is impelling "soldiers to wage war to defend an idea" (144). On the Black Douglases' use of *Howlat* to cultivate their connection to the James Douglas who carried Robert the Bruce's heart into battle against Muslim enemies, see Brown, *Black Douglases,* 128–30.

70. Brown, *Black Douglases,* 134.

71. J. A. Tuck, "War and Society in the Medieval North," *Northern History* 21

(1985): 33–52 [42]. For a sociological exploration of Anglo-Scottish borderlands culture, see John Gray, "Lawlessness on the Frontier: The Anglo-Scottish Borderlands in the Fourteenth to the Sixteenth Century," *History and Anthropology* 12.4 (2001): 381–408.

72. On the socio-economic benefits associated with constant militarization in the English North, see Tuck, "War and Society," 43–48. On similar developments in Scotland and in the Anglo-Scottish marches, see Brown, *Black Douglases*, 157–82.

73. Madden, ed., *Syr Gawayne*, xli. On traditions associating Gawain with Scotland, see Martin B. Shichtman, "Sir Gawain in Scotland: A Hometown Boy Made Good," in *King Arthur through the Ages*, ed. Valerie M. Legurio and Mildred Leake Day (New York: Garland, 1990), 234–67.

74. The Orkneys were pledged to the Scottish Crown by Christian I, King of Denmark and Norway, in a 1468 marriage treaty, after which Scottish kings treated them as Scottish territory; see A. D. M. Barrell, *Medieval Scotland* (Cambridge: Cambridge University Press, 2000), 171–72.

75. On the ambiguity of national divisions in medieval Europe, see Robert Bartlett, *The Making of Europe: Conquest, Colonization, and Cultural Change, 950–1350* (Princeton, NJ: Princeton University Press, 1993), 24–59.

76. Shichtman, "Sir Gawain," 236–37. Flora Alexander cautions that hostility to Arthur is not uniform in Scottish chronicles and romances, in "Late Medieval Scottish Attitudes to the Figure of King Arthur: A Reassessment," *Anglia* 93 (1975): 17–34. On trends in Scottish treatment of Arthur in romance and chronicle, see Royan, "Fine Art," in *Scots*, ed. Purdie and Royan, 43–54.

77. Malory, *Morte*, in *Works*, ed. Vinaver, 671. On Malory's channeling of English contempt for Scots in representations of knights responsible for the dissolution of Arthur's regime, see Cory J. Rushton, "'Of an uncouthe stede': The Scottish Knight in Middle English Arthurian Romances," in *Scots*, ed. Purdie and Royan, 109–19.

78. Nicola Royan, "'Na les vailyeant than ony uthir princis of Britane': Representations of Arthur in Scotland, 1480–1540," *Scottish Studies Review* 3 (2002): 9–20 [16]. Gawain's ethnic ambiguity seems appropriate, considering the multi-ethnic nature of Scottish and English identities. See Keith Stringer's linkage of Scottish nation-formation with the unification of multiple ethnicities, in "The Emergence of a Nation-State, 1100–1300," in *Scotland*, ed. Wormald, 39–76 [74–75]. On the multi-ethnic nature of English identity, see Kumar, *Making of English National Identity*, 9–12.

79. *Awntyrs*, 418; 419–20. Though textual variation makes identification of the entire list of Galeron's territories impossible, the scribes agree on identifying Carrick, Cunningham, and Kyle, which are located in Ayrshire, just northwest of the powerful lordship of Galloway. For textual variants, see Gates, ed., *Awntyrs*, 150, and Amours, ed., *Scottish Alliterative Poems*, 354. On Galloway's perennial ascendancy over its neighbors, see Barrell, *Medieval Scotland*, 86–90.

80. George Mackay, *Scottish Place Names* (New Lanark: Geddes and Grosset, 2000), 39.

81. Barrell, *Medieval Scotland*, 86.

82. Brown, *Black Douglases*, 60. For a history of Galloway before the Wars of Independence, see Richard Oram, *The Lordship of Galloway: c. 900 to c. 1300* (Edinburgh: John Donald, 2000).

83. On Galloway's traditions of unity and resistance to the Scottish Crown, see Barrell, *Medieval Scotland*, 86–91. On Galloway during the Wars of Independence, see Brown, *Wars*, 304–6.

84. On Anglo-Norman settlement in Galloway, see D. D. R. Owen, ed. and trans., *Fergus of Galloway: Knight of King Arthur*, by Guillaume le Clerc (London: J. M. Dent, 1991), x–xi.

85. On Black Douglas respect for Galloway's distinct customs, see Brown, *Black Douglases*, 60–64; 171–75. The Douglas conquest of the Galwegians is commemorated in Holland's thirteen-line stanzaic *Howlat*. If Turville-Petre is correct in suggesting that the *Awntyrs* brought the thirteen-line stanza into Scotland ("'Summer Sunday,'" 3), then the *Awntyrs* is also a borderlands text in literary history. On the conquest of Galloway as depicted in the Douglas arms, see Brown, *Black Douglases*, 62–64; and Amours, ed., *Scottish Alliterative Poems*, 303n. On wild men as arms-bearers, see Husband, ed., *Wild Man*, 171–95.

86. On "social logic" and the irreducibly local nature of texts as "lived events," see Spiegel, "History," 77.

87. Goodman, "Anglo-Scottish Marches," 29; 18.

88. Regardless of one's acceptance of the existence of medieval nation-states, the trend of late-medieval political centralization throughout Western Europe is clear. Gellner argues that state centralization made medieval nation formation possible—but that the necessary binding of cultural identity and political power simply did not occur, in *Nationalism*, 16–17. On political centralization in England, see W. M. Ormrod, *Political Life in Medieval England, 1300–1450* (New York: St. Martin's Press, 1995), 18–60. On centralization in Scotland, see Brown and Boardman, "Survival and Revival," 101–6.

89. Tuck ties the emergence of a "northern nobility" to wealth generated by cross-border conflicts and alliances, in "War and Society," 43–45. On the Douglases' transnational identity, see Brown, *Black Douglases*, 203–26.

90. Goodman, "Anglo-Scottish Marches," 19; 23.

91. On knightly combats in borderland areas, see Richard Barber and Juliette Barker, *Tournaments: Jousts, Chivalry and Pageants in the Middle Ages* (Woodbridge: Boydell, 1989), 34–44; and Rosamund Allen, "*The Awntyrs off Arthure*: Jests and Jousts," in *Romance Reading on the Book*, ed. Jennifer Fellows et al. (Cardiff: University of Wales Press, 1996), 129–42 [131–32]. Edward III twice challenged the French king to fight for the French realm, demonstrating his commitment to the chivalric ethos—though with little expectation of being taken seriously; see Prestwich, *Three Edwards*, 207.

92. Ingham, *Sovereign Fantasies*, 186.

93. Hahn, ed., *Sir Gawain: Eleven Romances*, 217n. Amours argues that Galeron's possessions cluster around Ayrshire, in *Scottish Alliterative Poems*, 417n. For relevant variants, see Gates, ed., *Awntyrs*, 150n.

94. As with the list of lands through which Galeron identifies himself, the lands that Arthur offers to Gawain are not easily identified and display significant textual variation. For variants, see Gates, ed., *Awntyrs*, 188n; for discussion of the difficulty of deciphering the locations, see Hanna, ed., *Awntyrs*, 140n.

95. Hahn, ed., *Sir Gawain: Eleven Romances*, 224n.

96. The Welsh territory of Glamergan [Glamorgan] is the first territory mentioned in all of the manuscripts, followed by the "worship of Wales" as the primary gift; "Gryffones castelle" [Griffon's castle] (Lincoln MS) and "Criffones castelle" (in both the Douce MS and the Ireland MS), both unidentified, approximate Welsh orthography; and "Wales" is again mentioned in line 669 of the Douce MS (Gates, ed., *Awntyrs,* 188–89).

97. See Davies, *First English Empire,* 79–80.

98. Goodman, "Anglo-Scottish Marches," 29.

99. Hulbert argues for a "baronial" patronage for the *Awntyrs,* suggesting an attempted "revival" of an anti-monarchical aristocratic culture, in "Hypothesis," 414.

100. Brown, *Black Douglases,* 146–51.

101. Ibid.

102. Barrell, *Medieval Scotland,* 134.

103. On largely unsuccessful efforts to impose national consolidation, see Goodman, "Anglo-Scottish Marches," 23–26.

104. After James II murdered Earl William Douglas at the Stirling Castle "Black Dinner," the Black Douglas house became fractured by internecine conflict. On James II's subsequent, brutally successful campaigns against Black Douglas threats, see Brown, *Black Douglases,* 283–311. Bawcutt and Riddy's conservative dating of the *Howlat* from 1445 to 1452 (*Howlat,* 42) supports the view that it served as Black Douglas propaganda aimed at reviving their marcher power-base. On dating Holland's *Howlat,* see Felicity J. Riddy, "Dating *The Buke of the Howlat,*" *Review of English Studies* 37 (1986): 1–10.

105. Hanna, ed., *Awntyrs,* 52.

106. On the waning of Douglas family fortunes as border violence decreased after 1389, see Brown, *Black Douglases,* 327–32.

107. On the mobilization of border-family interests against Richard II's efforts to secure a treaty with the Scots, see J. A. Tuck, "Richard II and the Border Magnates," *Northern History* 3 (1968): 27–52.

108. Gates, ed., *Awntyrs,* 228n.

109. See the variants to lines 683–85 (Gates, ed., *Awntyrs,* 190). The Lambeth manuscript also has Gawain refer to "oure" (that is, Arthurian) "lordscip" [lordship]; the Douce manuscript, with its reading of "your," has surely contributed to the editorial confusion addressed by Gates (228n).

110. Arthur E. Smailes, *North England,* rev. ed. (London: Thomas Nelson and Sons, 1968), 103.

111. On the stakes of Edward I's imperial experiments in the British Isles, see Davies, *First English Empire,* 22–30. Prestwich argues that Edward I's failure to bring sufficient occupying forces precluded him from colonizing Scotland as he had Wales, in "Colonial Scotland: The English in Scotland Under Edward I," in *Scotland and England: 1286–1815,* ed. Roger A. Mason (Edinburgh: John Donald, 1988), 6–17.

112. The ghost asserts that the knight who will "encroche" [seize] Arthur's sovereignty will be "crowned" at "Carlele" [Carlisle] (287–88). Malory makes "Carlyle" [Carlisle] the site of the surprise of Lancelot that triggers the Arthurian civil war (*Morte,* in *Works,* ed. Vinaver, 675).

113. On Hadrian's Wall marking the frontier of the "Empire's jurisdiction," with its "defensive function" interrelated with an effort to manage "transfrontier traffic," see

Norman Davies, *The Isles: A History* (Oxford: Oxford University Press, 1999), 126–31.

114. On Carlisle's military and economic history, see Smailes, *Northern England*, 121–22; and Henry Summerson, "Responses to War: Carlisle and the West March in the Late Fourteenth Century," in *War and Border Societies in the Middle Ages*, ed. Anthony Goodman and Anthony Tuck (London: John Donald, 1992), 155–77 [156–61].

115. See Malory, *Works*, ed. Vinaver, 675. Arthur is encamped in Viterbo, readying to take Rome, when he hears news from Craddok of the treason of Mordred, which drives him back to Britain (*Alliterative 'Morte,'* 3522–56).

116. See Alexander Grant, *Independence and Nationhood: Scotland, 1306–1469* (Edinburgh: Edinburgh University Press, 1985), 56–57.

117. See Goldstein, *Matter of Scotland*, 88–103.

118. The Latin text and bracketed translation derive from the *Declaration of Arbroath*, ed. and trans. James Fergusson (Edinburgh: Edinburgh University Press, 1970), 8–9.

119. Barrell, *Medieval Scotland*, 122. On the ideological project of the *Declaration*, see Goldstein, *Matter of Scotland*, 88–103.

120. Hahn, ed., *Golagros*, 227; 231.

121. See Wales, *Northern English*, 5.

122. Hahn, ed., *Golagros*, 227n.

123. The mention of Tuscany is one key textual link shared by the *Awntyrs* (284), the *Morte Arthure* (3150), and *Golagros* (2).

124. Hanna emends from Chepman and Myllar's "Rome" (57n), following suggestions by Amours (261n) and Hahn (286n).

125. Musgrove analyzes these regions as part of a generally militarized North, in *North of England*, 118–54. On the *Morte*-poet's dialect, see McIntosh, "Textual Transmission," 240; Andrew, "Dialect," 418–23; and Oakden, *Alliterative Poetry*, II.87–88.

126. Hodges discusses Malory's adaptation of the *Morte*-poet's narrative of the Roman campaign, arguing for a medieval nation in Anderson's sense, in *Forging Chivalric Communities in Malory's 'Le Morte Darthur'* (New York: Palgrave Macmillan, 2005), 67–68.

127. See Anderson, *Imagined Communities*, 164–75.

128. That Arthur is holding court at Carlisle links the Alliterative *Morte* with a number of northerly Arthurian romances, including the *Awntyrs*. On Carlisle as a site of frequent Anglo-Scottish conflict, see Musgrove, *North of England*, 140–54.

129. On Welsh mercenaries, see Walker, *Medieval Wales*, 62–63.

130. Edward I's conquest of Wales was completed by 1284; Owain's uprising, beginning in 1400 and remaining explosive through 1410, could be contemporary with the Alliterative *Morte*. On the Edwardian conquest and Owain's later rebellion, see Walker, *Medieval Wales*, 111–38; 165–74.

131. Ingham, *Sovereign Fantasies*, 88–89.

132. While Matthews's assertion that Edward III is the intended figure behind the *Morte*-poet's Arthur fits awkwardly with the poem's decidedly general, non-topical critique of militarism, Matthews argues compellingly for Arthur's status as an English warlord in the Alliterative *Morte* and the *Awntyrs* (*Tragedy of Arthur*, 178–92). On various efforts to assert an English-dominated unity for imperial holdings throughout a medieval Britain destabilized by competing ethnicities, each of which was complex,

see Smyth's preface to *Medieval Europeans,* xii–xiv; and Kumar, *Making of English National Identity,* 60–88.

133. *Golagros*'s two plotlines derive from the *First Continuation* of Chrétien de Troyes's *Perceval;* see Nigel Bryant, ed. and trans., *Perceval: The Story of the Grail* (Cambridge: D. S. Brewer, 1982), 122–23. Spearing challenges Hanna's view of the *Awntyrs* as "composite," arguing that its two incidents form a "diptych," in *"Awntyrs,"* 183–202.

134. R. D. S. Jack argues that Arthur's releasing of his claim to Golagros's lands reveals his having benefitted spiritually from visiting Jerusalem, in "Arthur's Pilgrimage: A Study of *Golagros and Gawane,"* *Studies in Scottish Literature* 12.1 (1974): 3–20 [19].

135. Hanna here replaces the printed text's "lord" with "maister," on metrical grounds (51n). I restore the text's reading because the term "lord" seems intended to create a link with Golagros's introduction as the "lord" who holds the desirable property that Arthur besieges (255–65). A failure in alliteration in this line calls attention to the term, highlighting the diptychal relation of the Arthurian armies' encounters with provincial lords.

136. This unnamed lord of *Golagros*'s opening encounter displays the aristocratic virtue of generosity, the value of which is only increased by Arthur's status as both a great conqueror and his "cousing of kyn" [relative] (191).

137. Hahn, ed., *Sir Gawain: Eleven Romances,* 291n. Such "routis" are synonymous with the *chevauchée,* a tactic in medieval warfare involving the destruction of goods, and the starvation and plundering of civilians. Such warfare was common in the Anglo-Scottish borderlands, where raids and counter-raids were aimed primarily at villages and outlying farms; see Brown, *Black Douglases,* 138–39. On literary and chronicle evidence that pillaging and property destruction were common practice throughout late-medieval Europe, despite chivalric idealism, see Richard W. Kaeuper, *Chivalry and Violence in Medieval Europe* (Oxford: Oxford University Press, 1999), 176–85. The Alliterative *Morte* offers numerous examples of Arthur's brutal campaigns, such as when Arthur overturns towers and "turmentez the pople" [torments the people], making many "wedwes" [widows] worry and wring their hands (3153–55).

138. Considering the popularity of the *Siege of Jerusalem* (clear from the nine extant medieval texts), and considering the northerly origins of the geographic spread of the poem (Hanna and Lawton, eds., xiii–xxxvii; lxvii–lxviii), the *Golagros*-poet may have known the *Siege*-poet's brutal depictions of the Roman siege and sack of Jerusalem. Chism argues that the *Siege*-poet uses Jews to found a Christian empire, with anxieties about Judaism's anteriority to Christianity magnifying the violence, in *Alliterative Revivals,* 155–88 (updating her *"The Siege of Jerusalem:* Liquidating Assets," *Journal of Medieval and Early Modern Studies* 28 [1998]: 309–40). On anti-imperialist elements in the depiction of divinely-authorized warfare in the *Siege* as mirroring anti-militarism in the *Awntyrs* and *Golagros,* see Randy P. Schiff, "The Instructive Other Within: Secularized Jews in *The Siege of Jerusalem,"* in *Cultural Diversity,* ed. Cohen, 135–51 [137–42].

139. Even as *Golagros* gestures at the brutality of medieval warfare, it also smoothes over such violence with a conventional style of tournament combat common in Arthurian romances. On the pronounced theatricality of *Golagros*'s violence, see Fradenburg,

City, Marriage, Tournament, 182.

140. Hahn argues that Golagros's defeat is due partly to the happenstance of losing his footing on "an uneven battlefield," which calls attention to the "honorable conduct" that ensues (*Sir Gawain: Eleven Romances,* 302n).

141. On chivalry as an ideology that often insulated aristocratic knights from severe violence, while doing little to restrain the destructive practices of pillaging commoners' lands, see Kaueper, *Chivalry and Violence,* 169–88.

142. See Bourdieu, *Language and Symbolic Power,* 118–19.

Chapter 5

1. Backus and Shaw, *Shaw's New History,* 21.
2. Ibid., 31.
3. Ibid., 30–31.
4. Halleck, *History,* 47.
5. On the influence of Carlyle's view of Germanic superiority in Britain, and on Nott's arguments against a single Creation and that interbreeding weakens Saxon purity, see Horsman, *Race and Manifest Destiny,* 64–65; 129–33.
6. On theories of a Germanic identity encompassing Saxons and Normans, see Horsman, *Race and Manifest Destiny,* 36–41.
7. William J. Long, *English Literature: Its History and Its Significance for the Life of the English-Speaking World* (1909; Boston: Ginn and Company, 1919), 46.
8. Ibid., 49.
9. Ibid.
10. Saintsbury, *History,* I.110.
11. Ibid.
12. I take this phrasing from Christopher Cannon, who introduces technology as a key concern for medieval culture in *Middle English Literature: A Cultural History* (Cambridge: Polity, 2008), 8. While Cannon, discussing writing technology, focuses on medieval confessional narrative as an uncannily modern "technology of the self" (27–35), I will explore a related but contrary movement, whereby book culture enables the self's multiplication and extension.
13. On *Piers Plowman* as a "national" poem, see Anne Middleton, "The Audience and Public of *Piers Plowman,*" in *Middle English Alliterative Poetry,* ed. Lawton, 101–23; 147–54 [103–4]; and see Burrow's argument that *Piers Plowman* alone intended a "Reading Public" that transcended any "specific locality," whereas the "Revival" was otherwise "a local affair" ("Audience of Piers Plowman," 373–77).
14. Larry Scanlon argues that this transition presents a "national vision" juxtaposing the "agrarian west" and the "more mercantile, more industrialized southeast," in "King, Commons, and Kind Wit: Langland's National Vision and the Rising of 1381," in *Imagining a Medieval English Nation,* ed. Lavezzo, 191–233 [200].
15. On biographical evidence for Langland, see Ralph Hanna, *William Langland* (Aldershot: Variorum, 1993), 1–10; 17–26. Hanna links Will's self-presentation as a hermit with the "relative discursive freedom" of a wandering minstrel (24–25), in "Will's Work," in *Written Work,* ed. Justice and Kerby-Fulton, 23–66 [24–25]. Fiona

Somerset argues that Will authorizes his clerkly role through the negotiation of "lewed" [lay] texts with Latin discursive modes, in *Clerical Discourse and Lay Audience in Late Medieval England* (Cambridge: Cambridge University Press, 1998), 22–61. See Kellie Robertson's argument that Langland conceives of literary labor as hybrid, being both "immaterial" (like preaching) and "material" (like agriculture), in *The Laborer's Two Bodies: Literary and Legal Productions in Britain, 1350–1500* (New York: Palgrave Macmillan, 2006), 49–50. Ethan Knapp maintains that Langland's Will conflates scribal and agricultural labor in the C-Text's autobiographical passage (V.42–48) by intentionally "misapplyin[g]" the trope of pastoral spirituality to books, in "Poetic Work and Scribal Labor in Hoccleve and Langland," in *The Middle Ages at Work: Practicing Labor in Late Medieval England,* ed. Michael Uebel and Kellie Robertson (New York: Palgrave Macmillan, 2004), 209–29 [214–15].

16. See Anne Middleton's analysis of Langland's increasingly sophisticated forms of autobiographical self-presentation, in "William Langland's *Kynde Name:* Authorial Signature and Social Identity in Late Fourteenth-Century England," in *Literary Practice and Social Change in Britain, 1380–1530,* ed. Lee Patterson (Berkeley: University of California Press, 1991), 15–82 [55–60]. On late-medieval economic emigration from rural areas to London, see Saul, "Medieval Britain," 137–42.

17. On the circulation of *Piers Plowman* manuscripts within the London book market, see Ralph Hanna, *London Literature, 1300–1380* (Cambridge: Cambridge University Press, 2005), 243–314. On the provenance of *Piers Plowman,* see A. I. Doyle, "Some Remarks on Surviving Manuscripts of *Piers Plowman,*" in *Medieval English Religious and Ethical Literature,* ed. Kratzmann and Simpson, 35–48. On manuscript evidence for Langland's return to Malvern, see Derek Pearsall, "Langland's London," in *Written Work,* ed. Justice and Kerby-Fulton, 185–207 [198]; M. L. Samuels, "Langland's Dialect," *Medium Aevum* 54 (1985): 232–247 [240]; and Hanna, *William Langland,* 14–17.

18. After London, which dwarfed all other late-medieval British cities in size and wealth, Bristol and York were the two most important towns. On the distribution of population and wealth in medieval towns, see Saul, "Medieval Britain," 133–37. Simon Horobin argues for a Bristol dialectal origin for both *Richard* and *Mum* in "The Dialect and Authorship of *Richard the Redeless* and *Mum and the Sothsegger,*" *Yearbook of Langland Studies* 18 (2004): 133–52.

19. *The Crowned King* is uniquely attested in Bodleian Douce MS 95, a miscellany dated by Barr to the mid-fifteenth century. It features English and Latin poetic and prose contents with "explicit connections with Westminster and London," including lists and descriptions of London churches and their staff. See Helen Barr, ed., *The 'Piers Plowman' Tradition: A Critical Edition of 'Pierce the Ploughman's Crede,' 'Richard the Redeless,' 'Mum and the Sothsegger' and 'The Crowned King'* (London: J. M. Dent, 1993), 30.

20. A. I. Doyle, "An Unrecognized Piece of *Piers the Ploughman's Creed* and Other Work by Its Scribe," *Speculum* 34 (1959): 428–36 [434]. Doyle here adds to the known output of the scribe identified by Eleanor Prescott Hammond in articles such as "A Scribe of Chaucer," *Modern Philology* 27 (1929): 26–33.

21. Kerby-Fulton and Justice, "Langlandian Reading Circles," 59–76. On bureaucratic culture and political centralization in late-medieval Britain, see M. T. Clanchy,

From Memory to Written Record, 2nd ed. (Oxford: Blackwell, 1993), 44–184.

22. On the spread of scribal culture through bureaucratic forms, see Kerby-Fulton and Justice, "Langlandian Reading Circles," 59–83. See also Frank Grady's study of bureaucratically informed poets, in "The Generation of 1399," in *The Letter of the Law: Legal Practice and Literary Production in Medieval England,* ed. Emily Steiner and Candace Barrington (Ithaca, NY: Cornell University Press, 2002), 202–29; and see Knapp's argument that bureaucratic identity shapes late-medieval English literary culture, in *Bureaucratic Muse,* 27–44.

23. I take this phrase from Emily Steiner, *Documentary Culture and the Making of Medieval English Literature* (Cambridge: Cambridge University Press, 2003), 10.

24. I take this phrase from Helen Barr, *Signes and Sothe: Language in the 'Piers Plowman' Tradition* (Cambridge: D. S. Brewer, 1994), 22; see Barr's survey of evidence for this Langland-generated community, 1–22. The concept of a "*Piers Plowman* tradition" is first explicitly offered by David A. Lawton in "Lollardy and the *Piers Plowman* Tradition," *Modern Language Review* 76 (1981): 780–93; Turville-Petre also groups works influenced by *Piers Plowman* in *Alliterative Revival,* 31–32. Kathryn Kerby-Fulton suggests adding the Wycliffite broadside poem "Heu quanta desolacio" to this tradition, seeing its Langlandian allusions as predated only by the 1381 rebel writings, in *Books Under Suspicion: Censorship and Tolerance of Revelatory Writing in Late Medieval England* (Notre Dame, IN: University of Notre Dame Press, 2007), 174–87.

25. Beginning with his edition of the A-text in 1868, Skeat produced six volumes covering the A-, B-, and C-texts, as well as an excerpt volume. Most scholars of *Piers Plowman* accept an A-B-C composition sequence. On the evidence for three discrete *Piers Plowman* texts, see Charlotte Brewer, *Editing 'Piers Plowman'* (Cambridge: Cambridge University Press, 1996), 182–209; and C. David Benson, *Public 'Piers Plowman': Modern Scholarship and Late Medieval English Culture* (University Park: Pennsylvania State University Press, 2004), 43–75. Jill Mann argues for a B-C-A sequence, in "The Power of the Alphabet: A Reassessment of the Relation between the A and B Versions of *Piers Plowman,*" *Yearbook of Langland Studies* 8 (1994): 21–50. On the vexed critical history concerning the authorship of *Piers Plowman,* see Bowers, *Chaucer and Langland,* 56–79.

26. See John Manly, "The Lost Leaf of *Piers the Plowman*" (EETS o.s. 135b, 1906).

27. Kane and Donaldson's eclectic edition of the B-Text weaves editorial intuition into the construction of a text from heterogeneous manuscript data; see their introduction to William Langland, *Piers Plowman: The B Version* (London: Athlone Press, 1975), 131. Assuming a consistent, multi-generational abyss between editor and the poet, Kane uses a stunning metaphor to explain his eclectic editing method: he likens Langland's authorial "quality" to an invisible sun that "shines through the damage done at the archetypal stage," penetrating the darkness of inferior scribal work; see "The Text," in *A Companion to 'Piers Plowman,'* ed. John A. Alford (Berkeley: University of California Press, 1989), 175–200 [175; 194]. On debate surrounding Kane and Donaldson's enabling idealization of Langland, see Tim William Machan, "Middle English Text Production and Modern Textual Criticism," in *Crux and Controversy in Middle English Textual Criticism,* ed. A. J. Minnis and Charlotte Brewer (Cambridge:

D. S. Brewer, 1992), 1–18 [10–17]; and see Lee Patterson's seminal analysis of Kane and Donaldson's reliance on editorial intuition concerning authorial writing habits, in a systematic rescue of Langland's uniqueness from the "ruins" of scribal noise (*Negotiating the Past*, 77–116 [97]).

28. Rigg and Brewer maintain that the text in MS Bodley 851 is an authorial draft that pre-dates the A-text; see *Piers Plowman: The Z Version*, by William Langland (Toronto: Pontifical Institute of Medieval Studies, 1983), 2. Few critics have supported the Rigg-Brewer hypothesis. See George Kane's virulent reaction, in "The 'Z Version' of *Piers Plowman*," *Speculum* 60 (1985): 910–30; Kane's argument that the "puerile" readings of Bodley MS 851 fail to meet the "Langlandian" standard (920) ironically reinforces Rigg and Brewer's basic contention that the A-Text improves a Z-Text deemed unready for release by an aesthetically uncompromising Langland. On dating the A-Text, see Hanna, *William Langland*, 14–17.

29. See Lawton, "Diversity of Middle English Alliterative Poetry," 143–72; and Lawton, "Unity of Middle English Alliterative Poetry," 72–94.

30. See Duggan, "Alliterative Patterning," 85; Duggan also excludes *Pierce the Ploughman's Crede* (79).

31. E. Talbot Donaldson, "*Piers Plowman*: Textual Comparison and the Question of Authorship," in *Chaucer und seine Zeit: Symposion für Walter F. Schirmer*, ed. Arno Esch (Tübingen: Max Niemeyer Verlag, 1968), 241–47 [241].

32. Foucault, "What Is an Author?," 159.

33. Donaldson, "*Piers Plowman*," 245; 244; 241.

34. Ibid., 245.

35. Bowers, *Chaucer and Langland*, 23. See Bowers's analytical survey of appropriations of Langland's work (103–56). On the use of *Piers Plowman* in rebel communications, see Steven Justice, *Writing and Rebellion: England in 1381* (Berkeley: University of California Press, 1994), 231–54.

36. Kerby-Fulton, "*Piers Plowman*," 524.

37. On the tense political conditions surrounding Richard II's 1399 deposition, see Michael Bennett, *Richard II and the Revolution of 1399* (Phoenix Mill, Gloucestershire: Sutton, 1999). On the censorious atmosphere for theologically oriented texts in late-medieval England, see Nicholas Watson, "Censorship and Cultural Change in Late-Medieval England: Vernacular Theology, the Oxford Translation Debate, and Arundel's Constitutions of 1409," *Speculum* 70 (1995): 822–64; and Kerby-Fulton, *Books under Suspicion*, 11–37; 71–124. James Simpson sets satirical literature in the context of sociopolitical tensions in "The Constraints of Satire in *Piers Plowman* and *Mum and the Sothsegger*," in *Langland, the Mystics, and the Medieval English Mystic Tradition: Essays in Honour of S. S. Hussey*, ed. Helen Phillips (Cambridge: D. S. Brewer, 1990), 11–30.

38. On the 1381 rebels' demands, see Rodney Hilton, *Bond Men Made Free: Medieval Peasant Movements and the English Rising of 1381* (New York: Viking, 1973), 195–98; 224–28.

39. Fradenburg, *Sacrifice Your Love*, 75–77. Fradenburg urges scholars to eschew fantasies of absolute alterity and instead to channel their inevitably subjective investments into connecting modern and medieval political desires (43–78). For an alternative view, see George Kane's argument that contemporary political concepts such as

"protest" are "unhistorical" except in clearly Wycliffite works, in "Some Fourteenth-Century 'Political' Poems," in *Medieval English Religious and Ethical Literature*, ed. Kratzmann and Simpson, 82–91 [82].

40. Hardt and Negri, *Empire*, 150–54. Hardt and Negri here question postcolonial critics' tendency to celebrate hybridity, with "circulation, mobility, diversity, and mixture" proving key to global capital and the logic of Empire (143–51). On postcolonial theorists' over-confidence in determining sites of resistance, see James Holstun, *Ehud's Dagger: Class Struggle in the English Revolution* (London: Verso, 2000), 42–45; 76–84.

41. Simpson, *Reform*, 214–19.

42. For an epochal analysis of transformations in communications techniques and their impact on social relations in the digital age, see Deibert, *Parchment*, 137–216. For comparison of digital and scribal textualities, see David Burnley, "Scribes and Hypertext," *Yearbook of English Studies* 25 (1995): 41–62; and see D. C. Greetham's argument that electronic editions enable reproduction of the "mouvance" of manuscript culture that print cannot capture, in "Reading in and Around *Piers Plowman*," in *Texts and Textuality: Textual Instability, Theory, and Interpretation*, ed. Philip Cohen (New York: Garland, 1997), 25–57 [40–43].

43. Scanlon critiques the view that Langland's C-revisions reveal a "latent social conservatism," in "Langland, Apocalypse and the Early Modern Editor," in *Reading the Medieval in Early Modern England*, ed. Gordon McMullan and David Matthews (Cambridge: Cambridge University Press, 2007), 51–73; 238–43 [54–55]. On Langland's revisions to the C-Text of *Piers Plowman*, see George Russell and George Kane's introduction to *Piers Plowman: The C Version* (London: Athlone Press, 1997), 62–88.

44. On rebel appropriation of Piers Plowman, see Justice, *Writing and Rebellion*, 231–54. Andrew Galloway links Langland's work with late-medieval communal struggles concerning law and authority, in "Making History Legal: *Piers Plowman* and the Rebels of Fourteenth-Century England," in *Piers Plowman: A Book of Essays*, ed. Kathleen M. Hewett-Smith (New York: Routledge, 2005), 7–31. On Langland's response to 1381, see Bowers, *Chaucer and Langland*, 115–22.

45. See William Langland, *The Vision of William Concerning Piers Plowman: The 'Vernon' Text: or Text A*, ed. Walter W. Skeat, Early English Text Society O.S. 28 (1867). In each version a knight, while leading a communal plowing project, is moved by Piers Plowman's speech to abandon allegorical for actual plowing. Piers tells him that it is his class-based duty to protect the community from "wastoures" [wasters] and "wikked men," and tells him to go and hunt hares and foxes (C.VIII.27–29), leaving agricultural labor to peasants.

46. On the topical evidence for dating *Crede* to 1393–1400, see Barr, ed., *Piers Plowman Tradition*, 9–10. For descriptions of the three manuscripts and two prints in which *Crede* survives, see ibid., 8–10; and Walter W. Skeat, ed., *Pierce the Plowman's Creed* (EETS o.s. 30, 1867), i–vi.

47. All citations from *Mum*, and all from *Crede, Richard*, and the *Crowned King* are from Barr's edition; my translations.

48. On Langland's reactions to contemporary socioeconomic conditions, see Helen M. Jewell, "*Piers Plowman*—A Poem of Crisis: an Analysis of Political Instability in Langland's England," in *Politics and Crisis in Fourteenth-Century England*, ed. John

Taylor and Wendy Childs (Gloucester: Alan Sutton, 1990), 59–80 [63–67]. Anima spiritualizes agricultural labor, glossing "Piers the Plowman" as "Petrus, id est Christus" [Peter—that is, Christ] (B.xv.12, ed. Kane and Donaldson).

49. On tensions between an upwardly mobile peasantry and a reactionary landholding class in fourteenth- and fifteenth-century England, see E. B. Fryde, *Peasants and Landlords in Later Medieval England* (Phoenix Mill, Gloucestershire: Alan Sutton, 1996), 6; 49–50. Fryde's studies of West Midlands estates (54–75; 185–208), especially of the Worcestershire in which Langland introduces his dreamer (135–44; 169–84), provide a crucial background for the *Piers Plowman* tradition. On describing the socioeconomically diverse 1381 insurgency as "the Rising" rather than "the Peasants' Revolt," see Hilton, *Bond Men,* 176–213. Paul Strohm analyzes chroniclers' efforts to efface the Rising's socioeconomic diversity by stigmatizing all critics of the economic status quo as peasants, in *Hochon's Arrow: The Social Imagination of Fourteenth-Century Texts* (Princeton, NJ: Princeton University Press, 1992), 33–56.

50. In what is typically read as an autobiographical insertion unique to the C-text, Will argues to Reason that society should not "constrayne" a clerk to "knaues werkes" [peasants' labors] and claims that clerks should come only from the classes "of frankeleynes and fre men and of folke ywedded" [gentry and noble men and married people], while "bondemen and bastardus and beggares children . . . bylongeth to labory, and lordes kyn to serue" [bondmen, bastards and beggars' children belong to a laboring class who serve the land-owning class] (V.54–66). Will proceeds to lament current examples of laborers' upward social mobility in a passage beginning, "Ac sythe" [However, lately] (53–80), and looks forward to when these patterns will have "ychaunged" [changed] (81). All citations from *Piers Plowman,* unless otherwise noted, are from Derek Pearsall's C-Text edition (rev. ed.; Exeter: University of Exeter Press, 1994); my translations. See Kerby-Fulton's analysis of the *Crede*-poet's and Langland's C-Text classist rants against self-improving laborers, in *"Piers Plowman,"* in *Cambridge History,* ed. Wallace, 513–38 [537].

51. *Crede* is openly Lollard: the narrator urges readers to "wytnesse" the "trewth" [truth] delivered by "Wycliff" (528–30), and refers to the "sothe" [truth] told by Walter Brut, whose heretical status is firmly denied (657–62). On indirect evidence for Lollardy elsewhere in the *Piers Plowman* tradition, see Lawton, "Lollardy," 780–93; and Barr, *Signes and Sothe,* 95–132.

52. John Scattergood, *"Pierce the Ploughman's Crede:* Lollardy and Texts," in *Lollardy and the Gentry in the Later Middle Ages,* ed. Margaret Aston and Colin Richmond (Stroud, Gloucestershire: Sutton, 1997), 77–94 [83].

53. N. Katherine Hayles, *Writing Machines* (Cambridge, MA: MIT Press, 2002), 30–31. Media Specific Analysis analyzes the inflection of content by medium, tracking how a "rhetorical form mutates when it is instantiated in different media" (31). The *Crede*-poet's strategic management of multiple media in critiquing spiritual culture is also seen in his analysis of the ecclesiastical exploitation of individuals' desire to see their identities etched in stained-glass windows (118–33) and in his social reading of secular patronage and architectural style (192–218).

54. Scattergood, *"Pierce the Ploughman's Crede,"* 83–84.

55. Hayles, *Writing Machines,* 30.

56. On legal texts and their relation to *Piers Plowman* and Langland-influenced

works, see Steiner, *Documentary Culture*, 143–90; Barr, *Signes and Sothe*, 133–66; and Grady, "Generation of 1399," 222–29.

57. See Knapp's argument that Hoccleve's literary sensibilities were shaped by training in the Privy Seal office, where documents accumulated writing as they passed through departments, in *Bureaucratic Muse*, 181–82.

58. Grady, "Generation of 1399," 204–6; 227.

59. The practice of maintenance (the use of liveries and fees to form associations between a powerful individual and retainers, who agree to support the power-broker's interests in legal and political venues) was the subject of much satirical complaint in late-medieval England; see Strohm, *Hochon's Arrow*, 179–85.

60. Mabel Day and Robert Steele, eds., *Mum and the Sothsegger* (EETS o.s. 199, 1936), x.

61. Barr, ed., *Piers Plowman Tradition*, 16.

62. See Barr's discussion of *Piers Plowman* received "not as an 'auctored' act of literary play but as a communal work for society," in *Signes and Sothe*, 22.

63. Day and Steele, eds., *Mum*, x.

64. Ibid.

65. Ibid.

66. Horobin, "Dialect and Authorship," 133–52. The dialect of *Richard* has elsewhere been localized only very generally as Southwest Midlands, with the scribe's Cambridgeshire language presenting editorial difficulties. See *A Linguistic Atlas of Late Mediaeval English*, ed. Angus McIntosh, M. L. Samuels, and Michael Benskin, 4 vols. (Aberdeen: Aberdeen University Press, 1986), III.111; and Samuels, "Langland's Dialect," 241. Doyle argues that there is "no firm localization" for the *Mum*-poet's dialect, in "Manuscripts," 98.

67. Day and Steele do not significantly distinguish the prosody of the fragments from that of either *Piers Plowman* or *William of Palerne* (xlii-xlvi).

68. Dan Embree discusses layout as a factor dissociating these two texts, in "*Richard the Redeless* and *Mum and the Sothsegger*: A Case of Mistaken Identity," *Notes and Queries* 220 (1975): 4–12 [5].

69. Ibid., 9

70. Day and Steele, eds., *Mum*, ix.

71. Ibid., xii. Barr corrects Day and Steele's claim that two folios of text have been lost after folio 12 (*Piers Plowman Tradition*, 340).

72. Day and Steele, eds., *Mum*, xii.

73. Ibid., ix–x. The full note reads, "Mum, soth segger id est Taciturnitas, verorum dictrix. Liber est Anglicus, qui incipit 'Dum orans ambularem presbyteris altari astantibus, Bristollensi in vrbe,' etc. *Ex venatione Nicolai Brigani*'" [*Mum* and *Soth Segger*, which means Taciturnity and Teller of Truths. The book is English, and it begins, "While I was walking in prayer by the priests standing by the altar, in the city of Bristol,' etc. *From the collection of Nicholas Brigham*], in John Bale, *Index Britanniae Scriptorum*, ed. Reginald Lane Poole and Mary Bateson (1902; Cambridge: D. S. Brewer, 1990), 479; my translation.

74. Day and Steele, eds., ix. Doyle argues that BL Additional MS 41666 dates "probably" from the "third quarter" of the fifteenth century, in "Manuscripts," 98.

75. On the dating of *Richard* and *Mum*, see Barr, ed., *Piers Plowman Tradition*,

14–16; 22–23. Barr discusses topical evidence for dating *Mum* around 1409, in "The Dates of *Richard the Redeless* and *Mum and the Sothsegger*," *Yearbook of Langland Studies* 4 (1990): 270–75.

76. Embree, "*Richard the Redeless*," 11.

77. Ibid., 4. *Richard the Redeless* is uniquely attested in Cambridge University Library MS. L1.4.14 (ff. 107b-119a), a paper manuscript dated to the second quarter of the fifteenth century. The manuscript is a miscellany, with items as disparate as treatises on arithmetic (ff. 127a–148b) and on "physionomie" (ff. 156b–159b), a C-Text of *Piers Plowman* (ff. 1–107a), Psalms in Latin (ff. 161a–163a), and a "doctrine of Fishing and foulyng" (ff. 173a–174b). For a full description, see Kane and Donaldson, eds., *Piers Plowman*, 4.

78. Brewer, *Editing 'Piers Plowman,'* 185–86. On the impact of printed editions on later scholarship, see Matthews, *Making of Middle English*, xvii–xxi; and Stephanie Trigg, *Congenial Souls: Reading Chaucer from Medieval to Postmodern* (Minneapolis: University of Minnesota Press, 2002), 109–43.

79. Brewer, *Editing 'Piers Plowman,'* 186. Embree lists Helen M. Cam, V. J. Scattergood, and Arthur Ferguson as scholars who assume single authorship, in "*Richard the Redeless*," 6. For further examples, see Alcuin G. Blamires, "*Mum & the Sothsegger* and Langlandian Idiom," *Neuphilologische Mitteilungen* 76 (1975): 583–604 [583]; Kane and Donaldson, eds., *Piers Plowman*, 4; and Ruth Mohl, "Theories of Monarchy in *Mum and the Sothsegger*," *PMLA* 59 (1944): 26–44 [26].

80. Such "collaborative" authorship differs strikingly from the "multiple" authorship proposed for *Piers Plowman* by Manly, who posits separate authors for distinct *Piers Plowman* texts. Collaborative composition entails multiple authorship within *each* manuscript instantiation of a poem. On trends in theorizing scribal participation in *Piers Plowman*, see C. David Benson, "Another Fine Manuscript Mess: Authors, Editors and Readers of *Piers Plowman*," in *New Directions in Later Medieval Manuscript Studies*, ed. Derek Pearsall (Woodbridge: York Medieval Press, 2000), 15–28. On long-running editorial assumptions of Langland's individual authorship, see Bowers, *Chaucer and Langland*, 64–79.

81. Kerby-Fulton and Justice speculate that *Richard* circulated in Westminster circles, in "Langlandian Reading," 77–78.

82. Spiegel, "History," 84. *Richard*'s thinly veiled topical references, such as the appearance of Richard II's executed favorites, Bushy, Green, and Scrope, in puns on "busshes," "grene," and "schroup" (II.152–54), are numerous enough to lead Oakden to describe the poem as a "pamphlet of the hour" (*Alliterative Poetry*, II.61).

83. Barr argues that the text was to remain "secrette" due to "strictures on writing political poetry," in *Piers Plowman Tradition*, 252n. See Judith Ferster's survey of "camouflage" techniques used to avoid constraints on literary speech, in *Fictions of Advice: The Literature and Politics of Counsel in Late Medieval England* (Philadelphia: University of Pennsylvania Press, 1996), 8–9. See also Ann W. Astell's discussion of the "material" concerns related to audience and circulation in late-medieval political satire, in *Political Allegory in Late Medieval England* (Ithaca, NY: Cornell University Press, 1999), 4–6.

84. For a critical survey of texts deployed to advise princes, ranging from philosophical to historical treatises, see Richard Firth Green, *Poets and Princepleasers: Lit-*

erature and the English Court in the Late Middle Ages (Toronto: University of Toronto Press, 1980), 135–67; see also Ferster, *Fictions of Advice*, 3–35. For both written and iconographic examples of addressing Richard II, see Lynn Staley, *Languages of Power in the Age of Richard II* (University Park: Pennsylvania State University Press, 2005), 118–39.

85. *'Piers the Plowman,' Text C, 'Richard the Redeles,' and 'The Crowned King,'* ed. Walter W. Skeat (EETS o.s. 54, 1873), 505n. Skeat has "not the slightest hesitation in ascribing" *Richard* to "William, the author of Piers the Plowman," claiming it "must be his, and his only" (cvii).

86. Barr argues that the narrator urges the reader to use his or her "faculty for counsel, together with clerkly help," to "correct" the text (Barr, ed., *Piers Plowman Tradition*, 251n). Clanchy's view that "in manuscript culture reading and writing were separate skills" (*From Memory to Written Record*, 47n; see also 225–52) supports Barr's argument that these "clerkys" need not represent the king's administrators: audience members who could read the text might be expected to engage a clerk to write out their corrections.

87. Skeat argues in his edition that this is "really the first line of the Poem, since the Prologue may be looked upon as a sort of preface" (ciii). Barr's argument that there is no "firm" manuscript "authority" for Skeat's and Day and Steele's "insertion" of a "Prologue" before line 88 is unconvincing (Barr, ed., *Piers Plowman Tradition*, 247n). A red capital is used for the initial letter of the line; such initial red capitals introduce *passus* 2–4 of *Richard*, as well as the *passus* of *Piers Plowman* immediately preceding *Richard*.

88. The narrator of *The Crowned King* similarly addresses his audience: "And ye like to leer and listen a while" [And if it pleases you to learn and listen for a while], then "the soth y shall you shewe" [I shall show you the truth] (13–15), only later referring to the "crouned kyng" of his dream (35). For other examples, see *Wynnere and Wastoure*, ed. Trigg, 31; and *Sir Gawain*, ed. Vantuono, 29.

89. Nicolas Jacobs argues that the "main culturally determined peculiarity of English textual traditions before Chaucer is the predominant anonymity of authors and the phenomenon of cumulative composition," in "Kindly Light or Foxfire? The Authorial Text Reconsidered," in *A Guide to Editing Middle English*, ed. Douglas Moffat and Vincent P. McCarren (Ann Arbor: University of Michigan Press, 1998), 3–14 [14].

90. A. I. Doyle, "The Social Context of Medieval Literature," in *The Pelican Guide to English Literature, vol. 1: The Age of Chaucer*, ed. Boris Ford (Harmondsworth: Penguin), 83–103 [88–90].

91. Recognizing the "gret diversite / In Englissh and in writing of oure tonge," Chaucer's narrator prays in *Troilus and Criseyde* that no one "myswryte" his "litel bok" (V.1793–96).

92. See Doyle, 'Social Context," 88–90.

93. For a comparison of John But, who added 19 lines to *Passus* XII of a *Piers Plowman* A-text, with a Westminster scribe who contributed to the close of an A-text manuscript, see Anne Middleton, "Making a Good End: John But as a Reader of *Piers Plowman*," in *Medieval Studies Presented to George Kane*, ed. Edward Donald Kennedy, Ronald Waldron, and Joseph S. Wittig (Cambridge: D. S. Brewer, 1988), 244–46. John Bowers speculates that John But authored both *Richard* and *Mum*, in "*Piers*

Plowman's William Langland: Editing the Text, Writing the Author's Life," *Yearbook of Langland Studies* 9 (1995): 87–124. On scribes behaving like editors in copying a *Piers Plowman* C-text released without a final "authorial, and hence authoritative, formal structure," see George Russell, "Some Early Responses to the C-Version of *Piers Plowman*," *Viator* 15 (1984): 275–303.

94. On the risks assumed by critics of policy in Lancastrian England, see Andrew Wawn's reflection on the proverb, "who sayth soth shalbe shent" [who tells the truth will be harmed], in "Truth-telling and the Tradition of *Mum and the Sothsegger*," *Yearbook of English Studies* 13 (1983): 270–87 [273–75].

95. James Simpson, "The Power of Impropriety: Authorial Naming in *Piers Plowman*," in *Piers Plowman: A Book of Essays*, ed. Kathleen M. Hewett-Smith (New York: Routledge, 2005), 145–65 [148].

96. Kerby-Fulton, *Books under Suspicion*, 17–18.

97. See Elizabeth J. Bryan's study of the collaborative enterprise of producing the "enjoining" text of Laʒamon's *Brut* in BL MS Cotton Caligula A.ix.38, which reveals a communal process lacking print culture's fixed author–copyist hierarchy, in *Collaborative Meaning in Medieval Scribal Culture* (Ann Arbor: University of Michigan Press, 1999), 3–46. See also Carol Braun Pasternack's study of scribal collaboration as the norm in a fundamentally intertextual tradition that precluded individual authorship in Old English texts, in *The Textuality of Old English Poetry* (Cambridge: Cambridge University Press, 1995), 12–21.

98. See Kerby-Fulton and Justice's discussion of Westminster scribal habits, as well as their argument that the author and scribe of *Richard* worked in the Chancery, in "Langlandian Reading," 76–80.

99. Knapp, *Bureaucratic Muse*, 1–9.

100. Ibid., 181.

101. *Mum* is the sole text in the manuscript, which consists of nineteen vellum leaves and is dated by Barr as "probably" from the "third quarter of the fifteenth century" (*Piers Plowman Tradition*, 22). On the editorial hand in BL Additional 41666, see Barr's critical notes (291–368). My own analysis of the manuscript leads me to concur with Barr's view of a "single hand" being responsible for the corrections and insertions (36). Doyle suggests that the manuscript represents preparation for recopying the poem, in "Manuscripts," 98.

102. On the physical risks run by Lancastrian satirists, see V. J. Scattergood, *Politics and Poetry in the Fifteenth Century* (London: Blandford Press, 1971), 21.

103. The *OED* traces Definition A2 to an allegorical use made in 1562 by John Heywood. The use of "mummer" follows the same trajectory of sound to silence in "mum": the earliest recorded instance (1440) is "one who mutters or murmurs"; by 1502 a "mummer" is an actor performing the silence of the "dumb-show."

104. On Bale's note, see n73 (above). The *OED*'s speculative dating of *Mum* to 1399 would be a decade too early, according to Barr ("Dates," 205–10).

105. The primary *MED* definition of "mum" (listed under the heading "mom") includes the "poetic character" Mum. On anxiety concerning mumbling as a dangerous force competing with plain speech, ranging from medieval Titivullus stories to early modern dramatic works, see Carla Mazzio, *The Inarticulate Renaissance: Language Trouble in an Age of Eloquence* (Philadelphia: University of Pennsylvania Press, 2009),

20–31.

106. Langland, *Piers Plowman*, ed. Pearsall.

107. I take this phrase from Steve McCaffery's description of the poetic "adventure" opened up by the violent dislodging of sound from meaning, in *Prior to Meaning: The Protosemantic and Poetics* (Evanston: University of Illinois Press, 2001), 161–86.

108. Frank Grady exposes the fantasy of such sonically figured politics, arguing that the *Fürstenspiegel* genre's "mutually reinforcing fictions" are the "presumption that the king's subordinate has worthwhile advice to give, and that the monarch virtuously desires to follow it," in "The Lancastrian Gower and the Limits of Exemplarity," *Speculum* 70.3 (1995): 552–75 [554].

109. As the *Mum*-text is fragmentary, we do not know for how long the narrator's opening monologue has gone on before Mum's self-referential interruption.

110. Strohm lists, among "the notes most consistently congenial to Lancastrian legitimacy," imagery of unquestioned majesty set against threats of popular rebellion (*England's Empty Throne: Usurpation and the Language of Legitimation, 1399–1442* [New Haven, CT: Yale University Press, 1998], 178).

111. On the interplay of literary complaint and legal reforms allowing increased peasant access, see Wendy Scase, *Literature and Complaint in England, 1272–1553* (Oxford: Oxford University Press, 2007), 5–41.

112. On "entropy-resistance" as the use of identifiable features to consolidate class divisions, and on its dominance in the medieval world and persistence as an obstacle to modern industrialization, see Gellner, *Nations and Nationalism*, 64–67.

113. See Barr's analysis of Mum as "the personification of the self-interested use of speech," in *Signes and Sothe*, 80.

114. Day and Steele (*Mum*, xxiv) and Barr (*Piers Plowman Tradition*, 326) link this insistence on a proactive clergy, as well as Mum's statement that he who knows of a storm and does not warn others to take shelter is "auctor of al the harme and th'ache / And so pryuy to the peynes that peeres induren" [engenderer of all the harm and pain, and responsible for the pain that peers endure] (733–42), with rebellious activities organized against Henry IV.

115. See Giancarlo's analysis of the *Mum*-poet's focus on political "health" and parliamentary rhetoric concerning civic remedy, in *Parliament and Literature in Late Medieval England* (Cambridge: Cambridge University Press, 2007), 237–52.

116. Barr argues that lines 760–62 refer to tensions between Henry IV and the Percy family (*Piers Plowman Tradition*, 327n).

117. Luke, traditionally held to be the author of the eponymous *Gospel* and *Acts*, is often identified as a physician, based on Paul's reference to "Lucas medicus carissimus" [Luke, dearest doctor] (*C01*.4:14) [*Biblia Sacra Vulgata*; my translation]. On the tradition of Luke as physician, see James G. Walsh, *Old-Time Makers of Medicine: The Story of the Students and Teachers of the Sources Related to Medicine during the Middle Ages* (New York: Fordham University Press, 1911), 7–8; 301–18.

118. Day and Steele, eds., *Mum*, 120n.

119. Oakden exemplifies the Revivalist reduction of the *Piers Plowman* tradition to works of merely "historical interest," deeming *Richard*, *Mum*, and *The Crowned King* merely "topical," while holding that the *Piers Plowman* that they imitate is "timeless" (*Alliterative Poetry*, II.61–63). Marsh, who does not mention *Mum*, describes *Richard*

as an "imitation" of *Piers Plowman* that is "exclusively political in character" (*Origin and History,* 334). After speaking at length of *Piers Plowman* (301–27) as the key work sustaining the "revived" Anglo-Saxon meter (317), Marsh displays a signal lack of interest in Langlandian poems: he confines his discussion of *Richard* to a single passage of *nautical* interest (334).

120. Simpson argues that legislation, dating from the late 1370s, restricting communication rendered any criticism of the Council politically dangerous, in "Constraints of Satire," 17–20.

121. The transnational dimension of the *Mum*-narrator's travels emerges in the treatment of his Orléans visit as an unexceptional stop in his corruption investigation (322–23).

122. Scanlon critiques the view that the B-text moves from a politically self-conscious *Visio* to an apolitical, purely spiritual *Vita,* in "Langland," 239n–40n.

123. While the Gardener seems a laborer, he hints at his possible legal control, stating "I am gardyner of this gate . . . the grovynde is myn owen" [I am the gardener of this plot . . . the ground is mine] (976).

124. On the *Mum*-poet's use of Bartholomaeus and of John Trevisa's translation, see Helen Barr, *Socioliterary Practice in Late Medieval England* (Oxford: Oxford University Press, 2001), 163–66.

125. On the complex understanding of justice in late-medieval political theory, see Ormrod, *Political Life,* 109–29.

126. The *Mum*-poet derives the Genghis Khan exemplum from Mandeville. On Mandeville's virtual travels and the text's literary-historical impact, see Ian Macleod Higgins, *Writing East: The 'Travels' of Sir John Mandeville* (Philadelphia: University of Pennsylvania Press, 1997), 1–27.

127. On the *Mum*-poet's discomfort with the implications of such political philosophy, see Grady, "Generation of 1399," 220–22.

128. The Gardener's combination of timeless political wisdom and practical publishing advice suggests that it participates in what Steven F. Kruger sees as polar opposites of the traditional dream vision—both the transcendent moral instruction of the "educative vision" typified by Cicero's *Somnium Scipionis* and the gravitation "toward the things of the world" seen in Ovid's *Amores;* see *Dreaming in the Middle Ages* (Cambridge: Cambridge University Press, 1992), 124–26. Such a unique blend of dream-vision extremes contributes to the jarring effect created by presenting a bag of books rather than a transcription of the Gardener's speech.

129. Lucien Febvre and Henri-Jean Martin, *The Coming of the Book,* trans. David Gerard (1958; London: Verso, 1976), 24.

130. Richard Firth Green, "Medieval Literature and Law," in *Cambridge History,* ed. Wallace, 407–31 [419–21]. See also Barr, *Signes and Sothe,* 43–44; 70–72; 165; and Giancarlo, *Parliament and Literature,* 179–208; 228–54.

131. See Steiner's analysis of public availability as key to the *Mum*-poet's presentation of the archive, in *Documentary Culture,* 178.

132. Wawn, "Truth-telling," 280; 284.

133. See Barr's analysis of the poet's strategic use of multiplicity, in *Piers Plowman Tradition,* 348n. In terms of medieval literary theory, the *Mum*-narrator can be seen as strategically avoiding the coincidence of attribution and responsibility in the *auctor* by

presenting the transcription of the dream vision as produced by the activities of a *compilator* [compiler], who inserts "no opinion of his own" into the work; see Alastair Minnis, *Medieval Theory of Authorship: Scholastic Literary Attitudes in the Later Middle Ages,* 2nd ed. (1988; Philadelphia: University of Pennsylvania Press, 2010), 94–95.

134. J. A. Alford, *'Piers Plowman': A Glossary of Legal Diction* (Cambridge: Cambridge University Press, 1988), 108 [cited in Barr, ed., *Piers Plowman Tradition,* 349n].

135. Grady, "Generation of 1399," 227.

136. Kerby-Fulton, "Langland," 106. Kerby-Fulton argues that Langland's target audience, the unbeneficed clergy, produced circles of readers and rewriters much like those imagined in *Richard* (122).

137. Middleton historicizes the ambiguous authorial presence in *Piers Plowman,* observing that, despite his having produced the first "national" poem, Langland appears to disappear in the sixteenth century, supplanted by the fictional Piers Plowman "widely taken to be the center and source of authority for the poet's powerful innovation" ("William Langland's *Kynde Name,*" 15–16).

138. See Nichols's discussion of the "manuscript matrix" and "social context" generating a dialectics of meaning, in "Introduction," 9; and see Bernard Cerquiglini's argument that scribal variation is a medieval norm obscured by nineteenth-century philology's obsession with single, stable authorship, in *In Praise of the Variant: A Critical History of Philology,* trans. Betsy Wing (Baltimore: Johns Hopkins University Press, 1999), 1–11.

Epilogue

1. Blake, "Middle English Alliterative Revivals," 206.

2. Ibid.

3. See Anderson, *Imagined Communities,* 9–65. For medievalist critiques of Anderson's reductive view of medieval culture, see Davis, "National Writing," 612–13; 628–29; Kathleen Biddick, "Coming out of Exile: Dante on the Orient Express," in *Postcolonial Middle Ages,* ed. Cohen, 35–52 [36–37]; and Scanlon, "King, Commons, and Kind Wit," 191–93. See also Lisa Lampert's argument that alteritist insistence on a secular modernity postdating a religious Middle Ages leads scholars to underestimate the role of modern religious identity in racialist discourse, in "Race, Periodicity, and the (Neo-) Middle Ages," *Modern Literary Quarterly* 65 (2004): 391–421 [410–16].

4. See Ingham's discussion of Anderson's evolutionary historiography, in *Sovereign Fantasies,* 70–71. On capitalism as an ongoing, progressively developing set of forces, see Benedict Anderson, *The Spectre of Comparisons: Nationalism, Southeast Asia and the World* (London: Verso, 1998), 66–70.

5. Ingham, *Sovereign Fantasies,* 70–71.

6. Such a reconfigured timeline, conjoining the medieval and the early modern, argues against Davis's claim that modernist theories of the nation such as Anderson's depend upon a "totalizable Middle Ages" ("National Writing," 613)

7. Kathleen Davis, *Periodization and Sovereignty: How Ideas of Feudalism and Secularization Govern the Politics of Time* (Philadelphia: University of Pennsylvania Press, 2008), 5.

8. On the Anglo-Saxon origins of English nationalism, see Hastings, *Construction of Nationhood*, 35–44; and Davis, "National Writing," 614–28.

9. On Reformation England as the first nation, see Greenfeld, *Nationalism*, 29–87; on a range of cultural forms of self-writing, including cartography and jurisprudence, producing a sixteenth-century English nationalist discourse, see Helgerson, *Forms of Nationhood*, 1–18.

10. On eighteenth-century Francophobic intellectual culture spurring English nationalism, see Newman, *Rise of English Nationalism*, 87–156; on the 1707 union of Scotland and England triggering British nationhood, see Colley, *Britons*, 1–9.

11. While Hastings criticizes Anderson for emphasizing technology, he himself foregrounds religious identity in suggesting Bede as an origin for English identity (see *Construction of Nationhood*, 26–38). All interpretations of modernity, whether Hastings's or Anderson's, are arbitrary.

12. On the ongoing impact of global migration in shaping nationalist culture, see Anderson, *Spectre of Comparisons*, 58–74.

13. Michael Hardt and Antonio Negri, *Multitudes: War and Democracy in the Age of Empire* (New York: Penguin, 2004), 162–63 (emphasis in original); see also their analysis of current crises concerning borders (314–15).

14. Nichols, "Introduction," 9.

15. On parallels between manuscript and digital cultures, see Deibert, *Parchment, Printing, and Hypermedia*, 137–216; and Burnley, "Scribes and Hypertext," 41–62. The New Medievalist return to the "manuscript matrix" (Nichols, "Introduction," 9) would benefit immeasurably from Hayles's analyses of the dynamic interrelation of text and material context in the digital epoch, in *Writing Machines* (19–33).

16. See especially Gellner's argument for nationalism's equation of culture and politics, in *Nationalism*, 20–21.

17. Turville-Petre outlines his argument for medieval English nationalism, in *England the Nation*, v–vii.

18. See Newman's distinction between patriotism, which is of great antiquity and is oriented exclusively toward external threats, and the more systematic nationalism, in *Rise of English Nationalism*, 52–54.

19. Pearsall argues that late-medieval statements of vernacular pride imagined as a general "wave of English nationalism" are just as readily interpreted as "fragmentary, sporadic, regional responses to particular circumstances," in "Chaucer and Englishness," 288–89.

20. See Derrida's analysis of Jean-Jacques Rousseau's and Friedrich Nietzsche's opposed hermeneutic views, with the former paralyzed by guilt over his inability to offer a totalizing view and the latter reveling in the possibilities for interpretive play produced by awareness of the impossibility of totalization, in "Structure, Sign, and Play in the Discourse of the Human Sciences," in *Writing and Difference*, trans. Alan Bass (1967; Chicago: University of Chicago Press, 1978), 278–93 [292].

21. See Smith's study of nationalist critics' appropriation of ethnic history for "poetic, didactic and integrative purposes," in *Ethnic Origins*, 25.

22. See Anderson, *Imagined Communities*, 47–65.

23. Gellner, *Nations and Nationalism*, 125.

24. D. Vance Smith, "*Piers Plowman* and the National Noetic of Edward III," in

Imagining a Medieval English Nation, ed. Lavezzo, 214–54 [214]. On the crucial role of forgetting in the modern imagination of the nation, see Renan, *Qu'est-ce Qu'une Nation?*, 25–26; Anderson, *Imagined Communities*, 197–205; and Gellner, *Nationalism*, 45–47.

25. See Gellner's argument that nationalism "preaches and defends cultural diversity, when in fact it imposes homogeneity," in *Nations and Nationalism*, 125.

26. Smith, *Ethnic Origins*, 212. Smith insists that a past sense of ethnic homogeneity and territorialism is part of the modern nation (11), producing a temporally complex entity (see 212–14).

27. Lawton, "Diversity of Middle English Alliterative Poetry," 27.

BIBLIOGRAPHY

Primary Sources

The Alliterative 'Morte Arthure.' Ed. Valerie Krishna. New York: Burt Franklin, 1976.
Amours, F. J., ed. *Scottish Alliterative Poems in Riming Stanzas.* The Scottish Text Society 27; 38. 1897. London: Johnson Reprint Corporation, 1966.
Andreas Capellanus. *On Love.* Ed. and trans. P. G. Walsh. London: Duckworth, 1982.
Andrew of Wyntoun. *The Original Chronicle of Andrew of Wyntoun.* Ed. F. J. Amours. 6 vols. Edinburgh: W. Blackwood and Sons, 1903–14.
Of Arthour and Merlin. Ed. O. D. Macrae-Gibson. Vol. 1. EETS o.s. 268. 1973.
Arthur and Gorlagon. Ed. George L. Kittredge. *Studies and Notes in Philology and Literature* 8 (1903): 149–275.
———. Trans Frank A. Milne. In *A Lycanthropy Reader: Werewolves in Western Culture.* Ed. Charlotte F. Otten. Syracuse: Syracuse University Press, 1986. 234–55.
The Avowyng of Arthur. Ed. Thomas Hahn. In Hahn, ed. 113–68.
The Awntyrs off Arthure at the Terne Wathelyn. Ed. Ralph Hanna. Manchester: Manchester University Press, 1974.
The Awntyrs off Arthure at the Terne Wathelyne. Ed. Robert J. Gates. Philadelphia: University of Pennsylvania Press, 1969.
Bale, John. *Index Britanniae Scriptorum.* Ed. Reginald Lane Poole and Mary Bateson. 1902. Introduction by Caroline Brett and James P. Carley. Cambridge: D. S. Brewer, 1990.
Barbour, John. *The Bruce.* Ed. and trans. A. A. M. Duncan. Edinburgh: Canongate, 1997.
Barr, Helen, ed. *The 'Piers Plowman' Tradition: A Critical Edition of 'Pierce the Ploughman's Crede,' 'Richard the Redeless,' 'Mum and the Sothsegger' and 'The Crowned King.'* London: J. M. Dent, 1993.
Biblia Sacra Vulgata: Iuxta Vulgata Versionem. Ed. Robert Weber et al. 4th ed. Stuttgart: Deutsche Bibelgesellschaft, 1994.
Bryant, Nigel, ed. and trans. *Perceval: The Story of the Grail.* Cambridge: D. S. Brewer, 1982.
Camden, William. *Remains Concerning Britain.* 1605. Rpt. London: John Russel Smith, 1870.

Chaucer, Geoffrey. *The Riverside Chaucer.* 3rd ed. Ed. Larry D. Benson et al. Boston: Houghton Mifflin, 1987.
Cicero. *Cato Maior, De Senectute.* Ed. J. G. F. Powell. Cambridge: Cambridge University Press, 1988.
———. *De Senectute.* In *De Senectute, De Amicitia, De Divinitatione.* Ed. and trans. William Armistead Falconer. Cambridge, MA: Harvard University Press, 1923.
Conlee, John W., ed. *Middle English Debate Poetry.* East Lansing, MI: Colleagues Press, 1991.
The Death of King Arthur. Ed. and trans. James Cable. London: Penguin, 1971.
The Declaration of Arbroath. Ed. and trans. James Fergusson. Edinburgh: Edinburgh University Press, 1970.
Dunbar, William. *Selected Poems.* Ed. Priscilla Bawcutt. London: Longman, 1996.
Eachtra Uilliam: An Irish Version of 'William of Palerne.' Ed. Cecile O'Rahilly. Dublin: Dublin Institute for Advanced Studies, 1949.
"Francis Joseph Amours, Obituary." *Scottish Historical Review* 8 (1911): 101–4.
Gaston Phébus. *Livre de Chasse.* Ed. Gunnar Tilander. Cynegetica 18. Karlshamn, Sweden: E. G. Johanssons, 1971.
Geoffrey of Monmouth. *The History of the Kings of Britain.* Ed. Michael D. Reeve. Trans. Neil Wright. Woodbridge: Boydell, 2007.
The Gest Hystoriale of the Destruction of Troy. Ed. George A. Panton and David Donaldson. EETS o.s. 39, 86. 1869; 1874.
Ginsberg, Warren, ed. *'Wynnere and Wastoure' and 'The Parlement of the Thre Ages.'* Kalamazoo: Medieval Institute Publications, 1992.
Gottfried von Strassburg. *Tristan.* Ed. and trans. A. T. Hatto. Baltimore: Penguin, 1960.
Guillaume de Palerne: An English Translation of the 12th Century French Verse Romance. Ed. and trans. Leslie A. Sconduto. Jefferson, NC: McFarland, 2004.
Guillaume de Palerne: Roman du XIIIe Siècle. Ed. Alexandre Micha. Geneva: Librairie Droz, 1990.
Guillaume le Clerc. *Fergus of Galloway: Knight of King Arthur.* Ed. and trans. D. D. R. Owen. London: J. M. Dent, 1991.
Hahn, Thomas, ed. *Sir Gawain: Eleven Romances and Tales.* Kalamazoo: Medieval Institute Publications, 1995.
Hobbes, Thomas. *Leviathan.* 1651. Ed. Richard E. Flathman and David Johnston. New York: Norton, 1997.
Holland, Richard. *The Buke of the Howlat.* In *Longer Scottish Poems, Volume One: 1375–1650.* Ed. Priscilla Bawcutt and Felicity Riddy. Edinburgh: Scottish Academic Press, 1987. 43–84; 323–40.
Isidore of Seville. *Isidori Hispalensis episcopi Etymologiarum sive Originum.* Ed. William Lindsay. Oxford: Oxford University Press, 1911.
The Knightly Tale of Golagros and Gawane. Ed. Ralph Hanna (with material by W. R. J. Barron). Scottish Text Society Fifth Series 7. Woodbridge: Boydell, 2008.
Lancelot-Grail: The Old French Arthurian Vulgate and Post-Vulgate in Translation. Ed. and trans. Norris J. Lacy et al. 5 vols. New York: Garland, 1993–96.
———. Vol. 2. Ed. Norris J. Lacy. Trans. Samuel N. Rosenberg and Carleton W. Carroll. New York: Garland, 1993.
Langland, William. *Piers Plowman: The B Version.* Ed. George Kane and E. Talbot

Donaldson. London: Athlone Press, 1975.

———. *Piers Plowman: The C-text.* Ed. Derek Pearsall. Rev. ed. Exeter: University of Exeter Press, 1994.

———. *Piers Plowman: The Z Version.* Ed. A. G. Rigg and Charlotte Brewer. Toronto: Pontifical Institute of Medieval Studies, 1983.

Madden, Frederic, ed. *Syr Gawayne: A Collection of Ancient Romance Poems, by Scottish and English Authors.* 1839. New York: AMS, 1971.

Malory, Thomas. *Le Morte Darthure.* Ed. Stephen H. A. Shepherd. New York: W. W. Norton, 2004.

———. *Works.* Ed. Eugène Vinaver. 3 vols. Oxford: Clarendon Press, 1947.

Marie de France. *Lais.* Ed. Karl Warnke. Trans. Laurence Harf-Lancner. Paris: Librairie Générale Française, 1990.

———. *The Lais.* Ed. and trans. Glynn S. Burgess and Keith S. Busby. 2nd ed. New York: Penguin, 1999.

Mélion. In *Les Lais anonymes des XIIe et XIIIe siècles.* Ed. Prudence Mary O'Hara Tobin. Geneva: Librairie Droz, 1976.

Merlin. Ed. Henry B. Wheatley. 2 vols. EETS o.s. 10; 21; 36; 112. 1865–69.

Morris, Richard, ed. *Early English Alliterative Poems.* EETS o.s. 1. 1864.

La Mort le Roi Artu. Ed. Jean Frappier. Geneva: Librairie Droz, 1964.

Mum and the Sothsegger. Ed. Mabel Day and Robert Steele. EETS o.s. 199. 1936.

The Parlement of the Thre Ages. Ed. M. Y. Offord. EETS o.s. 246. 1959.

Pierce the Plowman's Creed. Ed. Walter W. Skeat. EETS o.s. 30. 1867

Les Prophecies de Merlin. Ed. Lucy Allen Paton. 2 vols. 1926. Rpt. New York: Kraus Reprint Corporation, 1966.

Prose Merlin. Ed. John Conlee. Kalamazoo: Medieval Institute Publications, 1998.

Puttenham, George. *The Arte of English Poesie.* 1589. Menston: Scolar Press, 1968.

Saint Erkenwald. Ed. Clifford Peterson. Philadelphia: University of Pennsylvania Press, 1977.

Sidney, Philip. "The Defence of Poesy." In *Sir Philip Sidney.* Ed. Katherine Duncan-Jones. Oxford: Oxford University Press, 1994.

———. *The Old Arcadia.* Ed. Katherine Duncan-Jones. Rev. ed. Oxford: Oxford University Press, 1994.

The Siege of Jerusalem. Ed. Ralph Hanna and David Lawton. EETS o.s 320. 2003.

Sir Gawain and the Carle of Carlisle. Ed. Thomas Hahn. In Hahn, ed. 81–112.

Sir Gawain and the Green Knight. Ed. Malcolm Andrew and Ronald Waldron. in *The Poems of the 'Pearl' Manuscript.* 4th ed. Exeter: University of Exeter Press, 2002.

———. Ed. J. R. R. Tolkien and E. V. Gordon. 1925. 2nd ed. Rev. by Norman Davis. Oxford: Clarendon Press, 1967.

———. Ed. and trans. William Vantuono. Rev. ed. Notre Dame, IN: University of Notre Dame Press, 1999.

Skeat, Walter W., ed. *'Piers the Plowman,' Text C, 'Richard the Redeles,' and 'The Crowned King.'* EETS o.s. 54. 1873.

The Stacions of Rome. Ed. F. J. Furnivall. EETS o.s. 24. 1867.

La Suite du Roman Merlin. Ed. Gilles Roussineau. 2 vols. Geneva: Librairie Droz, 1996.

Susannah: An Alliterative Poem of the Fourteenth Century. Ed. Alice Miskimin. New

Haven, CT: Yale University Press, 1969.
"Thomas of Erceldoune's Prophecy." In *Medieval English Political Writings*. Ed. James Dean. Kalamazoo: Medieval Institute Publications, 1996.
Turville-Petre, Thorlac, ed. *Alliterative Poetry of the Later Middle Ages: An Anthology*. Washington, DC: Catholic University Press of America, 1989.
The Vulgate Version of the Arthurian Romances. Ed. H. Oskar Sommer. 8 vols. 1908–16. New York: AMS Press, 1979.
The Wars of Alexander. Ed. Hoyt N. Duggan and Thorlac Turville-Petre. EETS s.s. 10. 1989.
The Wars of Alexander: An Alliterative Romance. Ed. Walter W. Skeat. EETS e.s. 47. 1886.
When Rome Is Removed into England. Ed. Reinhard Haferkorn. Leipzig: Verlag von Bernhard Tauchnitz, 1932.
William and the Werewolf. Ed. Frederic Madden. 1832. Rpt. New York: Burt Franklin, 1970.
William of Palerne: An Alliterative Romance. Ed. G. H. V. Bunt. Groningen, Netherlands: Bouma's Boekhuis, 1985.
Wynnere and Wastoure. Ed. Stephanie Trigg. EETS o.s. 297. 1990.

Secondary Sources

Aers, David. "A Whisper in the Ear of Early Modernists; or, Reflections on Literary Critics Writing the 'History of the Subject.'" In *Culture and History, 1350–1600: Essays on English Communities, Identities and Writing*. Ed. David Aers. Detroit: Wayne State University Press, 1992. 177–202.
Agamben, Giorgio. *Homo Sacer: Sovereign Power and Bare Life*. Trans. Daniel Heller-Roazen. Stanford, CA: Stanford University Press, 1998.
———. *The Open: Man and Animal*. Trans. Kevin Attell. Stanford, CA: Stanford University Press, 2004.
Akbari, Suzanne Conklin. "Between Diaspora and Conquest: Norman Assimilation in Petrus Alfonsi's *Disciplina Clericalis* and Marie de France's *Fables*." In Cohen, ed., *Cultural Diversity*. 17–37.
———. "Orientation and Nation in Chaucer's *Canterbury Tales*." In Lynch, ed. 102–34.
Alexander, Flora. "Late Medieval Scottish Attitudes to the Figure of King Arthur: A Reassessment." *Anglia* 93 (1975): 17–34.
Alford, J. A. *'Piers Plowman': A Glossary of Legal Diction*. Cambridge: Cambridge University Press, 1988.
Allen, Rosamund. "*The Awntyrs off Arthure*: Jests and Jousts." In *Romance Reading on the Book*. Ed. Jennifer Fellows et al. Cardiff: University of Wales Press, 1996. 129–42.
"Francis Joseph Amours, Obituary." *Scottish Historical Review* 8 (1911): 101–4.
Anderson, Benedict. *Imagined Communities: Reflections on the Origin and Spread of Nationalism*. Rev. ed. London: Verso, 1991.
———. *The Spectre of Comparisons: Nationalism, Southeast Asia and the World*.

London: Verso, 1998.

Andrew, Malcolm. "Theories of Authorship." In Brewer and Gibson, eds. 23–33.

Andrew, S. O. "The Dialect of *Morte Arthure.*" *Review of English Studies* 4 (1928): 418–23.

Archer, Rowena E. "'How ladies . . . who live on their manors ought to manage their households and estates': Women as Landholders and Administrators in the Later Middle Ages." In *Woman is a Worthy Wight: Women in English Society.* Ed. P. J. P. Goldberg. Phoenix Mill, Gloucestershire: Alan Sutton, 1992. 149–81.

Archibald, Elizabeth. *Incest and the Medieval Imagination.* Oxford: Oxford University Press, 2001.

Ashcroft, Bill, Gareth Griffiths, and Helen Tiffin. *Post-Colonial Studies: The Key Concepts.* London: Routledge, 2000.

Astell, Ann W. *Political Allegory in Late Medieval England.* Ithaca, NY: Cornell University Press, 1999.

Backus, Truman J., and Thomas B. Shaw. *Shaw's New History of English Literature together with A History of English Literature in America.* 1874. Rev. ed. New York: Sheldon and Company, 1884.

Barber, Richard, and Juliette Barker. *Tournaments: Jousts, Chivalry and Pageants in the Middle Ages.* Woodbridge: Boydell, 1989.

Barney, Stephen A. "Langland's Prosody: The State of Study." In Tavormina and Yeager, eds. 65–85.

Barr, Helen. "The Dates of *Richard the Redeless* and *Mum and the Sothsegger.*" *Yearbook of Langland Studies* 4 (1990): 270–75.

———. *Signes and Sothe: Language in the 'Piers Plowman' Tradition.* Cambridge: D. S. Brewer, 1994.

———. *Socioliterary Practice in Late Medieval England.* Oxford: Oxford University Press, 2001.

Barrell, A. D. M. *Medieval Scotland.* Cambridge: Cambridge University Press, 2000.

Barrett, Robert W., Jr. *Against All England: Regional Identity and Cheshire Writing, 1195–1656.* Notre Dame, IN: University of Notre Dame Press, 2009.

Barron, W. R. J. "Alliterative Romance and the French Tradition." In Lawton, ed. 70–87.

Barth, Fredrik. "Introduction." In *Ethnic Groups and Boundaries: The Social Organization of Cultural Difference.* Ed. Fredrik Barth. 1969. With new preface. Long Grove, IL: Waveland Press, 1998. 9–38.

Bartlett, Robert. *The Making of Europe: Conquest, Colonization, and Cultural Change, 950–1350.* Princeton, NJ: Princeton University Press, 1993.

Bartra, Roger. *Wild Men in the Looking Glass: The Mythic Origins of European Otherness.* Trans. Carl T. Berrisford. Ann Arbor: University of Michigan Press, 1994.

Beattie, Cordelia. *Medieval Single Women: The Politics of Social Classification in Late Medieval England.* Oxford: Oxford University Press, 2007.

Beckwith, Sarah. *Signifying God: Social Relation and Symbolic Act in the York Corpus Christi Plays.* Chicago: University of Chicago Press, 2001.

Bennett, Judith M. "Public Power and Authority in the Medieval English Countryside." In *Women and Power in the Middle Ages.* Ed. Mary Erler and Maryanne Kowaleski. Athens: University of Georgia Press, 1988. 18–36.

Bennett, Michael J. *Community, Class and Careerism: Cheshire and Lancashire Society in the Age of 'Sir Gawain and the Green Knight.'* Cambridge: Cambridge University Press, 1983.

———. "*Mandeville's Travels* and the Anglo-French Moment." *Medium Aevum* 75 (2006): 273–92.

———. *Richard II and the Revolution of 1399.* Phoenix Mill, Gloucestershire: Sutton, 1999.

Benson, C. David. "Another Fine Manuscript Mess: Authors, Editors and Readers of *Piers Plowman.*" In Pearsall, ed. 15–28.

———. *Public "Piers Plowman": Modern Scholarship and Late Medieval English Culture.* University Park: Pennsylvania State University Press, 2004.

Benzie, William. *Dr. F. J. Furnivall: A Victorian Scholar Adventurer.* Norman, OK: Pilgrim Books, 1983.

Bernheimer, Richard. *Wild Men in the Middle Ages: A Study in Art, Sentiment and Demonology.* Cambridge, MA: Harvard University Press, 1952.

Bestul, Thomas H. *Satire and Allegory in Wynnere and Wastoure.* Lincoln: University of Nebraska Press, 1974.

Biddick, Kathleen. "Coming Out of Exile: Dante on the Orient Express." In Cohen, ed., *The Postcolonial Middle Ages.* 35–52.

———. *The Shock of Medievalism.* Durham, NC: Duke University Press, 1998.

Birkholz, Daniel. *The King's Two Maps: Cartography and Culture in Thirteenth-Century England.* New York: Routledge, 2004.

Birrer, Doryjane. "A New Species of Humanities: The Marvelous Progeny of Humanism and Postmodern Theory." *Journal of Narrative Theory* 37.2 (2007): 217–45.

Blake, N. F. "Chaucer and the Alliterative Romances." *Chaucer Review* 3 (1969): 163–69.

———. *The English Language in Medieval Literature.* London: Methuen, 1977.

———. "Middle English Alliterative Revivals." *Review* 1 (1979): 205–14.

Blamires, Alcuin G. "*Mum & the Sothsegger* and Langlandian Idiom." *Neuphilologische Mitteilungen* 76 (1975): 583–604.

Blank, Paula. *Broken English: Dialects and the Politics of Language in Renaissance Writings.* London: Routledge, 1996.

Bloch, R. Howard. *Medieval Misogyny and the Invention of Western Romantic Love.* Chicago: University of Chicago Press, 1991.

——— and Stephen G. Nichols, eds. *Medievalism and the Modernist Temper.* Baltimore: Johns Hopkins University Press, 1996.

Borroff, Marie. *Sir Gawain and the Green Knight: A Stylistic and Metrical Study.* New Haven, CT: Yale University Press, 1962.

Bourdieu, Pierre. *Language and Symbolic Power.* Ed. John B. Thompson. Trans. Gino Raymond and Matthew Adamson. Cambridge, MA: Harvard University Press, 1991.

———. *Outline of a Theory of Practice.* Trans. Richard Nice. Cambridge: Cambridge University Press, 1977.

———. *Practical Reason.* Trans. Loïc Wacquant and Samar Farage. 1994. Stanford, CA: Stanford University Press, 1998.

Bowers, John. *Chaucer and Langland: The Antagonistic Tradition.* Notre Dame, IN:

University of Notre Dame Press, 2007.

———. "*Piers Plowman*'s William Langland: Editing the Text, Writing the Author's Life." *Yearbook of Langland Studies* 9 (1995): 87–124.

———. *The Politics of 'Pearl': Court Poetry in the Age of Richard II*. Cambridge: D. S. Brewer, 2001.

Bowers, R. H. "*Gawain and the Green Knight* as Entertainment." *Modern Language Quarterly* 24 (1963): 333–41.

Braude, Benjamin. "The Son of Noah and the Construction of Ethnic and Geographical Identities in the Medieval and Early Modern Periods." *William and Mary Quarterly* 54 (1997): 103–42.

Brewer, Charlotte. *Editing 'Piers Plowman.'* Cambridge: Cambridge University Press, 1996.

Brewer, Derek, and Jonathan Gibson, eds. *A Companion to the 'Gawain'-poet*. Cambridge: D. S. Brewer, 1997.

Brown, Michael. *The Black Douglases: War and Lordship in Late Medieval Scotland, 1300–1455*. East Linton, East Lothian: Tuckwell Press, 1998.

———. "'Rejoice to hear of Douglas': The House of Douglas and the Presentation of Magnate Power in Late Medieval Scotland." *Scottish Historical Review* 76.2 (1997): 161–84.

———. *The Wars of Scotland: 1214–1371*. The New Edinburgh History of Scotland. Edinburgh: Edinburgh University Press, 2004.

——— and Steve Boardman. "Survival and Revival: Late Medieval Scotland." In Wormald, ed. 77–106.

Bryan, Elizabeth J. *Collaborative Meaning in Medieval Scribal Culture*. Ann Arbor: University of Michigan Press, 1999.

Bunt, G. H. V. "Localizing *William of Palerne*." In *Historical Linguistics and Philology*. Ed. Jacek Fisiak. Berlin: Mouton de Gruyter, 1990. 73–86.

———. "Patron, Author and Audience in a Fourteenth-century English Alliterative Poem." In *Non Nova, sed Nove: Mélanges de civilisation médiévale dédiés à Willem Noomen*. Ed. Martin Grosman and Jaap van Os. Mediaevalia Groningana 5. Groningen, Netherlands: Bouma's Boekhuis, 1984. 25–36.

———, ed. *William of Palerne: An Electronic Edition*. Society for Early English & Norse Electronic Texts A:3. Ann Arbor: University of Michigan Press, 2002.

Burnley, David. "Scribes and Hypertext." *Yearbook of English Studies* 25 (1995): 41–62.

Burrow, John. "The Audience of Piers Plowman." *Anglia* 75 (1957): 373–84.

Butterfield, Ardis. "French Culture and the Ricardian Court." In *Essays on Ricardian Literature in Honour of J. A. Burrow*. Ed. A. J. Minnis, Charlotte C. Morse, and Thorlac Turville-Petre. Oxford: Clarendon Press, 1997. 82–120.

Bynum, Caroline Walker. *Metamorphosis and Identity*. New York: Zone Books, 2005.

Cable, Thomas. *The English Alliterative Tradition*. Philadelphia: University of Pennsylvania Press, 1991.

Camille, Michael. *Image on the Edge: The Margins of Medieval Art*. Cambridge, MA: Harvard University Press, 1992.

Cannon, Christopher. *Middle English Literature: A Cultural History*. Cambridge: Polity, 2008.

———. "The Rights of Medieval English Women: Crime and the Issue of Representation." In *Medieval Crime and Social Control.* Ed. Barbara A. Hanawalt and David Wallace. Minneapolis: University of Minnesota Press, 1998. 156–85.

Carson, Angela. "Morgain la Fée as the Principle of Unity in *Gawain and the Green Knight.*" *Modern Language Quarterly* 23 (1962): 3–16.

Cerquiglini, Bernard. *In Praise of the Variant: A Critical History of Philology.* Trans. Betsy Wing. Baltimore: Johns Hopkins University Press, 1999.

Chakrabarty, Dipesh. *Provincializing Europe: Postcolonial Thought and Historical Difference.* Princeton, NJ: Princeton University Press, 2000.

Chambers, R. W. *On the Continuity of English Prose from Alfred to More and his School.* EETS o.s. 191. 1932.

———. *The Papers of Raymond Wilson Chambers (1874–1942).* Ed. Janet Percival. London: Library of University College, London, 1978.

Chandler, Alice. *A Dream of Order: The Medieval Ideal in Nineteenth-Century English Literature.* Lincoln: University of Nebraska Press, 1970.

Chapman, Coolidge Otis. "The Authorship of the *Pearl.*" *PMLA* 47 (1932): 346–53.

Chism, Christine. *Alliterative Revivals.* Philadelphia: University of Pennsylvania Press, 2002.

———. "*The Siege of Jerusalem:* Liquidating Assets." *Journal of Medieval and Early Modern Studies* 28 (1998): 309–40.

———. "Too Close for Comfort: Dis-Orienting Chivalry in the *Wars of Alexander.*" In Tomasch and Gilles, eds. 116–39.

Clanchy, M. T. *England and Its Rulers, 1066–1272.* 2nd ed. Oxford: Blackwell, 1998.

———. *From Memory to Written Record.* 2nd ed. Oxford: Blackwell, 1993.

Coghill, Nevill. "The Pardon of Piers Plowman." *Proceedings of the British Academy* 30. London: Humphrey Milford, 1945.

Cohen, Jeffrey Jerome, ed. *Cultural Diversity in the British Middle Ages: Archipelago, Island, England.* Ed. Jeffrey Jerome Cohen. New York: Palgrave Macmillan, 2008.

———. *Hybridity, Identity, and Monstrosity in Medieval Britain: On Difficult Middles.* New York: Palgrave Macmillan, 2006.

———. *Medieval Identity Machines.* Minneapolis: University of Minnesota Press, 2003.

———. *Of Giants: Sex, Monsters, and the Middle Ages.* Minneapolis: University of Minnesota Press, 1999.

———, ed. *The Postcolonial Middle Ages.* New York: St. Martin's Press, 2000.

Colley, Linda. *Britons: Forging the Nation, 1707–1837.* New Haven, CT: Yale University Press, 1992.

Colls, Robert. *Identity of England.* Oxford: Oxford University Press, 2002.

Connor, Walker. *Ethnonationalism: The Quest for Understanding.* Princeton, NJ: Princeton University Press, 1994.

Cooper, Helen. *The English Romance in Time: Transforming Motifs from Geoffrey of Monmouth to the Death of Shakespeare.* Oxford: Oxford University Press, 2004.

Coss, Peter. *The Lady in Medieval England, 1000–1500.* Phoenix Mill, Gloucestershire: Sutton, 1998. 56–72.

Court, Franklin E. *The Scottish Connection: The Rise of English Literary Study in Early America.* Syracuse, NY: Syracuse University Press, 2001.

Craigie, William. "The Scottish Alliterative Poems." *Proceedings of the British Academy* 28. London: Humphrey Milford, 1942.
Crane, Susan. "Anglo-Norman Cultures in England, 1066–1460." In Wallace, ed. 35–60.
———. *The Performance of Self: Ritual, Clothing, and Identity during the Hundred Years War.* Philadelphia: University of Pennsylvania Press, 2002.
Crawford, Robert. *Devolving English Literature.* 2nd ed. Edinburgh: Edinburgh University Press, 2000.
Cummins, John. *The Hound and the Hawk: The Medieval Art of Hunting.* London: Phoenix Press, 1988.
Davies, Norman. *The Isles: A History.* Oxford: Oxford University Press, 1999.
Davies, R. R. *Domination and Conquest: The Experience of Ireland, Scotland and Wales, 1100–1300.* Cambridge: Cambridge University Press, 1990.
———. *The First English Empire: Power and Identity in the British Isles, 1093–1343.* Oxford: Oxford University Press, 2000.
Davis, Kathleen. "National Writing in the Ninth Century: A Reminder for Postcolonial Thinking about the Nation." *Journal of Medieval and Early Modern Studies* 28 (1998): 611–37.
———. *Periodization and Sovereignty: How Ideas of Feudalism and Secularization Govern the Politics of Time.* Philadelphia: University of Pennsylvania Press, 2008.
Day, Gary. *Class.* London: Routledge, 2001.
Deibert, Ronald J. *Parchment, Printing, and Hypermedia: Communication in World Order Transformation.* New York: Columbia University Press, 1997.
Deleuze, Gilles, and Félix Guattari. *A Thousand Plateaus: Capitalism and Schizophrenia.* Trans. Brian Massumi. Minneapolis: University of Minnesota Press, 1987.
Derrida, Jacques. "Structure, Sign, and Play in the Discourse of the Human Sciences." In *Writing and Difference.* 1967. Trans. Alan Bass. Chicago: University of Chicago Press, 1978. 278–93.
Diefendorf, Barbara B. *The St. Bartholomew's Day Massacre: A Brief History with Documents.* New York: Bedford/St. Martin's, 2009.
Dinshaw, Carolyn. *Getting Medieval: Sexualities and Communities, Pre- and Postmodern.* Durham, NC: Duke University Press, 1999.
———. "A Kiss Is Just a Kiss: Heterosexuality and Its Consolations in *Sir Gawain and the Green Knight.*" *Diacritics* (1994): 205–25.
Donaldson, E. Talbot. "*Piers Plowman:* Textual Comparison and the Question of Authorship." In *Chaucer und seine Zeit: Symposion für Walter F. Schirmer.* Ed. Arno Esch. Tübingen: Max Niemeyer Verlag, 1968. 241–47.
Donoghue, Daniel. "Laȝamon's Ambivalence." *Speculum* 65 (1990): 537–63.
Douglas, David C. *William the Conqueror: The Norman Impact upon England.* Berkeley: University of California Press, 1964.
Doyle, A. I. "The Manuscripts." In Lawton, ed. 88–100.
———. "The Social Context of Middle English Literature." In *The Pelican Guide to English Literature, vol. 1: The Age of Chaucer.* Ed. Boris Ford. Harmondsworth: Penguin, 1959. 83–103.
———. "Some Remarks on Surviving Manuscripts of *Piers Plowman.*" In Kratzmann and Simpson, eds. 35–48.

———. "An Unrecognized Piece of *Piers the Ploughman's Creed* and Other Work by Its Scribe." *Speculum* 34 (1959): 428–36.

Duggan, Hoyt N. "Alliterative Patterning as a Basis for Emendation in Middle English Alliterative Poetry." *Studies in the Age of Chaucer* 8 (1986): 73–105.

Dunn, Charles W. *The Foundling and the Werwolf: A Literary-Historical Study of 'Guillaume de Palerne.'* Toronto: University of Toronto Press, 1960.

Edwards, A. S. G. "The Manuscript: British Library MS Cotton Nero A.x." In Brewer and Gibson, eds. 197–219.

Embree, Dan. "*Richard the Redeless* and *Mum and the Sothsegger:* A Case of Mistaken Identity." *Notes and Queries* 220 (1975): 4–12.

Emerson, Ralph Waldo. *English Traits*. Boston: Phillips, Sampson, and Company, 1857.

Everett, Dorothy. "The Alliterative Revival." In *Essays on Middle English Literature*. Ed. Patricia Kean. London: Oxford University Press, 1959. 46–96.

———. Rev. of Israel Gollancz,' ed., *Winner and Waster, Death and Liffe*. *Review of English Studies* 9 (1933): 213–18.

Febvre, Lucien, and Henri-Jean Martin. *The Coming of the Book*. 1958. Trans. David Gerard. London: Verso, 1976.

Federico, Sylvia, and Elizabeth Scala. "Getting Post-Historical." In *The Post-Historical Middle Ages*. Ed. Elizabeth Scala and Sylvia Federico. New York: Palgrave Macmillan, 2009. 1–12.

Fein, Susanna G. "The Ghoulish and the Ghastly: A Moral Aesthetic in Middle English Alliterative Verse." *Modern Language Quarterly* 48 (1987): 3–19.

Ferster, Judith. *Fictions of Advice: The Literature and Politics of Counsel in Late Medieval England*. Philadelphia: University of Pennsylvania Press, 1996.

Field, Rosalind. "Romance in England, 1066–1400." In Wallace, ed. 152–76.

Finke, Laurie A., and Martin B. Shichtman. *King Arthur and the Myth of History*. Gainesville: University Press of Florida, 2004.

Fisher, Sheila. "Taken Men and Token Women in *Sir Gawain and the Green Knight*." In *Seeking the Woman in Late Medieval and Renaissance Writings*. Ed. Sheila Fisher and Janet E. Halley. Knoxville: University of Tennessee Press, 1984. 71–105.

Foucault, Michel. *The History of Sexuality*. Vol. 1. Trans. Robert Hurley. New York: Vintage, 1978.

———. "What Is an Author?" Trans. Josué V. Harari. In *Textual Strategies: Perspectives in Post-Structuralist Criticism*. Ithaca, NY: Cornell University Press, 1979. 141–60.

Fradenburg, L. O. Aranye. *City, Marriage, Tournament: Arts of Rule in Late Medieval Scotland*. Madison: University of Wisconsin Press, 1991.

———. *Sacrifice Your Love: Psychoanalysis, Historicism, Chaucer*. Minneapolis: University of Minnesota Press, 2002.

———. "The Scottish Chaucer." In *Writing after Chaucer*. Ed. Daniel J. Pinti. New York: Garland, 1998. 167–77.

———. "'So That We May Speak of Them': Enjoying the Middle Ages." *New Literary History* 28.2 (1997): 205–30.

Frakes, Jerold C. *Brides and Doom: Gender, Property, and Power in Medieval German Women's Epic*. Philadelphia: University of Pennsylvania Press, 1994.

———. *The Fate of Fortune in the Middle Ages: The Boethian Tradition.* Studien und Texte zur Geistesgeschichte des Mittelalters 23. Leiden: E. J. Brill, 1987.
Frame, Robin. *The Political Development of the British Isles, 1100–1400.* Oxford: Oxford University Press, 1990.
Frantzen, Allen J. *Desire for Origins: New Language, Old English, and Teaching the Tradition.* New Brunswick, NJ: Rutgers University Press, 1990.
——— and John D. Niles. "Anglo-Saxonism and Medievalism." In Frantzen and Niles, eds. 1–14.
——— and John D. Niles, eds. *Anglo-Saxonism and the Construction of Social Identity.* Gainesville: University Press of Florida, 1997.
Friedman, Albert B. "Morgan le Fay in *Sir Gawain and the Green Knight.*" *Speculum* 35 (1960): 260–74.
Fries, Maureen. "The Characterization of Women in the Alliterative Tradition." In Levy and Szarmach, eds. 25–45.
Fryde, E. B. *Peasants and Landlords in Later Medieval England.* Phoenix Mill, Gloucestershire: Alan Sutton, 1996.
Fuchs, Barbara. "Imperium Studies." In Ingham and Warren, eds. 71–90.
Gadamer, Hans-Georg. *Truth and Method.* 2nd ed. Rev. ed. Trans. Joel Weinsheimer and Donald G. Marshall. London: Continuum, 2004.
Galbraith, V. C. "Nationality and Language in Medieval England." *Transactions of the Royal Historical Society.* 4th ser. 23 (1941): 113–28.
Galloway, Andrew. "Latin England." In Lavezzo, ed. 41–95.
———. "Making History Legal: *Piers Plowman* and the Rebels of Fourteenth-Century England." In *Piers Plowman: A Book of Essays.* Ed. Kathleen M. Hewett-Smith. New York: Routledge, 2005. 7–31.
Ganim, John. "The Myth of Medieval Romance." In Bloch and Nichols, eds. 148–66.
Gates, Henry Louis, Jr. "Writing 'Race' and the Difference It Makes." *Critical Inquiry* 12.1 (1985): 1–21.
Geary, Patrick J. *The Myth of Nations: The Medieval Origins of Europe.* Princeton, NJ: Princeton University Press, 2002.
Gellner, Ernest. *Nationalism.* New York: New York University Press, 1997.
———. *Nations and Nationalism.* Ithaca, NY: Cornell University Press, 1983.
Giancarlo, Matthew. *Parliament and Literature in Late Medieval England.* Cambridge: Cambridge University Press, 2007.
Girouard, Mark. *The Return to Camelot: Chivalry and the English Gentleman.* New Haven, CT: Yale University Press, 1981.
Given-Wilson, Chris. *The English Nobility in the Late Middle Ages: The Fourteenth-Century Political Community.* London: Routledge & Kegan Paul, 1987.
Goldstein, R. James. *The Matter of Scotland: Historical Narrative in Medieval Scotland.* Lincoln: University of Nebraska Press, 1993.
Gollancz, Israel, ed. *A Good Short Debate between Winner and Waster: An Alliterative Poem on Social and Economic Problems in England in the Year 1352, with Modern English Rendering.* London: Humphrey Milford, 1920.
Goodman, Anthony. "The Anglo-Scottish Marches in the Fifteenth Century: A Frontier Society?" In *Scotland and England: 1286–1815.* Ed. Roger A. Mason. Edinburgh: John Donald, 1988. 18–33.

Grady, Frank. "The Generation of 1399." In *The Letter of the Law: Legal Practice and Literary Production in Medieval England.* Ed. Emily Steiner and Candace Barrington. Ithaca, NY: Cornell University Press, 2002. 202–29.

———. "The Lancastrian Gower and the Limits of Exemplarity." *Speculum* 70.3 (1995): 552–75.

Graham, John M. "National Politics and the Publishing of the Troubadours." In Bloch and Nichols, eds. 57–94.

Grant, Alexander. *Independence and Nationhood: Scotland, 1306–1469.* Edinburgh: Edinburgh University Press, 1985.

———. "Scotland's 'Celtic Fringe' in the Late Middle Ages: The Macdonald Lords of the Isles and the Kingdom of Scotland." In *The British Isles, 1100–1500: Comparisons, Contrasts and Connections.* Ed. R. R. Davies. Edinburgh: John Donald, 1988. 118–41.

Gray, John. "Lawlessness on the Frontier: The Anglo-Scottish Borderlands in the Fourteenth to the Sixteenth Century." *History and Anthropology* 12.4 (2001): 381–408.

Green, Richard Firth. "Medieval Literature and Law." In Wallace, ed. 407–31.

———. *Poets and Princepleasers: Literature and the English Court in the Late Middle Ages.* Toronto: University of Toronto Press, 1980.

Greenfeld, Liah. *Nationalism: Five Roads to Modernity.* Cambridge, MA: Harvard University Press, 1992.

Greetham, D. C. "Reading in and Around *Piers Plowman.*" In *Texts and Textuality: Textual Instability, Theory, and Interpretation.* Ed. Philip Cohen. New York: Garland, 1997. 25–57.

Guillory, John. *Cultural Capital: The Problem of Literary Canon Formation.* Chicago: University of Chicago Press, 1993.

Hahn, Thomas. "The Difference the Middle Ages Makes: Color and Race before the Modern World." *Journal of Medieval and Early Modern Studies* 31.1 (2001): 1–37.

Halleck, Reuben Post. *History of English Literature.* New York: American Book Company, 1900.

Hammill, Graham L. *Sexuality and Form: Caravaggio, Marlowe, and Bacon.* Chicago: University of Chicago Press, 2000.

Hammond, Eleanor Prescott. "A Scribe of Chaucer." *Modern Philology* 27 (1929): 26–33.

Hanawalt, Barbara A. "Men's Games, King's Deer: Poaching in Medieval England." *Journal of Medieval and Renaissance Studies* 18 (1988): 175–93.

Hanna, Ralph, III. "Alliterative Poetry." In Wallace, ed. 488–512.

———. "*The Awntyrs off Arthure:* An Interpretation." *Modern Language Quarterly* 31 (1970): 275–97.

———. "Defining Middle English Alliterative Poetry." In Tavormina and Yeager, eds. 43–63.

———. *London Literature, 1300–1380.* Cambridge: Cambridge University Press, 2005.

———. *William Langland.* Aldershot: Variorum, 1993.

———. "Will's Work." In Justice and Kerby-Fulton, eds. 23–66.

Hardt, Michael, and Antonio Negri. *Empire.* Cambridge, MA: Harvard University Press, 2000.

———. *Multitudes: War and Democracy in the Age of Empire.* New York: Penguin, 2004.
Harrington, David V. "Indeterminacy in *Winner and Waster* and *The Parliament of the Three Ages.*" *Chaucer Review* 20.3 (1986): 246–57.
Harriss, Gerald. *Shaping the Nation: England, 1360–1461.* Oxford: Oxford University Press, 2005.
Hastings, Adrian. *The Construction of Nationhood: Ethnicity, Religion and Nationalism.* Cambridge: Cambridge University Press, 1997.
Hayles, N. Katherine. *Writing Machines.* Cambridge, MA: MIT Press, 2002.
Helgerson, Richard. *Forms of Nationhood: The Elizabethan Writing of England.* Chicago: University of Chicago Press, 1992.
Heng, Geraldine. "Feminine Knots and the Other: *Sir Gawain and the Green Knight.*" *PMLA* 106 (1991): 500–514.
Hey, David. *A History of Yorkshire: 'County of the Broad Acres.'* Lancaster: Carnegie, 2005.
Higgins, Ian Macleod. *Writing East: The 'Travels' of Sir John Mandeville.* Philadelphia: University of Pennsylvania Press, 1997.
Higham, N. J. *King Arthur: Myth-Making and History.* London: Routledge, 2002.
Hill, Christopher. "The Norman Yoke." In *Puritanism and Revolution: Studies in Interpretation of the English Revolution of the Seventeenth Century.* 1958. Harmondsworth: Penguin, 1986. 58–125.
Hilton, Rodney. *Bond Men Made Free: Medieval Peasant Movements and the English Rising of 1381.* New York: Viking, 1973.
———. *A Medieval Society: The West Midlands at the End of the Thirteenth Century.* New York: John Wiley & Sons, 1966.
Hinchman, Walter S. *A History of English Literature.* New York: Century, 1916.
Hobsbawm, Eric. *Industry and Empire: The Birth of the Industrial Revolution.* Rev. ed. Ed. Chris Wrigley. New York: New Press, 1999.
———. *Nations and Nationalism since 1780: Programme, Myth, Reality.* 2nd ed. Cambridge: Cambridge University Press, 1992.
——— and Terence Ranger, eds. *The Invention of Tradition.* Cambridge: Cambridge University Press, 1983.
Hodges, Kenneth. *Forging Chivalric Communities in Malory's 'Le Morte Darthur.'* New York: Palgrave Macmillan, 2005.
Holsinger, Bruce W. "Medieval Studies, Postcolonial Studies, and the Genealogies of Critique." *Speculum* 77 (2002): 1195–1227.
Holstun, James. *Ehud's Dagger: Class Struggle in the English Revolution.* London: Verso, 2000.
Horobin, Simon. "The Dialect and Authorship of *Richard the Redeless* and *Mum and the Sothsegger.*" *Yearbook of Langland Studies* 18 (2004): 133–52.
Horsman, Reginald. *Race and Manifest Destiny: The Origins of American Racial Anglo—Saxonism.* Cambridge, MA: Harvard University Press, 1981.
Hudnall, Richard Henry. "Franklin Verzelius Newton Painter." In *Library of Southern Literature.* Ed. Edwin Anderson Alderman and Joel Chandler Harris. Vol. 9. New Orleans: Martin & Hoyt, 1917. 3889–94.
Hulbert, James R. "A Hypothesis Concerning the Alliterative Revival." *Modern Philol-*

ogy 28 (1931): 405–22.

———. Papers. Special Collections Research Center. University of Chicago Library.

———. "The Problems of Authorship and Date of *Wynnere and Wastoure*," *Modern Philology* 18 (1920–21): 31–40.

———. Syr Gawayn and the Grene Knyȝt." *Modern Philology* 13 (1915): 433–62; 689–730.

Hunt, Alan. *Governance of the Consuming Passions: A History of Sumptuary Law.* New York: St. Martin's Press, 1996.

Husband, Timothy, ed. *The Wild Man: Medieval Myth and Symbolism.* New York: Metropolitan Museum of Art, 1980.

Ingham, Patricia Clare. "Contrapuntal Histories." In Ingham and Warren, eds. 47–70.

———. *Sovereign Fantasies: Arthurian Romance and the Making of Britain.* Philadelphia: University of Pennsylvania Press, 2001.

——— and Michelle R. Warren, eds. *Postcolonial Moves: Medieval through Modern.* New York: Palgrave Macmillan, 2003.

Ingledew, Francis. "The Book of Troy and the Genealogical Construction of History: The Case of Geoffrey of Monmouth's *Historia regum Britanniae.*" *Speculum* 69 (1994): 665–704.

Jack, R. D. S. "Arthur's Pilgrimage: A Study of *Golagros and Gawane.*" *Studies in Scottish Literature* 12.1 (1974): 3–20.

Jacobs, Nicolas. "Kindly Light or Foxfire? The Authorial Text Reconsidered." In *A Guide to Editing Middle English.* Ed. Douglas Moffat and Vincent P. McCarren. Ann Arbor: University of Michigan Press, 1998. 3–14.

———. "The Typology of Debate and the Interpretation of *Wynnere and Wastoure.*" *Review of English Studies* n.s. 36 (1985): 481–500.

James, Jerry D. "The Undercutting of Conventions in *Wynnere and Wastoure.*" *Modern Language Quarterly* 25 (1964): 243–58.

Janssen, Anke. "The Dream of the Wheel of Fortune." In *The Alliterative Morte Arthure: A Reassessment of the Poem.* Ed. Karl Heinz Göller. Cambridge: D. S. Brewer, 1981. 140–52.

Jewell, Helen M. *The North-South Divide: The Origins of Northern Consciousness in England.* Manchester: Manchester University Press, 1994.

———. "*Piers Plowman*—A Poem of Crisis: an Analysis of Political Instability in Langland's England." In *Politics and Crisis in Fourteenth-Century England.* Ed. John Taylor and Wendy Childs. Gloucester: Alan Sutton, 1990. 59–80.

Johnston, Arthur. *Enchanted Ground: The Study of Medieval Romance in the Eighteenth Century.* London: Athlone Press, 1964.

Jusserand, J. J. *A Literary History of the English People from the Origins to the End of the Middle Ages.* New York: G. P. Putnam's Sons, 1893.

Justice, Steven. "Introduction: Authorial Work and Literary Ideology." In Justice and Kerby-Fulton, eds. 1–12.

———. "Lollardy." In Wallace, ed. 662–89.

———. *Writing and Rebellion: England in 1381.* Berkeley: University of California Press, 1994.

——— and Kathryn Kerby-Fulton, eds. *Written Work: Langland, Labor, and Authorship.* Philadelphia: University of Pennsylvania Press, 1997.

Kaeuper, Richard W. *Chivalry and Violence in Medieval Europe.* Oxford: Oxford University Press, 1999.
Kane, George. *Piers Plowman: The Evidence for Authorship.* London: Athlone, 1965.
———. "Some Fourteenth-Century 'Political Poems.'" In Kratzmann and Simpson, eds. 82–91.
———. "The Text." In *A Companion to 'Piers Plowman.'* Ed. John A. Alford. Berkeley: University of California Press, 1989. 175–200.
———. "The 'Z Version' of *Piers Plowman*," *Speculum* 60 (1985): 910–30.
Kant, Immanuel. *Critique of Judgement.* Trans. J. H. Bernard. New York: Hafner Press, 1951.
Kay, Sarah. "Analytical Survey 3: The New Philology." In *New Medieval Literatures.* Vol. 3. Ed. Wendy Scase, Rita Copeland, and David Lawton. Oxford: Clarendon Press, 1999. 295–326.
Kedourie, Elie. *Nationalism.* 3rd ed. London: Hutchinson, 1966.
Keiser, George R. "Lincoln Cathedral Library MS 91: Life and Milieu of the Scribe." *Studies in Bibliography* 32 (1979): 158–79.
———. "More Light on the Life of Robert Thornton." *Studies in Bibliography* 36 (1983): 11–19.
Ker, W. P. *The Dark Ages.* 1904. Rpt. New York: Mentor, 1958.
Kerby-Fulton, Kathryn. *Books under Suspicion: Censorship and Tolerance of Revelatory Writing in Late Medieval England.* Notre Dame, IN: University of Notre Dame Press, 2007.
———. "Langland and the Bibliographic Ego." In Justice and Kerby-Fulton, eds. 67–143.
———. "*Piers Plowman.*" In Wallace, ed. 513–38.
———. "Professional Readers of Langland at Home and Abroad: New Directions in the Political and Bureaucratic Codicology of *Piers Plowman.*" In Pearsall, ed. 103–29.
——— and Steven Justice. "Langlandian Reading Circles and the Civil Service in London and Dublin, 1380–1427." In *New Medieval Literatures.* Ed. Wendy Scase, Rita Copeland, and David Lawton. Oxford: Clarendon Press, 1997. 59–83.
Kinser, Samuel. "Wildmen in Festival, 1300–1550." In *Oral Tradition in the Middle Ages.* Ed. W. F. H. Nicolaisen. Binghamton, NY: Center for Medieval and Early Renaissance Studies, 1995. 145–60.
Kiser, Lisa. "Elde and His Teaching in *The Parlement of the Thre Ages.*" *Philological Quarterly* 66 (1987): 303–14.
Kittredge, George Lyman. *A Study of 'Gawain and the Green Knight.'* Cambridge, MA: Harvard University Press, 1916.
Knapp, Ethan *The Bureaucratic Muse: Thomas Hoccleve and the Literature of Late Medieval England.* University Park: Pennsylvania State University Press, 2001.
———. "Poetic Work and Scribal Labor in Hoccleve and Langland." In *The Middle Ages at Work: Practicing Labor in Late Medieval England.* Ed. Michael Uebel and Kellie Robertson. New York: Palgrave Macmillan, 2004. 209–29.
Kratzmann, Gregory, and James Simpson, eds. *Medieval English Religious and Ethical Literature.* Cambridge: D. S. Brewer, 1987.
Kruger, Steven F. *Dreaming in the Middle Ages.* Cambridge: Cambridge University

Press, 1992.

Kumar, Krishan. *The Making of English National Identity.* Cambridge: Cambridge University Press, 2003.

Lampert, Lisa. "Race, Periodicity, and the (Neo-) Middle Ages." *Modern Literary Quarterly* 65 (2004): 391–421.

Larrington, Carolyne. *King Arthur's Enchantresses: Morgan and Her Sisters in Arthurian Tradition.* London: I. B. Tauris, 2006.

Lavezzo, Kathy. *Angels on the Edge of the World: Geography, Literature, and English Community, 1000–1534.* Ithaca, NY: Cornell University Press, 2006.

———, ed. *Imagining a Medieval English Nation.* Minneapolis: University of Minnesota Press, 2004.

———. "Introduction." In Lavezzo, ed. vii–xxxiv.

———. Review of Cohen, ed., *Postcolonial Middle Ages,* in *Journal of Colonialism and Colonial History* 3.1 (2002).

Lawton, David. "The Diversity of Middle English Alliterative Poetry." *Leeds Studies in English* 20 (1989): 143–72.

———. "Lollardy and the *Piers Plowman* Tradition." *Modern Language Review* 76 (1981): 780–93.

———. "Middle English Alliterative Poetry: An Introduction." In Lawton, ed. 1–19; 125–29.

———, ed. *Middle English Alliterative Poetry and Its Literary Background.* Cambridge: D. S. Brewer, 1982.

———. "The Unity of Middle English Alliterative Poetry." *Speculum* 58 (1983): 72–94.

Lerer, Seth. *Chaucer and His Readers: Imagining the Author in Late-Medieval England.* Princeton, NJ: Princeton University Press, 1993.

Levy, Bernard S., and Paul Szarmach, eds. *The Alliterative Tradition in the Fourteenth Century.* Kent, OH: Kent State University Press, 1982.

Lewis, Charlton T. *An Elementary Latin Dictionary.* 1890. Oxford: Oxford University Press, 1998.

A Linguistic Atlas of Late Mediaeval English. Ed. Angus McIntosh, M. L. Samuels, and Michael Benskin. 4 vols. Aberdeen: Aberdeen University Press, 1986.

Lochrie, Karma. *Heterosyncrasies: Female Sexuality When Normal Wasn't.* Minneapolis: University of Minnesota Press, 2005.

Long, William J. *English Literature: Its History and Its Significance for the Life of the English-Speaking World.* 1909. Boston: Ginn and Company, 1919.

Loomis, Laura Hibbard. "*Gawain and the Green Knight.*" In *Arthurian Literature in the Middle Ages: A Collaborative History.* Ed. Roger Sherman Loomis. Oxford: Clarendon Press, 1959. 528–40.

Lynch, Kathryn L., ed. *Chaucer's Cultural Geography.* New York: Routledge, 2002.

MacCracken, Henry Noble. "Concerning Huchown." *PMLA* 25 (1910): 507–34.

MacDougall, Hugh. *Racial Myth in English History: Trojans, Teutons, and Anglo-Saxons.* Hanover, NH: University Press of New England, 1982.

Machan, Tim William. "Middle English Text Production and Modern Textual Criticism." In *Crux and Controversy in Middle English Textual Criticism.* Ed. A. J. Minnis and Charlotte Brewer. Cambridge: D. S. Brewer, 1992. 1–18.

Mack, Ruth. *Literary Historicity: Literature and Historical Change in Eighteenth-Century Britain.* Stanford, CA: Stanford University Press, 2009.

Mackay, George. *Scottish Place Names.* New Lanark, South Lanarkshire: Geddes and Grosset, 2000.

Manly, John. "The Lost Leaf of *Piers the Plowman.*" EETS o.s. 135b. 1906.

Mann, Jill. "The Power of the Alphabet: A Reassessment of the Relation between the A and B Versions of *Piers Plowman.*" *Yearbook of Langland Studies* 8 (1994): 21–50.

Mardorossian, Carine M. *Reclaiming Difference: Caribbean Women Rewrite Postcolonialism.* Charlottesville: University of Virginia Press, 2005.

Marsh, George Perkins. *Origin and History of the English Language.* London: Sampson Low, 1862.

Marvin, William Perry. *Hunting Law and Ritual in Medieval English Literature.* Cambridge: D. S. Brewer, 2006.

Mate, Mavis E. *Women in Medieval English Society.* Cambridge: Cambridge University Press, 1999.

Matthews, David, ed. *The Invention of Middle English: An Anthology of Primary Sources.* University Park: Pennsylvania State University Press, 2000.

———. *The Making of Middle English, 1765–1910.* Minneapolis: University of Minnesota Press, 1999.

Matthews, William. *The Tragedy of Arthur: A Study of the Alliterative Morte Arthure.* Berkeley: University of California Press, 1960.

Mazzio, Carla. *The Inarticulate Renaissance: Language Trouble in an Age of Eloquence.* Philadelphia: University of Pennsylvania Press, 2009.

McCaffery, Steve. *Prior to Meaning: The Protosemantic and Poetics.* Evanston: University of Illinois Press, 2001.

McFarlane, K. B. "The English Nobility, 1290–1536." 1953. In *The Nobility of Later Medieval England: The Ford Lectures for 1953 and Related Studies.* Oxford: Oxford University Press, 1973. 1–141.

McIntosh, Angus. "Early English Alliterative Verse." In Lawton, ed. 20–33.

———. "A New Approach to Middle English Dialectology." *English Studies* 44 (1963): 1–11.

———. "The Textual Transmission of the Alliterative *Morte Arthure.*" In *English and Medieval Studies Presented to J. R. R. Tolkien.* Ed. Norman Davis and C. L. Wrenn. London: Allen & Unwin, 1962. 231–40.

Middleton, Anne. "The Audience and Public of *Piers Plowman.*" In Lawton, ed. 101–23; 147–54.

———. "Making a Good End: John But as a Reader of *Piers Plowman.*" In *Medieval Studies Presented to George Kane.* Ed. Edward Donald Kennedy, Ronald Waldron, and Joseph S. Wittig. Cambridge: D. S. Brewer, 1988. 243–63.

———. "William Langland's *Kynde Name:* Authorial Signature and Social Identity in Late Fourteenth-Century England." In *Literary Practice and Social Change in Britain, 1380–1530.* Ed. Lee Patterson. Berkeley: University of California Press, 1991. 15–82.

Miles, David. *The Tribes of Britain: Who Are We? And Where Do We Come From?* Rev. ed. London: Phoenix, 2005.

Minnis, Alastair. *Medieval Theory of Authorship: Scholastic Literary Attitudes in the*

Later Middle Ages. 2nd ed. 1988. Philadelphia: University of Pennsylvania Press, 2010.

Mohl, Ruth. "Theories of Monarchy in *Mum and the Sothsegger.*" *PMLA* 59 (1944): 26–44.

Moody, William Vaughn, and Robert Morss Lovett. *A History of English Literature.* New York: Charles Scribner's Sons, 1905.

Moorman, Charles. "The English Alliterative Revival and the Literature of Defeat." *Chaucer Review* 16.1 (1981): 85–100.

———."The Origins of the Alliterative Revival." *Southern Quarterly* 7 (1969): 345–72.

Morrison, Susan Signe. *Excrement in the Late Middle Ages: Sacred Filth and Chaucer's Fecopoetics.* New York: Palgrave Macmillan, 2008.

Musgrove, Frank. *The North of England: A History from Roman Times to the Present.* Oxford: Basil Blackwell, 1990.

Narin, Elisa Marie. "'Þat on . . . þat oþer': Rhetorical Description and Morgan le Fay in *Sir Gawain and the Green Knight.*" *Pacific Coast Philology* 23 (1988): 60–66.

Neilson, George. *Huchown of the Awle Ryale, the Alliterative Poet: A Historical Criticism of Fourteenth Century Poems Ascribed to Sir Hew of Eglintoun.* Glasgow: James MacLehose and Son, 1902.

Neville, Cynthia J. *Violence, Custom and Law: The Anglo-Scottish Border Lands in the Later Middle Ages.* Edinburgh: Edinburgh University Press, 1998.

Newman, Gerald. *The Rise of English Nationalism: A Cultural History, 1740–1830.* Rev. ed. New York: St. Martin's Press, 1997.

Nichols, Stephen G. "Introduction: Philology in a Manuscript Culture," *Speculum* 65 (1990): 1–10.

———. "Modernism and the Politics of Medieval Studies." In Bloch and Nichols, eds. 25–56.

———. "Writing the New Middle Ages." *PMLA* 120.2 (2005): 422–41.

Nietzsche, Friedrich. *'The Twilight of the Idols' and 'The Anti-Christ.'* 1889; 1895. Ed. and trans. R. J. Hollingdale. New York: Penguin, 1968.

Nolan, Maura. "'With Tresone Withinne': *Wynnere and Wastoure,* Chivalric Self-Representation, and the Law." *Journal of Medieval and Early Modern Studies* 26.1 (1996): 1–28.

Oakden, J. P. *Alliterative Poetry in Middle English.* 2 vols. Manchester: Manchester University Press, 1930–35.

Oram, Richard. *The Lordship of Galloway: c. 900 to c. 1300.* Edinburgh: John Donald, 2000.

Ormrod, W. M. *Political Life in Medieval England, 1300–1450.* New York: St. Martin's Press, 1995.

———. *The Reign of Edward III.* Rev. ed. Charleston: Tempus, 2000.

Painter, F. V. N. *Introduction to English Literature, Including a Number of Classic Works with Notes.* Boston: Leach, Shewell, and Sanborn, 1894.

Paris, Gaston. "La Sicile dans la littérature française du moyen âge." *Romania* V (1876): 108–13.

Pasternack, Carol Braun. *The Textuality of Old English Poetry.* Cambridge: Cambridge University Press, 1995.

Paton, Lucy Allen. *Studies in the Fairy Mythology of Arthurian Romance.* 1903. Rev. ed. Afterword by Roger Sherman Loomis. New York: Burt Franklin, 1970.
Patterson, Lee. *Negotiating the Past: The Historical Understanding of Medieval Literature.* Madison: University of Wisconsin Press, 1988.
Pearsall, Derek. "The Alliterative Revival: Origins and Social Backgrounds." In Lawton, ed. 34–53.
———. "Chaucer and Englishness." In Lynch, ed. 281–301.
———. "Langland's London." In Justice and Kerby-Fulton, eds. 185–207.
———, ed. *New Directions in Later Medieval Manuscript Studies.* Woodbridge: York Medieval Press, 2000.
———. *Old English and Middle English Poetry.* London: Routledge & Kegan Paul, 1977.
———. "The Origins of the Alliterative Revival." In Levy and Szarmach, eds. 1–24.
Peck, Jeffrey M. "'In the Beginning Was the Word': Germany and the Origins of German Studies." In Bloch and Nichols, eds. 127.
Pelletreau, William S. *A History of Long Island.* Vol. 3. New York: Lewis Publishing, 1903.
Percy, Thomas, ed. *Reliques of Ancient English Poetry.* 1765. Rpt. Philadelphia: Porter & Coates, 1869.
Perkins, David. *Is Literary History Possible?* Baltimore: Johns Hopkins University Press, 1992.
Platt, Colin. *King Death: The Black Death and its Aftermath in Late-Medieval England.* Toronto: University of Toronto Press, 1997.
Prestwich, Michael: "Colonial Scotland: The English in Scotland under Edward I." In *Scotland and England: 1286–1815.* Ed. Roger A. Mason. Edinburgh: John Donald, 1988. 6–17.
———. *Edward I.* Rev. ed. New Haven, CT: Yale University Press, 1997.
———. *Plantagenet England: 1225–1360.* Oxford: Oxford University Press, 2005.
———. *The Three Edwards: War and State in England, 1272–1377.* 2nd ed. New York: Routledge, 2003.
Purdie, Rhiannon. "The Search for Scottishness in *Golagros and Gawane*." In Purdie and Royan, eds. 95–107.
——— and Nicola Royan, eds. *The Scots and Medieval Arthurian Legend.* Arthurian Studies LXI. Cambridge: D. S. Brewer, 2005.
Putter, Ad. *'Sir Gawain and the Green Knight' and French Arthurian Romance.* Oxford: Clarendon Press, 1995.
Reese, Jesse Byers. "Alliterative Verse in the York Cycle." *Studies in Philology* 48 (1951): 639–68.
Renan, Ernest. *Qu'est-ce Qu'une Nation?* 1882. Paris: R. Helleu, 1934.
———. "What Is a Nation?" 1882. Trans. Martin Thom. In *Nation and Narration.* Ed. Homi K. Bhabha. London: Routledge, 1990. 8–22.
Revard, Carter. "Was the *Pearl* Poet in Aquitaine with Chaucer? A Note on *Fade,* L. 149 of *Sir Gawain and the Green Knight.*" *SELIM* 11 (2001–2): 5–26.
Reynolds, Susan. *Kingdoms and Communities in Western Europe, 900–1300.* Oxford: Oxford University Press, 1984.
Riddy, Felicity J. "Dating *The Buke of the Howlat.*" *Review of English Studies* 37

(1986): 1–10.

Rigby, Marjory. "*Sir Gawain and the Green Knight* and the Vulgate *Lancelot*." *Modern Language Review* 78.2 (1983): 357–66.

Robertson, Kellie. *The Laborer's Two Bodies: Literary and Legal Productions in Britain, 1350–1500*. New York: Palgrave Macmillan, 2006.

Rosenthal, Joel T. *Old Age in Late Medieval England*. Philadelphia: University of Pennsylvania Press, 1991.

Ross, Trevor. *The Making of the English Literary Canon: From the Middle Ages to the Late Eighteenth Century*. Montreal: McGill-Queen's University Press, 1998.

Royan, Nicola. "The Fine Art of Faint Praise in Older Scots Historiography." In Purdie and Royan, eds. 43–54.

———. "'Na les vailyeant than ony uthir princis of Britane': Representations of Arthur in Scotland, 1480–1540." *Scottish Studies Review* 3 (2002): 9–20.

Rushton, Cory J. "'Of an uncouthe stede': The Scottish Knight in Middle English Arthurian Romances." In Purdie and Royan, eds. 109–19.

Queller, Donald E., and Thomas F. Madden. *The Fourth Crusade: The Conquest of Constantinople*. 2nd ed. Philadelphia: University of Pennsylvania Press, 1997.

Russell, George. "Some Early Responses to the C-Version of *Piers Plowman*." *Viator* 15 (1984): 275–303.

Saintsbury, George. *A History of English Prosody, from the Twelfth Century to the Present Day*. 3 vols. London: Macmillan, 1906–10.

Salisbury, Joyce E. *The Beast Within: Animals in the Middle Ages*. New York: Routledge, 1994.

Salter, Elizabeth. "The Alliterative Revival." *Modern Philology* 64 (1966–67): 146–49; 233–37.

———. "The Timeliness of *Wynnere and Wastoure*." *Medium Ævum* 47 (1978): 40–65.

Samuels, M. L. "Langland's Dialect." *Medium Ævum* 54 (1985): 232–47.

Sapora, Robert William, Jr. *A Theory of Middle English Alliterative Meter with Critical Applications*. Cambridge, MA: Medieval Academy of America, 1977.

Saul, Nigel. "Medieval Britain." In *The National Trust Historical Atlas of Britain: Prehistoric to Medieval*. Ed. Nigel Saul. Phoenix Mill, Gloucestershire: Alan Sutton, 1994. 115–204.

Saunders, Corinne J. *The Forest of Medieval Romance: Avernus, Broceliande, Arden*. Cambridge: D. S. Brewer, 1993.

Scala, Elizabeth. *Absent Narratives, Manuscript Textuality, and Literary Structure in Late Medieval England*. New York: Palgrave Macmillan, 2002.

Scanlon, Larry. "King, Commons, and Kind Wit: Langland's National Vision and the Rising of 1381." In Lavezzo, ed. 191–233.

———. "Langland, Apocalypse and the Early Modern Editor." In *Reading the Medieval in Early Modern England*. Ed. Gordon McMullan and David Matthews. Cambridge: Cambridge University Press, 2007. 51–73; 238–43.

Scase, Wendy. *Literature and Complaint in England, 1272–1553*. Oxford: Oxford University Press, 2007.

Scattergood, John. "*Pierce the Ploughman's Crede*: Lollardy and Texts." In *Lollardy and the Gentry in the Later Middle Ages*. Ed. Margaret Aston and Colin Richmond. Stroud, Gloucestershire: Sutton, 1997. 77–94.

---. *Politics and Poetry in the Fifteenth Century.* London: Blandford Press, 1971.
Schiff, Randy P. "Holland as Howlat: Shadow Self and Borderland Homage in *The Buke of the Howlat.*" *Mediaevalia* 29.2 (2008): 91–116.
---. "The Instructive Other Within: Secularized Jews in *The Siege of Jerusalem.*" In Cohen, ed., *Cultural Diversity.* 135–51.
---. "The Loneness of the Stalker: Poaching and Subjectivity in *The Parlement of the Thre Ages.*" *Texas Studies in Literature and Language* 51.3 (2009): 263–93.
Schofield, William Henry. *English Literature from the Norman Conquest to Chaucer.* New York: Macmillan, 1906.
Shaw, Thomas B. *Outlines of English Literature.* Philadelphia: Lea and Blanchard, 1849.
Shepherd, Geoffrey. "The Nature of Alliterative Poetry in Late Medieval England." *Proceedings of the British Academy* 56 (1970): 57–76.
Shichtman, Martin B. "Sir Gawain in Scotland: A Hometown Boy Made Good." In *King Arthur through the Ages.* Ed. Valerie M. Legurio and Mildred Leake Day. New York: Garland, 1990. 234–67.
Shoaf, R. A. *The Poem as Green Girdle: Commercium in Sir Gawain and the Green Knight.* Gainesville: University Press of Florida, 1984.
Silverstein, Theodore. "*Sir Gawain,* Dear Brutus, and Britain's Fortunate Founding: A Study in Comedy and Convention." *Modern Philology* 62 (1965): 189–206.
Simmons, Clare A. *Reversing the Conquest: History and Myth in Nineteenth-Century British Literature.* New Brunswick, NJ: Rutgers University Press, 1990.
Simpson, James. "The Constraints of Satire in *Piers Plowman* and *Mum and the Sothsegger.*" In *Langland, the Mystics, and the Medieval English Mystic Tradition: Essays in Honour of S. S. Hussey.* Ed. Helen Phillips. Cambridge: D. S. Brewer, 1990. 11–30.
---. "The Power of Impropriety: Authorial Naming in *Piers Plowman.*" In *Piers Plowman: A Book of Essays.* Ed. Kathleen M. Hewett-Smith. New York: Routledge, 2005. 145–65.
---. *Reform and Cultural Revolution: The Oxford English Literary History, Vol. 2: 1350–1547.* Oxford: Oxford University Press, 2002.
Skeat, Walter W. "An Essay on Alliterative Poetry." In *Bishop Percy's Folio Manuscript: Ballads and Romances.* Vol. 3. Ed. John W. Hales and Frederick J. Furnivall. London: N. Trübner and Co., 1868. xi–xxxix.
Smailes, Arthur E. *North England.* Rev. ed. London: Thomas Nelson and Sons, 1968.
Smith, Anthony D. *The Ethnic Origins of Nations.* Oxford: Blackwell, 1986.
Smith, D. Vance. "*Piers Plowman* and the National Noetic of Edward III." In Lavezzo, ed. 214–54.
Smyth, Alfred P., ed. *Medieval Europeans: Studies in Ethnic Identity and National Perspectives in Medieval Europe.* New York: St. Martin's Press, 1998.
Somerset, Fiona. *Clerical Discourse and Lay Audience in Late Medieval England.* Cambridge: Cambridge University Press, 1998.
Spearing, A. C. "*The Awntyrs off Arthure.*" In Levy and Szarmach, eds. 183–202.
Speirs, John. *Medieval English Poetry: The Non-Chaucerian Tradition.* London: Faber and Faber, 1957.
Spiegel, Gabrielle M. "History, Historicism, and the Social Logic of the Text in the

Middle Ages." *Speculum* 65 (1990): 79–86.
Staley, Lynn. *Languages of Power in the Age of Richard II.* University Park: Pennsylvania State University Press, 2005.
Stanbury, Sarah. *Seeing the 'Gawain'-Poet: Description and the Act of Perception.* Philadelphia: University of Pennsylvania Press, 1991.
Steadman, J. M. "The Date of 'Winnere and Wastoure.'" *Modern Philology* 19 (1921): 211–19.
———. Review of *Winner and Waster,* ed. Israel Gollancz. *Modern Language Notes* 36 (1921): 103–10.
Stein, Robert M. "Making History English: Cultural Identity and Historical Explanation in William of Malmesbury and Laʒamon's *Brut.*" In Tomasch and Gilles, eds. 97–115.
Steiner, Emily. *Documentary Culture and the Making of Medieval English Literature.* Cambridge: Cambridge University Press, 2003.
———. "Medieval Documentary Poetics and Langland's Authorial Identity." In *Crossing Boundaries: Issues of Communal and Individual Identity in the Middle Ages and Renaissance.* Ed. Sally McKee. Turnholt: Brepols, 1999. 79–105.
Stott, Andrew. *Comedy.* New York: Routledge, 2005.
Strayer, Joseph R. *The Albigensian Crusades.* 1971. Epilogue by Carol Lansing. Ann Arbor: University of Michigan Press, 1992.
Stringer, Keith. "The Emergence of a Nation-State, 1100–1300." In Wormald, ed. 39–76.
Strohm, Paul. *England's Empty Throne: Usurpation and the Language of Legitimation, 1399–1442.* New Haven, CT: Yale University Press, 1998.
———. *Hochon's Arrow: The Social Imagination of Fourteenth-Century Texts.* Princeton, NJ: Princeton University Press, 1992.
Summerson, Henry. "Responses to War: Carlisle and the West March in the Later Fourteenth Century." In *War and Border Societies in the Middle Ages.* Ed. Anthony Goodman and Anthony Tuck. London: 1992. 155–77.
Suzuki, Eiichi. "A Note on the Age of the Green Knight." *Neuphilologische Mitteilungen* 78 (1977): 27–30.
Sykes, Bryan. *Saxons, Vikings, and Celts: The Genetic Roots of Britain and Ireland.* New York: W. W. Norton, 2006.
Taine, Hippolyte. *History of English Literature.* Trans. H. van Laun. New York: Grosset & Dunlap, 1908.
———. *L☐Histoire de la littérature anglaise.* 4 vols. Paris: Librairie Hachette, 1863–64.
Tavormina, Teresa M., and R. F. Yeager, eds. *The Endless Knot: Essays on Old and Middle English in Honor of Marie Borroff.* Cambridge: D. S. Brewer, 1995.
ten Brink, Bernhard. *Early English Literature (to Wiclif).* 2 vols. Trans. Horace M. Kennedy. London: George Bell & Sons, 1891.
———. *History of English Literature (from the Fourteenth Century to the Death of Surrey).* Trans. L. Dora Schmitz. Vol II.2. New York: Henry Holt and Company, 1896.
———. *Geschichte der Englischen Litteratur.* Ed. Alois Brandl. 2 vols. Berlin: Robert Oppenheim, 1877.

Terrell, Katherine H. "Subversive Histories: Strategies of Identity in Scottish Historiography." In Cohen, ed., *Cultural Diversity*. 153–72.
Thompson, John J. *Robert Thornton and the London Thornton Manuscript*. Cambridge: D. S. Brewer, 1987.
Tibbals, Kate Watkins. "Elements of Magic in the Romance of William of Palerne." *Modern Philology* 1 (1903–4): 355–71.
Tilly, Charles. *Coercion, Capital, and European States, A.D. 990–1992*. Rev. ed. Oxford: Blackwell, 1992.
Tolhurst, Fiona. "The Britons as Hebrews, Romans, and Normans: Geoffrey of Monmouth's British Epic and Reflections on Matilda." *Arthuriana* 8.4 (1998): 69–87.
Tolman, A. H. "Obituary: Bernhard ten Brink." *Modern Language Notes* 7 (1892): 191–92.
Tomasch, Sylvia, and Sealy Gilles, eds. *Text and Territory: Geographical Imagination in the European Middle Ages*. Philadelphia: University of Pennsylvania Press, 1998.
Trautmann, Moritz. "Der Dichter Huchown und seine Werke." *Anglia* 1 (1878): 109–49.
Traversi, Derek. "Langland's *Piers Plowman*." In *The Pelican Guide to English Literature, vol. 1: The Age of Chaucer*. Ed. Boris Ford. Harmondsworth: Penguin, 1959. 127–45.
Trigg, Stephanie. *Congenial Souls: Reading Chaucer from Medieval to Postmodern*. Minneapolis: University of Minnesota Press, 2002.
———. "Israel Gollancz's *Wynnere and Wastoure*: Political Satire or Editorial Politics?" In Kratzmann and Simpson, eds. 115–27.
Tuck, Anthony. *Crown and Nobility: England 1272–1461*. 2nd ed. Oxford: Blackwell, 1999.
———. "The Emergence of a Northern Nobility, 1250–1400." *Northern History* 22 (1986): 1–17.
———. "Richard II and the Border Magnates." *Northern History* 3 (1968): 27–52.
———. "War and Society in the Medieval North." *Northern History* 21 (1985): 33–52.
Turville-Petre, Thorlac. *The Alliterative Revival*. Cambridge: Cambridge University Press, 1977.
———. "The Author of *the Destruction of Troy*." *Medium Aevum* 57 (1988): 264–69.
———. "The Brutus Prologue to *Sir Gawain and the Green Knight*." In Lavezzo, ed. 340–46.
———. *England the Nation: Language, Literature, and National Identity, 1290–1340*. Oxford: Oxford University Press, 1996.
———. "Humphrey de Bohun and *William of Palerne*." *Neuphilologische Mitteilungen* 75 (1974): 260–62.
———. "The Prologue of *Winner and Waster*." *Leeds Studies in English* 18 (1987): 19–29.
———. 'Summer Sunday,' 'De Tribus Regibus Mortuis,' and 'The Awntyrs off Arthure: Three Poems in the Thirteen-Line Stanza.' *Review of English Studies* 25 (1970): 1–14.
Twomey, Michael W. "Morgain la Fée in *Sir Gawain and the Green Knight*." In *Text and Intertext in Medieval Arthurian Literature*. Ed. Norris J. Lacy. New York: Garland, 1996. 91–115.

———. "Morgan le Fay at Hautdesert." In *On Arthurian Women: Essays in Memory of Maureen Fries.* Ed. Bonnie Wheeler and Fiona Tolhurst. Dallas: Scriptorium, 2001. 103–19.

Utz, Richard J. "Enthusiast or Philologist? Professional Discourse and the Medievalism of Fredrick James Furnivall." In *Studies in Medievalism XI—Appropriating the Middle Ages: Scholarship, Politics, Fraud.* Ed. Tom Shippey and Martin Arnold. Woodbridge: Boydell and Brewer, 2001. 188–212.

VanHoosier-Carey, Gregory A. "Byrthnoth in Dixie: The Emergence of Anglo-Saxon Studies in the Postbellum South." In Frantzen and Niles, eds. 157–72.

Wales, Katie. *Northern English: A Cultural and Social History.* Cambridge: Cambridge University Press, 2006.

Walker, David. *Medieval Wales.* Cambridge: Cambridge University Press, 1990.

Wallace, David, ed. *The Cambridge History of Medieval English Literature.* Cambridge: Cambridge University Press, 1999.

———. *Premodern Places: Calais to Surinam, Chaucer to Aphra Behn.* Malden: Blackwell, 2004.

Walsh, Elizabeth. "*Golagros and Gawane:* A Word for Peace." In *Bryght Lanternis: Essays on the Language and Literature of Medieval and Renaissance Scotland.* Ed. J. Derrick McClure and Michael R. G. Spiller. Aberdeen: Aberdeen University Press, 1989. 90–103.

Walsh, James G. *Old-Time Makers of Medicine: The Story of the Students and Teachers of the Sources Related to Medicine during the Middle Ages.* New York: Fordham University Press, 1911.

Warner, Lawrence. "Langland and the Problem of *William of Palerne.*" *Viator* 37 (2006): 397–415.

Warren, Michelle R. *History on the Edge: Excalibur and the Borders of Britain.* Minneapolis: University of Minnesota Press, 2000.

Warton, Thomas. *The History of English Poetry, from the Close of the Eleventh to the Commencement of the Eighteenth Century.* 3 vols. London: J. Dodsley, 1774–81.

———. *History of English Poetry, from the Twelfth to the Close of the Sixteenth Century.* 4 vols. Rev. ed. Ed. W. Carew Hazlitt. 1871. Rpt. New York: Haskell House, 1970.

Waswo, Richard. "The History That Literature Makes." *New Literary History* 19 (1988): 541–64.

Watson, Andrew G. *The Manuscripts of Henry Savile of Banke.* London: The Bibliographical Society, 1969.

Watson, Nicholas. "Censorship and Cultural Change in Late-Medieval England: Vernacular Theology, the Oxford Translation Debate, and Arundel's Constitutions of 1409." *Speculum* 70 (1995): 822–64.

Waugh, Scott L. *England in the Reign of Edward III.* Cambridge: Cambridge University Press, 1991.

Wawn, Andrew. "Truth-telling and the Tradition of *Mum and the Sothsegger.*" *Yearbook of English Studies* 13 (1983): 270–87.

Webster, A. Blyth. "A Biographical Memoir." In *A Saintsbury Miscellany.* Ed. Augustus Muir et al. New York: Oxford University Press, 1947. 27–73.

Whitehurst, Edith Williams. "Morgan la Fée as Trickster in *Sir Gawain and the Green*

Knight." *Folklore* 96 (1985): 38–56.
Williams, Deanne. *The French Fetish from Chaucer to Shakespeare.* Cambridge: Cambridge University Press, 2004.
Wormald, Jenny, ed. *Scotland: A History.* Oxford: Oxford University Press, 2005.

INDEX

advice, 121–22, 137, 154, 156, 225n128; to princes, 137, 140–42, 221–22n84, 224n108
Aers, David, 170n82
aesthetics, 38–39; critical, 5, 14, 23–24, 33, 35, 51–52, 74, 90, 97, 99, 132, 151, 161, 200nn92–94, 217n28; and textuality, 131, 136, 143; and war, 124
Agamben, Giorgio, 49, 57, 60–61, 186n31, 188n76, 189n90
Akbari, Suzanne Conklin, 20, 101, 172–73n29
Alexander and Dindimus, 177n116
Alexander, Flora, 209n76
Alexandrine, 50, 54–55, 57, 61–66, 71, 190n97
Alfred, King, 8, 78
allegory: and age, 14–15, 76–77, 94–99, 202n130; animalized, 14, 54, 56, 61, 66; and dream-vision, 41–43, 182n186; and law, 136, 152; political, 15, 135, 144, 152–53, 218n45
Allen, Rosamund, 210n91
Alliterative *Morte Arthure* (Anonymous), 14, 28, 76, 77, 83, 87–89, 99, 100, 106–11, 119, 121–24, 126–27, 198n68, 198n79, 199nn82–84, 199n88, 205–6nn33–35, 206n37, 212n115, 212n123, 212n128, 212nn130–32, 213n137; authorship of, 27, 29, 175n86, 176nn99–100;

dialect of, 196n50, 197–98n67, 206n43, 212n125; manuscript of, 107, 169n74, 197n65
alliterative prosody, 1–4, 13–14, 17–18, 23–24, 28, 32–36, 44, 47–48, 51, 127–29, 142–43, 162, 163n5, 167n52, 168n59, 168n61, 168nn73–74, 171nn9–10, 179n44, 182–83n2, 197n65; and alliteration, 1, 18, 23, 33, 124, 213n135; caesura in, 1, 18, 178n135; as heteromorphic, 195n44, reception of, 9–10, 167nn55–57, 171n10; stress in, 1, 4, 10, 18, 33–34, 39–40, 73, 178–79n135, 179n137, 179n145, 192n6; syllables in, 33; thirteen-line, 12, 15, 24, 107, 174–75n65, 206n40, 210n85
Alliterative Revivalism, 2–17, 20–36, 46–47, 50, 62, 80–81, 128–31, 135–36, 147–48, 151, 153, 156, 157–62, 164n11, 168n61, 170n79, 173n34, 174n57, 179nn149–50, 184n15, 196nn49–50, 211n99, 214n13, 225n119; and authenticity, 1, 33–34, 37, 40–41; and dating, 44, 48, 68, 164n15, 180n158, 183n8, 185n26, 190n117; and editing, 37–44, 131–32, 136; and empire, 103–4, 111–12; and gender, 14, 61, 74, 77, 91, 99; and language, 7, 45–49; on love, 68–69, 77,

255

82, 99; and modernity, 4, 19, 32, 35–37, 167n57, 185n22; and nation, 8–9, 17, 21, 32, 57, 79, 113, 161, 193n17; as reductive, 15–17, 34–35, 38–39, 44–45, 132, 139, 162, 164n15, 181n174, 182n183, 193n22, 195n45; and race, 185n21; and region, 80–83, 103, 106–7, 130, 171n4, 177n113, 182n197, 196n49, 206n40; and war, 11, 69, 83, 89–90, 200n91. *See also* death; nostalgia; race

alterity, 6, 66, 78, 110, 133, 187n52; and alteritism, 8, 29, 32, 101–3, 157–59, 217–18n39; and criticism, 170n82, 186n27, 191n118; and ethnicity, 7, 33, 50, 71, 104, 112, 121, 129, 165n29, 166n31, 226n3; and gender, 99; and Revivalism, 3, 32, 68

America, 2, 103; and Civil War, 32, 178n22; and England, 184n15; and empire, 4, 5, 175n84; and Mexico, 165n23; and Native Americans, 11, 165n23; and race, 12, 21, 169n67, 169n69; and Revivalism, 21, 26–27, 29–32, 47, 161; the South of, 31–32, 177–78n122

Amours, F. J., 29, 113–14, 175–76nn86–87, 176nn98–100, 208n66, 210n85, 210n93

Anderson, Benedict, 7, 8, 19–21, 31–32, 45–46, 100–101, 104, 109, 121, 158–59, 161, 166n35, 173n33, 175n84, 183–84nn8–9, 191n118, 203–204n7, 207n48, 212n126, 226nn3–6, 227nn11–12, 228n24

Andreas Capellanus, 66

Andrew, Malcolm, 195n45; and Ronald Waldron, 201n101

Andrew of Wyntoun, 27, 175n86

Anglo-Saxonism, 26–27, 31, 165n23, 169n67, 169n69, 173n40, 190n113; and empire, 5, 175n84; and racism, 12, 21, 48, 161, 173n32, 214nn5–6

Anglo-Saxons, 161, 173n40, 194n33, 198n71; character of, 14, 20, 22, 24, 40, 69, 88, 128–30, 172n27; and Englishness, 11, 103, 161–62, 177n109; neo-Saxons, 2–3, 4–5, 7, 11, 24, 32, 45–49, 78, 156; and nation, 8, 158, 227n8; and poetics, 13, 18, 22, 80, 172n16, 173n34, 225n119; study of, 78, 171n10; and war, 83, 89–90, 99. *See also* Alliterative Revivalism; nostalgia; Saxon-Norman

animals, 14, 49–50, 56, 188n76; bears, 50, 53–55, 61, 64–67, 188n65, 189n92, 190n103; bees, 152–53; boar, 189n94; deer, 50, 54, 59, 63, 66–67, 70, 94, 142, 189n94, 190n97, 191n123; dogs, 63, 188n79; eagles, 128, 142; and fables, 54, 152, 187n53; goats, 190n97; horses, 66; and humanity, 58–62, 65–67; leopards, 42; monkeys, 56; oxen, 40, 128; serpents, 190n97; sheep, 60; skins of, 14, 54, 56–57, 61–68, 185–86n30, 188n65, 189n92, 189n95, 191n123; wild, 57; wolves, 50, 58, 59–61, 188n69. *See also* werewolves

anonymity: and agency, 15, 133, 141, 142, 156, 159, 192n15, 222n89; and nation, 26

antiquarianism, 18–19, 28, 32, 69, 163–64n10, 164n12, 171n11, 190n117

antiquity, 3–5, 21–23, 28, 43, 129, 161, 184n15; and ancestry, 18, 28, 30, 103; and archaism, 190n117; and desire, 180n158; factitious, 7, 40, 46, 76–77, 103–4; Germanic, 2, 19, 21, 33, 44, 74; and language, 6, 7, 19–20, 45–46; Northern, 37. *See also* traditionalism

Apulia, 54–55, 59, 71

Archer, Rowena E., 75, 192nn15–16, 201n108

Archibald, Elizabeth, 199n83

aristocracy, 14, 22, 38, 48–50, 54–70, 125–26, 152–53, 191n121; baronial, 30–31, 211n99; English, 177n121,

187n43; and history, 30. *See also* feudalism; patronage
Arthour and Merlin (Anonymous), 52
Arthur, King, 29, 91–93, 175n86, 176n100, 191–92n4, 196n53, 199nn82–84, 207n55, 211n112, 212n115, 213n137; Celtic, 194n28; and empire, 15, 43–44, 73, 76–78, 84–89, 94–99, 100–127, 160, 175n86, 199n86, 212n132; and England, 111–12, 121–22, 207–8n56, 208n60, 212n128; and Scotland, 209nn76–78. *See also* civil war; romance
Arthur and Gorlagon (Anonymous), 59–60, 188n73
Ashcroft, Bill, Garreth Griffiths, and Helen Tiffin, 204n21
assimilation, 5, 20, 45, 95, 112, 119, 121; of outsiders, 112
Astell, Ann W., 221n83
authorship, 79–80, 181n179, 195n45, 221n80; and editing, 132, 136, 216–17nn27–28, 226n138; and minstrelsy, 38–39, 135; and origins, 27–29, 141, 156, 170n79; and responsibility, 154–55, 225–26n133. *See also* anonymity; collaboration; multiplicity; scribes; singularity
Avowyng of Arthur (Anonymous), 112, 208n58, 208n59
Awntyrs off Arthure (Anonymous), 15, 27, 35, 100, 103–19, 122, 126–27, 196n52, 198n68, 199n80, 199n86, 205–6n35, 207n55, 208n66, 209n79, 210n94, 211n96, 211n99, 212n123, 212n128, 212n132, 213n138; date of, 205n32; dialect of, 206n43; manuscripts of, 107, 118, 169n74, 206n42; and prosody, 24, 206n40, 210n85

Backus, Truman J., 47, 184n15. *See also* Shaw
backwardness, 5, 37, 38, 40, 47, 50, 81, 128; and vision, 4, 15, 33, 36, 44, 129. *See also* technology
Bale, John, 138, 144, 164n12, 220n73, 223n104
Balliols, 113, 115
banning, 49, 50, 57, 61, 71
barbarism, 5, 10, 15, 128; and language, 22, 36, 47, 51; and prosody, 23, 174n54
Barber, Richard, and Juliette Barker, 210n91
bare life, 57, 63–64, 189n90
Barney, Stephen A., 179n135, 179n144, 197n65
Barr, Helen, 136, 154–55, 215n19, 216n24, 218n46, 219n51, 219–20n56, 220n62, 220n71, 220–21n75, 221n83, 222nn86–87, 223n101, 224n114, 224n116, 225n124, 225n130, 225n133
Barrell, A. D. M., 114, 117, 209n74, 209n79, 210n83
Barrett, Robert W., Jr., 170n78, 194n31, 197n59, 201n112
Barth, Fredrik, 183n5
Bartra, Roger, 38
Bartholomaeus Anglicus, 152, 225n124
Bartlett, Robert, 114, 209n75
Beattie, Cordelia, 201n108
beauty, 55, 60, 64, 71, 76–77, 86, 90, 92, 94–96, 98, 116, 202n124
Beckwith, Sarah, 169n74
becoming, 49; animal, 14, 56–68; and class, 14, 63, 70–71, 191n123
Bede, 13
Bennett, Judith M., 99
Bennett, Michael J., 41, 68, 74–75, 81, 182n189, 192n8, 195–96n47, 196nn50–51, 196n54, 197nn60–62, 199n86, 217n37
Benson, C. David, 216n25, 221n80
Benzie, William, 176nn90–91
Bernheimer, Richard, 180n170
Bertilak, 15, 72–75, 76–77, 79, 84–87, 89–93, 96–97, 98–99, 191–92nn2–4, 198n75, 200n92, 201n101,

202n132, 203n138
Bestul, Thomas H., 180n158, 182n186
Bible, Vulgate, 6, 80, 165n29, 224n117
Biddick, Kathleen, 3, 175n84, 226n3
biopolitics, 8, 153, 186n31
Birkholz, Daniel, 207–8n56
Birrer, Doryjane, 188n69
Blake, N. F., 12, 107, 157, 167n52, 167n55, 169n72, 179n150
Blank, Paula, 168n62
Bloch, R. Howard, 94; and Stephen G. Nichols, 1, 173n31
book production, 15, 136–37, 153–54, 157; and markets, 40, 44, 81, 131, 167n55, 215n17; and multiplicity, 154–55. *See also* collaboration; manuscripts; print; scribes
borderlands, 3, 58–59, 108–9; Anglo-Scottish, 15, 81, 83, 88, 100–127, 159, 198n68, 199n86, 205n31, 208n57, 209nn71–72, 210n91, 212n128; Anglo-Welsh, 23, 81–82, 196n53, 204n23; and Arthur, 116, 196n53; and cities, 118–19; and fluidity, 103, 106, 159; and power, 105–17, 127, 211n104; and war, 104–7, 112–13, 122, 168n59, 196n54, 206–7n45, 208n61, 211nn106–7, 213n137
Borroff, Marie, 178n135
boundaries, 8, 63–64; class, 57, 147–48; and Empire, 204n18; ethnic, 183n5; gender, 76
Bourdieu, Pierre, 9, 49, 57, 76–77, 96, 126, 186n34, 193n18, 205n30
Bowers, John, 167n55, 194n40, 216n25, 217n35, 218n44, 221n80, 222–23n93
Bowers, R. H., 90
Bradley, Henry, 28, 176n94
Braude, Benjamin, 165n29
Braunde, 54–55, 58, 61–62, 71
Brewer, Charlotte, 139, 216n25. *See also* Rigg
Brigham, Nicholas, 138, 220n73
Bristol, 130, 131, 137, 215n18, 220n73.

See also Southwest Midlands
Britain, 20–22, 78, 93, 96, 100, 104, 114, 161, 164n12, 168n64, 169n69, 214n5, 215–16n21; and community, 6, 10, 12, 36, 44, 82, 169–70n69, 175n80, 190–91n118, 194n33, 227n10; and empire, 4, 5, 8, 19, 87–89, 105–6, 111, 166n43, 182n194, 199nn82–84, 207n56, 211n111, 212–13n132; and nation, 11–12, 26, 29, 36, 158, 166n34, 166n39, 172n18, 205n26
Brown, Michael, 114, 117, 205n31, 206–7n45, 207n49, 208nn61–62, 208n69, 209n72, 209–10nn82–83, 210n85, 210nn88–89, 211n104, 211n106, 213n137; and Steve Boardman, 109
Bruce (Barbour), 113, 119–20, 208n69
Bruce, Robert the, 106, 112–13, 208n69
Brutus, 27, 43
Bryan, Elizabeth J., 223n97
Buke of the Howlat (Holland), 108, 113, 117, 206–7n45, 208n69, 210n85, 211n104
Bunt, G. H. V., 52, 186nn37–38
bureaucracy, 15, 207n48; and nation, 6, 100, 166n39, 170n78; and poetry, 129–31, 136, 142, 154, 156, 216n22, 220n57; and states, 215–16n21; and Westminster, 130–31, 170n80, 215n19, 221n81, 222n93, 223n98. *See also* centralization; clergy; scribes
Burnley, David, 218n42, 227n15
Burrow, John, 177n116, 214n13
But, John, 141, 222–23n93. *See also* scribes
Butterfield, Ardis, 183n7
Bynum, Caroline Walker, 58, 59, 186n36, 188n69

Cable, Thomas, 33, 182–83n2, 197n65
Caedmon, 22
Camden, William, 69, 184n13

INDEX · 259

Camelot, 76–78, 82, 84–85, 87, 91–93, 96, 98–99. *See also* Arthur
Camille, Michael, 56
Cannon, Christopher, 93, 129, 214n12
capital, 42, 74–75, 82, 85, 205n30; cultural, 5, 134; and Empire, 218n40; and force, 205n30; symbolic, 76, 94, 96, 98–99, 102. *See also* capitalism; wealth
capitalism, 7, 19–20, 158–59, 166n39, 191n118, 226n4; and anxiety, 51; and biopower, 186n31; corporate, 204n21; and difference, 133; print-, 7, 45–46, 100–101, 158, 168n58, 183n8; proto-, 52, 59, 69–70, 187n50. *See also* industrialism
Carlisle, 105, 110–12, 114, 117–19, 121, 208n58, 211n112, 212n114, 212n128. *See also* North
Carlyle, Thomas, 128, 214n5
Carson, Angela, 90
Celts, 11, 20, 78, 87, 90, 114–15, 121–22, 194n28, 194n33, 197n60, 202n119
censorship, 133, 141–42, 156, 217n37, 221n83, 225n120; and surveillance, 139–44
centrality: authorial, 131–32; and peripheries, 15, 44, 79, 130, 168n58; metropolitan, 39, 76, 80, 193n17; narrative, 61, 84–85, 90–91, 97, 105, 200n94; royal, 208n68. *See also* provincialism; London
centralization, state, 6, 13, 36, 78, 100–102, 106, 115–17, 119, 127, 166n39, 168n58, 207n49, 210n88, 215–16n21. *See also* state
Cerquiglini, Bernard, 226n138
Chakrabarty, Dipesh, 5, 37
Chambers, R. W., 29–30, 36–37, 45, 46, 177n103, 177nn108–9
Chandler, Alice, 11, 168n64, 175n80
Chapman, Coolidge Otis, 79–81
Chaucer, Geoffrey, 3, 9–12, 19, 23, 68, 79, 80, 129, 161–62, 167n53, 167n57, 168n59, 172n16, 180n173, 184–85n21; and modernity, 2–5, 11–13, 21, 25–26, 33, 36, 37, 185n22; and the Pardoner, 98; and the Parson, 9–10, 11, 40, 167nn54–55; and *Troilus and Criseyde,* 10, 40, 141, 198n77, 222n91; and the Wife of Bath, 77, 95, 203n137
Chepman, Walter, and Andrew Myllar, 107, 108, 205n33, 206n44
Chester, 82, 197n59. *See also* Northwest Midlands
Cheuelere Assigne (Anonymous), 169n74
Chism, Christine, 3–4, 91, 94, 190n117, 195n46, 213n138
chivalry, 49, 79, 110, 115, 118, 125–26, 180n170, 195n46, 210n91, 212n137, 214nn140–41
Christendom, 101, 125, 207n48. *See also* community; religion
chronicle, 112, 194n36, 208n57, 209n76, 213n137, 219n49. *See also* romance
Cicero, 77, 93, 96–97, 193n21, 201n113, 202n119, 202–3n133, 225n128
civil war, 174n52, 224n110, 224n114; Arthurian, 87–89, 111, 119, 121, 199n83, 211n112; and France, 31–32; metrical, 5, 7, 11, 16, 17, 23, 25, 31, 36, 38, 129; U. S., 32, 178n22
civilization, 21, 38, 43, 49, 126; Chaucer and, 47; and class, 125–26; and the French, 5, 22, 29–30, 128–29; as Western, 5; and war, 43, 126. *See also* courtliness
Clanchy, M. T., 13, 215–16n21, 222n86
class, 6, 13, 20, 30–31, 46, 157, 159, 167–68n58, 170n78, 208n69; and difference, 57, 64, 125–26, 186n34, 187n60, 224n112; hierarchy, 55, 125, 135, 147–48, 159, 218n45; instability, 41–42, 50–52, 56, 64, 69–70, 219n49, 249n50; and land, 42; and language, 51–52; and power, 22, 56, 63, 75, 89, 104; and

260 · INDEX

socioeconomic mobility, 7, 14, 41–42, 50–52, 69–70, 130, 135, 148, 187n60, 218n40, 219nn49–50; working, 52–56. *See also* aristocracy; labor; peasants; violence
Cleanness (Anonymous), 27, 79, 80
clergy, 41, 48–49, 149–50, 195–96n47, 219n50; and aristocracy, 52, 58, 70, 191n123; and coteries, 131, 139; and intellect, 76–77, 193n26, 193n19, 193n21; and literature, 130, 214–15n15, 226n136; and rebellion, 150, 224n114; and women, 14, 72, 76, 96–97; and writing, 222n86
Clerk of Tranent, 27, 176n88
clothing, 38, 50, 55–57, 59, 62–67, 77, 86–87, 181n182, 188n65, 191n120, 198n78
Coghill, Nevill, 37
Cohen, Jeffrey Jerome, 8, 49, 61, 105, 165n29, 188n79, 204n22, 205n26
collaboration: on estates, 75, 86–90; textual: 50, 68, 132, 136–43, 155–56, 184n15, 221n80, 223n97
Colley, Linda, 172n18, 227n10
Colls, Robert, 173n40
comedy, 49, 96, 180n173, 187n60
communication, 59, 70, 159, 218n42; and nation, 166n39, 170n38; networks, 3, 15, 81, 134, 156; political, 134–56, 217n35, 225n120; symbolic, 42, 76–77, 84, 94–99, 193n18; and technology, 15, 129–31, 136, 142, 153, 156, 162. *See also* censorship; media
community, 5–8, 100–104, 207n48; and language, 7; local, 79, 113, 159, 172–73n29; political, 13, 16, 19, 32, 48–49, 158, 165n26, 166n34, 168n58, 169–70n77, 173n33, 175n84, 196n53, 218n45; and textuality, 80–81, 131, 216n24, 220n62, 223n97. *See also* Britain
Conlee, John W., 181n177, 201n18
Connor, Walker, 5, 165n26, 166n41, 194n38, 197n59
conservatism, 24, 41–42, 50, 54, 62, 74, 80, 129, 133–34, 153, 182n183, 187n52, 218n43
consumption: of material goods, 14, 41–42, 58, 73–75, 89, 93, 97; of poetry, 51–52, 80, 197n62
continuity, 20, 56, 120, 173n30, 194n33; and desire, 13, 33; and ethnicity, 4–5, 11–12, 18, 22–23, 29–30, 45–47, 78, 82, 178n30; and historiography, 7–9, 36–37, 171n11; and land, 121; medieval-modern, 100–103, 158, 161, 185n27; and prosody, 18, 33, 182–83n2. *See also* epochality; genealogy
Cooper, Helen, 189n82
Coss, Peter, 192n16
courtliness, 38, 56–57, 77, 82, 92–93; and empire, 112; and hunting, 50, 65, 67, 99, 191n2; and love, 50, 56, 66, 68–70, 80, 85, 94, 96, 99, 189n95, 190n101; and romance, 52, 197n62
Craigie, William, 168n59, 206n40
Crane, Susan, 38, 56, 84, 183n8, 191n120, 198n72
Crawford, Robert, 36, 175n83
Creole identity, 7, 8, 19, 158–59, 161, 166n35; and America, 175n84
Crowned King (Anonymous), 131, 215n19, 222n88, 225n119
Crusade: Albigensian, 31, 178n124; Fourth, 71, 191n124
Cummins, John, 65, 190n98, 190n102

Davies, Norman, 211–12n113
Davies, R. R., 78, 100, 109, 166n43, 169–70n77, 194n28, 198n69, 204n22, 211n111
Davis, Kathleen, 8, 158, 226n3, 226n6, 227n8
Davis, Norman, 167n53
Day, Mabel, and Robert Steele, 136–39, 150–51, 220n67, 220n71, 222n87,

224n114
death: and identity, 98, 202n130; and language, 45–46; and Revivalism, 2–4, 15, 18–19, 32–33, 35, 36–37, 39, 48, 157, 171n9, 182–83n183
Declaration of Arbroath, 106, 114, 117, 119, 120, 126, 212n119
Deibert, Ronald J., 168n62, 218n42, 227n15
Deleuze, Gilles, and Félix Guattari, 186n33, 189n83
demographics, 13, 78, 186n31, 194n33; and anxiety, 37; and immigration, 20, 42–43, 132, 159, 173n40, 210n84, 215n17, 227n12; and militarism, 14, 73, 197n61; rural, 181n180, 192n8
Derrida, Jacques, 160, 227n20
desire, 77, 86, 88, 95, 139, 186n36, 219n53; and criticism, 2–3, 13, 30, 34, 35, 41, 75, 103, 159, 170n82, 180n158, 202n125, 218–19n39; imperial, 93, 106, 123, 153, 194n30, nationalist, 16, 28; occlusion of, 17, 36, 39; recovering, 9, 12, 16, 50, 62, 68, 71, 75, 157
Diefendorf, Barbara B., 178n124
Dinshaw, Carolyn, 92–93, 103, 170n82
documents, 131, 136, 142–43, 154–55, 183n7, 220n57. *See also* bureaucracy; law; scribes
Donaldson, E. Talbot, 132. *See also* Kane
Donoghue, Daniel, 182–83n2
doom, 4, 5, 11, 16, 19, 161
doubleness, 4, 14, 63, 78, 89–93, 98, 199n83, 200n96
Douglas, David C., 173n30
Douglases (Black), 108, 115, 117, 206–7n45, 208n69, 210n85, 210n89, 211n104, 211n106
Doyle, A. I., 131, 141, 182n196, 206n42, 215n17, 215n20, 220n66, 220n74, 223n101
dreams, 37–38, 41–43, 54, 61–62, 77, 88, 96, 108, 110, 151–53,

189n84, 219n49, 222n88, 225n128, 225–26n133; and criticism, 156, 174n52
Duggan, Hoyt N., 34, 132, 192n6, 217n30; and Turville-Petre, 195n46
Dunbar, William, 10, 162, 176n88
Dunn, Charles W., 187n57
dynamism, 185n27; economic, 42, 74, 76; medieval, 6, 8, 16, 21, 101

Early English Text Society (EETS), 27–28, 37, 132, 136, 176n90, 176n92
Eastern culture, 14, 50, 71, 187n57, 195n46, 208n69; Byzantine, 71, 191n124
Edinburgh, 107–8
editions, 16, 20, 132, 136–43, 179n144, 171n11, 216–17n27; digital, 218n42; EETS, 28; emendation in, 34, 39–40, 181n177, 201n101; and gender, 50, 189n82; and print, 221n78; Revivalist, 34, 37–38, 179n143; and titles, 61, 74, 189n82; and variation, 118, 211n109
education: and nation, 7, 9, 19, 22, 32, 46–47, 70, 100, 159, 166n39, 175n84; religious, 135
Edward I, 8, 81, 106, 112–13, 119, 122, 166n43, 196n53, 205n31, 207n47, 207–8n56, 211n111, 212n130
Edward III, 38, 42, 51, 112, 158n80, 184n13, 207n56, 208n62, 210n91, 212n132
Edwards, A. S. G., 194n39
Embree, Dan, 138, 220n68, 221n79
Emerson, Ralph Waldo, 169n71
empire, 5, 6, 12, 14–15, 19, 50, 100–104, 108–9, 127, 172n18; and anti-imperialism, 2, 15, 108–11, 199nn85–86; and collapse, 88, 105, 110–11, 118–19; and ethnicity, 121–22; and literary history, 4, 204n22, 204–5n26; post-national, 8, 159; and power, 43, 84, 110, 112,

126; and race, 175n84; rulers of, 54–55, 71. *See also* Arthur; England; Scotland; state
England, 5, 8, 13, 79, 128, 148; and class, 52, 219n49; and criticism, 1, 26; and empire, 8, 14–15, 42–44, 77–78, 87, 104, 109, 117, 122, 175n84, 207n47, 211n111, 212–13n132; and Englishness, 7, 9, 11–13, 20, 22, 29–30, 33, 45–48, 79, 83, 170n78, 177n109, 184n15; and law, 73, 75; and modernity, 4–5, 8–9, 32–36, 161; and nation, 4, 7, 13, 111, 167–68n58, 170n78, 209n78, 227nn8–11, 227n17; and patriotism, 28; and race, 20–26, 29–30, 128–29, 169n67, 169n71; and Revivalism, 1, 27–32, 36, 171n16; as state, 115, 210n88; and war, 14, 106–7, 114. *See also* Alliterative Revivalism; Anglo-Saxons; Arthur; borderlands; Britain; militarism; Normans
English, language, 5, 7, 10; and French, 45–49, 183n7, 184n13; Middle, 2, 4, 14, 17, 20, 39, 51–52, 68–69, 184–95nn7–8, 194n36, 222n91; Old, 2, 171n10; Northern, 39, 175–76n87; and Scots, 7, 20, 36, 107, 120, 175n83
English Channel, 48, 68, 71, 104, 189–90n96
Enlightenment, 6, 9, 164n21, 195n45, 204n21
epochality, 1, 7, 9, 15, 17, 115, 164n11, 186n31; and conquest, 18, 21–22; and historiography, 22, 37, 47, 157–62, 218n42; medieval, 8, 9, 23; and modernity, 2–3, 7; and nation, 18, 20, 102
estate: management, 52, 75, 85–87, 90–92, 99, 192–93n16, 201n108; residents, 56, 69–70, 219n49
ethnicity, 3, 15, 78, 101–104, 183n5; and anxiety, 14, 18; and assimilation, 112; and difference, 12, 26, 172n26, 178n130, 194n33, 209n78, 212–13n132; and empire, 109, 112–15, 121–22, 161; and ethnie, 6; and history, 4, 5–6, 18, 20–26, 29–32, 44, 69; and nation, 6, 7, 13, 19, 24, 101–103, 105, 158, 170n78, 227n21, 228n26. *See also* alterity; continuity; genealogy; language; race
Europe, 43, 48, 50, 79, 114, 182n194, 185n27, 187n50, 192–93n16, 199n87, 204n21, 210n88; as Continental culture, 9, 14, 17, 31, 33, 36, 47, 66, 129, 173n34, 185n18; and nation, 2, 7, 19, 20, 46, 158, 161, 166n35, 177n105, 209n75; and war, 88, 121–22, 196n54, 213n137
Everett, Dorothy, 17, 69, 80, 181n177, 197n62, 200n91
evolutionary criticism, 5, 11, 25–26, 128, 169n68, 169n71; and atavism, 2, 33, 128
exceptionalism: aristocratic, 14, 48–50, 56–57, 62, 69–70, 125, 147, 160; English, 5, 13, 21, 22, 25, 161
expansionism, 15, 46–47, 87, 89, 100–101, 104–5, 109, 110, 121–22, 126, 199n86

fantasy, 46, 99, 140, 164n19; and criticism, 2, 4, 13, 23, 14, 103, 132, 161–62, 174n52, 202n125, 217n39; medieval, 6, 43, 105, 109, 190–91n118, 224n108; and nation, 5, 9, 16, 20, 30, 103–4; Revivalist, 2–4, 7, 9–12, 16, 19, 25, 30–31, 25–37, 39, 44, 68–69, 74, 103, 129, 135, 157–60; and race, 22, 26–28, 32
Febvre, Lucien, and Henri-Jean Martin, 154, 225n129
Federico, Sylvia, and Elizabeth Scala, 163n6
Fein, Susanna G., 35
Ferster, Judith, 221–22nn83–84
feudalism, 51–53, 64, 69–70; and

gender, 86, 91–92; and lordship, 3, 15, 42, 72, 76, 110–15, 117–18, 123–26, 205n31, 213nn135–36; and maintenance, 136, 142, 155, 220n59; and modernity, 50–51
Field, Rosalind, 111–12, 196n56, 205n34
filth, 53–54, 56, 67, 80, 187n52
Finke, Laurie A., and Martin B. Shichtman, 199n82, 204–5n26
Fisher, Sheila, 86, 90–92, 188–89n91, 200n94
food, 41, 54, 57–58, 63–64
foreignness, 5, 9, 24–25, 83, 114, 169n69; and empire, 87–88, 121–22; and language, 22, 45–49; and poetry, 11, 36; and queens, 87; and xenophobia, 31
forest, 43, 49, 54–66, 174n52, 188n67, 200–1n97; agents, 191n121; Wirral, 32, 78, 94, 194n31
Fortune (Lady), 77, 88–89, 99, 108, 110, 127, 199n85, 199nn87–88
Foucault, Michel, 132, 186n31, 195n45
Fradenburg, L. O. Aranye, 4, 66, 87, 103, 133, 164n19, 168n59, 174n52, 190n101, 199n80, 202n121, 213–14n139, 217n39
Frakes, Jerold C., 192–93n16, 199n87
Frame, Robin, 205n31
France, 14, 21, 42–43, 186n31; and aristocracy, 14, 52, 194–95n40; and Chaucer, 5, 47–48, 161, 185n21; and England, 19, 68–70, 74, 82, 189–90n96, 192n4, 194–95n40, 210n91; and Francophilia, 4, 7, 13, 23, 30, 44, 68, 80; and Francophobia, 14, 46, 99, 227n10; and nation, 29, 31, 49, 178nn124–25, 183n3; and race, 25; and Revivalism, 2, 5, 33, 185n22, 192n4. *See also* civilization; Normans
Frantzen, Allen J., 171n10, 190n13; and John D. Niles, 165n23
freedom, 15, 20, 23, 112–13, 119–20, 124–26, 173n32, 174n52; and

gender, 73, 85
French (language), 46, 177n116, 185n25; in England, 51–52, 183n7, 183–84n9, 184n13
Friedman, Albert B., 90, 200n92
Fries, Maureen, 200n96, 202n124
Fryde, E. B., 219n49
Fuchs, Barbara, 205n26
Furnivall, F. J., 28, 163–64n10, 176n90, 176n92

Gadamer, Hans-Georg, 164n13
Galbraith, V. C., 184n11, 184n13
Galeron, 15, 105, 110–19, 126, 160, 208n63, 209n79, 210nn93–94,
Galloway, 15, 105, 114–16, 118–19, 160, 209n79, 209n81, 210nn83–85
Galloway, Andrew, 48–49, 183n7, 218n44
Ganim, John, 178n133
Gardener, 134, 152–56, 225n123, 225n128
Gaston Phébus, 65–66, 190n96
Gates, Henry Louis, Jr., 21, 29, 177n104
Gates, Robert J., 118, 206n42, 211n109
Gawain, 15, 27, 32, 63, 72, 74, 76–77, 78, 84–87, 90–93, 95–98, 105–6, 110–18, 123–27, 191n2, 194n30, 198n68, 198n78, 202n127, 208n58, 209n73, 209n78, 210n94, 211n109
Geary, Patrick J., 22, 182n194
Gellner, Ernest, 7, 8–9, 19–20, 22, 26, 31, 46–47, 49, 148, 158–59, 161, 166n39, 172n25, 175n79, 186n30, 187n60, 191n118, 210n88, 224n112, 227n16, 228nn24–25
gender, 3, 14, 63–64, 157; and anxiety, 73–74, 77, 85–87, 192n10, 203n138; and criticism, 50, 90, 96, 189n82; and female power, 62, 72–78, 83–99, 192–93nn15–16, 193n26, 199n88; and masculinity, 14, 50, 61, 74, 76–78, 83, 89–90, 99, 202n125; and misogyny, 86–87
genealogy, 104, 145; Biblical, 6,

165n29; and class, 55–56, 183n7; and criticism, 4, 80, 163–64n10, 170n82; and ethnicity, 6, 22–23, 78, 85, 114, 165n23, 178n30, 182n194, 183n3, 198n71, 227n10, 228n21, 228n26; and Revivalism, 2, 9, 12, 18–19, 27–28, 32, 35–39, 49, 74, 171n4
Genghis Khan, 153, 225n126
gentry, 42, 75, 219n50; as audience, 31, 197n62
Geoffrey of Monmouth, 8, 43, 76, 78, 87, 121, 167n47, 182n194, 193n19, 194n28, 199n84, 207n56
geography, 169–70n77, 206n38; and desire, 93; and ethnicity, 22; medieval, 68, 79, 114,120, 131, 165n29, 193nn26–27, 201n112, 207–8n56, 208n58, 213n138, 214n14; Revivalist 3, 15, 80–81
Germanic culture, 2, 21; and England, 48, 160; and nation, 164n20, 183n3; and poetry, 39; and race, 11, 19, 21, 23, 25–26, 47, 48, 69, 74, 89–90, 128–29, 161, 165n23, 169n69, 173n32, 214nn5–6. *See also* Anglo-Saxonism; antiquity
Gest Hystoriale of the Destruction of Troy (Clerk), 14, 81, 85–86, 87, 175n86, 179n145, 195n46, 197n58, 198n77; and Guido delle Colonne, 81
ghosts, 132; and Guinevere's mother, 108, 110–11, 118, 122, 127, 199n86, 211n112
Giancarlo, Matthew, 150, 224n115
Ginsberg, Warren, 181n177
Girouard, Mark, 168n64
Given-Wilson, Chris, 187n43
Golagros, 15, 103, 108–9, 120, 122–27, 213n134, 213n135, 214n140
Golagros and Gawane (Anonymous), 15, 27, 100, 103–9, 111, 119–27, 198n68, 205n33, 207n50, 207n53, 212n123, 213nn134–36, 213nn138–39, 214n140; date of, 109; meter of, 107, 206n40; print of, 107–8, 206n44; source for, 213n133
Goldstein, R. James, 106, 207n47, 208n57, 208n69, 212n119
Gollancz, Israel, 28, 34, 37–41, 176n90, 176n94, 179n143, 179–80n158, 181n177, 182n183
Goodman, Anthony, 115, 205n31, 211n103
Gottfried von Strassburg, 65, 189n94
Gower, John, 10
Grady, Frank, 136, 155, 216n22, 219–20n56, 224n108, 225n127
Graham, John M., 183n3
Grant, Alexander, 207n47, 212n116
Gray, John, 209n71
Greeks, 50, 57, 71, 87, 198n77
Green, Richard Firth, 154, 221–22n84
Greenfeld, Liah, 158–59, 167n48, 174n44, 227n9
Greetham, D. C., 218n42
grotesquerie, 38, 55–56, 187n60, 203n137
Guillaume de Palerne (Anonymous), 14, 46–71, 187n60, 188n65, 189n92, 189–90nn96–97, 191n123; dating of, 184n10; dialect of, 51; manuscript of, 184n10; reception of, 185n25
Guillory, John, 5
Guinevere, 76–77, 87–99, 92–94, 96, 99, 114, 116, 189n84, 198–99nn79–80, 199n84; False, 191–92n4. *See also* ghosts

Hadrian's Wall, 119, 211–12n113
Hahn, Thomas, 112, 116, 120, 166n31, 198n68, 208n58, 214n140
Halleck, Reuben Post, 12, 25, 40, 89, 128
Hammill, Graham, 189n95
Hammond, Eleanor Prescott, 215n20
Hanawalt, Barbara A., 191n120
Hanna, Ralph, III, 3, 4, 17–18, 34, 68, 81, 107, 117, 163n5, 163n15,

169n73, 171n10, 179n145, 193n22, 195n44, 205n32, 206nn42–43, 213n133, 213n135, 214n15, 215n17, 217n28; and David Lawton, 81, 196n50, 213n138
Hardt, Michael, and Antonio Negri, 8, 103, 133, 159, 204n18, 218n40, 227n13
Harrington, David V., 182n183
Hastings, Adrian, 13, 174n44, 227n8
Hautdesert, 72–73, 75–79, 85, 90–93, 97–99
Hayles, N. Katherine, 135, 219n53, 227n15
Helgerson, Richard, 10, 167–68n58, 227n9
Henry IV, 133, 137, 142, 146–47, 150, 151, 224n114, 224n116
heraldry, 38, 42–43, 67, 108, 180n158, 182n191, 210n185; and the green girdle, 198n78
Hey, David, 197n63
Higgins, Ian Macleod, 225n126
Higham, N. J., 207n56
Hill, Christopher, 172n27
Hilton, Rodney, 195n41, 217n38, 219n49
Hinchman, Walter S., 69, 83, 200n91
historiography, 5, 15–16, 157–62, 166nn33–34, 204nn21–23, 208n68; and desire, 103; and historicism, 3, 5, 17, 38; and ideology, 119, 208n57; and invasions, 21–22, 173n40; and politics, 158; and positivism, 21. *See also* alterity; continuity; epochality; literary history
Hobbes, Thomas, 60–61
Hobsbawm, Eric, 20, 102, 166n39, 168n58, 177n105, 183n8, 184n11
Hoccleve, Thomas, 142, 222n57
Hodges, Kenneth, 121, 212n126
Holsinger, Bruce W., 204n21
Holstun, James, 218n40
homogeneity, 6; cultural, 7, 9–11; economic, 7, 19–20, 46–47, 159, 166n39; ethnic, 7, 36, 78, 162;
and nation, 6–11, 13, 21, 26, 100–101, 148, 158, 46–47, 192, 228nn25–26
homo sacer, 14, 57, 60–61, 63, 189n90
Horobin, Simon, 137, 215n18
Horsman, Reginald, 4, 21, 78, 164n21, 165n23, 169n67, 169n69, 172n27, 173nn31–32, 175n84, 178n122, 194n33, 198n71, 214n6
Huchown of the Awle Ryale, 27–29, 175n83, 175–76nn86–87, 176n94, 176nn99–100, 208n66
Hulbert, J. R., 29, 30–31, 177n103, 180n158, 200n92
Humphrey de Bohun, 51–52, 54, 69–70
Hundred Years' War, 74, 81–82, 105–6, 117, 124, 194–95n40, 196n54
Hunt, Alan, 181n181
hunting, 50, 57, 59, 63, 70, 92, 97, 99, 188n79, 189n94, 190n97, 190n101, 191n2, 202n132, 218n45; manuals, 65, 189–90n96, 221n77
Husband, Timothy, 182n191, 210n85
hybridity, 135, 165n29, 218n40; bodily, 49, 58–59, 61, 63, 67, 188n69; cultural, 7, 20–21, 26,114, 117–18; metrical, 11, 24–25, 48, 80, 135, 162, 215n15; and race, 5, 12, 25, 129, 169n71

industrialism, 6–9, 11, 19, 21–22, 26, 46–47, 100, 103, 158–59, 162, 166n39, 204n21, 224n112
Ingham, Patricia Clare, 6, 77, 78, 93, 95, 102, 104, 111, 116, 122, 158, 166n34, 185n27, 190–91n118, 193–94nn27–28, 194n30, 199n82, 199n86, 202n121, 204n23, 205n34, 206n37, 207n55, 226n4; and Michelle R. Warren, 104, 204n22, 206n38
Ingledew, Frances, 182n194
Ireland, 43, 59–60, 76, 79, 81–82, 87–88, 114, 116, 166n33, 185n25, 193n19, 196n51, 207n47

irony, 38–40, 53, 66, 68
Isidore of Seville, 165n29

Jack, R. D. S., 213n134
Jacobs, Nicolas, 42, 182n183, 222n89
James, Jerry D., 180n173
Janssen, Anke, 89
Jerusalem, 120, 122–24, 213n134, 214n138. *See also Siege of Jerusalem*
Jewell, Helen, 170n78, 198n69, 208n60, 218–19n48
John of Fordun, 114
Johnston, Arthur, 171n8, 171n11
Joseph of Arimathie (Anonymous), 28
Jusserand, J. J., 185n22
Justice, Steven, 217n35, 217n44. *See also* Kerby-Fulton

Kaeuper, Richard W., 213n137
Kane, George, 216–17nn27–28, 217–18n39; and E. . Donaldson, 132, 216–17n27. *See also* Russell
Kant, Immanuel, 98, 203n136
Kay, Sarah, 1, 163n8
Kedourie, Elie, 164n20, 165n30
Keiser, George, 169n74
Ker, W. P., 33, 178n133
Kerby-Fulton, Kathryn, 133, 141, 156, 181n179, 216n24, 217n37, 219n50, 226n136; and Steven Justice, 131, 170n80, 216n22, 221n81, 223n98
kingdoms, 46–47, 114, 115, 160, 165n26. *See also* sovereignty; state
Kinser, Samuel, 180n170
Kiser, Lisa, 202n130
kitchens, 50, 51, 63–66, 70, 190n97
Kittredge, George Lyman, 191n2, 200n92
Knapp, Ethan, 136, 142, 170n80, 215n15, 216n22, 220n57
Kruger, Steven F., 225n128
Kumar, Krishan, 20, 173n30, 209n78, 212–13n132

labor, 82–83, 219n50, 225n123; agricultural, 134, 219n48; and anxiety, 52–56, 63, 66–67; clerkly, 148; literary, 214–15n15; scribal, 132, 215n15. *See also* class; peasants
Lady (*Sir Gawain*), 14, 73–78, 85–87, 89–94, 97–99, 191n2, 200n96, 202n124
Lady of the Lake, 95–96, 99, 203n139
Lampert, Lisa, 226n3
Lancelot, 114, 119, 189n84, 202n127, 211n112
Lancelot (Vulgate), 90189n84, 191–92n4, 200–1n97, 202n127, 202n132
land, 15, 22, 32, 37, 82, 100–101, 159, 197n59; and desire, 122–23; and dispossession, 105, 108–19, 122–25; and empire, 109, 113; grants, 15; and nation, 19, 21, 43, 48–49; and power, 104–5, 113, 219nn49–50; sales, 42; as territory, 6, 13, 56, 77, 95, 116–17, 194n30, 209n79, 210n94, 211n96
language, 6, 59; and class, 51, 187n43; and dialect, 10–11, 27, 168n62, 182n184; and ethnicity, 14, 22–23, 29–30, 45–49; and nation, 7, 10, 17, 19, 20, 45–49, 79, 184n11, 194n36; and power, 133–34, 144–45; and vernacularity, 7, 13, 25, 35, 45–46, 79
Larrington, Carolyne, 193n26
Latin, 26, 31, 46, 59, 138, 183n7, 183–84n8, 184n11, 185n25, 214–15n15, 215n19, 221n77
Lavezzo, Kathy, 5, 165n27, 168n58, 191n118, 204n22
law, 14, 73, 114, 133, 152, 166n33, 208n68, 218n44; and class, 147; and corruption, 130; forest, 70, 191n121; and jurisdiction, 43, 49, 88–91, 101, 109, 207n48, 212–13n113; and justice, 153, 225n125; and language, 150, 224n115; and literature, 136, 139, 154, 218n44, 219–20n56, 224n111; and marriage,

75, 85, 90, 93, 201n108; and nation, 166n33; records, 75; and speech, 150; sumptuary, 70, 181n181, 191n120
Lawton, David, 35, 84–85, 132, 162, 170n79, 174–75n65, 179nn149–50, 190n109, 200n93, 206n40, 216n24, 217n29, 219n51. *See also* Hanna
Laȝamon, 182–83n2, 199n82, 223n97
legitimacy (political), 76–77, 84, 87, 114, 147, 193n18; and empire, 101, 121; Lancastrian, 147, 224n110; and nation, 9, 31, 203–4n7; and violence, 106, 153
Lerer, Seth, 184–85n17
libraries, 31, 177n121, 194n39; and archives, 154–55, 225n131
literary history, 9, 12, 18–36, 103, 106, 133, 157–62, 164n14, 166n33, 167n52, 169n68, 185n27, 204–5n26; and disciplinarity, 1–4, 13, 45, 157, 163n6, 171n8; foundational, 18–21, 47, 164n12, 164–65n22, 171n11; militarized, 11, 13, 15, 21, 24–26, 29, 69, 82–83, 85–86, 200n91; and modernity, 2–3, 5, 7–9, 21, 25–26, 128; and nation, 2–4, 6–7, 9, 11, 19, 21, 26–32, 35–37, 44, 70, 161, 164n19, 184n15; pressure of, 38–44, 48, 68; and race, 2–5, 13, 20–26, 177n104. *See also* Alliterative Revivalism; historiography; philology
Loathly Lady, 77, 95, 98, 199n80, 202n121, 203n137
locality: and audience, 214n13; and criticism, 2, 12, 16, 44, 106, 160–61, 185n27, 210n86; and demographics, 78; and identity, 75–76, 85, 108, 115–17, 119–20, 123, 127, 130, 136, 141, 160, 172–73n129, 205n31, 208n61; and patronage, 30, 182n197; and war, 104–5, 113, 127
Lochrie, Karma, 201n117
Lollardy, 135, 201n117, 216n24, 217–18n39, 219n51

London, 39, 44, 80, 81–82, 133, 160, 167n55, 170n80, 193n17, 194–95n40, 195–96n47, 197n57, 197n62, 198n79, 215nn16–18, 215n19; and the Midlands, 15, 129–31, 136, 154, 156
Long, William J., 128–29
Loomis, Laura Hibbard, 90,
loyalties (political), 6, 12–13, 14, 79, 101–2, 112–13, 117, 125, 130, 156, 159–60, 169–70n77, 173n30, 184n11, 193n27, 194n38
Luke, 224n117
Lydgate, John, 10

MacCracken, Henry Noble, 28–29, 176n87
Macdougall, Hugh A., 190n113, 194n28, 198n71, 207n56
Machan, Tim William, 216–17n27
Mack, Ruth, 171n11
Madden, Frederic, 27–28, 61, 95–96, 114, 189n82
magic, 59, 61–63, 71, 72, 77, 84, 94–96, 175n84, 193n26, 202n124, 203n139
Malory, Thomas, 63, 114, 119, 197–98n67, 209n77, 211n112, 212n126
Man (Isle), 14, 76, 79, 81, 196n51
Mandeville, John, 225n126
Manly, John, 132, 221n80
Mann, Jill, 216n25
manuscripts, 13, 15, 34, 40, 83, 107, 130–41, 156, 159, 182n196, 195nn46–47, 206n42, 226n138, 227n15; Arsenal Fr. 6565, 184n10; BL Additional 31042, 37, 39, 169n74; BL Additional 41666, 137–38, 142–43, 220n74, 223n101; Bodley 851, 217n28; CUL L1.4.14, 137–38, 221n77, 222n87; Cotton Caligula A.ix.38, 223n97; Cotton Nero A.x, 27, 79–81, 191–92nn4–5, 194–95nn39–40, 195n45; Digby 202, 177n116; Douce 95, 215n19; Douce 324, 206n42; Harley 78,

131; Harley 2253, 181n182; Hunterian 38, 195n46; illuminated, 56, 65; Ireland Blackburn, 118, 105n32, 206n42; King's College Cambridge MS 13, 184n10; Lambeth Palace 491, 206n42; Lincoln Cathedral 91, 107, 169n74, 197n65, 206n42. *See also* book production; editions; media; scribes

Mardorossian, Carine, 166n45

marginality, 8, 68, 168n58, 193n26; artificial, 81; and centrality, 15, 44

Marie de France, 60–61, 63, 77, 188n79, 193n26

marriage, 38, 50, 54–55, 68, 70–71, 75, 77, 85, 87, 117, 188n79, 201n117, 209n74

Marsh, George Perkins, 21, 25, 172n16, 173n34, 224–25n119

Marvin, William Perry, 190n96

Mate, Mavis E., 85, 201n108

Matthews, David, 163–64n10, 171n8, 171n11, 176n90, 176n92, 221n78

Matthews, William, 198n68, 198n79, 199n85, 205–6n35, 206n37, 212n132

Mazzio, Carla, 223–24n105

McCaffery, Steve, 145, 224n107

McFarlane, K. B., 105–6

McIntosh, Angus, 83, 171n10, 192n5, 195n44, 196n50, 197n67, 212n125

media, 15, 129, 155; digital, 133, 156, 159, 218n42, 227n15; mass, 160; and Media Specific Analysis, 135–36, 142, 154, 219n53. *See also* communication; manuscripts; print

medicine, 150, 224n115, 224n117

medievalism, 4, 8–12, 13–14, 26–27, 74, 83, 168n64, 204m22; amateur, 1, 13, 27, 28, 61, 176n90; and nation, 100–101, 112, 158–60, 164n19, 165n23, 173n31, 206n38; and New Medievalism, 1–2, 163n6, 227n15; Pre-Raphaelite, 11, 44; professional, 19, 163n9; and Romanticism, 11, 13, 164n21. *See also* antiquarianism; literary history

Mélion (Anonymous), 59–60

memory, 6, 148, 158, 173n34; ethnic, 23, 103; and forgetting, 19, 31, 178n124. *See also* trauma

merchants, 41, 52, 59, 82, 130, 183n7, 197n61, 214n14

Merlin, 72, 76, 94–95, 99, 155, 193n19, 194n28, 202n119, 202n124, 203n139

metamorphosis, 50, 58, 60, 62, 63, 94–95, 186n36, 188n69, 202n119

Middleton, Anne, 130, 214n13, 215n16, 222n93, 226n137

Miles, David, 172n26, 194n33

militarism, 24–25, 54, 69, 83, 89, 101, 160, 205n30, 213n137; anti-, 108–11, 197n57, 207n53; and arbitrariness, 15, 108; and class, 66–67, 70; and conquest, 21–22, 43–44, 81–82, 106, 112, 116, 122–27, 173n40, 177–78n122, 210n85; and economics, 14, 41–44, 73–76, 85, 105–6, 117, 122, 196n56, 212n129; and ethics, 106, 110–11; and fear, 113; natural, 60–61; and poetry, 208n69. *See also* borderlands; literary history; Northwest Midlands; suffering

Milton, John, 22

Minnis, Alastair, 225–26n133

Miskimin, Alice, 176n87

monolithic criticism. *See* singularity

Moody, William Vaughn, and Robert Morss Lovett, 47–48, 185n21

Moorman, Charles, 31–32, 69, 181n174, 200n91

morality, 11, 21, 35, 53–54, 62, 64, 69, 126, 153, 155–56, 172n16, 181n174, 225n128

Mordred, 87–88, 114, 118–19, 121, 198n79, 199n83, 212n115

Morgan le Fay, 14–15, 61, 62, 72–79, 83, 84–87, 88–99, 189n84, 191n3, 193n26, 199n88, 200–201nn92–97, 201n117, 202n124, 202n126,

202n128, 203n135, 203nn137–39
Morris, Richard, 27–28
Morrison, Susan Signe, 187n52
Mort le Roi Artu (Anonymous), 87, 198n79
multiplicity: and books, 137, 154–55; and criticism, 2, 105; and ethnicity, 209n78; and reduction, 29, 35; socio-material, 76, 82, 193n27, 101, 197n62, 199n82; and textuality, 131–33, 136–43, 146, 154–59, 195n45, 214n12, 219n53, 221n80, 225–26n133. *See also* collaboration
Mum, 143–46, 148–53, 156, 223n105, 224nn113–14
Mum and the Sothsegger (Anonymous), 15, 129, 134–39, 142–56, 220n73, 224n109, 224nn114–16, 225n121, 225n124, 225nn126–28, 225n131, 225–26n133; authorship of, 136–43, 221n79, 222–23n93; dating of, 220–21n75, 223n104; dialect of, 215n18, 220n66; manuscript of, 220n68, 220n74, 223n101, 224n119
Musgrove, Frank, 196n53, 206n36, 212n125, 212n128

Narin, Elisa Marie, 200n94
nations, 5–7, 13, 21–22, 26, 105, 161–62, 168n58, 173n40, 184n11; and anachronism, 31, 105–6; and capitalism, 50–51, 159; and fantasy, 190–91n118; and locality, 112–18; medieval, 5–6, 12–13, 48–49, 121, 160; and modernity, 5, 8, 11, 19, 23, 44, 100–102, 157–59, 161, 166n35, 166n39, 175n84, 191n118, 204n23, 210n88, 228n24; as natural, 164n20; and poetry, 15, 18, 214n13; and state, 8, 101, 205n30. *See also* education; ethnicity; homogeneity; language; sovereignty
nationalism, 2, 19, 26, 79, 102–3, 158–60, 161–62, 166n39, 186n30, 187n60, 190–91n118, 194n38, 227nn16–19, 228n25; and desire, 16; and empire, 14; and forgetting, 19, 31, 178n124; and language, 45–49, 177n105, 183–84n8; and mythology, 11, 20–21, 31–32, 103; and origins, 4, 6–7, 9, 102–3, 227nn8–11, 227n21; and race, 5–6; and Romanticism, 4, 164n20. *See also* Alliterative Revivalism; Anderson; ethnicity; Gellner; industrialism; literary history; philology; rhetoric
nativism, 2–5, 7, 9, 11, 12, 14, 16, 21 27, 46–48, 68, 74, 81, 146, 156, 157, 160, 162
nature, 11, 38, 48, 49, 53, 56–61, 63–65, 83, 87, 96, 126, 132, 143–44, 147, 152, 164n20, 168n64, 200n91
Neilson, George, 28–29, 176n94
Neville, Cynthia J., 205n31
Newman, Gerald, 172n27, 227n10, 227n18
Nichols, Stephen G., 4, 159, 164n20, 183n3, 226n138, 227n15. *See also* Bloch
Nietzsche, Friedrich, 169n68, 227n20
noise, 144–45, 156, 217n27, 224n107; and anxiety, 223–24n105
Nolan, Maura, 180n170
Normans, 20–27; character of, 25, 40; and Conquest, 11, 13, 18, 20–22, 29, 32, 45–48, 128, 173n40, 184n13, 184n15, 186n35; Norman Yoke, 20, 172n27. *See also* Saxon-Norman
North (English), 14, 39, 44, 79, 80, 106, 124, 170n78, 206n36; and Cumberland, 82, 107; and poetry, 195n41, 208n60; and war, 115, 196n53, 209n72, 210n89. *See also* borderlands
Northernness, 22, 25, 38, 175–76n87
Northeast Midlands, 14, 76, 83, 182n184, 196n50; and Lincolnshire, 83, 196n50, 197n67
Northwest Midlands, 12, 78–85,

93–94, 106, 122, 130, 182n184, 194–95n40, 195n46, 196nn49–51, 197n58, 197nn61–63, 206n36; and Cheshire, 41, 74, 81, 192n5; and Lancashire, 41, 74, 81, 195n46, 206n42; and militarism, 14, 41–44, 73–76, 85, 106, 111, 127, 182n189, 192n8, 196nn53–54, 198n69, 199n86. *See also* empire; England
nostalgia, 3, 11–14, 36, 37, 40–42, 44, 68, 77, 99, 105, 129, 135, 151, 157, 160
Nott, Josiah C., 128, 214n5

Oakden, J. P., 17, 30, 69, 80, 81, 83, 171n4, 177n113, 179n145, 180n158, 185n26, 195n41, 196nn49–50, 197nn65–66, 206n40, 212n125, 221n82, 224n119
old age, 33, 38–39, 76–77, 94–99, 193nn21–22, 202n130, 202n132, 203n137. *See also* allegory
opposition, 9, 134; binary, 49, 125, 151, 225n128, 227n20; political, 30–31, 133–34, 147, 194n28, 211n99; prosodic, 10, 19, 68, 80. *See also* struggle
orality, 13, 15, 18, 32, 37, 45, 84, 129, 135–36, 156, 170n79, 181–82n183; and transcription, 154–55
Oram, Richard, 209n82
origins. *See* genealogy
Orkneys, 87, 113, 114, 209n74
Orléans, 160, 225n121
Ormrod, W. M., 210n88, 225n125
otherworldliness, 35, 62–63, 66, 77, 88, 90, 110–11, 193n26. *See also* alterity; ghosts
Owain Glyn Dŵr, 122, 212n130

Painter, F. V. N., 11, 169n67
Paris, Gaston, 62–63
Parlement of the Thre Ages (Anonymous), 77, 81, 96–97, 169n74, 196n50, 202n130
parliament, 41, 131, 147, 150, 152, 155, 224n115
Pasternack, Carol Braun, 223n97
Patience (Anonymous), 27, 79, 80
Paton, Lucy Allen, 193n26, 202n119
patronage, 14, 45, 51–52, 54, 69–70, 108, 117–18, 143, 152, 153–54, 207–8n45, 211n99, 219n53; and Revivalism, 30–31, 81, 83, 182n197, 196n55, 197n62, 211n99; and pleasure, 51
patriotism, 105, 113, 160, 184n13, 227n18; and criticism, 26–32, 46, 47, 176n90, 183–84n8, 200n91
Patterson, Lee, 1, 163n9, 170n82, 182n194, 217n27
Pearl (Anonymous), 27, 79, 80, 195n44
Pearsall, Derek, 2, 9, 17, 27, 51, 160, 164n11, 170n79, 176n87, 185n26, 190n109, 194n37, 215n17, 227n19
peasants, 22, 63, 131, 134–35, 147, 218n45, 219n48; and complaint, 147; contempt for, 52–56, 66–67, 187n60, 219nn49–50; oppression of, 60, 64. *See also* rural life
Peck, Jeffrey M., 183n3
Percies, 115, 117–18, 224n116
Percy, Thomas, 18, 171nn8–10
performance, 59, 92, literary, 38–40; and power, 94–99; public, 57, 125–26; and theatricality, 38, 50, 56, 184, 180n170, 198n72
Perkins, David, 164n14, 169n68
philology, 33, 45, 174n52, 226n138; and nationalism, 4, 20–21, 33, 173n31, 183n3
Pierce the Ploughman's Crede (Anonymous), 15, 28, 129, 131, 134–35, 217n30, 218n46, 219nn50–53
Piers Plowman (Langland), 18, 30, 37, 130–35, 143–45, 148, 151–54, 156, 214n13, 218n45, 218–19n48, 219n50, 219–20n56, 221n80; editions of, 28, 131–32, 216n25, 216–17nn27–28, 218n43; Langland,

17–19, 23, 25, 38, 47–48, 128–34, 167n57, 177n108, 181n174, 185n22, 185–86n29, 196n47, 214–15nn15–16, 222n85; manuscripts of, 130–31, 141, 177n116, 215n17, 221n77, 222n87, 222–23n93; and prosody, 18, 171n10, 172n16; reception of, 35, 156, 167n57, 185n22, 217n35, 218n44, 220n62, 222n93, 226nn136–37
Piers Plowman tradition, 15, 129–56, 216n24, 219nn49–51, 219–20n56, 224–25n119, 226–27n133
Pilate, Pontius, 149–50
Pistill of Swete Susane (Anonymous), 27, 107, 175–76n87, 176n99
plague, 41, 43, 98, 130, 134, 198n74
Platt, Colin, 181n180, 198n74
play, 14, 38–40, 44, 85, 118, 160, 185n26, 220n62, 227n20; and games, 57, 60, 68, 72, 74, 84, 86, 198n78; identity, 3, 49–50, 63–69, 71, 94–99, 126, 151, 159; and policing, 191n121
postcolonialism, 8, 103, 105, 204n22, 204–5n26, 206n38, 218n40
pragmatism, 15, 24, 63, 66–67, 144, 152, 156, 173n30
prejudice, 2, 3, 54, 103, 164n13, 187n60
Prestwich, Michael, 196n54, 205n31, 207n56, 208n62, 210n91, 211n11
print, 7, 10–11, 185n25, 221n78; and authorship, 223n97; and criticism, 159, 162; and language, 45–46, 183n8. *See also* book production; capitalism; Chepman; editions; manuscripts
propaganda, 117, 119, 120, 133, 211n104
Prophecies de Merlin (Anonymous), 95–96, 99, 203n139
prophecy, 38, 41, 110–11, 118, 155, 181n182, 194n28, 199n80, 201n118
Prose Merlin (Anonymous), 94, 96, 201n118
prosody, 1, 7, 19, 168n61; and ex-change, 107; heteromorphic, 171n10, 195n44; homomorphic, 195n44; syllabic, 2, 5, 9, 11, 13, 17, 25–26, 33, 80, 167n53. *See also* alliterative prosody
Protestantism, 22, 23, 172n18, 174n44
provincialism: claims of, 4, 15, 24, 30–32, 36–37, 41, 48, 52, 76, 79–83, 130, 157, 161, 175n83, 177n13, 181n174; and empire, 19, 213n35
Purdie, Rhiannon, 109, 205n33, 207n50
Puttenham, George, 167n57, 171n10
Putter, Ad, 52, 192n4

Quatrefoil of Love (Anonymous), 169n74
Queller, Donald E., and Thomas F. Madden, 191n124
quest, 63, 134–35, 137, 143, 148, 151, 152

race, 4–5, 11, 16, 29, 157, 165–66n31, 169n71, 194n33, 226n3; and England, 18, 169n69, 175n84, 184n15, 185n22, 198n71, 214n6; and language, 29–30; and nation, 6, 20–26, 175n84; and philology, 183n3; and prosody, 2, 4, 7; racism, 5, 12, 21, 48, 128, 161, 173n32, 183n3, 214n5; and Romanticism, 46, 78, 177n104, 194n33; and science, 161, 172n26. *See also* America; Anglo-Saxonism; ethnicity; genealogy; Germanic culture; literary history; Saxon-Norman
recovery, 2, 16, 36, 38, 40, 48, 74, 75–76, 83, 91, 93, 103, 104, 157, 160, 170n82, 186n31
recursivity, 15, 133, 135–36, 137, 139–43, 153–55. *See also* media
Reese, Jesse Byers, 169n74
region, 12, 35, 43–44, 115; and difference, 10, 107; and identity, 6, 37, 39, 81, 169–70n77, 170n78; and

networks, 73, 79–90, 117, 142, 197n62; and power, 14–15, 72–78, 83–99; regionalism, 3, 13, 29–31, 181n174. *See also* geography; land; locality
religion, 2, 145, 148–49, 155, 219n53, 202n130; and community, 6–7, 13, 22, 158–59, 203–4n7, 207n48; and heresy, 133; and historiography, 8, 175n84, 226n3, 227n11; and identity, 101, 115, 125, 130, 156; and texts, 135; and theology, 133–35, 217n37. *See also* clergy; spirituality
Renan, Ernest, 31–32, 178nn124-n25
Revard, Carter, 194–95n40
Reynolds, Susan, 165n26
rhetoric, 151; critical, 164n11; courtly, 92; and flattery, 129–30, 143, 145–47, 151literary, 10, 52, 77, 160, 200n94, 219n53; legal, 150, 224n115; nationalist, 1, 3, 10, 15–16, 21, 159–61; political, 221–22n84; and race, 16, 29; and speech instruction, 148–51, 152–54
rhyme, 10, 18–19, 23, 24–25, 80, 128, 129, 162, 167n53
Richard the Redeless (Anonymous), 15, 129, 131, 134, 136–43, 147–48, 155–56, 224–25n119; authorship of, 221n79, 222n85, 222–23n93; dating of, 220–21n75; dialect of, 215n18, 220n66; manuscript of, 138, 220n68, 221n77
Richard II, 118, 131, 133, 137–38, 140, 142, 147–48, 211n107, 217n37, 221n82, 222n84
Riddy, Felicity J., 211n104
Rigby, Marjory, 202n127
Rigg, A. G., and Charlotte Brewer, 132, 217n28
Rising of 1381, 132–34, 214n14, 216n24, 217n35, 217n38, 218n44, 219n49
ritual, 38, 56, 191n123; and passage, 49–50, 54, 57–61, 62–68, 71, 126, 186n34; and social power, 14, 56–68, 70, 186n34; and violence, 188n76
Robertson, Kellie, 215n15
Robin Hood, 24, 174n52
romance, 51, 61, 114; and aristocracy, 14, 48, 191n123; Arthurian, 15, 29, 59, 109, 72–127, 130, 160, 192n4, 193n26, 196n53, 208n58, 212n128, 213–14n139; and class, 52, 54, 60; and chronicle, 106, 114, 121, 196n56, 205n34; and criticism, 1, 163n9, 172n14, 178n133; and Revivalism, 69
Romanticism, 4, 6, 26, 164n20, 183n3. *See also* medievalism; nationalism; race
Rome, 8, 20, 21, 54–55, 57, 71, 87–88, 111, 119, 121–22, 181n182, 182n194, 194n33, 199n84, 212n115, 212n126, 213n138
Rosenthal, Joel T., 193n21
Ross, Trevor, 171n11
Rousseau, Jean-Jacques, 227n20
Royan, Nicola, 112, 114, 209n76
rupture. *See* epochality
rural life, 118, 130–31, 134–35, 214n14, 215n16; disregard for, 55–56, 60; and poverty, 134–35; and raiding, 213n137; as Revival locale, 76, 130
Rushton, Cory J., 209n77
Russell, George, 223n93; and George Kane, 218n43

Saint Erkenwald (Anonymous), 81, 195–96n47, 197n57
Saintsbury, George, 9, 11, 17, 24–26, 29, 36, 81, 129, 175n77, 178n133
Salisbury, Joyce E., 187n53
Salter, Elizabeth, 30–31, 177n121, 180n158, 182n197, 193n17, 197n62
Samuels, M. L., 215n17, 220n66
Sapora, Robert, Jr., 178–79n135
satire, 37–38, 41, 134, 154, 182n186, 217n37, 220n59, 221n83, 223n102
Saul, Nigel, 181n180, 192n8, 215n16,

215n18
Saunders, Corinne J., 188n67
Savile, Henry, 79, 194n39
Saxon-Norman conflict, 4–5, 11, 12, 20–27, 29–30, 32, 45–49, 161, 164–65n22, 169n69, 174n52, 177n109, 183n6, 184n11, 185n21. *See also* Anglo-Saxons; Normans
Scala, Elizabeth, 98, 200n94, 203n135. *See also* Federico
Scanlon, Larry, 214n14, 218n43, 225n122, 226n3
Scandinavia, 20, 173n40; and Danes, 88, 29; and Norse identity, 114–15, 128–29, 169n69
Scase, Wendy, 224n111
Scattergood, John, 135, 221n79, 223n102
Schiff, Randy P., 202n130, 207n45, 213n138
Schofield, William Henry, 17, 83, 200n91
school (literary), 2, 7, 9, 17, 31, 44, 130–32; and competition, 24–25
Scotland, 12, 14, 205n31, 211n111; and Chaucer, 168n59; and criticism, 26–29, 36, 161, 169n83; and empire, 8, 15, 100, 104, 109, 117, 122, 210n83; and ethnicity, 113–15, 209n78; and literary history, 10, 107, 175n86, 195n41; and nation, 13, 103, 106, 111, 114, 117, 119–20, 166n33, 209n78; and race, 27, 169n67; southern, 81, 102; and Scottishness, 15, 120; as state, 115; and Stewart power, 109, 207n49, 211n104; and war, 196n53. *See also* borderlands
scribes, 12, 34, 215n20, 218n42; and anxiety, 141, 222n91; and authorship, 141–43, 221n80, 222–23n93, 223n97, 226n138; clerks as, 222n86; and labor, 215n15, 216–17n27; and layout, 137
Seeley, John Robert, 28, 176n91
sexuality, 38, 56, 65–66, 72, 87, 99, 189n92, 189n95, 201n117, 202n128, 203nn138–39
Shaw, Thomas B., 184n13, 184n15; and Truman J. Backus, 128, 184n15
Shepherd, Geoffrey, 33, 193n22
Shichtman, Martin B., 114, 209n73. *See also* Finke
Shoaf, R. A., 198n78
side-switching, 15, 78–79, 105, 117–18, 126–27
Sidney, Philip, 167n57, 171n10
Siege of Jerusalem (Anonymous), 35, 81, 83, 124, 169n74, 196n50, 213n138
Silverstein, Theodore, 197n58
Simmons, Clare A., 12, 164–65n22, 172n27
Simpson, James, 2, 49, 133, 141, 151, 164n12, 172n14, 197n57, 217n37, 225n120
singularity, 2, 13, 16, 21–22, 34; and authorship, 27–29, 132, 136, 195n45, 221n80; and prosody, 32–36; and Revivalism, 12, 17, 24–26, 30–31, 38, 44, 139, 157; textual, 136–43
Sir Gawain and the Carle of Carlisle (Anonymous), 112, 208n58
Sir Gawain and the Green Knight (Anonymous), 12, 14–15, 27, 65, 68–69, 72–99, 189n94, 191–92nn2–4, 192n10, 193n27, 196n52, 197n58, 198n68, 198n78, 200nn92–97, 222n88; dialect of, 192n5; editions of, 28, 61, 74, 201n101, 202n132; the *Gawain*-poet, 79–80, 177n108, 194–95n40, 197n62, 202n127; manuscript of, 79–81, 191–92nn4–5, 194–95nn39–40, 195n45; and prosody, 168n61, 178n135, 192n6, 206n40
Skeat, Walter W., 1, 18, 25, 28, 34, 132, 139, 140–41, 163n2, 172n16, 192n6, 195n46, 216n25, 218n46, 222n85, 222n87
Smailes, Arthur E., 118, 212n114
Smith, Anthony D., 6, 103, 161–62,

165–66n31, 170n78, 227n21, 228n26
Smith, D. Vance, 161
Smyth, Alfred P., 166n33, 208n68, 212–13n132
Somerset, Fiona, 214–15n15
sophistication, 4, 14, 15, 38–41, 44, 47, 49–51, 56, 62, 80, 83, 92, 99, 130, 151, 156, 182n183
South, England, 2, 9–10, 13, 30, 31, 33, 37, 80; and Scotland, 175n83
Southwest Midlands, 12, 80, 131, 134, 220n66; and London, 15, 129–31, 136, 154, 156; and the Malvern Hills, 130, 144–45; and Worcestershire, 170n79, 186n37, 219n49
sovereignty, 49, 55, 57, 60–64, 70, 88–89, 95, 104, 124, 199n80, 199n88, 202n121; national, 7, 21, 32, 100–101, 104, 109, 121, 159, 173n33; and royalty, 42–44, 59, 67–68, 77, 87, 111, 114, 141, 146–47, 173n33, 188n79, 201n101, 211n112; and anti-royalism, 30, 43, 211n99
Spain, 43, 54–55, 67–68, 70
Spearing, A. C., 207n54, 213n133
Speirs, John, 37, 181–82n183
Spiegel, Gabrielle M., 16, 139, 210n86
spirituality, 57, 80, 110–11, 143, 148, 213n134, 215n15, 219n53, 225n122; and authority, 134, 152, 219n48; and ethnicity, 48; and Revivalism, 35. *See also* religion
Staley, Lynn, 222n84
Stanbury, Sarah, 97
state, 2, 13, 77, 106, 115; imperial, 5, 6, 8, 19, 42–43, 78–79, 88, 100, 103–4, 108–9; power, 6, 43, 47, 49, 57, 61, 84, 101, 110–12, 116–17, 126, 152–53, 186n31. *See also* centralization
Steadman, J. M., 179n143, 180n158
Stein, Robert M., 177n109
Steiner, Emily, 131, 216n23, 219–20n56, 225n131

sternness, 14, 32, 39, 47; and penance, 35, 68–69, 132
Stott, Andy, 187n60
Strayer, Joseph R., 178n124
Stringer, Keith, 209n78
Strohm, Paul, 147, 219n49, 220n59, 224n110
struggle, 35–36, 204n23; and ethnicity, 183n5; imperial, 100–101; and law, 218n44; metrical, 7–13, 18–32; regional, 31, 111, 116. *See also* militarism; opposition; Saxon-Norman
sublimity, 56, 77, 98, 203n136
subversion, 3, 63, 77, 88, 94, 133, 134, 194n28
suffering, 31, 53, 58–61, 66, 130, 141, 150, 190n101; civilian, 70, 85–86, 105–7, 199n86, 206n37; and empathy, 116; and truth-telling, 143–45
Suite du Merlin (Anonymous), 96, 202n174
Summerson, Henry, 212n114
Suzuki, Eiichi, 202n132
Sykes, Bryan, 183n3, 194n33

Taine, Hippolyte, 9, 21–23, 24, 46 173n38, 183n5, 183n6
technology, 129, 214n12; and backwardness, 15, 24–26, 36, 128–29; literary, 128; and nation, 100–101, 159, 161, 170n78, 227n11. *See also* communication
teleology, 166n33; and historiography, 13, 15–16, 25–26, 129; and nation, 6–7, 100, 175n79, 204n23
Ten Brink, Bernhard, 21, 23–24, 39, 173n36, 174n57, 176n87
Terrell, Katherine H., 208n57
terror, 31, 35, 52–53, 57, 60, 65, 84, 98, 148, 186n36
Thompson, John J., 197n64
Thornton, Robert, 12, 83, 169n74, 197n64, 197n65, 197–98n67
Tilly, Charles, 187n50

topicality, 37–38, 140, 150, 156, 179–80n158, 212n132, 221n82, 224–25n119
Tolhurst, Fiona, 199n84
Tolkien, J. R. R., and E. V. Gordon, 91, 96, 201n101, 202n124
totalization, 2–3, 12, 36, 162, 170n82, 226n7, 227n20. *See also* singularity
tournaments, 115–16, 124, 210n91, 213–14n139. *See also* borderlands; chivalry; violence
traditionalism, in Revivalism, 2–3, 7, 10, 20, 30, 32–33, 37, 39–42, 47–48, 62, 80, 135, 151, 178n133, 181n174, 181–82n183, 200n91. *See also* conservatism; nostalgia
translation, 42, 46, 48, 49–52, 62, 81, 138, 167n54, 185n25–26, 191n3, 196n55, 225n124; and class, 14, 59, 69–71; of French, 66, 68–70, 160, 184n10, 185n26, 188n65, 189–90n96
transnationality, 3, 12, 16, 50, 69–71, 102–4, 130, 160, 166n45; and class, 14, 48, 125, 147, 194–95n40; and England, 42–44, 182n189; and learning, 79, 225n121; and networks, 8, 101, 159; and post-nationality, 2, 3, 6, 8, 101, 103, 159; and region, 76, 81–83, 108–9, 182n189, 196n51, 196n54; and religion, 125. *See also* borderlands; community
trauma, 31–32, 54, 178nn124–25. *See also* memory
Trautmann, Moritz, 29, 176n99
Traversi, Derek, 181n174
Trigg, Stephanie, 34, 37–38, 40, 43, 180n158, 182n184, 196n50, 221n78, 222n88
Tristan and Iseult, 58, 65, 188n67, 189n94
Troy, 78, 82, 85–86, 194n182, 197nn57–58; and origins, 43, 78, 82, 85, 87–88, 182n194, 196n55
truth-telling, 136; and risk, 143, 223n94; and the Sothsegger, 138,
143–44, 148, 151, 152, 155
Tuck, Anthony, 113, 196n54, 209n72, 210n89, 211n107
Turville-Petre, Thorlac, 2, 17, 31, 37, 44, 51–52, 70, 79–80, 157, 160, 164n11, 168n61, 169n72, 174n65, 177n116, 181n174, 181n177, 183–84nn7–8, 194nn36–37, 195n46, 196n55, 197n62, 206n40, 210n85, 216n24, 227n17. *See also* Duggan
Tuscany, 120, 212n123
Twomey, Michael W., 74, 188–89n91, 191n3, 192n10, 202n126

urban life, 144, 151, 160; and economics, 76, 82, 130–31, 169m74, 187n50, 215n18, 220n73; and ritual, 61, 63; and war, 60, 85–86, 118–19, 123–24
Utz, Richard J., 176n90

VanHoosier-Carey, Gregory A., 177–78n122
violence, 1, 106, 153, 127, 191n124, 213–14nn138–39; and brutality, 15, 54, 58, 105, 110–11, 121–24, 178n124, 211n104, 213n137, and class, 52, 58–61, 70; predatory, 58–60, 65, 189n95; and prosody, 69–70, 83, 200n91; and ritual, 188n76; state, 152–53. *See also* militarism

Wales, 14, 23, 59, 74, 76, 78–79, 81–82, 87, 93, 116–17, 121–22, 166n33, 188n73, 194n30, 196n51, 196nn53–54, 197n60, 204n23, 207n47, 211n96, 211n111, 212nn129–30
Wales, Katie, 38, 170n78
Walker, David, 197n60, 212nn129–30
Wallace, David, 22
Walsh, Elizabeth, 207n53
Walsh, James G., 224n117
War. *See* militarism

Warner, Lawrence, 62, 185–86n29, 187n41
Warren, Michelle R., 178n130, 196n53. *See also* Ingham
Wars of Alexander (Anonymous), 81, 195n46
Warton, Thomas, 18–19, 47, 171n11, 172n14, 172n16, 184–85nn17–18
Waswo, Richard, 182n194
Watson, Nicholas, 217n37
Waugh, Scott L., 198n74
Wawn, Andrew, 154, 223n94
wealth, 14, 41, 51, 73–77, 82–89, 91–94, 99, 111, 133, 149, 192–93n16, 193n26, 210n89, 215n18
Wedding of Sir Gawain and Dame Ragnell (Anonymous), 77, 95, 203n137
werewolves, 14, 49, 50, 54–55 56–61, 63–68, 188n79, 189n82
West, England, 17, 32, 37, 39–42, 80, 171n4, 177n113, 214n14; Midlands, 27, 195n41, 197n67, 219n49
Western culture, 2, 5, 9, 21, 50, 57, 66, 68, 71, 104, 126, 157–58, 165n29, 196n55, 205n26, 210n88
Westminster. *See* bureaucracy
When Rome is Removed into England (Anonymous), 181n182
widows, 14–15, 73, 75, 85, 90, 108, 124, 192n16, 198n74, 213n137
wild man, 38–39, 43, 115, 180n170, 182n191, 210n85; Edward, the Black Prince as, 38, 180n58

William of Palerne (William), 14, 46–71, 74, 125, 130, 147, 152, 160, 185n26, 186n38, 187n60, 188n65, 190n97, 190n103; dating of, 48; dialect of, 186n37; manuscript of, 184n10; reception of, 28, 185n25, 189n82; William (poet), 14, 51–54, 68–71, 168n61, 185–86n29
William I (Conqueror), 19, 32, 47, 173n30. *See also* Normans
Williams, Deanne, 20, 48, 52, 68, 186n35
Williams, Edith Whitehurst, 200n96
Wynnere and Wastoure (Anonymous), 13–14, 34, 37–44, 62, 68, 76, 81, 83, 129, 151, 160, 169n74, 179n143, 180n170, 180nn173–74, 181n177, 181–82n183, 182n186, 196n56; dating of, 37, 179–80n158; dialect of, 182n184, 196n50, 222n88; manuscript of, 196n64

York, 12, 76, 81, 215n18; and drama, 169n74
Yorkshire, 12, 79–81, 83, 107, 169n73, 196n50, 197n63, 206n42

zones, alliterative, 12, 74–76, 79, 82–83, 104, 107, 108, 113, 115–17, 122, 127, 130, 160, 206n35

Interventions: New Studies in Medieval Culture

Ethan Knapp, Series Editor

Interventions: New Studies in Medieval Culture publishes theoretically informed work in medieval literary and cultural studies. We are interested both in studies of medieval culture and in work on the continuing importance of medieval tropes and topics in contemporary intellectual life.

Revivalist Fantasy: Alliterative Verse and Nationalist Literary History
　RANDY P. SCHIFF

Inventing Womanhood: Gender and Language in Later Middle English Writing
　TARA WILLIAMS

Body Against Soul: Gender and Sowlehele *in Middle English Allegory*
　MASHA RASKOLNIKOV

www.ingramcontent.com/pod-product-compliance
Lightning Source LLC
Chambersburg PA
CBHW021835220426
43663CB00005B/263